IN THE MATTER OF KAREN QUINLAN

Volume II

The Complete Briefs, Oral Arguments,
and Opinion
in the New Jersey Supreme Court

IN THE MATTER OF KAREN QUINLAN

Volume II

The Complete Briefs, Oral Arguments, and Opinion in the New Jersey Supreme Court

Introduction by
Daniel N. Robinson
Professor of Psychology
Georgetown University

UNIVERSITY PUBLICATIONS OF AMERICA, INC.
1976

Contents

INTRODUCTION

This is the second and final volume addressed to the matter of Karen Ann Quinlan. Neither the Attorney General for the State of New Jersey nor the Prosecutor for Morris County decided to appeal the decision of the New Jersey Supreme Court. Yet, while the U.S. Supreme Court will not confront this case, it is plausible to anticipate that cases akin to this will finally require judgment by the U.S. Supreme Court. The issues involved are among the most fundamental not only in constitutional respects but in their larger ethical and moral projections. And in an age that has perfected nothing less than the method of invention itself, one may reasonably expect that imminent achievements in medical science and medical engineering will render the issues in *Quinlan* even more vexing.

Readers of this and of the first volume may be taxed by the weight and the complexity of the medical testimony and by the apparent lack of clarity in those remarks intended to disclose the prevailing canons of "bioethics". To some—and perhaps because of this—it may also be difficult to penetrate the meaning and the significance of what the New Jersey Supreme Court decision takes as the "focal point" in this case; namely, the possibility of Karen Quinlan's ". . .return to cognitive and sapient life. . .". If readers are to form defensible opinions on the ethical, legal, and social implications of *Quinlan*, some guidance would seem to be in order.

I.

Karen Quinlan's Condition:

At the time of the arguments before the New Jersey Supreme Court (January 26, 1976) and for approximately eleven months prior, Karen Quinlan was in a state described as "comatose" and "chronically vegetative". The cause of her symptoms could not be determined in *two* respects: (a) the trauma initiating her condition is unknown and (b) the precise nature of her neurological impairment is also unknown. There is presumptive evidence of drug toxicity in that her urine was found to contain traces of quinine, salicylates (presumably from aspirin), and barbiturates. However, none of these was, itself, in the toxic range. Assuming, however, that the quinine was ingested with alcoholic beverages, the combination of barbiturates and alcohol certainly could have had toxic effects. There was also evidence, from police reports and from attending friends, that Karen Quinlan had been in a state of anoxia for at least thirty minutes prior to the institution of mechanically supported respiration.

It is important to note that expressions such as "comatose" and "chronically vegetative" are *descriptive* and not diagnostic. The diagnostic methods employed in this case were (a) gross clinical-neurological examination, (b) electroencephalography, (c) cerebral angiography and (d) brain-scanning. With respect to the first, it is too obvious to note that a clinical assessment of a comatose patient can only be of limited informativeness. Ordinarily, the experienced neurologist, by interrogating the conscious patient, is able to discern even very subtle varieties of neuropathology. However, as the patient's ability to cooperate wanes, the range of tests becomes commensurately narrow. In her abiding condition, however, Karen Quinlan did offer the following signs: rigidity of posture often seen in cases of severe insults to the cerebral cortex and especially in those instances in which the insults are diffuse; reflex-responding to stimuli which the normal person would describe as sharply painful; reflexive chewing and lip-smacking, also seen in patients with diffuse cortical anomalies; rotary movements of the eyes, sometimes conjugate and sometimes disconjugate (that is, sometimes with both eyes moving in the same direction, by the same amount and at the same time vs. each eye moving in a way that is independent of the movements of the other). She also displayed facial and postural reflexes which suggest the diminished capacity of inhibitory mechanisms known to be of cortical origin. All in all, then, the gross clinical picture is one of diffuse cortical pathology which, in fact, *could* result from prolonged oxygen starvation. Added to these symptoms is the fact that Miss Quinlan's respiratory mechanisms were (are) not able to sustain life without the aid of nearly continuous artificial supports.

Electroencephalography can offer almost conclusive evidence of certain forms of neurological impairment (e.g., particular types of epilepsy) but it is of only marginal consequence in a case such as this. At no time in the period of hospitalization did Karen Quinlan's brain cease to provide recordable electrical activity. Her EEG traces were reported to show signs of "slowing", meaning that the oscillatory or rhythmic components in her EEG were at frequencies below the expected rate for one her age. Still, the most that could be said of the EEG data was that they were "abnormal". Taken by itself, however, the EEG evidence in this case would not allow *any prediction at all* regarding the "return to cognitive and sapient life" nor does it shed light on the initial or current status of Karen Quinlan's mind. From the description of her EEG profile offered by testifying neurologists, one would be safe in concluding that a similar profile could be obtained from any number of patients enjoying excellent prognoses or suffering from diseases of minor importance.

Angiography involves the injection of a dye that is opaque to radiation. With the dye present in the cerebral circulation, the position of the major blood vessels of the head can be visualized. Since space-occupying lesions (e.g., tumors) will generally displace these vessels, the technique is a useful means of detecting such masses. "Brain scans", too, permit the visualization of masses since tumors tend to absorb radioactive material at a greater rate than does normal tissue. By injecting radioactive material into the cerebral blood supply, the physician is able to detect areas of high radioactive "uptake". In the case of Karen Quinlan, both the angiograms and the brain-scans were normal. So, too, were measures of her cerebro-spinal pressure.

The overall clinical picture presented here will not and cannot support a claim of "brain death", even on the loosest acceptation of the term. Miss Quinlan's brain is electrically active; is not enduring the lethal effects of increased intra-cranial pressure; is not, apparently, invaded by tumors, benign or malignant. No testifying expert, either for the State or for the Plaintiff, sought to challenge this contention. No existing standard in the field of neurology challenges this contention. Indeed, the evidence taken as a whole, does not conduce to the conclusion that Miss Quinlan's cerebrum or cerebral cortex is "dead" either. Her clinical signs suggest a severe cortical dysfunction but there is no evidence to suggest that she lacks functioning cortical cells. But here, too, little more can be said in the absence of more elaborate and potentially dangerous diagnostic procedures. Strong EEG signals can be recorded from experimental animals whose cerebral hemispheres have been surgically removed or chemically depressed. Thus, the mere presence of regular EEG waves is not proof positive of cerebral vitality. Nor, of course, is a diminished or "abnormal" EEG proof positive of cerebral morbidity.

A saddening side-effect of Miss Quinlan's neurological impairment is, of course, her inability to ingest food voluntarily. Thus, in addition to mechanically aided respiration, her body must be sustained by nasogastric feeding. If infections can be prevented, a surprising degree of general, systemic health can be maintained for some time, even under these unusual and melancholy conditions. Nonetheless, clinical experience leads most of the experts to conclude that the life Karen Quinlan now displays would not survive another year. In those cases where patients are similarly "chronically vegetative" and where, nevertheless, life is supported for as many as five years, the ability to breathe without mechanical assistance is the rule. In this respect, Karen Quinlan's case borders on the *sui generis*. Because of the need for artificial respiration and for artificial feeding, she cannot be moved much or often. As a result, her muscles are wasting. Because of the artificially created passages for air and food, her *interieur milieu* is in precarious commerce with the outer world. All in a position to make a judgment will conclude that, no matter what action is taken by the Quinlan family or by Miss Quinlan's physicians, her days are numbered. Yet, the mere fact of human mortality does not provide a legal defense for homicide. Accordingly, decisions regarding the medical services performed in behalf of Karen Quinlan must be based on some consideration other than the imminence of her final decline. And this consideration, or what the Justices of the New Jersey Court called the "focal point", turns out in this case to be the likelihood of Karen Quinlan's "return to cognitive and sapient life".

II.

Qualities of Life:

If human judgment in its perfected form were no more than language and logic, justice could be administered by any literate person in possession of a dictionary and the valid forms of the syllogism. That this is not the case is rudely certified by the words "life" and "death".

In the Brief filed by the Prosecutor of Morris County with the Superior Court of New Jersey, Mr. Collester argued that Karen Quinlan did not satisfy either historic or current criteria of "death"; that she was, therefore, alive and that the relief sought by Mr. Quinlan would violate State laws governing homicide. The Plaintiff, whose *Factual and Legal Contentions* initially asserted that Miss Quinlan was dead, did not claim this in the Brief filed in Superior Court nor did he, as Appellant, argue this before the New Jersey Supreme Court. Instead, the argument sought refuge in the fact—or putative fact—that no extant therapeutic procedure held out any possibility of restoring Miss Quinlan to *cognitive* and *sapient* status. As such, the procedures being invoked in her behalf were not "treatments" at all since her prognosis, in the stated respects, was hopeless. The Appellant argued, further, that the "extraordinary" measures invoked were not required by the canons of Roman Catholic belief—a belief adopted by the Appellant and by Karen Quinlan in the years of her intellectual competence.

The terms "cognitive" and "sapient" are neither legal nor medical but are *psychological*. Loosely, they refer to the capacity of human beings and lower organisms to behave in purposeful ways in response to environmental demands which must be perceived and remembered. There is, however, no unequivocal definition of these terms in the one professional discipline that has explored such capacities with experimental rigor and theoretical insight. It is not uncommon for specialists in Comparative Psychology to describe the performance of organisms as relatively simple as reptiles in "cognitive" terms. Nor is it even necessary for observable behavior to occur in order to obtain evidence of a kind of learning. For example, experimental animals (e.g., dogs) can be conditioned to withdraw a limb when a tone is sounded. Once this conditioned response has been established, the dogs can be reversibly paralyzed by the application of a drug which, while rendering movement impossible, has no effect upon the sensory and perceptual capacities of the animal. If, in this paralyzed state, the dog is exposed to repeated presentations of the conditioning tone—but with the tone not followed by the shock that initially produced the limb-withdrawal—the conditioned response can be extinguished. That is, when the drug has worn off and the dog is again presented with the tone, withdrawal of the limb does not occur. This indicates that the extinction was taking place during that period of paralysis when, to all outward appearances, the animal was capable of learning nothing. The point here is that neither organismic complexity nor overt behavior is a *sufficient* or a *necessary* condition for the proof of "cognitive" or "sapient" capacity. Indeed, fetal heart-rate can be conditioned and this form of "learning" is taking place under the most "extraordinary" life-supporting conditions available to the human race.

It is also depressing but important to recall the "cognitive" and "sapient" impoverishment of many thousands of brain-damaged individuals and individuals suffering from genetic or congenital neurological disease. There are forms of mental incapacitation which are, for all practical and definable purposes, as extreme as that displayed by Karen Quinlan. That in these cases normal breathing is possible is a fact whose significance is difficult to interpret. And in such cases, the symptoms may be as unequivocally described as "irreversible" as Miss Quinlan's. There is no treatment for the Mongoloid idiot, for the anencephalic child, for the infant born with massive, malignant invasions of the brain. On the question of how "extraordinary" are the means needed to keep such tragic cases alive, one again confronts the Delphic nature of ordinary words when applied to rare instances. The Mongoloid idiot may require 24-hour supervision, intravenous feeding, mechanically aided forms of exercise. Even the most severe cases of catatonic withdrawal—in the absence of *any* detectable organic disease—may require care of this sort. Thus, men and women who explore issues of this kind will be frustrated but quick to perceive that terms such as "cognitive", "sapient", and "extraordinary" are likely to be no more than *ad hocisms* where decisions of ethical weight and legal consequence are involved. The law must pursue justice and in that pursuit it often becomes necessary to draw lines at arbitrary boundaries but, in the matter of Karen Quinlan, it is not clear even where the unavoidably arbitrary boundary has been drawn. What would Karen Quinlan have to do to offer evidence of "cognitive" or "sapient" life? How often would she have to do it? If, as she was reported to have done early in her hospitalization, she were to blink twice on command, would this earn her a reprieve? And if the combination of naso-gastric feeding and mechanical respiration are, in the circumstance, "extraordinary" procedures, what ruling would follow in the case of the Mongoloid idiot who *happened* to require naso-gastric feeding as a result of some other condition and mechanical respiration as well? While it may be stipulated that, in such a case, the Mongoloid idiot could be restored to his initial state, the initial state in question may not be one of "cognitive" and "sapient" life.

As the briefs and arguments indicate, this issue was not ignored. Mr. Hyland, for the State of New Jersey, does ask what "quality" of life must be proved for one to cling to whatever life he has and he asks further who will set this standard. As raised by Mr. Hyland, the questions are excusably rhetorical and they promise to be raised again. Nor is the matter settled, either in law or in logic, by stipulatively denying "cognitive" and "sapient" capacities to those in a "chronic vegetative state". This, alas, can only yield a tautology, not a medical or legal criterion. It is surely true that one would have every reason to consider a patient to be in a "vegetative" state if one were sure that there was no semblance of cognition. Similarly, one might plausibly conclude that there is no evidence of cognition in a "chronically vegetative" patient. But both conclusions depend upon the availability of meaningful—if arbitrary— criteria. There are techniques in neuropsychology and the neural sciences which might be of use here but the arbitrariness would still endure. It is known, for example, that statistically averaged responses recorded from the brain will provide evidence of the formation of mental associations. In principle, data of such a sort could serve as presumptive evidence of at least the neurophysiological equivalent of "cognition" or the capacity to learn. This is noted for illustrative purposes and with the *caveat* that such data would not yield unarguable evidence. The point, however, is that where the judicial fulcrum is set according to inferences regarding the "cognitive" and the "sapient", it is no longer necessary to rely upon merely clinical or medical estimations. The neural and the behavioral sciences can, in certain cases, offer methods and perspectives capable of lending greater and desired precision to the largely *psychological* terms which played so great a part in *Quinlan*.

III.

Consent:

Students of this case whose particular interest is in the ethical dimensions of the judgment will be careful to note comments on both sides regarding what Miss Quinlan's own wishes might be were she in a position to voice them. The Supreme Court, in taking as the focal point of the case Miss Quinlan's current and likely (alleged) *mental* capacities, has supported the unanimous opinion with the belief that most people in Miss Quinlan's condition and facing the same odds would elect to die. This part of the opinion draws upon common sense, medical opinion and medical testimony. One must note that in framing this portion of the opinion, the Justices allude several times to patients with incurable cancer suffering from intractable pain—although, in the matter of Karen Quinlan, there has never been any evidence adduced in support of the claim that *she* is in pain. Nonetheless, there is at least a basis for the assertion that many people, when actually or hypothetically confronted by the fate that surrounds Miss Quinlan, would elect not to live and would consent to the termination of life-sustaining measures. But it seems equally arguable that some people, if assured that they would endure no pain or conscious suffering, would ask that their bodies be kept alive for research purposes or that their organs be made available to others in need or that the most radical inventions of science be brought to bear on their conditions in the remotest possibility of salutary effects. The plain fact is that neither the Justices of the Supreme Court of New Jersey nor the parents of Karen Quinlan nor her doctors nor anyone else can claim to know what she might have decided had she the chance and the competence. No one knows, that is, if she might have blinked twice in response to the question, "Do you want us to keep you alive?"

The appointment of guardians is the customary procedure invoked when the party at issue is not competent. It has been decided in *Quinlan* or, better, reaffirmed in *Quinlan* that the patient's right of privacy would allow her to refuse the treatment she is now getting and that this right "should not be discarded solely on the basis that her condition prevents her conscious exercise of the choice." As the Court perceives the matter, the right can only be preserved by extending the proprietorship of this right to the guardian (*Appellant* in this case) and the family. The constraint on the exercise of this proxy is set by the most informed available medical counsel.

As the concept of *consent* here raises a set of traditional ethical questions, it also illuminates the widening area occupied by "privacy rights". In *Quinlan* as in *Roe* v. *Wade*, the State is called upon to demonstrate a compelling interest if its intervention is to be sanctioned. In *Quinlan*, the State's assertion of its interest in the life of every citizen is not upheld. The Justices decide,

> ". . .that the State's interest *contra* weakens and the individual's right to privacy grows as the degree of bodily invasion increases and prognosis dims."

But in this, the connection with *Roe* v. *Wade* can only be very thin for, in seeking to prevent an abortion, the State is the *non-invader* and the prognosis in cases of pregnancy is at least as good as that in abortion. Moreover, by extant medical standards, neither a tracheotomy nor a nasogastric tube would constitute a radical "bodily invasion". And, finally, on this question of *consent*, it is worth noting that the Court again seeks an analogy in the cancer ward, insisting that the State has no compelling interest in requiring Miss Quinlan "to endure the unendurable" where her choice is much like that made, ". . .by a competent patient, terminally ill, riddled by cancer and suffering great pain. . .". The chain of argument here, in including "great pain", would seem to fall beyond the facts in *Quinlan* although, were there evidence of great suffering on Karen Quinlan's part, guesses as to the choice she might make for herself could be improved.

IV.

Medical Ethics—Public and Private:

One of the more persistent themes in the Supreme Court decision involves the chilling effect malpractice suits have had on the general tone of medical ethics and the need for the Court to write an opinion that might free physicians ". . .from contamination by self-interest and self-protection. . .". What the Court has recognized in the medical testimony is a double-standard—a private, intra-professional standard and a public "official" standard—where euthanasia, "death with dignity" and related issues are involved. How easily the physician can be caught in the middle of such issues is dramatically revealed in *Quinlan* where the attending physicians sought to *continue* the life-sustaining measures.

What the Court has sensed in contemporary collisions between doctors and litigants is a growing tendency toward expensive, extraordinary, and interminable measures adopted by the medical community *not* on the basis of the best and most thoughtful medical opinion but on the basis of potential litigation. The decision in *Quinlan* promises some protection for the medical community by treating the death ensuing from the termination of life-supporting measures not as a homicide "...but rather expiration from existing natural causes." Indeed, the Court goes on to say that, ". . .even if it were to be regarded as homicide, it would not be unlawful." The Court, that is, distinguishes between *homicide*, which is the *unlawful* killing of another, and the suspension of mechanical assistance in cases where the patient is "doomed". The ethical foundation for such a distinction is old, if not firm. It is rooted in the well-known "double-effect" analysis which allows one to distinguish between actions that intend to kill and otherwise moral and necessary actions which lead inescapably to the death of another but where that death was not the intended or desired result of the actions. Instances of the "double-effect" are easily conjured. A common illustration finds a group of people trapped in a cave, the mouth of which is blocked by a person who is accidentally and immoveably wedged in place. The group has a stick of dynamite and can free itself by destroying the person now blocking passage. Granting that it is morally sound to save the lives of a group that will otherwise starve and granting that the dynamite is not detonated in order to kill the man in the way, some have argued that the action is not culpably homicidal. But the applicability of "double-effect" reasoning in cases such as *Quinlan* remains to be developed. Miss Quinlan is no threat to the life of any other person nor will her own death save the life of any other person. Moreover, to remove the current sources of her life could only be to end her life since no *other* reason for the action appears in the briefs and arguments.

It is also of interest that the Court urges greater reliance on the counsel of ethics committees in these difficult cases. The Court recognizes the need for the ". . .diffusion of professional responsibility" if the malpractice climate is to weigh less heavily on the individual physician. But social scientists will note that it is precisely because of the diffusion of responsibility that occurs in groups that groups tend to propose actions of a more radical or risky nature than those proposed or adopted by the members of the group taken one-at-a-time. Here too, then, another of the many sides of this enormous issue presents itself. If the suggestive findings in the social sciences apply in contexts such as *Quinlan*, one might be tempted to expect that the maxim, *primum non nocere*, would bind the conscience of the individual physician more surely in the solitary application of his art than it would "in committee".

The Court in *Quinlan* cites expert testimony on the effect that modern technology has had on traditional concepts and practices in medicine; effects that have led to what some perceive to be new ethical dilemmas. One physician is constrained to observe that Karen Quinlan would not have been a problem just a decade or two ago because the care she is now receiving was not then available. But the Court does not go beyond this fact to the principle implicitly recommended by it. There is no doubt but that, in any other century, Karen Quinlan's death and burial would have taken place soon after the appearance of her first symptoms. But this is true of contemporary patients undergoing cardiac surgery, dialysis, organ-transplants. And it is true of the first patients whose diabetes was brought under the control of insulin. It is equally true of those residents of the Second Kingdom of Egypt whose conditions were reversed by trephination. Medicine in each of its stages, from remote antiquity to the present, can achieve results that would startle physicians in an earlier epoch and that would be described as "extraordinary" by them. The plain fact is that "extraordinary" is statistical in meaning; "extraordinary" actions become ordinary ones when adopted by the majority of persons competent to take the actions in question. In matters such as *Quinlan*, it is the courts themselves which will determine "extraordinary" for the future.

V.

The "Common Moral Judgment":

The Court in *Quinlan* must establish grounds in principle by which to set limits—or, at least, to assert that there are limits—on the extent to which what medicine *can* do it *does* do. Wisely, the Court acknowledges the unique status of the qualified physician in the matter of what is best for his patient. But having benefitted from the physician's expert judgment, the Court must test this advice against, ". . .the common moral judgment of the community at large ... equity and justice must not themselves quail in the face of modern technological marvels. . .".

Here, at last, the determining factor is not the nuances of the EEG or the fraction of Karen Quinlan's cortical cells still functioning or the learned analyses conducted by professional ethicists. Rather, the Court reasons, all these must be weighed against the moral sensibilities of men and women whose authority in such matters derives from their very humanity. And how might "the common moral judgment" find in the case of Karen Quinlan?

On the one hand, there is a twenty-two year old woman, twisted in coma, able to whimper and groan, bereft of any ray of reason, and sinking with horrific gradualness to the inevitable state of the flesh. To the parents who love her, the spectre of this living death has already gone beyond the bearable and has entered the realm of nightmare. To the nurses and doctors attending her, she is but a vivid and macabre reminder of the limitations nature imposes even on good will and technical genius. To those at a greater distance, she fills a bed and requires services that might better be reserved for a hopeful case. The odds are such that only the more churlish and sophistical would contest the prognosis. And even those, driven by chivalric devotion to protect the weak, search in vain for Karen Quinlan's assailant. Karen Quinlan has no avowed enemy in this case; her parents love her, her Church stands ready to commend her soul, her physicians labor with tireless enthusiasm over her wasting body. By what canon of conscience or sympathy can one refuse to let her go?

On the other hand, this young woman lives. Her heart beats, her brain flickers with an uncertain light, her emaciated fingers grope aimlessly, for what cannot be known. When pricked by a pin, she is resistless but seems hurt. Her eyes roll hither and thither but none knows what they see. She was for many years a person—an uncontested claim—and there is no fact of science able at this time to take that title from her. And no matter how bravely whatever is left of her fights to live, and no matter how valiantly her healers struggle to preserve the life she has, her final and doubtless death cannot be far off. There is, out there in that "common moral judgment", more than one citizen pulling for Karen Quinlan; more than one citizen richer to be living in a State that will go so far to save a life whose only claim is that it is.

What is to be learned from the case of Karen Quinlan is that matters of life and death will not dissolve in a well of data or in the wake of committee deliberations. The Courts have ultimate authority but not the ultimate wisdom for, in cases such as this, there is no "ultimate" wisdom. The "common moral judgment" of which the Court in *Quinlan* speaks is, itself, not a static or monolithic agency. It is an expression of a nation's character, shaped by education, superstition, material needs, and the press of coping. It can be informed by ethical principles and by scientific facts but it cannot be controlled by them alone. If the most thoughtful and competent members of society are to serve the best interests of mankind by cultivating this "common moral judgment", they will do well to avoid extremes in cases such as *Quinlan*. They will do well to convey to those who are newly interested in or even simply curious about cases such as *Quinlan* the staggering complexity of the questions and the equally staggering implications that attach to *any* position taken on a matter of this kind. They will do well, that is, to make it clear that the Court has settled the matter of Karen Quinlan but not the issue.

Daniel N. Robinson
Georgetown University
April, 1976

In The

SUPREME COURT OF NEW JERSEY

September Term, 1975

Docket No. A-116

IN THE MATTER OF KAREN ANN QUINLAN, AN ALLEGED INCOMPETENT

ON APPEAL FROM JUDGMENT OF THE SUPERIOR COURT OF
NEW JERSEY, CHANCERY DIVISION (MORRIS COUNTY)
SAT BELOW: HONORABLE ROBERT MUIR, JR., J.S.C.

BRIEF AND APPENDIX FOR APPELLANT

Paul W. Armstrong
Attorney for Plaintiff-Appellant
801 Lindsley Drive,
Morristown, New Jersey 07960

Of Counsel:

James M. Crowley
Of the New York Bar

Dated: December 16, 1975

1

Procedural History

On September 12, 1975, the Plaintiff, Joseph Quinlan, filed with the Superior Court, Chancery Division, Morris County, a Complaint (Pa11), supported by an Affidavit of Plaintiff (Pa14) and Affidavits of Physicians (Pa15 through 18) Doctor Robert Morse and Doctor Arshad Javed. The Complaint prayed for a judgment (i) adjudicating Plaintiff's daughter, Karen Quinlan, to be mentally incompetent and (ii) granting to the Plaintiff letters of guardianship with the express power of authorizing the discontinuance of all extraordinary medical procedures sustaining Karen's vital processes.

On September 15, 1975, pursuant to Rule 4:26 the Honorable Robert Muir, Jr., Judge of the Superior Court, Chancery Division, Morris County, appointed Daniel R. Coburn, Esq., to represent Karen Quinlan in the instant proceeding as her guardian *ad litem* (Pa19).

On September 17, 1975, pursuant to Rule 4:67-2 a Supplemental Complaint (Pa20) and Order to Show Cause (Pa23) was filed joining the Defendants Donald G. Collester, Jr., Morris County Prosecutor, Doctor Robert Morse and Doctor Arshad Javed, Karen's treating physicians, and Saint Clare's Hospital, Denville, New Jersey, to this action.

On September 19, 1975, an Answering Affidavit (Pa25) was filed with the Court by the guardian *ad litem*.

On September 22, 1975, upon completion of the pretrial conference, the Pretrial Order (Pa33) was issued by the Court. On the same date, during the pretrial conference, the Honorable William F. Hyland, Attorney General of the State of New Jersey, intervened as of right pursuant to Rule 4:33-1; and James M. Crowley of the New York Bar was admitted *pro hac vice* pursuant to Rule 1:21-2 as co-counsel for the Plaintiff in the instant proceeding. On October 2, 1975, the Factual and Legal Contentions of the Plaintiff (Pa37) were filed.

On October 20, 21, 22, 23 and 27, 1975, the trial in this cause was held before the Honorable Robert Muir, Jr., Judge of the Superior Court, Chancery Division, Morris County at the Courthouse in Morristown, New Jersey.

On October 22, 1975, the Court entered an Order Amending the Pretrial Order (Pa41) to set forth that under any legal standard recognized by the State of New Jersey and also under standard medical practice, Karen Ann Quinlan is presently alive.

On October 23, 1975, the Court entered an Order Amending the Pretrial Order (Pa42) to set forth a request for (i) a declaratory judgment as to the effect of the granting of the requested relief upon the criminal laws of the State of New Jersey and (ii) a declaratory judgment as to whether the use of the criteria developed by the Ad Hoc Committee of the Harvard Medical School, and similar criteria, in connection with the determination of the death of a patient whose cardio-pulmonary functions are being artificially sustained is in accordance with ordinary and standard medical practice.

On November 10, 1975, a Judgment (Pa44) and Opinion (Pa40) were entered by the Court adjudicating Karen Ann Quinlan a mental incompetent and appointing her father, Joseph Quinlan, the guardian of her property and the guardian *ad litem,* Daniel Coburn, the guardian of her person. The Judgment further denied with prejudice the requested authorization to terminate the respirator supporting Karen Quinlan's cardio-respiratory functions and all corollary relief sought in connection therewith.

On November 12, 1975, a Supplemental Opinion (Pa89) clarifying the position of the guardian of Karen's person was issued by the Court.

On November 17, 1975, a Notice of Appeal (P90a) and Request to Stenographic Reporter for Preparation of Transcript (Pa94) were filed with the Superior Court,

Appellate Division, in Trenton. On the same day, the Supreme Court of New Jersey issued an order, pursuant to Rule 2:12-1, certifying this appeal then pending in the Superior Court, Appellate Division, directly to the Supreme Court for review and requiring all parties to file a supplemental brief within 21 days of the entry of the order. (Pa96-97).

On November 24, 1975, the defendant State of New Jersey, pursuant to Rule 2:3-4, filed a Notice of Cross Appeal (Pa98) from that portion of the decision and judgment of the Chancery Division of the Superior Court which held admissible various hearsay statements allegedly made by Karen Quinlan.

On November 21, 1975, an Acceptance of Guardianship (Pa101) was filed with the Superior Court, Chancery Division, by the guardian *ad litem,* Daniel R. Coburn, Esq.

On November 24, 1975, an Acceptance of Guardianship (Pa101) was filed with the Superior Court, Chancery Division, by the Plaintiff, Joseph Quinlan.

On November 24, 1975, a Notice of Motion for Stay of Judgment Appointing Guardian of the Person and for Substitution of Guardian of the Person (Pa102) along with the supporting Affidavit (Pa104) and Certification of Service (Pa104) were filed by the Plaintiff with the Superior Court, Chancery Division, Morris County.

On December 2, 1975, the Supreme Court of New Jersey, pursuant to the request of the Plaintiff dated December 2, 1975 (Pa107), entered an Order (Pa108) extending the time for the simultaneous filing of the initial briefs in this matter from December 9, 1975, to December 16, 1975, and allowing service of the responsive briefs within 10 days therafter.

On December 2, 1975, the Clerk of the Superior Court of New Jersey, Chancery Division, issued Letters of Guardianship (Pa109) to the Plaintiff, Joseph Quinlan.

4

On December 3, 1975, the counsel for the Plaintiff filed with the Supreme Court, pursuant to Rule 2:6-12, an Affidavit of Proof of Service (Pa110) of the transcript of the trial held in this matter before the Honorable Robert Muir, Jr., Judge of the Superior Court, Chancery Division, Morris County.

On December 10, 1975, Daniel R. Coburn, Esq., resigned as guardian of the person of Karen Quinlan, and Thomas Curtin, Esq., was appointed in his place (Pa112).

Statement of the Facts

Karen Quinlan is one of three children of Joseph and Julia Quinlan, residents of Landing, New Jersey (T334-20; T466-25; Pa11). The Quinlans, including Karen, are members of the Roman Catholic Church (T335-6 *et seq.*; T467-3 *et seq.*; T468-5). Karen was baptized as an infant and attended parochial and diocesan schools near Landing (T335-15 *et seq.*). She and her family are members of Our Lady of the Lake parish in Mount Arlington, New Jersey (T399-8).

On April 15, 1975, Karen, then twenty-one, was taken ill. She had difficulty breathing, and friends summoned a rescue squad. While awaiting the arrival of help, they attempted to administer artificial respiration to Karen (T245-25; *et seq.*; T305-3 *et seq.*).

An ambulance took her to Newton Memorial Hospital in Newton, New Jersey. She was in an unresponsive state and showed evidence of brain damage (T247-10; T250-24; 251-2). At Newton Memorial a variety of tests were performed (T55-15 *et seq.*; T56 through T69; T249-21). On April 24, 1975, she was transferred to the intensive care unit of St. Clare's Hospital in Denville, New Jersey, where she remains to date (T56-1 through 9).

The physicians who treated her have never been able to determine what caused Karen to have her initial respiratory

5

difficulties (T105-4 through 10; T138-10; T151-7). Absence of a clear history can seriously hamper diagnostic and prognostic efforts in the early or acute stages of an illness, but lack of such information assumes an ever diminishing importance as a patient's condition passes from the acute to the sub-acute to the chronic stage[1] (T286-9; 286-21 through T287-6). At present, more than six months after Karen became ill, the initial cause of her breathing difficulty is of no medical significance in formulating a prognosis (T292-13 through T293-6; T577-10 through 13).

Karen's condition is described as a persistent vegetative state (T73-10; T107-24; T255-6; T576-4; 597-1 through 598-3). It is the result of extensive and irreparable brain damage brought on by an insufficiency of oxygen (T79-11 through T80; T82-13; T101-21; T147-13; T153-9; T246-2 through 8; T259-13; T265-15; T287-1; T568-18; T576-1 through T577-18; T601-2 through 17; T634-5; T635-9 through 16; T639-6 through 8; T640-20 through 22; Pa18-6).

Such a state is characterized by total loss of cognitive functions (T597-22); there is no sapient behavior, no awareness of self or surroundings (T330-8 through 20; T601-2 through 14). There may be, and in Karen's case there is, a pattern similar to wakefulness and sleep, even though the patient is never conscious (T70-22 through 25; T71-1 through 4). There may be, and in Karen's case there are, reactions to stimuli of various types. She moves her head, opens her mouth, blinks and grimaces. All of these movements, however, follow the same patterns and are not related to any mental awareness of the stimuli or of their various intensities (T72-1 through 25; T73-2 through 25; T74-8; T108-1 through 5; T109-6; T232-13; T233-18; T234-6 through 8; T597-21 through 25).

---

[1] Acute = hours to days after onset.

Sub-acute = days to weeks after onset.

Chronic = weeks to months to years after onset (T286-12).

6

In addition to being totally unconscious, Karen is unable to breathe properly. At times she does not breathe at all; the rest of the time her breathing is not strong enough to maintain an adequate level of oxygen in her blood (T181-24 through 25; T182-1 and 2).

Because of this her doctors have inserted a respirator tube into her trachea through an opening in her throat (T176-20; T550-16; T587-4). The respirator forces air through the tube, into her lungs, and assists her ventilation process in two ways. If she breathes on her own, the respirator simply increases the volume of air which reaches her lungs. If she does not breathe at all, the respirator takes over that function entirely (T178-11 through 16; T179-5 through 10; T615-7 through 20).

Without the respirator Karen would die. (T182-12 through 16; T617-24 through 25; T618-1 through 3). There is, in addition, a constant danger of infection because of the opening in Karen's throat, and this danger is aggravated by the fact that she is in an intensive care ward with other critically ill patients (T87-21 through 25; T88-1 through 14; T143-1; T566-24).

The general care given to Karen by the hospital staff has been outstanding (T78-7 through 25; T79-1 through 10; T552-5 through 16; T553-2; T575-15; T576-1 through 13; T628-10 through 13).

Karen's condition is hopeless (T344-24; T568-18 through 23; Pa18-6; Pa113); her coma is irreversible (T468-25 through T469-5; T576-22; T601-15 through 17). No treatment is suggested or even known (T80-20 through 25; T265-22 through 25). She is terminally ill[2] (T87-7 through 21; T366-15; T370-24), and even with the aid of the respirator she will not live for so long as another year (T87-7 through 21; T110-6 through 8).

There is sound medical tradition to the effect that care of the type being administered to Karen is properly used only in acute situations where a possibility of recovery ex-

_____
[2] "Terminal illness" will be used to describe a disorder which is incurable and which will cause the patient's death.

7

ists, that withdrawal of such treatment in situations like Karen's is medically acceptable and that the family and physicians are properly cooperators in making the necessary decisions (T269 through T273; T297-25; T298-3; T299-6 through 13; T300-1 through 11; T333-5 through 13).

From the first days of Karen's illness the family was in regular and frequent communication with Doctors Morse and Javed, the treating physicians (T91-12 through 18; T153-11; T184-16). Both doctors stated that Karen's condition was hopeless and that she would not survive (T344-24; Pa18). Dr. Morse continually stated that Karen's condition was irreversible, and a consulting physician agreed (T468-23 through 25; T469-1 through 5). Dr. Javed advised that Karen should be removed from the respirator (T345-8; T391-8).

As part of his ongoing spiritual counsel and advice, the Quinlans' pastor, Father Thomas Trapasso, was able to provide them with a deeper understanding of the Church's approach to life-influencing decisions (T366-9 *et seq.;* T408-17 through 24); Father Caccavalle, the hospital chaplain, also advised Mr. and Mrs. Quinlan and the doctors within the framework of a Papal allocution dealing with the prolongation of life and delivered by His Holiness Pope Pius XII in 1957 (T442-9 through 25; T443-1; Pa1).

Not long before falling ill Karen had, on at least three occasions, made statements to the effect that were she in a hopeless medical condition, she would not want her life prolonged by the futile use of extraordinary medical measures (T484-7 through T492-23; T495-23 through T497-7; T516-25 through T518-19).

Over a period of time the entire Quinlan family reached the conclusion that Karen would never recover (T469-6 through 19). They felt the best course of action was to discontinue the use of the respirator and allow her to return to her natural state where, if it was God's will, she would die peacefully and pass to a better, more perfect life in the gentle, loving hands of the Lord (T356-25 through 361-25; T473-20).

In late July or early August of 1975 a meeting was held among the Quinlans, the treating physicians and Father Caccavalle. It was agreed by all present that the use of of the respirator would be discontinued. Dr. Morse did not advise one way or the other but said he would carry out the Quinlans' request (T346-9 through 22).

After this meeting the Quinlans were asked to sign a release in favor of Dr. Morse and the hospital. This they did (T347-6; Pa10).

Within a few days after the meeting Dr. Morse informed the Quinlans that he would not carry out their wishes. He stated that he could find no medical precedent with regard to such action (T117-9 through 17; T118-1 through 18).

If he had found a favorable precedent, he would have honored the request (T117-14; T157-14; T390-3). He feels that the Court may have to lay down some criteria (T118-2).

Consulting once again with the hospital authorities, Mr. Quinlan was advised that as a first step he would have to be appointed guardian of his daughter in order to be able to authorize the proposed withdrawal of treatment (T374-2 through 16). He would not take it upon himself to act without legal sanction (T353-24; T355-19). Accordingly, on September 12, 1975, he commenced the instant proceeding in the Superior Court, Chancery Division, Morris County, New Jersey (Pa11).

ARGUMENT

POINT I

Appellant Joseph Quinlan should be appointed sole guardian of the person of his daughter Karen.

New Jersey law requires that Appellant, as next of kin, be appointed guardian of his incompetent daughter unless it is proven to the Court that such appointment would not be to the best interest of the incompetent. N.J.S.A. 3A:6-36.

9

Within the framework of the trial Court's Opinion (Pa47, Pa85) and Supplemental Opinion (Pa90), the appointment of a guardian other than Appellant is (i) superfluous because the trial Court has in its Supplemental Opinion properly committed to Appellant and his wife the functions normally exercised by a guardian (Pa90-25); any future inability of either or both of them to perform such functions, especially with regard to concurrence in medical treatment, is speculative and can be more properly dealt with as circumstances arise; and (ii) unwarranted because Appellant has abundantly and without controversion demonstrated both his general fitness to serve as guardian (Pa86; T695-7 through 25) and his intention not to act in any manner which the Court feels inconsistent with Karen's best interests (T353-24; T355-19). *See, In re Roll,* 117 N.J. Super. 122, 283 A. 2d 764 (App. Div. 1971).

POINT II

The testimony regarding Karen's prior statements is of sufficient probative weight to compel the conclusion that she would elect to remove the futile medical measures presently being administered to her.

Not long before falling ill Karen had on at least three occasions made statements to the effect that were she in a hopeless medical condition, she would not want her life prolonged by the futile use of extraordinary medical measures (T484-7 through 492-23; T495-23 through T497-7; T516-25 through T518-19; Pa 65).

The trial Court, on the admission into evidence of these uncontroverted statements, advised, in overruling defendant's objections to their admissibility, that it would deal solely with the question of their probative weight rather than their probative force, relevancy or materiality. (T483-1 through 25; T484-1 through 5).

In rendering its opinion, the Court concluded that these proofs do not meet a standard clear enough to have the probative weight sufficient to convince the Court that Karen Quinlan, in full command of the facts, would elect her own removal from the respirator. (Pa75; Pa80). In so doing the Court advanced no criteria with which to assess their probative weight.

It is the contention of the appellant that the trial court erred in ruling that the testimony concerning Karen's statements is without sufficient probative weight to compel the conclusion that she would elect her own removal from the respirator.

In *Day* v. *Hopping*, 95 N.J. Eq. 680, 123 A. 869 (E. & A. 1924) the Court of Errors and Appeals held, at page 681, that:

"Express testimony cannot be rejected on the sole ground of its improbability. The testimony of a competent witness cannot be capriciously rejected. There must appear some good reason for such action, as, for example, that his story was inherently improbable, or that it was contradicted by some other testimony or by some proven fact or circumstances, or by testimony impeaching his truth and veracity."

In addressing itself to the question of improbability the Court of Errors and Appeals, in the case of *Gilson* v. *Gilson*, 116 N.J. Eq. 556, 174 A. 685 (E. & A. 1934), set forth, at page 560 of its decision, that:

"Testimony to be worthy of belief, must not only be offered by a credible witness, but must be such as the common experience and observation of reasonable men can approve as probable under the circumstances. There is no test of truth of testimony, except its conformity to our knowledge, observation, and experience. Improbable testimony is such as imputes conduct inconsistent with those principles by which persons, similarly situated, are governed."

Karen's mother, Julia Quinlan, her sister, Mary Ellen, and her friend and confidant, Lori Gaffney, testified that

11

Karen had expressed to each of them that should fate find her in the tragic circumstances which bring her father before this Court, she would elect and request the discontinuance of the futile medical measures presently being employed (T484-7 through 492-23; T495-23 through T497-7; 516-25 through T518-19; Pa65). This testimony is uncontradicted.

The Supreme Court of New Jersey, in *Ferdinand* v. *Agricultural Insurance Company*, 22 N.J. 482 (1956) addressed itself to such an evidentiary circumstance at page 498:

> ". . . Where the uncontradicted testimony of a witness, interested or otherwise, is unaffected by any conflicting inferences to be drawn from it and is not improbable, extraordinary or surprising in its nature, or there is no other ground for hesitating to accept it as truth, there is no reason for denying the verdict dictated by such evidence."

Despite the absence of inherent improbability or any contradiction of this testimony the trial Court felt it lacked a probative weight sufficient to persuade the Court that Karen would elect her own removal from the respirator (Pa75; Pa80).

This Court has laid down a standard by which such a conclusion may be weighed. In *Bernstein* v. *Metropolitan Bottling Co.*, 26 N.J. 263 (1958) it held on pages 274 and 275:

> "The burden of persuasion is sustained if the evidence demonstrates the tendered hypothesis as a rational inference, that is to say, a presumption grounded in a preponderance of the probabilities according to the common experience of mankind."

It is submitted that under the foregoing standard the Trial Court erred in not concluding that the prior statements of Karen conclusively show that she would elect her own removal from the respirator.

POINT III

Appellant and his family, including his irreversibly comatose and terminally ill daughter Karen, have a constitutionally protected right to cause the discontinuance of certain life-sustaining medical treatment which Karen presently receives.

1. Individuals are sovereign over their own persons and can ordain the disposition of their bodies.

As early as 1891, the United States Supreme Court spoke of a right of privacy[3] when it stated that individuals are sovereign over their own persons.

> "No right is held more sacred, or is more carefully guarded, by the common law, than the right of every individual to the possession and control of his own person, free from all restraint or interference of others, unless by clear and unquestionable authority of law" *Union Pacific Railway Company* v. *Botsford,* 141 U.S. 250, 251 (1891).

Mr. Justice Brandeis, in his dissent to *Olmstead* v. *United States,* 277 U.S. 438, 478 (1927), further elucidated this evolving concept:

> "The protection guaranteed by the Amendments is much broader in scope. The makers of our Constitution undertook to secure conditions favorable to the pursuit of happiness. *They recognized the significance of man's spiritual nature, of his feelings and of his intellect. They knew that only a part of the pain, pleasure, and satisfactions of life are to be found in material things.* They sought to protect Americans in their beliefs, their thoughts, their emotions and their sensations. They conferred, as against the Government, the right to be let alone—the most compre-

---

3. It does not appear necessary in the present circumstances to make a distinction between the right of privacy and the right of self-determination. The principle *non sunt multiplicanda entia sine necessitate* has constitutional implications unforeseen, perhaps, by Occam.

hensive of rights and the right most valued by civilized men.'' (emphasis added).

In *Griswold* v. *Connecticut,* 381 U.S. 479 (1965), the United States Supreme Court presented a comprehensive treatment of the constitutional right to privacy. The Court invalidated (as violative of the fundamental right to privacy) a Connecticut statute prohibiting the use of contraceptives by married couples and the distribution of birth control information and devices to them. The majority rendered four separate opinions, upholding that right under three distinct theories.

Mr. Justice Douglas, who authored the opinion of the Court, viewed the right to privacy as constitutionally created. He explained with reference to several of the first ten Amendments that ''specific guarantees in the Bill of Rights have penumbras, formed by emanations from those guarantees that help give them life and substance . . . Various guarantees create zones of privacy.'' *Id.* at 484 (citation omitted).

He further reasoned that although the Constitution nowhere specifically mentions a right to privacy, various expressly stated guarantees embody aspects of that right.

In placing the marital and familial relationship within the protective zone of privacy the Court held:

''We deal with a right of privacy older than the Bill of Rights—older than our political parties, older than our school system. Marriage is a coming together for better or for worse, hopefully enduring, and intimate to the degree of being sacred. It is an association that promotes a way of life, not causes; a harmony in living, not political faiths; a bilateral loyalty, not commercial or social projects. Yet it is an association for as noble a purpose as any involved in our prior decisions.'' *Id.* at 486.

Mr. Justice Goldberg, in his concurring opinion, concentrated his analysis on the Ninth Amendment and viewed it as an expression by the framers of the Constitution that certain personal rights should not be denied simply because they are not expressly stated in the first eight Amendments. He classified the right to privacy as one of those unenumerated rights emanating "from the totality of the constitutional scheme under which we live." *Id.* at 494 (quoting *Poe* v. *Ullman,* 367 U.S. 497, 521 (1961) (Douglas, J., dissenting)).

In determining which rights are fundamental and thus to be afforded protected status, Justice Goldberg set forth the following test:

> "judges are not left at large to decide cases in light of their personal and private notions. Rather, they must look to the 'traditions and [collective] conscience of our people' to determine whether a principle is 'so rooted [there] . . . as to be ranked as fundamental' . . . . The inquiry is whether a right involved 'is of such a character that it cannot be denied without violating those fundamental principles of liberty and justice which lie at the base of all our civil and political institutions' ". *Id.* at 493 (citations omitted).

Justices Harlan and White, concurring in separate opinions, reaffirmed the principle that due process, as set forth in the Fourteenth Amendment, can serve as a vehicle for protecting rights not enumerated in the Constitution. Mr. Justice White pointed out that "there is a 'realm of family life which the state cannot enter' without substantial justification". *Id.* at 502 (quoting *Prince* v. *Massachusetts,* 321 U.S. 158, 166 (1944)).

The right to familial and, *a fortiori,* individual privacy has grown to include not only decisions as to education and religious upbringing but also decisions bearing directly on the inception or the continuance of life; and it cannot be denied that a family is legally competent to make the decisions implicit in Petitioner's request. *Eisenstadt* v. *Baird,* 405 U.S. 438 (1972) (decision to bear or beget a child) ; *Roe*

v. *Wade,* 410 U.S. 113 (1973) (decision to terminate pregnancy). *See,* 3. below, p. 18.

2. There is no obligation to submit to medical treatment which offers no hope of relief or cure.

In his trial brief Appellant states at page 17:

"There is no New Jersey statute, nor any court decision, that requires a competent adult to submit to medical treatment which offers no reasonable hope of relief or cure."

Appellant also contends at page 25:

"The State has no compelling secular interest in prohibiting [the withdrawal of the treatment currently being administered to Karen Ann Quinlan]".

Learned counsel for other parties to the instant proceeding have disputed such contentions. Their argument has been based in large part on the case of *John F. Kennedy Memorial Hospital* v. *Heston,* 58 N.J. 576 (1971). In that case an unmarried young woman who had been severely injured in an automobile accident was admitted to the plaintiff hospital, where it was determined that surgery and a blood transfusion would be necessary to save her life. The patient's family informed the hospital that the transfusion was forbidden by the religion to which they all belonged and objected to the administration thereof. The hospital petitioned for the appointment of a guardian to consent to the transfusion. The Petition was granted, the transfusion was administered, surgery was performed and the patient recovered.

In affirming the denial of a motion to vacate the guardianship order, the Court observed:

"it seems correct to say there is no constitutional right to choose to die . . . nor is a constitutional right estab-

16

lished by adding that one's religious faith ordains his death" 58 N.J. at 580.

The Heston case, however, is clearly distinguishable from the one at hand. The above-quoted dicta of *Heston* should not be considered as dispositive of the instant proceeding.

In cases dealing with patients' rights it appears that three questions have been relevant in deciding whether a patient may refuse treatment.

 1. What is the nature and the prognosis of the ailment?

 2. What is the nature of the proposed treatment?

 3. What are the social responsibilities of the patient?

Depending on the answers to the foregoing questions, State interest may or may not be sufficiently compelling to overbalance individual choice.

Where a patient is considered to have a poor prognosis without treatment, a good chance of recovery with such treatment, and the treatment is not deemed essential, the right of a patient to refuse treatment has been upheld. *Erickson* v. *Dilgard,* 44 Misc. 2d. 27, 252 N.Y.S.2d. 705 (Sup. Ct. 1962); *In re Nemser,* 51 Misc. 2d. 616, 273 N.Y.S. 2d. 1964 (Supp. Ct. 1966).

Even in an emergency situation, where the prognosis was that death would ensue if treatment were not administered, the court, in *In re Estate of Brooks,* 32 Ill. 2d. 361, 205 N.E.2d 435 (1965), upheld a patient's refusal of treatment where such refusal created no clear and present danger to public health, welfare or morals. 32 Ill. 2d. at 373, 205 N.E.2d at 441.

Even more clear is the situation where death is inevitable despite any proposed treatment. In *Palm Springs*

General Hospital, Inc. v. *Martinez,* Civil No. 71-12687 (Dade Co. Cir. Ct., filed July 2, 1971) the court refused to order surgery for a 72-year old woman where such medical procedures might have prolonged her life, but there was no hope of a cure. The patient had "begged her family not to 'torture me any more' with further surgery". *Wash. Post,* July 5, 1971 at 1, Column 1. The Court stated:

> "Based upon [her] physical condition . . . and the fact that performance of surgery . . . and the administration of further blood transfusions would only result in the painful extension of her life for a short period of time, it is not in the interest of justice for this Court of Equity to order that she be kept alive against her will". *Palm Springs Gen. Hosp., Inc.* v. *Martinez, supra,* citing *Erickson* v. *Dilgard, supra,* at 27 and 705.

The Heston situation on the other hand was quite different. In *Heston* treatment was relatively uncomplicated, and the prognosis for recovery with such treatment was very good. In such a case it is not difficult to see that the state's admitted interest in preserving life could overcome a patient's objection to treatment. Moreover, if a patient, in addition to being quite curable, had significant social or familial responsibilities, the state's case would be even stronger, *Raleigh Fitkin-Paul Morgan Memorial Hospital* v. *Anderson,* 42 N.J. 421 (1964), *cert. den.* 377 U.S. 985 (1964).

In the instant proceeding, however, the situation is more similar to *Erickson, Nemser, Brooks* and *Martinez* than it is to *Heston.* Karen Quinlan is in an irreversible coma. (T468-25 through T469-5; T576-22; T601-15 through 17) The chances for her recovery are nil (T576-14 through 25; T577-1 through 17), she has no family to provide for, no children (Pa12), and the advent of her death is merely a matter of time. (T87-7 through 21; T366-15; T370-24) For the court to accept the above-quoted statements from

18

Heston as controlling in the present case would be to mis-apply an uncontested general principle. A more profitable use of the Court's opinion in *Heston* could be made by realizing that while the Court considered refusal of treatment in Miss Heston's case to be tantamount to suicide, it realized that the situation would be "arguably different when an individual, overtaken by illness, decides to let it run a fatal course." 58 N.J. at 582.

In summary, while Appellant agrees with and venerates the principle that life is sacred and that it is to be preserved through all reasonable means, he feels that there is no reason to continue treatment in the present circumstances, that Karen could lawfully discontinue such treatment if competent, that her family (see 3. below) and the Court (see Point VI below, p. 26) can thus consent thereto on her behalf and that the cases which are relied upon for the opposite proposition cannot support a denial of Appellant's request if proper weight is given to the facts before this Court.

3. Decisions with regard to continued medical treatment of terminally ill and irreversibly comatose patients are properly made by those closest to the patient.

Familial autonomy, the right of the family to make fundamental decisions affecting the lives of its members, received initial acceptance in *Meyer* v. *Nebraska,* 262 U.S. 390 (1923). Here the court recognized the right of parents to educate their children as they chose when it struck down a state statute forbidding the teaching of the German language to school children below the eighth grade. In rendering its opinion based upon the liberty guaranteed by the Fourteenth Amendment the Court stated:

> "While this Court has not attempted to define with exactness the liberty thus guaranteed, the term has received much consideration and some of the included things have been definitely stated. Without doubt, it denotes not merely freedom from bodily restraint but

19

also the right of the individual to contract, to engage in any of the common occupations of life, to acquire useful knowledge, to marry, establish a home and bring up children, to worship God according to the dictates of his own conscience, and generally to enjoy those privileges long recognized at common law as essential to the orderly pursuit of happiness by free men." *Id.* at 399.

Two years later in *Pierce* v. *Society of Sisters,* 268 U.S. 510 (1925), the court, citing the *Meyer* decision, upheld the right of parents to send their children to private schools despite a state statute forbidding such action. In so doing it held that the Fourteenth Amendment guarantees the "liberty of parents and guardians to direct the upbringing and education of children under their control." *Id.* at 534-35. The court stated:

"As often heretofore pointed out, rights guaranteed by the Constitution may not be abridged by legislation which has no reasonable relation to some purpose within the competency of the State. The fundamental theory of liberty upon which all governments in this Union repose excludes any general power of the State to standardize its children by forcing them to accept instruction from public teachers only. The child is not the mere creature of the State; those who nurture him and direct his destiny have the right, coupled with the high duty, to recognize and prepare him for additional obligations." *Id.* at 535.

The foregoing principles form the basis for Appellant's contention that the right of self determination (or privacy) vouchsafed to an individual can and in the instant circumstances should be exercised on the individual's behalf by those closest to the individual. The constitutional protection afforded to individual choice is based on a recognition of the fact that the individual is initially in the best position to decide how any course of action will affect the totality of his thoughts, decisions, plans, values and abilities. Realizing this the law has become ever more clearly aware that constitutionally protected individual decisions can in certain circumstances have death as a concomitant. (*See,* 2. above p. 15) Once that possibility is recognized, the law must then determine how such right may be made effective with regard to the irreversibly comatose and terminally ill. Appellant contends that those in a position to know and appreciate the totality of a comatose person's approach to life are the ones who should be entrusted with decision-making power in her regard. Only in this way can the right of self-determination be adequately protected. If a decision is called for and ''self'' cannot make it, then those most closely identified with ''self'' must act instead. As between competing decision makers the Court should favor those most likely to konw how a given course of action would be judged by the incompetent subject.

Within such a framework the role of a physician, as such, is to provide the decision maker with a medically exact diagnosis and prognosis which the decision maker can utilize in arriving at an informed choice with regard to the continuation of treatment.

Indeed, society at present recognizes that a physician should not and may not impose on a decision maker the values held by the physician or by some section of the medical profession. *Cobbs* v. *Grant,* 8 Cal. 3d 229, 502 P.2d 1, 104 Cal. Rptr. 505 (1972). *Canterbury* v. *Spence,* 150 U.S. App. D.C. 263, 464 F.2d 772, *cert. den.* 409 U.S. 1064 (1972). While this principle has been utilized chiefly in the area of medical malpractice, the fundamental values it protects have been critically endangered by the Lower Court's decision, which placed sole and exclusive authority in the hands of the medical profession. (Pa75-76).

Testimony has shown that while medical tradition does in fact support Appellant's position (T269 through T273; T297-25; T298-3; T299-6 through 13; T300-1 through 11; T333-5 through 13), the treating physician was apparently not aware of such tradition, or else, it was not accepted by the medical community to which he belonged (T117-9 through 17; T118-1 through 18).

Appellant submits, however, that the treating physician's view of medical tradition cannot control or limit Appellant's constitutionally protected decision making authority.

4. Reasonable medical judgment with regard to irreversibility is a standard sufficiently precise to support a decision to terminate treatment.

A physician is required to use the standard of care common to that of his profession or specialized field. This standard never requires absolute certainty with regard to a diagnosis or prognosis. In fact such certainty is unattainable (Pa72; Pa73; Pa74).

In the light of such a standard the Trial Court erred in not finding that Karen's condition is medically hopeless (Pa74). No physician knew of any cure or treatment, and the only qualifications that any of the testifying physicians would put on their unanimous judgment of irreversibility (T468-25 through T469-5; T576-22; T601-15 through 17) were those represented by the possibility of a miracle (T110-16) or a total suspension of known physical laws (T82-14; T280-8 through 18). Yet the Trial Court gave significant weight to these infinitesimally small and medically meaningless possibilities[4] (T287-1 through 5; Pa74).

5. Appellant's decision is rooted in religious belief and its effectuation is protected by the Free Exercise Clause of the First Amendment to the United States Constitution.

The First Amendment to the United States Constitution as applied to the States through the Fourteenth Amendment prohibits the States from interfering with the free exercise of religious beliefs absent a compelling contrary secular interest.

---

[4] The Trial Court also felt it significant that "none of the doctors testified there was no hope" (Pa74). In point of fact, while most spoke in terms of "irreversibility", two doctors out of six used the term "hope" or "hopeless" (T568-18; Pa18). In addition the Trial Court specifically ruled, in response to an objection from counsel, that testimony as to hopelessness in a medical context was inadmissible (T266-1 through 12).

In *Sherbert* v. *Verner,* 374 U.S. 398 (1963), the United States Supreme Court held that an individual's right to the free exercise of his religion is secured against state interference under the Fourteenth Amendment.

Mr. Justice Brennan, in delivering the opinion of the Court, stated that "[t]he door of the Free Exercise Clause stands tightly closed against any governmental regulation of religious *beliefs* . . ." *Id.* at 402.

In weighing the individual's right against the interest advanced on behalf of the State Justice Brennan concluded that "any incidental burden on the free exercise of . . . religion may be justified by a 'compelling state interest within the State's constitutional power to regulate . . .' " *Id.* at 403 (quoting *NAACP* v. *Button,* 371 U.S. 415, 438 (1963)).

He then set forth the following test as determinative of a "compelling state interest":

"It is basic that no showing merely of a rational relationship to some colorable state interest in the regulation of a subject would suffice; in this highly sensitive constitutional area, '[o]nly the gravest abuses, endangering paramount interests, give occasion for permissible limitation.' " *Id.* at 406 (quoting *Thomas* v. *Collins,* 322 U.S. 516, 530 (1945)).

As stated above, the Quinlans desire to carry out a decision which is rooted in religious belief. It was reached after months of prayer and spiritual counselling. It is conceived of as being a cooperation in carrying out the Lord's will. It is an application of Christian and Catholic principles to one of the most important aspects of human existence. The decision does not spring from personal preference merely, but from deep religious conviction, shared by an organized group and intimately related to daily living. (T337-12 through 13; T343-5 through 14; T345-18 through 25; T346-1 through 25; T349-1 through 25; T350-1 through 10; T353-9 through 20; T354-5 through 20; T357-1 through 20; T359-2 through 13; T361-1 through 8; T366-9 through

25; T367-1 through 5; T379-6 through 19; T382-14 through 25; T383-1 through 12; T393-14 through 20; T394-1 through 25; T395-1 through 16; T402 through T410; T442-1 through 25; T469-1 through 19; T470-13 through 25; T473-8 through 25; Pa1 through 10) The fact that there is no positive religious mandate to discontinue treatment is irrelevant. The state may not make determinations as to the doctrinal status of any beliefs. *Watson* v. *Jones,* 13 Wall 679, 728, 20 L. Ed 666 (1871). So long as a course of action is taken or chosen within the framework of a religious quest for spiritual good, it makes no difference whether that course of action is obligatory or merely optional. It is entitled to the protection offered by the Free Exercise clause of the First Amendment and can be overcome only by a state interest no less compelling than that required to overcome a positive command. Nor is it true that action as opposed to belief is automatically outside the protection of the Free Exercise clause. *Wisconsin* v. *Yoder,* 406 U.S. 221 (1972). The same compelling state interest test must apply to both.

As applied to the dying patient and his family the Christian and Catholic principles referred to above reveal that:

"Life, health and temporal activities are in fact subordinated to spiritual ends . . . The rights and duties of the doctor are correlative to those of the patient. The doctor, in fact, has no separate or independent right where the patient is concerned. In general, he can take action only if the patient explicitly or implicitly, directly or indirectly, gives him permission. The technique of resuscitation, which concerns us here, does not contain anything immoral in itself. Therefore, the patient, if he were capable of making a personal decision, could lawfully use it and, consequently, give the doctor permission to use it. On the other hand, since these forms of treatment go beyond the ordinary means to which one is bound, it cannot be held that there is an obligation to use them, nor,

24

consequently, that one is bound to give the doctor permission to use them.

"The rights and duties of the family depend in general upon the presumed will of the unconscious patient if he is of age and *sui juris*. Where the proper and independent duty of the family is concerned, they are usually bound only to the use of ordinary means.

"Consequently, if it appears that the attempt at resuscitation constitutes in reality such a burden for the family that one cannot in all conscience impose it upon them, they can lawfully insist that the doctor should discontinue these attempts, and the doctor can lawfully comply. There is not involved here a case of direct disposal of the life of the patient, nor of euthanasia in any way: This would never be licit. Even when it causes the arrest of circulation, the interruption of attempts at resuscitation is never more than an indirect cause of the cessation of life, and one must apply in this case the principle of double effect and of *voluntarium in causa*." Pa5; Pa7; Pa8 *et seq.*)

POINT IV

Failure to grant Appellant's Petition subjects Appellant and his family, including his daughter Karen, to cruel and unusual punishment.

In *Furman* v. *Georgia*, 408 U.S. 238 (1972), the United States Supreme Court presented a detailed and scholarly analysis of the Eighth Amendment's "Cruel and Unusual Punishment" Clause.

Mr. Justice Brennan, in his concurring opinion, asserted that the challenged punishment must be examined in the light of the basic prohibition against inhuman treatment embodied in this Clause and held:

"At bottom then, the Cruel and Unusual Punishments Clause prohibits the infliction of uncivilized and inhuman punishments. The State, even as it punishes, must treat its members with respect for their intrinsic

25

worth as human beings. A punishment is 'cruel and unusual', therefore, if it does not comport with human dignity.'' *Id.* at 270.

He then enunciated four principles, standards, or guidelines to be followed in assessing the constitutional validity of State imposed punishments.

''The primary principle is that a punishment must not be so severe as to be degrading to the dignity of human beings.

* * *

''[T]he State must not arbitrarily inflict a severe punishment. This principle derives from the notion that the State does not respect human dignity when, without reason, it inflicts upon some people a severe punishment that it does not inflict upon others.

* * *

''A third principle inherent in the Clause is that a severe punishment must not be unacceptable to contemporary society. Rejection by society, of course, is a strong indication that a severe punishment does not comport with human dignity.

* * *

''The final principle inherent in the Clause is that a severe punishment must not be excessive. A punishment is excessive under this principle if it is unnecessary: The infliction of severe punishment by the State cannot comport with human dignity when it is nothing more than pointless infliction of suffering.'' *Id.* at 271, 274, 277 and 279.

The Trial Court held (i) that the Eighth Amendment has no applicability to this civil action since that Amendment is primarily directed to State-imposed criminal sanctions (Pa84; Pa85) and (ii) that the continuation of medical treatment in whatever form is not proscribed by the provisions of the Amendment (Pa85).

While it is conceded by the Appellant that historically, both in its adoption and application, the Eighth Amendment has been primarily directed towards the constitutional permissibility of criminal sanctions imposed by the State, a scrutiny of the implementing decisions reveals nothing to preclude its application to the instant civil proceeding.

In analyzing the substance rather than the form of the Trial Court's decision, it becomes clear that for the Court to require Karen, who is terminally ill and irreversibly comatose (T87-7 through 21; T370-24; T468-25 through T469-5; T576-22; T601-15 through 17), to be kept alive against her will (T487-7 through 492-23; T495-23 through T497-7; T516-25 through T518-19; Pa65) and the will of her family (T356-25 through 361-25; T473-20), and to deny their pleas for the suspension of the futile use of extraordinary medical measures (Pa45; Pa46) after the dignity, beauty, promise and meaning of earthly life have vanished, is to subject them to a cruel and unusual punishment in violation of the Eighth Amendment of the United States Constitution.

POINT VI

Withdrawal of treatment would not constitute homicide.

The fact that the withdrawal of treatment is in the best interests of Karen and is the result of a constitutionally protected decision leads to the conclusion that the court should authorize consent to such withdrawal; the fact that such consent may be lawfully given is based on the determination that (i) in the face of hopeless and irreversible coma (T344-24; T568-18 through 23; T468-25 through T469-5; T576-22; T601-15 through 17; Pa18-6), where life processes are sustained only by the use of extraordinary and futile medical measures (T80-20 through 25, T265-22 through 25; T273-19 through 25), continued treatment serves no valid medical purpose and may be re-

27

fused on the patient's behalf and that (ii) withdrawal of such extraordinary means would not constitute homicide since the causality implicit in such withdrawal is not predicated upon any breach of duty to Karen and is therefore not culpable. Criminal liability, in fact, requires duty, knowledge, and proximate cause. Withdrawal of treatment quite arguably can cause death, but if such withdrawal is done pursuant to a constitutional right or judicial determination of best interests, it cannot be said to involve a breach of duty and can therefore not be culpable. (Pa77, footnote 11). Such determinations of the rights of parties *inter sese* are the proper subject of a declaratory judgment, and may properly serve as a basis for enjoining both criminal prosecution and civil or administrative suits or proceedings (Pb6 through 11).

POINT VII

1. Withdrawal of the medical treatment presently being administered to Karen Quinlan is the only course of action which will promote her best interests.

In determining whether a course of action is in the "best interests" of an incompetent the court must consider the physical, mental, moral, spiritual, and financial welfare of the person and her estate. Fraser, *Guardianship of the Person*, 45 Ia. L. Rev. 239 (1960).

While there is a clear duty incumbent upon a guardian to provide necessary medical care for his ward, a court of equity will not compel the doing of a futile or useless act. *Cf., In re Barr's Guardianship*, 156 N.E.2d 357, 359 (Ohio Prob. 1958). Evidence adduced at trial made it clear that Karen Ann Quinlan has, since falling ill, received the best medical care obtainable; that her condition continues to deteriorate and that medical science holds no hope for her recovery. (T80-20 through 25; 87-7 through 21; 110-6 through 8; T265-22 through 25; T366-15; T370-24; T468-25 through T469-5; T576-22; T601-15 through 17; T344-24; T568-18 through 23; Pa18-6). For the court to mandate continued treatment in such circumstances would violate one of the most fundamental principles of equity and would
28

create a precedent requiring that the vital functions of all persons in similar circumstances be indefinitely sustained— a grotesque distortion of Hippocratic ideals.

The Court must not seek to impose a purely external standard in determining Karen's best interests; it must look to Karen's own needs and her previously expressed desires. See, Strunk v. Strunk, 445 S.W. 2d 145 (Ky. Ct. App. 1969); In re Green, 448 Pa. 338, 292 A.2d 387, 392 (1972). At Present Karen is in an irreversible coma. The natural tendencies of her body are being thwarted, and the treatment to which she is being subjected does no more than retard the inevitable collapse of a now disunified or-. ganism. It is axiomatic that life is sacred and that he who protects life does justice, but continuance of the present treatment makes a parody of the essential human dignity which finds its expression in the individual's exercise of the constitutionally protected right of self determination.

Evidence adduced at trial demonstrated that it was Karen's desire, should she ever be in a hopeless medical condition, to be spared the administration of futile measures to prolong external aspects of life (T484-7 through 492-23; T495-23 through T497-7; T516-25 through T518-19; Pa65). Guardianship law does not require that the desires of a ward or an incompetent always be heeded; but Karen was not a child, she was a mature thoughtful adult, and for the court to ignore her wishes in the present circumstances would be an exercise in arbitrary behavior, rather than an exercise of sound judicial discretion. See, In re Brooks, supra, at 361; In re Green, supra at 392.

As supreme guardian, the court may properly look to the religious and spiritual belief and profit of the incompetent. 22 A.L.R.2d 696 (1952). Karen was comforted by her faith in a life beyond death, and the court offends that belief by needlessly and artificially forstalling death, especially if, as the evidence has shown the only rational basis for so doing is the contention that life is to be preserved at any cost, a position opposed to Karen's understanding of human existence.

29

CONCLUSION

In light of the foregoing, it is respectfully submitted that this Court grant the prayer of the petitioner.

Respectfully submitted,

By _____
PAUL W. ARMSTRONG, Esquire
801 Lindsley Drive,
Morristown, New Jersey

By _____
JAMES M. CROWLEY, Esquire
Of the New York Bar

Attorneys for the Plaintiff—
Appellant
    Joseph Thomas Quinlan

Dated this 16th day
of December, 1975.

Defendant's Exhibit DD-2

THE PROLONGATION OF LIFE

*An Address of Pope Pius XII to an
International Congress of Anesthesiologists*

Le Dr. Bruno Haid   *November 24, 1957*

DR. BRUNO HAID, chief of the anesthesia section at the
surgery clinic of the University of Innsbruck, has submitted to Us three questions on medical morals treating the
subject known as "resuscitation" [*la réanimation*].

We are pleased, gentlemen, to grant this request, which
shows your great awareness of professional duties, and your
will to solve in the light of the principles of the Gospel the
delicate problems that confront you.

PROBLEMS OF ANESTHESIOLOGY

According to Dr. Haid's statement, modern anesthesiology deals not only with problems of analgesia and
anesthesia properly so-called, but also with those of "resuscitation." This is the name given in medicine, and
especially in anesthesiology, to the technique which makes
possible the remedying of certain occurrences which seriously threaten human life, especially asphyxia, which for-
merly, when modern anesthetizing equipment was not yet
available, would stop the heart-beat and bring about death
in a few minutes. The task of the anesthesiologist has

Reported in Osservatore Romano, November 25-26, 1957. French
text.   Translation based on one released by N.C.W.C. News Service.

This is a response to three questions submitted to the Holy
Father by Dr. Bruno Haid, chief of the anesthesia section at the
surgery clinic of the University of Innsbruck.   It was delivered during
an audience granted delegates to an International Congress of Anesthesiologists, meeting at Rome's Mendel Institute.

Another recent address to anesthesiologists, delivered on February 24, 1957, appears on page 33 of the Summer 1957 issue of The
Pope Speaks, under the title "Anesthesia: Three Moral Questions."

therefore extended to acute respiratory difficulties, provoked by strangulation or by open wounds of the chest. The anesthesiologist intervenes to prevent asphyxia resulting from the internal obstruction of breathing passages by the contents of the stomach or by drowning, to remedy total or partial respiratory paralysis in cases of serious tetanus, of poliomyelitis, of poisoning by gas, sedatives, or alcoholic intoxication, or even in cases of paralysis of the central respiratory apparatus caused by serious trauma of the brain.

THE PRACTICE OF "RESUSCITATION"

In the practice of resuscitation and in the treatment of persons who have suffered headwounds, and sometimes in the case of persons who have undergone brain surgery or of those who have suffered trauma of the brain through anoxia and remain in a state of deep unconsciousness, there arise a number of questions that concern medical morality and involve the principles of the philosophy of nature even more than those of analgesia.

It happens at times—as in the aforementioned cases of accidents and illnesses, the treatment of which offers reasonable hope of success—that the anesthesiologist can improve the general condition of patients who suffer from a serious lesion of the brain and whose situation at first might seem desperate. He restores breathing either through manual intervention or with the help of special instruments, clears the breathing passages, and provides for the artificial feeding of the patient.

Thanks to this treatment, and especially through the administration of oxygen by means of artificial respiration, a failing blood circulation picks up again and the appearance of the patient improves, sometimes very quickly, to such an extent that the anesthesiologist himself, or any other doctor who, trusting his experience, would have given up all hope, maintains a slight hope that spontaneous breathing will be restored. The family usually considers this improvement an astonishing result and is grateful to the doctor.

If the lesion of the brain is so serious that the patient will very probably, and even most certainly, not survive, the anesthesiologist is then led to ask himself the distressing question as to the value and meaning of the resuscitation processes. As an immediate measure he will apply artificial respiration by intubation and by aspiration of the respiratory tract; he is then in a safer position and has more time to decide what further must be done. But he can find himself in a delicate position, if the family considers that the efforts he has taken are improper and opposes them. In most cases this situation arises, not at the beginning of resuscitation attempts, but when the patient's condition, after a slight improvement at first, remains stationary and it becomes clear that only automatic artificial respiration is keeping him alive. The question then arises if one must, or if one can, continue the resuscitation process despite the fact that the soul may already have left the body.

The solution to this problem, already difficult in itself, becomes even more difficult when the family—themselves Catholic perhaps—insist that the doctor in charge, especially the anesthesiologist, remove the artificial respiration apparatus in order to allow the patient, who is already virtually dead, to pass away in peace.

A FUNDAMENTAL PROBLEM

Out of this situation there arises a question that is fundamental from the point of view of religion and the philosophy of nature. When, according to Christian faith, has death occurred in patients on whom modern methods of resuscitation have been used? Is Extreme Unction valid, at least as long as one can perceive heatbeats, even if the vital functions properly so-called have already disappeared, and if life depends only on the functioning of the artificial-respiration apparatus?

THREE QUESTIONS

The problems that arise in the modern practice of resuscitation can therefore be formulated in three questions:

First, does one have the right, or is one even under the obligation, to use modern artificial-respiration equipment in all cases, even those which, in the doctor's judgment, are completely hopeless?

Second, does one have the right, or is one under obligation, to remove the artificial-respiration apparatus when, after several days, the state of deep unconsciousness does not improve if, when it is removed, blood circulation will stop within a few minutes? What must be done in this case if the family of the patient, who has already received the last sacraments, urges the doctor to remove the apparatus? Is Extreme Unction still valid at this time?

Third, must a patient plunged into unconsciousness through central paralysis, but whose life—that is to say, blood circulation—is maintained through artificial respiration, and in whom there is no improvement after several days, be considered *"de facto"* or even *"de jure"* dead? Must one not wait for blood circulation to stop, in spite of the artificial respiration, before considering him dead?

BASIC PRINCIPLES

We shall willingly answer these three questions. But before examining them We would like to set forth the principles that will allow formulation of the answer.

34

Natural reason and Christian morals say that man (and whoever is entrusted with the task of taking care of his fellowman) has the right and the duty in case of serious illness to take the necessary treatment for the preservation of life and health. This duty that one has toward himself, toward God, toward the human community, and in most cases toward certain determined persons, derives from well ordered charity, from submission to the Creator, from social justice and even from strict justice, as well as from devotion toward one's family.

But normally one is held to use only ordinary means— according to circumstances of persons, places, times, and culture—that is to say, means that do not involve any grave burden for oneself or another. A more strict obligation would be too burdensome for most men and would render the attainment of the higher, more important good too difficult. Life, health, all temporal activities are in fact subordinated to spiritual ends. On the other hand, one is not forbidden to take more than the strictly necessary steps to preserve life and health, as long as he does not fail in some more serious duty.

ADMINISTRATION OF THE SACRAMENTS

Where the administration of sacraments to an unconscious man is concerned, the answer is drawn from the doctrine and practice of the Church which, for its part, follows the Lord's will as its rule of action. Sacraments are meant, by virtue of divine institution, for men of this world who are in the course of their earthly life, and, except for baptism itself, presuppose prior baptism of the recipient. He who is not a man, who is not yet a man, or is no longer a man, cannot receive the sacraments. Furthermore, if someone expresses his refusal, the sacraments cannot be administered to him against his will. God compels no one to accept sacramental grace.

When it is not known whether a person fulfills the necessary conditions for valid reception of the sacraments, an effort must be made to solve the doubt. If this effort fails, the sacrament will be conferred under at least a tacit condition (with the phrase *"Si capax est,"* "If you are capable,"—which is the broadest condition). Sacraments are instituted by Christ for men in order to save their souls. Therefore, in cases of extreme necessity, the Church tries extreme solutions in order to give man sacramental grace and assistance.

THE FACT OF DEATH

The question of the fact of death and that of verifying the fact itself *("de facto")* or its legal authenticity *("de jure")* have, because of their consequences, even in the field of morals and of religion, an even greater importance. What We have just said about the presupposed essential elements for the valid reception of a sacrament has shown this. But the importance of the question extends also to effects in matters of inheritance, marriage and matrimonial processes, benefices (vacancy of a benefice), and to many other questions of private and social life.

It remains for the doctor, and especially the anesthesiologist, to give a clear and precise definition of "death" and the "moment of death" of a patient who passes away in a state of unconsciousness. Here one can accept the usual concept of complete and final separation of the soul from the body; but in practice one must take into account the lack of precision of the terms "body" and "separation." One can put aside the possibility of a person being buried alive, for removal of the artificial respiration apparatus must necessarily bring about stoppage of blood circulation and therefore death within a few minutes.

In case of insoluble doubt, one can resort to presumptions of law and of fact. In general, it will be necessary to presume that life remains, because there is involved here a fundamental right received from the Creator, and it is necessary to prove with certainty that it has been lost.

We shall now pass to the solution of the particular questions.

A DOCTOR'S RIGHTS AND DUTIES

1. Does the anesthesiologist have the right, or is he bound, in all cases of deep unconsciousness, even in those that are considered to be completely hopeless in the opinion of the competent doctor, to use modern artificial respiration apparatus, even against the will of the family?

In ordinary cases one will grant that the anesthesiologist has the right to act in this manner, but he is not bound to do so, unless this becomes the only way of fulfilling another certain moral duty.

The rights and duties of the doctor are correlative to those of the patient. The doctor, in fact, has no separate or independent right where the patient is concerned. In general he can take action only if the patient explicitly or implicitly, directly or indirectly, gives him permission. The technique of resuscitation which concerns us here does not contain anything immoral in itself. Therefore the patient, if he were capable of making a personal decision, could lawfully use it and, consequently, give the doctor permission to use it. On the other hand, since these forms of treatment go beyond the ordinary means to which one is bound, it cannot be held that there is an obligation to use them nor, consequently, that one is bound to give the doctor permission to use them.

The rights and duties of the family depend in general upon the presumed will of the unconscious patient if he is of age and *"sui juris."* Where the proper and independent duty of the family is concerned, they are usually bound only to the use of ordinary means.

Consequently, if it appears that the attempt at resuscitation constitutes in reality such a burden for the family that one cannot in all conscience impose it upon them, they can lawfully insist that the doctor should discontinue these attempts, and the doctor can lawfully comply. There is not involved here a case of direct disposal of the life of the patient, nor of euthanasia in any way: this would never be licit. Even when it causes the arrest of circulation, the interruption of attempts at resuscitation is never more than an indirect cause of the cessation of life, and one must apply in this case the principle of double effect and of *"voluntarium in causa."*

Extreme Unction

2. We have, therefore, already answered the second question in essence: "Can the doctor remove the artificial respiration apparatus before the blood circulation has come to a complete stop? Can he do this, at least, when the patient has already received Extreme Unction? Is this Extreme Unction valid when it is administered at the moment when circulation ceases, or even after?"

We must give an affirmative answer to the first part of this question, as we have already explained. If Extreme Unction has not yet been administered, one must seek to prolong respiration until this has been done. But as far as concerns the validity of Extreme Unction at the moment when blood circulation stops completely or even after this moment, it is impossible to answer "yes" or "no."

If, as in the opinion of doctors, this complete cessation of circulation means a sure separation of the soul from the body, even if particular organs go on functioning, Extreme Unction would certainly not be valid, for the recipient would certainly not be a man anymore. And this is an indispensable condition for the reception of the sacraments.

If, on the other hand, doctors are of the opinion that the separation of the soul from the body is doubtful, and that this doubt cannot be solved, the validity of Extreme Unction is also doubtful. But, applying her usual rules: "The sacraments are for men" and "In case of extreme necessity one tries extreme measures," the Church allows the sacrament to be administered conditionally in respect to the sacramental sign.

WHEN IS ONE "DEAD"?

3. "When the blood circulation and the life of a patient who is deeply unconscious because of a central paralysis are maintained only through artificial respiration, and no improvement is noted after a few days, at what time does the Catholic Church consider the patient "dead," or when must he be declared dead according to natural law (questions *de facto* and *de jure*)?"

(Has death already occurred after grave trauma of the brain, which has provoked deep unconsciousness and central breathing paralysis, the fatal consequences of which have nevertheless been retarded by artificial respiration? Or does it occur, according to the present opinion of doctors, only when there is complete arrest of circulation despite prolonged artificial respiration?)

Where the verification of the fact in particular cases is concerned, the answer cannot be deduced from any religious and moral principle and, under this aspect, does not fall within the competence of the Church. Until an answer can be given, the question must remain open. But considerations of a general nature allow us to believe that human life continues for as long as its vital functions—distinguished from the simple life of organs—manifest themselves spontaneously or even with the help of artificial processes. A great number of these cases are the object of insoluble doubt, and must be dealt with according to the presumptions of law and of fact of which We have spoken.

May these explanations guide you and enlighten you when you must solve delicate questions arising in the practice of your profession. As a token of divine favors which We call upon you and all those who are dear to you, We heartily grant you Our Apostolic Blessing.

Plaintiffs' Exhibit P-6

MEDICAL AUTHORIZATION AND RELEASE

July 31, 1975

We authorize and direct Doctor Morse to discontinue all extraordinary measures, including the use of a respirator for our daughter Karen Quinlan.

We acknowledge that the above named physician has thoroughly discussed the above with us and that the consequences have been fully explained to us. Therefore, we hereby release from any and all liability the above named physician, associates and assistants of his choice, Saint Clare's Hospital and its agents and employees.

Dated: July 31, 1975

/s/ JOSEPH QUINLAN
Joseph Quinlan

/s/ JULIA QUINLAN
Julia Quinlan

In The

SUPREME COURT OF NEW JERSEY

September Term, 1975

Docket No. 12,041

IN THE MATTER OF KAREN ANN QUINLAN, AN ALLEGED INCOMPETENT

ON APPEAL FROM JUDGMENT OF THE SUPERIOR COURT OF NEW JERSEY,
CHANCERY DIVISION (MORRIS COUNTY)
SAT BELOW: HONORABLE ROBERT MUIR, JR., J.S.C.

BRIEF AND APPENDIX ON BEHALF OF THE ATTORNEY GENERAL OF NEW JERSEY

WILLIAM F. HYLAND
Attorney General of New Jersey
David S. Baime   *Attorney for Defendant*
John De Cicco   State House Annex
Of Counsel and on the Brief   Trenton, New Jersey 08625

Jane E. Deaterly
Daniel Louis Grossman
Robert E. Rochford
Deputy Attorneys General
On the Brief

COUNTER-STATEMENT OF PROCEDURAL HISTORY

Karen Ann Quinlan was admitted to the Newton Memorial Hospital on April 15, 1975 in a coma of unknown etiology. Subsequently, on April 24, 1975 she was transferred to St. Clare's Hospital in Denville. Karen Quinlan has remained, until the present date, in a chronic or persistent vegetative state. Her respiratory functions, and consequently her life, are dependent on an assistor respirator.

Joseph Quinlan, the father of twenty-one year old Karen Quinlan, instituted this action in the Chancery Division, Morris County, by complaint and order to show cause seeking a declaration of incompetency and appointment as guardian of his daughter's person and property. Although the complaint initially asserted that Karen Quinlan was legally and medically dead, the claim was abandoned prior to trial. This demand, however, was overshadowed by the extraordinary request that appellant's guardianship be coupled "with the express power of authorizing the discontinuance of all extraordinary means of sustaining the vital processes of his daughter." Appellant additionally requested an injunction barring St. Clare's Hospital and the treating physicians from interfering with his intended termination of the assistor respirator. Lastly, appellant sought to enjoin the Morris County Prosecutor from invoking our homicide laws (*N.J.S.A.* 2A:113-1) in the event that the court authorized discontinuance of the life sustaining devices.

At the pretrial conference of this matter, the State of New Jersey, through its Attorney General, intervened as a party defendant. The court also appointed Daniel Coburn, Esq., guardian *ad litem* pursuant to *R.*4: 26-2. All parties stipulated that Karen Ann Quinlan is unfit and unable to manage her own affairs.

This matter was tried on October 20, 21, 22, 23 and 27, 1975 before the Honorable Robert Muir, Jr., J.S.C. Exhaustive expert medical testimony regarding both accepted standards of medical practice and the condition of the incompetent was elicited during trial. Decision was reserved, and on November 10, 1975 the trial court, in an extensive opinion, denied the requested relief. *In the Matter of Karen Quinlan, An Alleged Incompetent, ____ N.J. Super. ____ (Ch.Div. 1975).* The essence of the court's opinion was that the care being administered to Karen Ann Quinlan is consistent with, and indeed mandated by, accepted medical practice. The cessation of such care would be a medical determination. Moreover, the court rejected constitutional arguments designed to afford a guardian the ability to direct termination of his ward's life. Consequently, appellant was appointed guardian of his daughter's property and Daniel Coburn, Esq., was appointed guardian of her person.

A Notice of Appeal from Judge Muir's decision was filed on November 17, 1975. Thereafter, pursuant to *R.*2:12-1, the Court directly certified this case and provided for an expedited briefing and argument schedule.

COUNTER-STATEMENT OF FACTS

Introduction

This case presents questions of great public importance. The magnitude of this controversy cannot be gainsaid. The relief initially sought at the trial level, and now in this Court, is unique in jurisprudential history. Succinctly stated, the issue is whether a parent or guardian may authorize termination of the life of a child or ward and, simultaneously, bar others from providing life-sustaining treatment in circumstances clearly contrary to accepted medical practice.

The material facts are uncontroverted and are essentially a matter of record. Karen Ann Quinlan was admitted to the Newton Memorial Hospital on April 15, 1975 suffering from a coma of unknown etiology. Although not completely substantiated, various laboratory tests indicated that her condition may have been the result of the simultaneous ingestion of barbiturates and alcohol. Several days thereafter, on April 24, 1975, the patient was transferred to the Intensive Care Unit at St. Clare's Hospital in Denville where she was placed in the care of Doctors Robert Morse and Arshad Javed. At the time of her transfer Karen Quinlan's life was being sustained by an assistor respirator.

Doctors Morse and Javed were severely hampered by the paucity of available medical history. However, Doctor Morse, a neurologist, definitely concluded that Karen Quinlan was in a chronic or persistent vegetative state characterized by decortication of the brain, *i.e.*, the partial

43

destruction of neurons connecting the neocortex and the lower components of the brain. Moreover, a lesion, most probably in the mid-brain, was accountable for the patient's inability to spontaneously breathe without the respirator. Dr. Javed, a pulmonary internist, was unsuccessful in his attempts to "wean" Karen from the respirator for any significant period of time. On each occasion, she would experience "apnea", which is characterized by rapid-breathing with diminishing oxygenation of the blood. This necessitated placing the patient back on the respirator in order to avert further brain damage and ultimately death. Moreover, much of the time, Karen was unable to spontaneously breathe even while on the respirator. The hospital records indicated that these episodes have lasted for as long as 50 minutes. Thus, it is readily apparent that the continued existence of Karen Quinlan is entirely dependent upon the assistor respirator.

At the onset of Karen's illness, and for some time thereafter, the Quinlan family nourished hope for her recovery. However, as the months passed and her condition did not improve, various family members concluded that the medical devices sustaining Karen's life should be removed. Mrs. Quinlan and her children were the first to reach this decision. They were encouraged by the pastor of their church who informed them that their religion did not require the use of "extraordinary" means to sustain life. Mr. Quinlan, the "hold-out", was the last to decide that his daughter's life should no longer be sustained on the respirator. Mr. Quinlan had also been counseled by the pastor of the parish. Thereafter, the Quinlans requested the doctors to discontinue use of the respirator. The attending physicians and the hospital were unanimous in their rejection of this extraordinary demand. Mr. Quinlan then instituted this suit.

The trial of this matter consisted largely of the testimony of the attending physicians and expert neurologists. There was virtually unanimous agreement that the care presently being administered to Karen Quinlan was entirely consistent with accepted medical practice. Moreover, the testimony, particularly that of Dr. Sidney Diamond, an eminent neurologist, indicated that use of the respirator was not only consistent with, but mandated by, medical practice and ethics.

The appellant's case rested primarily upon an optional tenet of his religion and several statements attributed to his daughter. The Catholic religion permits its followers to determine whether "extraordinary" care should be continued in certain situations. However, it is uncontroverted that the Quinlans' religion does not mandate the requested relief. Rather, the Church teaches that there is no moral distinction between the use or discontinuance of extraordinary means of life support. The various statements attributed to Karen Quinlan indicated that she would not wish to be kept alive by the use of "extraordinary medical devices." However, these statements, although admitted over vigorous objection, were ascribed little probative value in view of the circumstances surrounding their utterance.

The Chancery Division denied the relief sought by appellant and this appeal followed.

Trial

Joseph Quinlan, the father of Ms. Quinlan, instituted the present action seeking authorization to discontinue the respirator sustaining his daughter's life. (T334-4 to 23). Mr. Quinlan is a follower of the Roman Catholic faith and a member of the Our Lady of the Lake parish in Mount Arlington. (T335-6 to 14). His three children, including Karen, were raised as members of the Catholic faith. (T335-14 to 15). In this regard, each of the children have received various sacraments of the Church. Further, they have all attended parochial elementary and secondary schools. (T336-12 to 16).

Mr. Quinlan's decision to resolve the plight of his daughter by terminating use of the respirator was months in the making. (T340-3 to 9). This determination was prompted by a series of meetings between Mr. Quinlan and the attending physicians. At these meetings the doctors described the condition of their patient and her prognosis. (T340-13 to T341-14). Dr. Morse had advised Mr. Quinlan that Karen could survive for as long as a year in her present condition. His response was that a year was "a long time." (T341-15 to 22). Believing that his daughter's illness was absolutely hopeless and that she was going to die, Mr. Quinlan ultimately decided to allow Karen to expire. Yet, it should be noted that he always maintained that his position would be materially altered if there was any hope. (T358-1 to 6).

Mr. Quinlan sought the advice of his pastor, Father Thomas Trapasso. (T343-1 to 14). According to appellant, his decision to urge discontinuation of "extraordinary" means of life support was made prior to his knowledge of the Church's position. (T372-4 to 11). After speaking with Father Trapasso and learning that his resolve did not deviate from Catholic tradition, Mr. Quinlan's decision became final. (T334-15 to 21; T372-22 to T373-1).

Mr. Quinlan conceded that his daughter had never informed him of

45

her religious convictions with regard to the use of extraordinary life sustaining treatment. However, as her parent, and in view of her incompetency, he believed that he had the right to "give her back to the Lord." (T349-2 to 6). Moreover, it was Mr. Quinlan's view that he had the authority to exercise Karen's right of self-determination regardless of her religious beliefs. (T350-11 to 23).

Julia Ann Quinlan, Karen's mother, vigorously supported her husband's decision to terminate use of the respirator. (T468-8 to 20). Indeed, Mrs. Quinlan was the first family member to decide that Karen's condition was hopeless and that her life should not be sustained by the respirator. She then discussed her decision with her two other children, Mary Ellen and John, who disagreed with her conclusion. Moreover, Mrs. Quinlan was aware that her husband was not ready to concede his daughter's life. Therefore, she determined to be patient until her family was able to reach a concensus. (T469-6 to 19). However, during this interval she confided, on a daily basis, with Father Trapasso regarding her dilemma. Father Trapasso advised that she should be patient with her family and that eventually her husband and children would agree with her decision. (T470-1 to 5). Father Trapasso informed Mrs. Quinlan that the Church did not require that Karen's life be extended by extraordinary means. Mrs. Quinlan became convinced that the respirator was an extraordinary device. (T473-13 to 17). Subsequently, she and Father Cacavalle, the hospital's chaplain, conversed with regard to the question of sustaining Karen's life. They also concluded that the matter should not be discussed with Mr. Quinlan until he demonstrated a readiness to accept this result. (T470-13 to 23).

Mrs. Quinlan maintained that on various occasions, she had discussed the concept of "extraordinary" means of sustaining life with her daughter, Karen. (T474-2 to 5). Approximately three years prior to Karen's illness, an aunt was dying of cancer of the breast and was in great pain. Miss Quinlan allegedly stated that she would never want to be kept alive by "extraordinary" means. (T484-12 to 16; T487-7 to 22). Karen Quinlan allegedly made the same statement in January 1974 when a girlfriend's father was also dying of cancer. (T476-21 to 23). A third statement was supposedly made in January 1975 when a close friend of the family requested that he be allowed to die at home rather than be sustained at a hospital by extraordinary means. (T486-4 to 14). He also was in great pain and dying of a brain tumor. (T489-1 to T490-14). Present during the first and third conversations was Laurie Gaffney, a friend of Karen. Mary Ellen Quinlan allegedly witnessed the second and third statements. (T477-12 to 16; T496-19 to T497-4). Mrs. Quinlan conceded that her daughter did not use the term "extraordinary" in its medical context. (T492-18 to 23).

In July, Mr. and Mrs. Quinlan agreed that it would be preferable to compel the removal of their daughter from the respirator. (T473-19 to 24). As previously discussed, Fathers Trapasso and Cacavalle played a dominant role in this momentous decision.

Father Thomas J. Trapasso, pastor of Our Lady of the Lake Parish advised the Quinlans that the Catholic Church does not require utilization of extraordinary means to prolong life and that they were not morally obliged to use such techniques. (T402-1 to 6). Father Trapasso defined "extraordinary" as "something that is very demanding, very prolonged, creating hardship either for the patient or the family." (T403-1 to 7).

Father Trapasso first addressed the subject of removal from the respirator at a meeting between Mr. Quinlan and Dr. Javed. The discussion concerned the possibility of weaning Karen from the machine. Father Trapasso was aware that Mr. Quinlan was "the one family holdout" regarding permanent withdrawal of the respirator. He also knew that Mrs. Quinlan had accepted the inevitability of the situation. However, she and Father Trapasso were concerned about Mr. Quinlan's grasp of the problem. Therefore, Father Trapasso felt obligated as a friend and religious advisor to broach the subject with Mr. Quinlan in order that the decision be made by an unanimous family. (T415-15 to 24). Thus, although Father Trapasso was requested to attend the meeting due to appellant's concern that the weaning process might be a risk to Karen's life, the occasion was utilized as a vehicle for informing Mr. Quinlan that the Church did not require Karen's maintenance on the respirator. Consequently, Father Trapasso advised Mr. Quinlan that he could risk weaning Karen from the machine and that this process would not be contrary to Catholic teaching. At this point in time, Mr. Quinlan still maintained hope for his daughter. (T480-10). However, as noted, Father Trapasso was of the view that the case was hopeless and that Mr. Quinlan was being unrealistic. (T408-11 to 14). After the meeting with Dr. Javed, Mr. Quinlan and Father Trapasso proceeded to a diner for coffee. Father Trapasso, still unsure whether Mr. Quinlan fully understood the Church's position, stated that, "if he should ever decide upon this course of action, according to my understanding of our faith, that this would be a moral stance that you could take." (T408-17 to 19).

Approximately two weeks after this conversation, Mr. Quinlan visited Father Trapasso and stated that he had decided to terminate the respirator. (T409-1 to 14). At this second meeting, Father Trapasso again

47

reassured Mr. Quinlan regarding the teachings of the Church. He stated that continuation of the respirator was optional and not mandatory. (T409-16 to T411-4).

Father Trapasso conceded that to his knowledge Karen Quinlan was not familiar with the doctrine of the Church regarding extraordinary life support devices. (T419-1 to 12). Father Trapasso also acknowledged that Pope Pius XII's statement in 1957, which recognized the distinction between extraordinary and ordinary care, was not binding as a matter of dogma with regard to those of the Catholic faith. (T431-23 to T432-4). Moreover, Father Trapasso readily admitted that the refusal of the treating physicians to discontinue treatment was not inconsistent with the position of the Church. (T424-20 to T425-15).

Mr. and Mrs. Quinlan, accompanied by Father Trapasso, requested a meeting with the attending physicians and hospital administrators in order to implement their decision regarding Karen. This meeting was also attended by Father Cacavelle, the hospital chaplain. Both Fathers Trapasso and Cacavelle advised the group regarding Church dogma. (T441-10 to T444-18; T345-11 to T346-22). There is some dispute as to whether the doctors and the hospital immediately refused the family's request. (T346-7 to 22). In any event, shortly thereafter, Dr. Morse and the hospital administrators unequivocally declined to discontinue treatment. (T387-19 to 25). It was at this juncture that the Quinlans enlisted the aid of the courts to implement their extraordinary request to allow their daughter to die.

Quite obviously, central to this case is the actual condition of Karen Quinlan and the relevant medical standards as related by the attending physicians and expert neurologists. Dr. Robert Joseph Morse, a neurologist and the principal treating physician of Karen Ann Quinlan, first examined his patient as a consultant at Newton Memorial Hospital on April 18, 1975. (T55-10 to 19). This examination occurred three days after her admission. (T60-9 to 10). Dr. Morse attempted to obtain a medical history relating to the etiology of Karen Quinlan's condition. However, after conferring with her parents and with the treating physicians, and following their review of the relevant hospital records, it became evident that there was a paucity of available information. This deficiency rendered Dr. Morse's task exceedingly difficult since the pertinent history is crucial in the field of neurology. (T56-13 to 25).

Dr. Morse's initial impression was that Karen Quinlan was comatose and that her physical manifestations indicated decortication of the brain.

(T60-4 to 7). Moreover, the assistor respirator seemed necessary to sustain the patient. However, she was able to maintain her own blood pressure and her body temperature. (T116-8 to 11). In his view, Karen's condition was the result of a prolonged period of anoxia, *i.e.*, lack of oxygen in the bloodstream. (T101-21 to 25). The Newton Memorial records indicated a presence of quinine, valium, and librium in the patient's blood. (T99-21 to T100-11). Therefore, Dr. Morse initially concluded that the anoxia was caused by a drug overdose. (T102-10 to 13).

On April 25, 1975, Karen Quinlan was transferred to Dr. Morse's service at St. Clare's Hospital in Denville. (T56-1 to 7). Dr. Morse immediately conducted extensive and detailed examinations of his patient. Initially, an electroencephalogram was performed. The electroencephalograph measures the cellular electrical cortex and cerebral activity of the brain (T129-6 to 11). Dr. Morse characterized the results as "slow for a girl of 21 years of age and ... consistent with her clinical state." (T62-18 to 21). Although the EEG was somewhat abnormal, it depicted electrical activity. (T62-25). Other significant neurological tests, including a brain scan, an angiogram and a lumbar puncture were all within normal ranges. (T63-3 to T65-21).

Dr. Morse's exhaustive examinations revealed that Karen Quinlan's comatose state was characterized by her inability to manifest normal states of arousal and her complete lack of contact with the environment. (T69-23 to T70-14). Specifically, in her case, the brain had experienced decortication. This infirmity involves lesions in the white matter and connecting neurons separating the cerebral cortex from the remainder of the brain. Decortication would account for most of the symptoms manifested by Karen Quinlan. (T133-4 to T-134-5). Moreover, these lesions are also present in the brain stem and are probably the cause of her respiratory disorder. (T147-5 to 8). Dr. Morse believed that the lesions were caused by a metabolic insult, such as anoxia, rather than by an external force, such as a fall or blow. (T151-7 to 18). The short form medical description of Karen's neurological state was denominated as a "chronic or persistent vegetative state." (T73-9 to 12).

When Karen was first admitted she manifested a "sleep like unresponsive coma." In a matter of weeks, her condition was altered to an "awake unresponsive coma." This type of coma is characterized by "sleep-wake" cycles. Although a patient in this type of coma completely lacks consciousness, that individual may yet experience varying stages of alertness. (T70-17 to T71-4). Thus, when Karen is in her "awake" cycle, her eyes are open and she blinks and moves. (T72-1 to 25). In her "sleep" cycle she is less active. (T72-25). More importantly, the "sleep-wake" cycles are decisive with respect to the patient's ability to spontaneously breathe. In this regard Dr. Morse determined that Karen Quinlan was dependent on the respirator. Dr. Morse's experience indicated that during her sleep periods Karen does not breathe spontaneously and the respirator must breathe for her. Since the respiratory system is a brain stem function, Karen's inability to spontaneously breathe indicates a disfunction of that part of her brain. (T86-3 to T87-6). Dr. Morse was unable to categorize utilization of the respirator as either "ordinary" or "extraordinary" due to the patient's obvious physcan dependence on that device for life. (T112-8 to 22).

Dr. Morse did not discount the possibility that Karen's condition was reversible. (T152-13 to 15). He was, however, pessimistic regarding the quality and level of functional existence which Miss Quinlan might regain. (T74-14 to 19).

The Quinlan family's decision to terminate use of the respirator was unexpected by Dr. Morse and rather sudden. Until that point, the treatment being administered to their daughter was completely consistent with the wishes of the parents. (T91-6 to 9). However, in July, the family requested Dr. Morse to cease using "extraordinary" means, in particular the respirator, to sustain their daughter's life. This request was made during a meeting between Dr. Morse, Mr. and Mrs. Quinlan, the family priest, a nurse, and hospital administrators. (T94-3 to 18; T94-12 to 12; T97-1 to 4). Dr. Morse, although a devout Catholic, was unfamiliar with the concept of antidysthanasia. However, at this meeting the family urged that such a course of action would not be inconsistent with the Catholic Church's teachings. (T97-1 to 8). Mention was also made of a release authorizing the removal of the extraordinary measures sustaining Karen Quinlan's life. (T154-18 to 155-8). Dr. Morse's position was unaffected by the release since he was concerned solely with the possibility of removal of the respirator from a medical viewpoint. (T155-11 to 21). In this regard, Dr. Morse carefully investigated the feasibility of discontinuance of the respirator. He concluded that the family's request could not be honored since he was unable to reconcile such action with accepted medical practice. He immediately notified the family of his decision not to break with medical tradition. (T94-19 to T95-10; T156-1 to 11; T158-1 to 11).

Dr. Morse indicated that he would not remove the respirator even should the court order him to do so. He stated that this stance was a matter of medical judgment. The witness testified that there were no medical precedents which would authorize the relief sought. (T117-3 to

25). Thus, in view of the fact that the patient was not brain dead, removal of the respirator was not supported by accepted medical practice. (T118-6 to 18).

Dr. Arshad Javed, a pulmonary internist, was solicited by Dr. Morse to assist in the treatment of Karen Quinlan. In view of the patient's respiratory difficulties, expert pulmonary care was required. Dr. Javed readily agreed to attend Miss Quinlan. (T169-14 to 20). Dr. Javed's initial examination of the patient occurred immediately subsequent to her transfer from Newton Memorial Hospital. At that time, the patient was not breathing spontaneously, and therefore, was totally dependent on the respirator. (T170-1 to 11). Dr. Javed learned that the patient had contracted pneumonia and that her condition was much improved. However, he ordered that the administration of antibiotics be continued. (T170-12 to 15).

Karen Quinlan's maintenance on the respirator was continued by Dr. Javed. The type of respirator being utilized delivers a fixed volume of air at a predetermined rate. Moreover, the device will deliver a "sigh" volume at specified intervals. This function prevents collection of excretions in those portions of the lungs which do not expand with normal tidal volume. (T176-23 to T177-7). On those occasions when the patient does not breathe simultaneously, the respirator completely takes over at a set rate and delivers a fixed volume of air. (T178-1 to 5).

Dr. Javed determined that Karen Quinlan's dependence on the respirator varies from total reliance to merely an assistive function. When the patient is in the awake cycle she is more apt to initiate her own breathing. However, even during this phase, her breathing is irregular in that she ingests varying quantities of air with each breath. (T178-19 to 25). During her sleep cycle she does not assist the respirator and the machine must completely assume her respiratory functions. (T179-6 to 10).

On various occasions during Dr. Javed's treatment of Karen Quinlan, he attempted to "wean" her from the respirator. The weaning process, if successful, would eventually result in complete reliance on the patient's own ability to breathe. However, prior to weaning a patient off a respirator, certain criteria must be met. The patient should be able to both maintain a stable respiratory pattern, and to move a certain volume of air without mechanical assistance. Karen Quinlan has dismally failed to meet these requirements. She has been removed from the respirator for short periods of time. On each occasion her respiratory rate increased. At the same time, her tidal volume, *i.e.,* the amount of air ingested, decreased. In each instance, it became necessary to place the patient back on the respirator to prevent further damage or even death. (T181-1 to T182-3).

Dr. Javed conducted a series of blood gas tests on the patient. The purpose of this test is to determine the quantitative level of carbon dioxide and oxygen in the blood. The results provide one of several methods of measuring the patient's ability to spontaneously breathe. (T175-7 to T176-12). While on the respirator, Karen demonstrated no abnormality. (T176-11 to 16). However, since Dr. Javed was only able to maintain the patient off the respirator for periods of up to a half hour, he could not obtain a definitive blood gas test. Nevertheless, he did observe a drop in the level of oxygen in the blood while off the respirator. (T181-14 to T182-3).

At the present time, Dr. Javed has abandoned his attempts to remove Karen Quinlan from the respirator. He views her respiratory difficulty as a secondary manifestation of her basic neurological problem. Since there has been no change in her neurological condition, he is of the opinion that no benefit could be derived from further weaning efforts. (T182-5 to 17). In Dr. Javed's considered medical judgment, removal of the respirator would cause anoxia leading to additional brain damage and ultimately death. (T197-13 to T198-8). Therefore, a court order directing removal of Karen from the respirator would violate traditional standards of medical practice in the field of pulmonary medicine. (T200-20 to 24). The physician has thus unequivocally refused to comply with the family's demand. (T184-5 to T185-19).

Subsequent to the inception of this action, Karen Quinlan was examined by a number of eminent neurologists. It is noteworthy that they were unanimous regarding the quality of care being administered to Karen. Virtually all of the experts agreed that Doctors Morse and Javed were treating Karen in a manner consistent with accepted medical practice. Indeed, no expert was able to testify that either medical practice or ethics would permit removal of the respirator in order to allow the patient to expire. Most instructive in this regard was the testimony of Doctor Sidney Diamond.

Dr. Diamond, a professor of neurology at Mt. Sinai School of Medicine in New York, performed an extensive neurological examination of Karen Quinlan on October 15, 1975. The physician's services were procured by defendant, the State of New Jersey (T607-20 to 24). Dr. Diamond's examination of the patient consumed approximately three hours. (T608-10). His examination was witnessed by Dr. Andrew Bender, Dr. Robert Morse, and Dr. Arshad Javed, as well as several nurses and hospital administrators. (T608-3 to 6).

Dr. Diamond also exhaustively reviewed the hospital charts and notes. (T608-19 to 21). In this manner he was able to obtain as complete a history of the patient as possible under the circumstances. (T608-19 to 25). The history as related by Dr. Diamond indicated that on April 15, 1975 Karen Quinlan lost consciousness and required respiratory assistance. There was evidence that artificial respiration was performed by an inexperienced individual. Although there was no reliable information concerning the cause of the comatose condition and accompanying respiratory distress, the laboratory evidence indicated that Miss Quinlan had ingested various sedatives, an analgesic, and alcohol. (T609-2 to 21). Upon admission to the hospital, the attending physicians took all necessary measures to support Karen's life. By April 18 it was evident that the patient was showing signs of decortication. (T610-4 to 12). This condition is manifested by certain paroxysms of movement in posturing that indicate a loss of continuity between the upper portion of the brain, *i.e.,* the cortex, and the mid-brain and brain stem. (T611-1 to 9).

Dr. Diamond's physical examination of the patient revealed that she was emaciated and that all her joints were bent in a flexion posture resembling a fetal position. (T612-2 to 8). Her eyes moved in a random fashion. Dr. Diamond observed her from afar for approximately five minutes. During that period he noted that the patient experienced approximately five episodes of paroxysms causing even greater flexion of her muscles. Upon closer observation Dr. Diamond noted that the patient would blink if challenged by stimuli in her visual field. (T612-22 to 25). He was unable to obtain any reflex activity because of the patient's rigid flexion. (T612-12 to 14). When he touched her face or applied other stimuli, the patient would experience the spasms described above. (T613-18 to 24). Dr. Diamond definitely concluded that Miss Quinlan did not meet any of the currently accepted brain death criteria. (T615-1 to 9).

Dr. Diamond observed the patient's sleep-wake cycles. During her more alert periods Miss Quinlan breathed spontaneously. However, Dr. Diamond indicated that this does not necessarily mean that she can breathe without use of the respirator. (T616-15 to 22). During the less alert or sleep phase, the patient was unable to spontaneously breathe. (T616-23 to 25). Indeed, during such periods Karen Quinlan had to be automatically respired for as long as an hour. (T617-1 to 7). If removed from the respirator while spontaneously breathing, the patient's respiration became increasingly rapid. If left off the machine in this state she would cease to breathe. (T617-17 to 19). Therefore, Dr. Diamond unequivocally concluded that removal of the respirator would terminate Karen Quinlan's physical existence. (T617-17 to T618-3).

Dr. Diamond concluded that continued use of the respirator under the circumstances of this case is in conformity with standard medical practice. He cogently observed that "no physician to my knowledge will ever interrupt a device which is performing a life saving measure." (T618-21 and 22). Therefore, removal of the respirator would only be warranted in situations where a patient has met the criteria of brain death. (T619-1 to 8). Doctor Diamond's examination of Miss Quinlan and his neurological expertise indicated that the treating physicians have acted in all respects in accordance with standard medical practice. Indeed, it is not within a physician's competence to determine when life support systems should be withheld and a life thereby terminated. (T619-9 to 11; T621-5 to 18).

The expert neurologist retained by the Quinlans did not contradict the conclusions reached by Dr. Diamond. Dr. Julius Korein, a Professor of Neurology at New York University, examined Karen Quinlan and reviewed the pertinent hospital records. The examination of the patient occurred on Friday, October 10, 1975. Dr. Korein obtained the history of the patient from the treating physicians and the medical reports (T221-1 to 10). He described Miss Quinlan as an emaciated woman with flexion contractures of the upper extremities and flexor contractures of the knees. (T224-10 to 18). During Dr. Korein's initial observations, the patient was not triggering the respirator and the machine was breathing for her. (T229-20 to 24). Dr. Korein applied various stimuli in order to elicit responses. With a minimal amount of stimulation, the patient would briefly trigger the respirator. Further stimulation would evoke eye-opening, eye-blinking and random disconjugated movements of the eyes. (T230-14 to T231-11). With application of noxious stimuli there would also be a marked arousal reaction. The patient's eyes would open and random eye movements would occur with maximal yawning. These reactions were characterized as stereotype. (T232-2 to 11).

An EEG was performed during Dr. Korein's examination. Dr. Korein interpreted the test results as demonstrating a moderate abnormal bilateral cerebral disfunction indicating moderate damage to the cerebral hemispheres. (T235-6 to 21).

Dr. Korein observed that the patient did not trigger the respirator during her sleep cycle and that the machine had to breathe for her. (T237-18 to T238-24). Dr. Korein learned that Karen had gone for periods of as long as fifty minutes without triggering the respirator. (T239-13 to 15). He reiterated however that various stimuli aroused the patient and that she would then activate the respirator. (T239-1 to 23). Dr. Korein conceded that the patient is dependent on the respirator. (T267-9 to 20).

The physician concluded from his consultation with the treating physicians and his review of the hospital records that the patient had suffered a sustained period of anoxia. Although the cause was not clear he indicated that a combination of drugs and alcohol could have been the offending agents. (T246-2 to 9).

Dr. Korein's impression as to Karen's condition was that the damage to her brain was localized in the high brain stem coupled with severe bilateral involvement. (T254-13 to 25). He generally described her condition as consistent with a persistent or chronic vegetative state. (T255-1 to 10). Dr. Korein typified the care being administered to Karen Quinlan as "extraordinary." However, the doctor recognized that treatment considered extraordinary in the recent past may now be commonplace or "ordinary." (T296-1 to T300-22). Moreover, the terms are not capable of precise definition. (T322-15 to 18).

Doctors Eugene Loeser, Stewart Cook, and Frederick Plum jointly examined Karen Quinlan on October 2, 1975 at the request of the guardian *ad litem*. (T549-7 to T550-5). Their conclusions and impressions were virtually identical to those of the treating physicians and Drs. Diamond and Korein, with one exception. They hypothesized that Karen could be removed from the respirator. They noted, however, that there were lengthy apneic periods. Further, they conceded that their opinion would be subject to verification by a pulmonary specialist. (T565-6 to 14). In this regard, it should be recalled that Dr. Javed's experience refuted such a possibility.

Based on the foregoing facts, the Chancery Division denied the relief sought and this appeal followed.

LEGAL ARGUMENT

Appellant's Request for Judicial Authorization to Terminate Extraordinary Means of Sustaining the Incompetent's Life Was Properly Denied.

A. The Chancery Division Correctly Delimited The Scope of Its Jurisdiction.

Preliminarily, we observe that appellant presented a "case or controversy" and that the Chancery Division had jurisdiction over the subject matter. In essence, appellant sought the issuance of declaratory relief whereby he would be appointed guardian for the incompetent with the express power to discontinue extraordinary life support systems. While not denominated a declaratory judgment action (*N.J.S.A.* 2A:16-50, *et seq.*), the gravamen of appellant's claim was a request for a judicial declaration of rights and obligations.

Initially, it is to be observed that appellant properly instituted this action in the Chancery Division. Original general jurisdiction in New Jersey is constitutionally vested in the various divisions of the Superior Court. *N.J. Const.*, Art. VI, §3, Paras. 2 & 3. Our Rules provide that a party seeking relief primarily equitable in nature must bring suit in the Chancery Division. *R.* 4:3-1(a)(1). However, the chancery court is not restricted to solely equitable matters. *N.J. Const.*, Art. VI, §3, Para. 4. It may exercise the Jurisdiction of the Law Division when such is necessary for a complete resolution of the controversy. *Id.*; *Unterman* v. *Unterman*, 19 *N.J.* 507 (1955); *Steiner* v. *Stein*, 2 *N.J.* 367 (1949); *Fleischer* v. *James Drug Stores*, 1 *N.J.* 138 (1948). Appellant's prayer for relief in the form of appointment of a guardian with instructions clearly invoked the equitable jurisdiction of the Chancery Division. *R.* 4:3-1(a)(1).

The authority of a court to honor a guardian's request for instructions by issuing declaratory relief is well established.[1] Such a procedure is especially appropriate where the guardian is in doubt as to the legality of a proposed course of action,[2] or when his private interest conflicts with that of his ward.[3] So too, one may enlist the aid of the judiciary in determining the propriety of the appointment of a guardian for an incompetent.[4] Significantly, as here, this remedy may be invoked to elucidate a guardian's duty with respect to his ward's medical treatment.[5]

The question remains whether this action was ripe for judicial resolution. Although our Constitution, unlike its federal counterpart, does not explicitly refer to a "case or controversy" requirement, this concept has been judicially incorporated into our jurisprudence.[6] A party must thus demonstrate a sufficient stake in the outcome of the litigation in order to invoke the aid of the courts.[7] The rendering of advisory abstract or hypothetical opinions is undisputably proscribed.[8] In short, a request for declaratory and equitable relief does not dispense with the requirement that the conflict be real and ripe for decision.[9] However, no existing or past wrong need be proved.[10] "The existence of a claim, or threat of a possible claim casting doubt upon [a party's] rights or status" satisfies the justiciability criterion.[11] Thus, where doubt arises as to the criminality of a proposed activity, a party need not assume the risk of prosecution by performing the act in question.[12] Rather, he may seek adjudication of his rights prior to embarking upon a questionable course of conduct.[13] This approach has been followed even in the absence of a specific threat of prosecution where the legality of the activity in issue is unclear.[14] Indeed, testing a criminal statute by conduct rather than by means of declaratory relief has been repeatedly disapproved by this Court.[15]

Here, it is evident that the requirement of justiciability has been amply satisfied. No discernible policy would have been furthered by compelling appellant to terminate life support systems at the risk of incurring criminal or civil penalties.[16] Since all parties, including the State, concede that Karen Ann Quinlan is incompetent, the power to dispose of her property and to determine the nature and extent of her medical treatment was properly vested in the court below. That court correctly bifurcated the duties of guardian with the result that the incompetent's father is now authorized to administer her property and the guardian *ad litem* is entrusted with the care of her person. This was eminently correct.

In addition, the court appropriately declined to render a declaratory judgment sanctioning medical adherence to a particular definition of "brain death" and its supporting criteria.[17] As noted previously, appellant initially claimed that the incompetent's condition met the definition of brain death. He subsequently abandoned that contention. However, during the course of trial, the hospital, while conceding that the incompetent was alive under any applicable standard, sought amendment of the pretrial order and requested the Chancery Division to rule that brain death was the proper criterion. Specifically, the hospital argued that the concept of brain death had been fully accepted by the medical profession and thus sought a declaratory judgment to that effect. The court noted that the "request [was] to make a determination in the abstract and [was] not a proper subject for judicial resolution." *In the Matter of Karen Quinlan, An Alleged Incompetent, ____ N.J. Super. ____, ____ (Ch. Div. 1975).*

In our view, the trial judge properly denied the hospital's request. The Declaratory Judgment Act, *N.J.S.A.* 2A:16-50 *et seq.*, was created to relieve uncertainty and insecurity of legal rights and to preclude costly and onerous multiple actions. *Union Cty. Bd. of Chosen Freeholders* v. *Union Cty. Park Comm.*, 41 *N.J.* 333 (1964); *Bergen Cty.* v. *Port of New York Auth.*, 32 *N.J.* 303 (1960). As we have noted, such a procedure may be employed to clarify a guardian's duties. However, declaratory relief cannot be employed as a vehicle to resolve a hypothetical dispute. *Crescent Park Tenant's Ass'n* v. *Realty Corp.*, 58 *N.J.* 98 (1971). Accordingly, the trial court's refusal to adopt a brain death standard with accompanying criteria was a proper and indeed sagacious exercise of judicial restraint.[18]

B.   The Chancery Division Properly Refused To Authorize The Termination of Extraordinary Life Support Systems.

i

We now turn to the grave question whether the judiciary may appoint a guardian with the express authorization to discontinue all extraordinary life-sustaining medical treatment. We approach this issue with great trepidation since there can be no doubt that the relief requested would ultimately result in the death of the incompetent. Appellant's claim is grounded upon the theory that there is a constitutional right to die. His present appeal is bottomed upon the assertion that a parent or guardian possess a derivative right to terminate a life by withholding medical care. Appellant's contention goes much further, however. In essence, he would bar the medical profession from providing life-sustaining treatment. Succinctly stated, appellant seeks to enlist the aid of the judiciary to prevent the treating physicians from administering medical care in accordance with their sound professional judgment. This request is all the more extraordinary in light of the testimony of medical experts that "no physician ... [would] interrupt" treatment under the circumstances present here. (T618-21 and 22). In sum, judicial intervention is sought despite the uncontroverted fact that the treating physicians have acted in accordance with standard medical practice. (T621-5 to 18).

The Chancery Division held that there was no legal basis to support appellant's request for relief. Finding no precedent which would permit a course of action designed to terminate life, the court concluded that the letter and spirit of the law express a profound concern with protecting human existence, irrespective of its quality. The Chancery Division thus refused to interfere with the doctors', the hospital's and the State's concomitant interests to protect the incompetent's most vital asset, her life. We agree.

ii

Preservation of life is government's primary mission. Indeed, "the right to life is inalienable in our society." *Glietman* v. *Cosgrove*, 49 *N.J.* 22, 30 (1967). Protection of human existence is deeply rooted in our jurisprudence and forms the very reason for government, as the preamble to the United States Constitution plainly says. See also *N.J. Const.*, Art. 1, para. 1, §21. Our judiciary has vigorously defended the State's compelling interest in preserving life. That interest has been held to outweigh the assertion of other constitutional rights.[19]

The Chancery Division relied in part upon the landmark case of *J.F.K. Memorial Hospital* v. *Heston*, 58 *N.J.* 576 (1971). There, this Court affirmed a trial judge's emergent grant of guardianship to a hospital for the purpose of administering a blood transfusion for an incompetent adult over the previously expressed objections of the patient and her family. The defendants were Jehovah's Witnesses and a tenet of their faith forbids blood transfusion.[20] It was undisputed that the patient would expire unless operated upon for a ruptured spleen. The operation would have been impossible unless whole blood was administered. This Court found that the religious beliefs of the patient and her family were insufficient to overcome the State's paramount interest in preserving life. Significantly, the Court concluded that "there is no constitutional right to choose to die." *Id.* at 580. "It is commonplace for the police and other citizens, often at great risk to themselves, to use force or strategem to defeat efforts at suicide, and it hardly could be said that thus to save someone from himself violated a constitutional right."[21] *Id.* The Court went on to note that a constitutional right cannot be asserted by adding, as here, that one's religious faith ordains his death. "Religious beliefs are absolute, but conduct" in their pursuance "is not wholly immune from governmental restraint." *Id.* If a court finds that death will be imminent unless treatment is administered, "the hospital and the physician should be permitted to follow that medical procedure." *Id.* at 583.

We recognize that *Heston* involved the administration of medical treatment designed to "cure" the patient, *i.e.,* to return the patient to a state of full health as a functioning human being. To be sure, use of the respirator in this case will not, by itself, restore the incompetent's cognitive functions. It would appear that the cerebral capacity of the incompetent has been irretrievably lost. Nevertheless, as we stated at trial, human life, in whatever form, is the principal concern of the State. It is not for the executive or judicial branches of government to evaluate the quality and usefulness of life, and based upon that assessment, to conclude that a citizen's existence is not worth preserving. If a person's life could be terminated because others have determined that it is unworthy of protection, no one in our society would be safe. In a similar context, this Court has opted for the preservation of human life despite what some might perceive to be its inferior quality. See *Gleitman* v. *Cosgrove, supra.* As this Court noted in *Gleitman* v. *Cosgrove, supra,* involving questions relating to eugenic abortions, "[t]he sanctity of the single human life is the decisive factor... ." *Id.* at 30. Though we sympathize with the unfortunate situation the Quinlan family finds itself in, "we firmly believe the right of [the]child to live is greater and precludes [the right of her family] not to endure emotional ... injury." *Id.* at 31.

Other New Jersey precedent strongly supports the result in *Heston*. No combination of individual rights with religious practice or tenets has ever been found sufficient to override the interest of the State in preserving the lives and safety of its citizenry.[22] Similar results have been reached in other jurisdictions.[23] In point of fact, extensive research has failed to reveal any decision permitting a guardian to withdraw or withhold consent to medical treatment necessary to sustain the life of an incompetent. Accordingly, the trial court's decision to preserve life is consistent with precedent and with the pervasive State policy of protecting human existence. As the court below recognized, no guardian may affirmatively discharge his obligation in such a manner so as to destroy the very life of his ward.

If, as this Court held in *Heston,* the State's interest in preserving life outweighs the expressed desire of the patient to die, it can hardly be argued that a guardian may choose to terminate the life of his ward. Surely, the guardian's right to practice religion freely does not include the liberty to expose his ward to ill health or death. See *Prince* v. *Massachusetts*, 321 *U.S.* 158, 166-67 (1944). Rather, the guardian is legally obliged to protect the interests of one entrusted to his care.[24] A guardian's primary duty is to advance and protect his ward's best interests. And, in determining the best interests of an incompetent, a guardian must act to protect the life and health of his ward, although his own private convictions and religious beliefs might suggest otherwise.[25] "It is basic to the human condition to seek life and hold on to it however heavily burdened." *Gleitman* v. *Cosgrove, supra* at 30. "For the living there is hope, but for the dead there is none." *Id.* at 30. It bears repeating that the "choice is not between being born with health or being born without it... ." *Id.* at 63. "Rather, the choice is between a worldly existence and none at all." *Id.* See also *In The Matter of Karen Quinlan, An Alleged Incompetent, supra* at ____. We submit that the sanctity of human life, however inferior the quality, must prevail.

iii

Appellant contends that the prior statements of the incompetent are relevant in defining the guardian's legal obligations. At trial, evidence was presented, over the vigorous objection of the Attorney General, that the incompetent had on several occasions expressed a wish that her life not be prolonged by extraordinary medical treatment in the event she were to suffer from a terminal illness. In essence, it is argued that these statements must be recognized and given effect under the principle of substituted judgment.

Appellant can take no solace in the doctrine of substituted judgment. Under that concept, a guardian is obliged to act in such a manner as the ward would have approved.[26] Thus, it is arguable that prior statements of the ward are pertinent in determining future care. However, as the court below ruled, the exercise of a guardian's authority must conform to the civil and criminal law of the jurisdiction. A guardian's authority flows from that of the State. Therefore, that authority can only be exercised pursuant to implicit and explicit regulations as established by public policy. See *Raleigh Fitkin-Paul Morgan Memorial Hospital* v. *Anderson, supra,* 42 *N.J.* at 423-24; *State* v. *Perricone, supra,* 37 *N.J.* at 477-78. The State, acting in the role of *parens patriae* is the ultimate guardian of all incompetents.[27] Clearly therefore, public policy must take precedence over the previously expressed desires of the incompetent, and as noted by this Court in *Heston,* there is no constitutional right to choose to die. For this reason, we submit Ms. Quinlan's prior statements, relied upon by appellant, are wholly immaterial and ought to be disregarded.

In any event, reliance upon the incompetent's statements would be improper for other reasons. First, Ms. Quinlan's statements do not tend to demonstrate her putative desires in the present circumstances and are thus irrelevant.[28] Quite plainly, the casual statements of a conscious, fully functioning, and healthy individual cannot logically prove that person's desires when actually confronted with the life-death decision. Moreover, it is significant that these statements were made in contemplation of a lengthy and painful terminal illness. They therefore reflect nothing more than the incompetent's general wish to avoid prolonged suffering. They do not bear any rational relationship to a constructive formulation of her current intentions as a comatose, nonsuffering individual. Rather, "our felt intuition of human nature tells us [the incompetent] would almost surely choose life with defects as against no life at all." *Gleitman* v. *Cosgrove, supra* at 30. Second, the conversations constituted unreliable hearsay and should not have been admitted at trial. It seems obvious that this evidence can only establish the state of mind of the incompetent when the statements were made. No evidence was presented from which it could properly be inferred that the incompetent's state of mind was a continuing one. In short, the circumstances surrounding the statements do not afford a sufficient guarantee of testimonial trustworthiness to justify admissibility. See *Evid. R.* 63(12)(a); *State* v. *Baldwin,* 47 *N.J.* 379, 394 (1966), *cert.* den. 385 *U.S.* 980 (1966); *In re Spiegelglass,* 48 *N.J.Super.* 265 (App.Div. 1958), certif. den. 26 *N.J.* 302

(1958). Third, the statements, as found by the trial court, "were not persuasive to establish a probative weight sufficient to [support a finding that the incompetent] would elect her own removal from the respirator." *In the Matter of Karen Quinlan, An Alleged Incompetent, supra* at _____. Thus, the statements of the incompetent have no bearing on the legal duties and obligations owed by the guardian.

Nor are the incompetent's statements material with respect to the legal obligations owed by the treating physicians. It is true that a physician's duty to his patient arises in part by contract. *Young* v. *Crescente*, 132 *N.J.L.* 223 (E. & A. 1944). If a doctor fails to perform his duties under a contract or to adequately inform the patient of the risk associated with a course of treatment, he may become exposed to civil liability. See *Lopez* v. *Swyer*, 115 *N.J.Super.* 237 (App.Div. 1971), aff'd and remanded 62 *N.J.* 267 (1973); *Cobbs* v. *Grant*, 8 *Cal.* 3d 229, 242, 502 *P.* 2d 19, 104 *Cal.Rptr.* 505, 513 (Sup.Ct. 1972); *Collins* v. *Itoh*, 160 *Mont.* 461, 503 *P.*2d 36, 40 (Sup.Ct. 1972); *Wilkinson* v. *Vesey*, 110 *R.I.* 606, 619, 295 *A.*2d 676, 685 (Sup.Ct. 1972); *Trogun* v. *Fruchtman*, 58 *Wis.*2d 569, 596 n.30, 207 *N.W.*2d 297, 311 n.30 (Sup.Ct. 1973). Thus, hypothetically, a patient's statements evidencing his expectations may have some bearing upon the physician's responsibilities. Nevertheless, in certain situations, this contractual duty must yield to the physician's fiduciary obligation to act in the patient's best interests. *Hammonds* v. *Aetna Cas. & Ins. Co.*, 237 *F.Supp.* 96 (N.D. Ohio 1965); *Moore* v. *Webb*, 345 *S.W.*2d 239 (Mo.App.Ct. 1963); *Stacey* v. *Patano*, 131 *N.W.*2d 163 (Neb.Sup.Ct. 1964); *Ison* v. *McFall*, 400 *S.W.*2d 243 (Tenn.App. 1964); *Allison* v. *Blewett*, 348 *S.W.*2d 182 (Tex.Civ.App. 1964). This trust relation arises from professionally imposed duties and from the obligation that is imposed by the State in the exercise of its police powers.[29] Quite plainly, the physician's duty to act as a fiduciary arises in emergent circumstances, *Hanig* v. *Orton*, 119 *N.J.L.* 248 (Sup.Ct. 1937), or when consent to medical treatment has been unlawfully withheld. *State* v. *Perricone, supra*. It is equally clear that a physician cannot contract to commit an unlawful act, a crime, or to perform his professional responsibilities in a manner repugnant to public policy. See, *e.g., Gleitman* v. *Cosgrove, supra* at 40, 48. *Cf. J.F.K. Memorial Hospital* v. *Heston, supra*.

We have previously alluded to the testimony of medical experts in this case and it would be superfluous to repeat it here in detail. Suffice it to say, it was uncontroverted that the treatment being administered to the incompetent did not deviate from medical tradition. Indeed, the firm refusal of the attending physicians to terminate use of the respirator was concurred in by an eminent physician at trial who aptly observed that to accede to the parents' demand would be tantamount to abdicating professional judgment and responsibility. See also Epstein, *The Role of the Physician In Prolongation of Life, Controversies in Medicine II* (1973). Judicial intervention to compel a physician to act contrary to his professional obligations would be irresponsible. Predilections of judges in such a sensitive technical area are no substitute for educated medical judgment.

iv

The Quinlans and the incompetent are Roman Catholics. That religion permits an individual (or his family if the individual is comatose) to reject extraordinary means of prolonging life. Pope Pius XII, "The Prolongation of Life," 4 *Pope Speaks* 393 (1958). See Elliot, *The Gods of Life* (1974); Flew, "The Principle of Euthanasia," in *Euthanasia and the Right to Death* (Downing ed., 1969), at 139; but see Martin, "Euthanasia: The Three-In-One Issue," 27 *Baylor L. Rev.* 62, 67 (1975). Clearly, no mandatory religious practice is involved in the acceptance or rejection of respirator treatment. *Id.* No sin is committed by voluntary or involuntary submission to such medical care.

Nevertheless, appellant argues that his First Amendment right to freely exercise his religion embraces the liberty to determine when heroic medical treatment is to be terminated. He first contends that his daughter, as a practicing Roman Catholic, could elect to cease extraordinary medical care although such a decision would ultimately lead to her demise. Appellant, as father of the incompetent, claims a derivative right.

The trial court was unpersuaded. Based upon the testimony, the Chancery Division found that, under Roman Catholic theory, "it is neither a mortal sin to continue nor discontinue 'extraordinary' means of support for the body functions." *In re Karen Quinlan, An Alleged Incompetent, supra* at ____. The decision to discontinue extraordinary treatment was thus considered to be "optional" with the individual involved. According to the court, to continue or discontinue heroic medical care "does not conflict with the teachings of the Church." *Id.* The trial judge therefore concluded that the thesis was "not a dogma of the Church ... rooted in religious belief" and that there was no governmental or other interference that "is caused by the court's refusal to authorize the termination of the respirator." *Id.*

In our view, the State's overriding interest in preserving human life must prevail. Simply stated, free exercise of religion encompasses no right to choose death. While the State may not regulate the formation of an individual's religious beliefs, it may, pursuant to the police power, control the manner in which those beliefs are exercised.[30] A person may not act in accordance with his religious beliefs to the detriment of himself or the general welfare. Even though his religion absolutely requires an activity, the sovereign may completely forbid its practice, so long as a compelling state interest is present.[31] *A fortiori*, when, as here, a religion merely permits a certain course of conduct but does not mandate it, no right may be successfully asserted to override the State's compelling interest.

Appellant's contention that a constitutional right of privacy encompasses the freedom to choose to die is equally unavailing. Since an explicitly protected right such as the free exercise of religion cannot overcome the State's interest in protecting the individual or the general welfare, no amorphous constitutional formulation could do so.[32] Several courts[33] and commentators[34] have purported to identify a "right to die." This "right" seems to have been extrapolated from the recently recognized right to privacy. That right has emerged from two leading United States Supreme Court decisions. In *Griswold* v. *Connecticut,* 381 *U.S.* 479, 485-86 (1965), a statute barring the use and distribution of contraceptives was invalidated on the ground that it violated the marital right to privacy. *Roe* v. *Wade,* 410 *U.S.* 130 (1973), overturned a Texas statute forbidding abortion on the ground that it violated a pregnant woman's right to privacy and to control her body until the second trimester. Neither case is absolute in its terms. *Griswold* rested on the absence of a compelling state interest. 381 *U.S.* at 484-86. *Roe* expressly recognized the right of states to define life and to extend or withhold legal protections in otherwise "gray" areas. See 410 *U.S.* at 162-64. *Roe* further sanctioned state regulation of medical procedures designed to protect the lives of its citizens. New Jersey legislation designed to effect this goal has been upheld. *State* v. *Norflett,* 67 *N.J.* 268 (1975).

Even if the right of privacy included a right to elect to die, the record plainly discloses that the incompetent is unable to make that choice. The trial court could find no convincing evidence that the incompetent would have desired termination of respirator treatment. In the absence of such a showing, the court relied in part upon a presumption favoring continuation of life. See *Gleitman* v. *Cosgrove, supra* at 30. This decision was the only ethically and legally sound course for the court to follow. *Cf. Bowman* v. *Redding & Co., Inc.* 449 *F.*2d 956 (D.D.C. 1971); *Fontenot* v. *Southern Farm Bureau Cas. Ins. Co.,* 304 *So.*2d 690, 693 (La. App.

1974). The incompetent was equally incapable of exercising any right to die that might have been reserved under the Ninth Amendment. *U.S. Const.*, Amend. IX. The judiciary has declined to accept the suggestions of several commentators that an independent right to die arises from the Ninth Amendment or the Due Process and Equal Protection Clauses of the Fourteenth Amendment.[35]

The absence of a constitutional guarantee embracing a right to die is consistent with the general scheme of American organic law. Life is explicitly protected by the Due Process Clause of the Fifth and Fourteenth Amendments. *U.S. Const.*, Amends. V, XIV. See *N.J. Const.*, Art. 1, para. 1. Thus, the right to live is fundamental and no state action in derogation of that right is permissible.[36] Arguably the State's failure to adequately defend a comatose terminal patient's last fundamental right might well deny that citizen equal protection of the law.[37] The decision below to refuse authorization to discontinue respirator treatment, and thereby terminate the incompetent's life, provided an appropriate judicial safeguard protecting the patient's constitutional rights.

The trial court properly dismissed as without merit appellant's claim that continued respirator treatment would constitute cruel and unusual punishment in contravention of the Eighth Amendment. *U.S. Const.*, Amend. VIII; see *Furman* v. *Georgia*, 408 *U.S.* 238 (1972). Appellant's contention is frivolous and is not deserving of extended treatment. It is beyond question that the State's defense of an individual's life cannot be considered a criminal sanction.

In sum, New Jersey has chosen to place a high regard on the sanctity of human life. See *J.F.K. Memorial Hospital* v. *Heston, supra*; *State* v. *Perricone, supra*. No mere guardian can strip an individual of the safeguards the State has created to protect life. These safeguards are consistent with the demands of the Federal and State Constitutions. If social ethics must be adjusted to meet medical advances, the Legislature and not the Judiciary is the only governmental entity equipped to make that adjustment.[38]

V

We cannot fully treat the issues raised without some reference being made to the concept of euthanasia. We realize that appellant is not in this case actively advancing the cause of euthanasia. Nevertheless, within the context of the arguments asserted, the concept of euthanasia deserves comment. Euthanasia literally means "happy death."[39] A leading exponent defines it as "... the deliberate easing into death of a patient suffering from a painful and fatal disease."[40] Commentators have sought to distinguish between "voluntary" and "involuntary" forms of euthanasia. Involuntary euthanasia is the termination of an individual's life without his consent. Voluntary enthanasia connotes the termination of an individual's life in accord with his wishes.[41] Voluntary enthanasia has attracted increasing support as the potential for prolonging life by use of "heroic" measures has increased.[42] The development of "heroic" measures to preserve life has engendered a distinction between ordinary and extraordinary treatment. Extraordinary treatment is the use of artificial means to prolong a patient's life once his vital processes have ceased their spontaneous functions.[43] The failure to take positive action to prolong the life of an incurable patient is termed antidysthanasia.[44]

Theoretically, a failure to take a positive step is deemed an act of omission rather than an act of commission. No other criminal sanctions attach to omissions which cause harm to others, unless there is a legal duty to act.[45] Proponents of euthanasia contend that antidysthanasia is nothing more than a human forebearance that permits nature to take its course. Accordingly, they consider the withholding of extraordinary life support measures to be a morally and legally acceptable form of passive euthanasia. They further embrace the theory that the termination of such measures is likewise permissible.[46] Support for these views is primarily based in theological and philosophical discussion.[47] Orthodox criminal law is to the contrary.

Criminal homicide is the unlawful killing of a human being by another.[48] If death results from an omission to act, that omission is non-culpable unless there was a preexisting duty.[49] But a knowing, intentional act which results in the death of another clearly subjects the actor to criminal liability.[50] It is axiomatic that "to shorten the life of one suffering from an incurable disease, or one already dying from a mortal injury..." is homicide. Perkins, *Criminal Law* (2d ed. 1969), at p. 31 citing *Commonwealth* v. *Bowen*, 13 *Mass.* 356 (Sup.Jud.Ct. 1816).[51] Proponents of antydysthanasia have sought to utilize the act/omission dichotomy to blur the distinction between culpable and non-culpable conduct.[52] Be that as it may, the facts here plainly reveal that the guardian owes the patient the duty of continuing extraordinary life-sustaining treatment. This was amply demonstrated by the testimony of the treating physicians and the medical experts that termination of respirator treatment would ultimately lead to the incompetent's death and be contrary to standard medical practice. Termination of life support systems currently sustaining the incompetent would thus constitute an omission contrary to the fiduciary obligation of the guardian.

Finally, it is of no consequence that the guardian is acting within what he deems to be the best interests of the ward. See *In re Richardson*, 254 *So.* 2d 185 (La.Ct.App. 1973), *cert.* den. 284 *So.* 2d 338 (Sup.Ct. 1973). We sympathize with the plight of the Quinlans. We do not wish to add to their anguish. However, humanitarian motives cannot justify the taking of a human life. See *State* v. *Ehlers*, 98 *N.J.L.* 236, 240 (E. & A. 1922); *People* v. *Roberts,* 211 *Mich.* 187, 178 *N.W.* 690 (Sup.Ct. 1920). New Jersey rejects humanitarian motives as a defense. *State* v. *Ehlers, supra* at 240. Other cases support this position.[53] Under these circumstances, we are constrained to oppose appellant's application for authorization to discontinue extraordinary life-sustaining treatment. We submit that the Chancery Division was eminently correct in its factual findings and conclusions of law. The decision below should therefore be affirmed.

CONCLUSION

For the foregoing reasons it is respectfully submitted that this Court affirm the Chancery Division's denial of appellant's application for judicial authorization to terminate the life support devices sustaining the vital functions of Karen Quinlan.

Respectfully submitted,

WILLIAM F. HYLAND
Attorney General of New Jersey

By: _____

DAVID S. BAIME
Deputy Attorney General

DAVID S. BAIME
JOHN DE CICCO
Deputy Attorneys General

Of Counsel and on the Brief

JANE E. DEATERLY
DANIEL L. GROSSMAN
ROBERT E. ROCHFORD
Deputy Attorneys General

On the Brief

[1]*In re Hosford's Estate*, 26 N.J. Super. 412 (App.Div. 1953); *In re Trott*, 119 N.J. Super. 436 (Ch.Div. 1972); *Fidelity Union Trust Co. v. Cavanagh*, 61 N.J. Super. 96 (Ch.Div. 1960), Rev'd 67 N.J. Super. 564 (App.Div. 1961), mod. 36 N.J. 561 (1962); *Trustees of Rutgers College* v. *Richman*, 41 N.J. Super. 259 (Ch.Div. 1956); *Hungerford & Terry, Inc.* v. *Geschwindt*, 24 N.J. Super. 385 (Ch.Div. 1953), aff'd 27 N.J. Super. 515 (App.Div. 1953); *Fidelity Union Trust Co.* v. *Cory*, 9 N.J. Super. 308 (Ch.Div. 1950); *Marsh* v. *Scott*, 2 N.J. Super. 240 (Ch.Div. 1949); *Taylor* v. *Errion*, 137 N.J. Eq. 495 (E. & A. 1947); *Pennsylvania Co.* v. *Gillmore*, 137 N.J. Eq.51 (Ch. 1945); *In re Fidelity Union Title and Mortgage Guaranty Co.*, 133 N.J. Eq. 320 (Ch. 1943), aff'd 134 N.J. Eq. 59 (E. & A. 1943); *In re Badenhop's Estate*, 61 N.J. Super. 526, 533 (Cty. Ct. 1960). *See also* N.J.S.A. 2A:16-52.

[2]*In re Conway's Estate*, 92 N.J. Super. 428 (App.Div. 1966), remanded 50 N.J. 525 (1967); *Fidelity Union Trust Co.* v. *Cavanagh, supra*; accord, *Pennsylvania Co.* v. *Gillmore, supra; In re Fidelity Union Title and Mortgage Guaranty Co., supra; Camden Trust Co.* v. *Thorne*, 141 N.J. Eq. 342 (Ch. 1948); *Trustees of Princeton University* v. *Wilson*, 78 N.J. Eq. 1 (Ch. 1910).

[3]*In re Badenhop's Estate, supra*; accord, *Hungerford & Terry, Inc.* v. *Geschwindt, supra; Fidelity Union Trust Co.* v. *Cory, supra; Taylor* v. *Errion, supra.*

[4]See *Marsh* v. *Scott, supra;* see also N.J.S.A. 3A:6-36.

[5]See *John F. Kennedy Memorial Hospital* v. *Heston*, 58 N.J. 576 (1971); *State* v. *Perricone*, 37 N.J. 463 (1962); *Muhlenberg Hospital* v. *Patterson*, 128 N.J.Super. 499 (Law Div. 1974); see also *Raleigh Fitkin— Paul Morgan Memorial Hospital* v. *Anderson*, 42 N.J. 421 (1964); *Hoener* v. *Bertinato*, 67 N.J.Super. 517 (J.D.R.C. 1961).

[6]U.S. Const., Art. III, §2; N.J. Const., Art. VI, §1; see also *Crescent Park Tenant's Ass'n* v. *Realty Equities Corp.*, 58 N.J. 98, 107 (1971); *Walker* v. *Stanhope*, 23 N.J. 658, 660 (1947); accord, *New Jersey Turnpike Auth.* v. *Parsons*, 3 N.J. 235 (1960).

[7]*Crescent Park Tenant's Ass'n* v. *Realty Equities Corp., supra* at 107; *Walker* v. *Stanhope, supra* at 660.

[8]*Id.*; see also *Hartford Indemnity Co.* v. *Selected Risks Indemnity Co.*, 65 N.J.Super. 328, 332 (App.Div. 1961); *Wagner* v. *Ligham*, 37 N.J. Super. 430, 431 (App.Div. 1955); *In re Seabrook's Will*, 90 N.J. Super. 553, 558 (Ch. Div. 1966).

[9]*Rego Industries, Inc.* v. *American Modern Metals Corp.*, 91 N.J. Super. 447, 452-53 (App.Div. 1966); *Euing* v. *Trenton*, 137 N.J. Eq. 109 (Ch.1945).

[10]*Lucky Calendar Corp.* v. *Cohen*, 19 N.J. 399 (1955), aff'd on rehearing 20 N.J. 451 (1966); *In re Seabrook's Will, supra* at 577-78; *New Jersey Home Builders Ass'n* v. *Division on Civil Rights*, 81 N.J. Super. 243, 251 (Ch.Div. 1963), aff'd sub nom. *David* v. *Vesta Co.*, 45 N.J. 301 (1965); *Dirabio* v. *Southard*, 106 N.J. Eq. 157, 159 (Ch.1930); *Tanner* v. *Boynton Lumber Co.*, 98 N.J. Eq. 85, 89 (Ch.1925).

[11]*Camarco* v. *Orange*, 111 N.J.Super. 400, 402 (Law Div. 1970), aff'd 116 N.J.Super. 531 (App.Div. 1971), aff'd 61 N.J. 463 (1972); accord *New Jersey Home Builders Ass'n* v. *Division on Civil Rights, supra; Trustees of Rutgers College* v. *Richman, supra.*

[12]See *State* v. *Baird*, 50 N.J. 376, 378 (1967); *Lucky Calendar Corp.* v. *Cohen, supra; Blackman* v. *Iles*, 4 N.J. 82 (1956); *Keuper* v. *Wilson*, 111 N.J.Super. 502, 506 (Ch.Div. 1970); *Camarco* v. *Orange, supra* at 402; *Thrillo, Inc.* v. *Scott*, 15 N.J.Super. 124, 129 (Law Div. 1951); see also *Sanitary Vendors, Inc.* v. *Byrne*, 72 N.J.Super. 276, 279-80 (Law Div. 1962).

[13]*State* v. *Baird, supra; Lucky Calendar Corp.* v. *Cohen, supra; Blackman* v. *Iles, supra* at 87-88; *Keuper* v. *Wilson, supra* at 506; *Camarco* v. *Orange, supra; Thrillo, Inc.* v. *Scott, supra* at 129-30; see also *Sanitary Vendors, Inc.* v. *Byrne, supra* at 279-90.

[14]*Blackman* v. *Iles, supra; New Jersey Home Builders Ass'n* v. *Division on Civil Rights, supra.*

[15]*State* v. *Baird, supra* at 378; *Lucky Calendar Corp.* v. *Cohen, supra.*

[16]Since the Chancery Division denied appellant the authority to terminate extraordinary life support systems it was unnecessary to reach the question whether the Morris County Prosecutor could be enjoined from instituting a criminal prosecution. Nevertheless, in this regard we would emphasize the well-established equitable maxim that ordinarily criminal prosecutions will not be enjoined. *Keuper* v. *Wilson, supra* at 504; *Eleuteri* v. *Richman*, 47 N.J.Super. 26 (App.Div. 1957), aff'd 26 N.J. 586 (1953), *cert.* den. 358 U.S. 843 (1955); *Frey* v. *Dixon*, 141 N.J. Eq. 481, 482 (Ch.1948); *Higgins* v. *Krogman*, 140 N.J. Eq. 518, 520 (Ch.1947), aff'd 142 N.J. Eq. 691 (E. & A. 1948); *Dell Publishing Co.* v. *Beggans*, 110 N.J. Eq. 72, 74 (Ch.1932); see also *Bantam Books, Inc.* v. *Melko*, 25 N.J.Super. 292, 298 (Ch.Div. 1953), mod. 14 N.J. 524 (1954).

[17]The traditional legal definition of death focused on the cessation of cardiovascular and respiratory functions. *Black's Law Dictionary* (4th ed. 1968), p. 488; *Dortland's Illustrated Medical Dictionary* (24 ed. 1965), p. 387. See, *e.g.*, *Schmitt* v. *Pierce*, 344 S.W.2d 120 (Mo.Sup.Ct. 1961); *Smith* v. *Smith*, 229 Ark. 479, 317 S.W.2d 275 (Sup.Ct. 1958); *Gray* v. *Sawyer*, 247 S.W.2d 496 (Ky.Ct.App. 1952); *In re Estate of*

Schmidt, 261 Cal. App. 2d 262, 67 Cal.Rptr. 847 (Ct.App. 1968); *Thomas* v. *Anderson*, 96 Cal. App. 2d 371, 215 P.2d 478 (Ct.App. 1950); Wasmuth and Stewart, "Medical and Legal Aspects of Human Organ Transplantation." 14 Cleve.-Mar. L. Rev. 442, 464 (1965); Note, "The Time of Death—A Legal, Ethical and Medical Dilemma," 18 Cath. Law. 242, 245 (1972).

The traditional legal definition of death has become outmoded due to medical technological advances and progress in the field of organ transplantation. Medicine now recognizes that death may occur when the brain ceases to function. This phenomenon has been denominated "brain death." See *e.g., Ad Hoc Committee of the Harvard Medical School to Examine the Definition of Brain Death, Report: A Definition of "Irreversible Coma,"* 208 J.A.M.A. 85 (1968); Corbett, "The Diagnosis of Cerebral Death in the Community Hospital," 74 J.A. Osteopathic A. 43, 44 (1974); Editorial, "Brain Death," Brit. Med. J. (Feb. 15, 1975), at p. 356; Editorial, "Brain Death vs. Heart Death," 3 Clin. Electroencephalogr. 318 (1972); Editorial, "The Harvard Criteria: An Appraisal," 221 J.A.M.A. 65 (1972); Editorial, "The Death of a Human Being," 2 Lancet 590 (Sept. 11, 1971); Harp, "Criteria for the Determination of Death," 40 Anesthesiol. 391 (1974); Maiyaziki et al., "Criteria of Cerebral Death," 13 Aeta. Radiol. [Diagn.] 318 (1972); Morison, "Dying," Sci. Am. (Sept. 1973), at p. 55; Ouaknine, et al., "Laboratory Criteria of Brain Death," 39 J. Neurosurg. 429 (1973); Paulson, "Determination of Brain Death," 68 Ohio St. Med. J. 39 (1972); Plum and Posner, *Stupor and Coma* (2d ed. 1972); Rosoff and Schwab, "The E.E.G. in Establishing Brain Death: a 10 Year Report With Criteria and Legal Safeguards in the 50 States," 24 Electroencephalogr. Clin. Neurophysiol. 283-84 (1968); Teraura, Handa, and Mori, "Determination of Death: Electrophysiological Background," 13 Int. Anesthesiol. Clin. 235 (1975); Task Force on Death and Dying of the Institute of Society, Ethics and Life Sciences, "Refinements in Criteria for the Determination of Death: An Appraisal," 221 J.A.M.A. 48 (1972); Note, 45 Chi.-Kent L. Rev. 202, 204 (1968).

[18]The State is in agreement with Judge Muir's position and urges now, as it did below, that gratuitous judicial adoption of a brain death standard would be highly inappropriate. The Legislature, with its ability to conduct hearings on the technical and ethical aspects of this question, is the body best equipped to formulate a response to advanced medical technology. Capron & Kass, "A Statutory Definition of the Standards for Determining Human Death: An Appraisal and a Proposal," 121 U.Pa.L.Rev. 87, 117-118 (1972); Compton, "Telling the Time of Human Death by Statute: An Essential and Progressive Trend," 31 Wash. & Lee L. Rev. 521, 540-542 (1974); Corday, "Life-Death in Human Transplantation," 55 A.B.A.J. 629, 632 (1969); Fried, "The Need for a Philosophical Anthropology," 48 Ind. L. J. 527, 531-532 (1973); Friloux, "Death, When Does It Occur?", 27 Baylor L. Rev. 10, 14 (1975); Sharp and Crofts, "Death with Dignity: The Physician's Liability," 27 Baylor L. Rev. 86, 108 (1975); Woodside, "Organ Transplantation," 31 Ohio St. L. J. 66, 93-97 (1970); Comment, "The Tell-Tale

Heart," 27 Baylor L. Rev. 157, 167-168 (1975); Note, 5 Cal.-W.L. Rev. 110, 122 (1968); Note, "A Survey of the Legal Aspects of Organ Transplantation," 50 Chi.-Kent L. Rev. 202, 205 (1968); Comment, "Liability and the Heart Transplant," 6 Houston L. Rev. 85, 100-12 (1968); Note, 51 N.C.L. Rev. 172, 182-84 (1972); Comment, "But When Did She Die? *Tucker* v. *Lower* and the Brain Death Concept," 12 San Diego L. Rev. 424, 431-45 (1975); Comment, "Medical and Legal Views of Death: Confrontation and Reconciliation," 19 St. Louis U.L.J. 172, 182 (1974). Legislation establishing a brain death standard was introduced in the New Jersey Legislature on July 31, 1975 by Senators Greenberg and McGahn. N.J. Sen. Bill No. 3314 (see Appendix).

[19]*State* v. *Krammes*, 105 N.J. Super. 345 (App.Div.), certif. den. 54 N.J. 257 (1969); *State* v. *Mele*, 103 N.J.Super. 353 (Cty.Ct. 1968). Accord, *Everhardt* v. *New Orleans*, 253 La. 285, 217 So.2d 400 (Sup.Ct. 1968), app. dism'd 395 U.S. 212 (1969); *Commonwealth* v. *Howie*, 354 Mass. 769, 238 N.E.2d 373 (Sup.Jud.Ct. 1968), cert. den. 393 U.S. 999 (1968); *People* v. *Carmichael*, 56 Misc. 2d 388, 288 N.Y.S.2d 931 (Cty.Ct. 1968); *People* v. *Brelmeyer*, 54 Misc. 2d 466, 282 N.Y.S.2d 797 (Cty.Ct. 1967); *People* v. *Schmidt*, 54 Misc. 2d 702, 283 N.Y.S.2d 290 (Cty.Ct. 1967), app. dism'd 295 N.Y.S.2d 936, 23 N.Y.2d 686, 243 N.E. 2d 154 (Ct.App. 1968); *State* v. *Anderson*, 3 N.C.App. 124, 164 S.E.2d 48 (Ct.App. 1968), aff'd 275 N.C. 168, 164 S.E.2d 48 (Sup.Ct. 1969); *State ex rel. Calvin* v. *Lombardi*, 104 R.I. 28, 241 A.2d 625 (Sup.Ct. 1968). But see *American Motor Cycle Ass'n* v. *Davids*, 11 Mich. App. 351, 158 N.W.2d 72 (Ct.App. 1968).

[20]This tenet is based primarily on an interpretation of *Leviticus* 17:10 (King James):

And whatsoever man there be in the house of Israel, or of the strangers that sojourn among you, that eateth any manner of blood; I will even set My face against that soul that eateth blood, and will cut him off from among his people.

[21]Chief Justice Weintraub reasoned that, "unless the medical option is laden with the risk of death or serious infirmity, the State's interest in sustaining life in such circumstances is hardly distinguishable from its interest in the case of suicide." *Id.* at 580. At the time of the decision in *Heston, supra*, N.J.S.A. 2A:70-25.6 made attempted suicide a disorderly persons offense. The New Jersey Legislature subsequently repealed all legislation prohibiting attempted suicide, N.J.S.A. 2A:85-5.1 (Supp. 1972), presumably for the reason stated in *Heston* that, "[o]rdinarily nothing would be gained by a prosecution, and hence the offense is rarely charged." *Heston, supra* at 580. Thus, repeal of the suicide statute in no sense affects the validity of *Heston*.

[22]*Raleigh Fitkin—Paul Morgan Memorial Hospital* v. *Anderson*, 42 N.J. 421, *cert.* den. 377 U.S. 985 (1964) (pregnant Jehovah's Witness ordered to submit to life sustaining blood transfusions); *State* v. *Perricone*, 37 N.J. 463, *cert.* den. 371 U.S. 890 (1962) (blood transfusions to

preserve life ordered for child of Jehovah's Witness parents); *Hoener* v. *Bertinato*, 67 N.J.Super. 517 (J.D.R.C. 1961) (blood transfusions ordered for infant over objections of Jehovah's Witness parents). See *Muhlenberg Hospital* v. *Patterson*, 128 N.J.Super. 498 (Law Div. 1974) (blood transfusions to prevent grievous bodily injury ordered for infant of Jehovah's Witness parents).

[23]See, *e.g.*, *Jehovah's Witnesses in the State of Washington* v. *King County Hosp.*, 390 U.S. 598, reh. den. 391 U.S. 961 (1968), aff'd 278 F.Supp. 488 (W.D.Wash. 1967); *Application of President and Director of Georgetown College, Inc.*, 331 F.2d 1000 (D.C.Cir.), reh. den. 331 F.2d 1010 (D.C.Cir.) (*en banc*), cert. den. 377 U.S. 978 (1964); *United States* v. *George*, 239 F.Supp. 752 (D.Conn. 1965); *People* v. *Labrenz*, 411 Ill. 618, 104 N.E.2d 769 (Sup.Ct.), cert den. 344 U.S. 824 (1952); *Morrison* v. *State*, 252 S.W.2d 97 (Ct.App. 1952); *Santos* v. *Goldstein*, 16 App. Div. 2d 755, 227 N.Y.S. 2d 450 (App.Div.), appeal dism. 232 N.Y.S.2d 1026 (1962); *Application of Brooklyn Hosp.*, 45 Misc. 2d 914, 258 N.Y.S.2d 62 (Sup.Ct. 1965); *Powell* v. *Columbia Presbyterian Medical Center*, 49 Misc. 2d 215, 267 N.Y.S. 2d 450 (Sup.Ct. 1965); *Collins* v. *Davids*, 44 Misc. 2d 622, 254 N.Y.S.2d 666 (Sup.Ct. 1964); *Battaglia* v. *Battaglia*, 9 Misc. 1067, 172 N.Y.S. 2d 361 (Sup.Ct. 1958); *In re Sampson*, 317 N.Y.S.2d 641 (Family Ct.), aff'd 323 N.Y.S.2d 253 (App. Div. 1971), aff'd *sub nom. Sampson* v. *Taylor*, 29 N.Y.S.2d 900, 278 N.E.2d 918 (Ct.At. 1972); *Mitchell* v. *Davids*, 205 S.W.2d 812 (Tex.Ct. Civ.App. 1947). See generally, *e.g.*, Cantor, "A Patient's Decision to Decline Life-Saving Medical Treatment: Bodily Integrity Versus The Preservation of Life," 26 Rutgers L. Rev. 228 (1973); Note, "Unauthorized Rendition of Life-Saving Treatment," 53 Calif. L. Rev. 860 (1965); Casenote, 60 N.W.U.L. Rev. 399 (1965); Note, "An Adult's Right to Resist Blood Transfusions: A View Through *John F. Kennedy Memorial Hospital* v. *Heston*," 47 Notre Dame Law 571 (1972); Note, 3 Seton Hall L. Rev. 444 (1972); Casenote, 25 S.W.L.J. 745 (1971); Annot. 9 A.L.R. 3d 1391 (1966). Only a few dissident notes have been struck against the vast weight of national precedent. *In re Osborne*, 294 A.2d 372 (D.C.Cir. 1972) (competent adult Jehovah's Witness could refuse emergency treatment); *In re Brooks Estate*, 32 Ill. 361, 204 N.E.2d 435 (Sup.Ct. 1965) (competent adult Jehovah's Witness permitted to refuse blood transfusion); *Erickson* v. *Dilgard*, 44 Misc. 2d 27, 252 N.Y.S.2d 705 (Sup.Ct. 1962) (adult patient permitted to refuse blood transfusion); *In re Maida Yetter*, 62 D.C. 2d 619, 623 (Pa.Dist.Ct. 1973) (competent adult could refuse diagnostic and corrective surgery). *Cf. In re Green*, 448 Pa. 338, 292 A.2d 387 (Sup.Ct. 1972), on remand 452 Pa. 373, 307 A.2d 279 (1973).

[24]See *e.g., In re Elmer*, 125 N.J.Eq. 148, 151 (E. & A. 1939); *Lippincott* v. *Lippincott*, 97 N.J.Eq. 517 (E. & A. 1925); *Gardner* v. *Hall*, 132 N.J.Eq. 64, 81 (Ch. 1942), aff'd 133 N.J.Eq. 287 (E. & A. 1943); *In re Hoppe*, 32 N.J.Super. 460, 462 (Cty.Ct. 1954).

[25]Assessment of a ward's best medical interests can present serious difficulties. A number of cases have been initiated by guardians seeking

judicial authorization to proceed with organ transplants from an incompetent donor. In *Strunk* v. *Strunk*, 445 S.E.2d 145 (Ky.Ct.App. 1969), parents of a 27 year old incompetent were granted permission to consent to a kidney transplant from the incompetent to his 28 year old brother. *Id.* at 145-46. The court recognized that while a guardian can act only in the best interest of the ward, under the circumstances of the case the transplant would be "to the best interest" of the incompetent since he was psychologically dependent on the otherwise doomed recipient. *Id.* at 149. The same result was reached in *Hart* v. *Brown*, 29 Conn.Sup. 368, 289 A.2d 386 (Super.Ct. 1972). There, the court approved donation of a kidney by an identical twin on the theory that the transplant would be "of some benefit" to the donor. 29 Conn.Sup. at 378, 289 A.2d at 391. Accord, *Bonner* v. *Moran*, 126 F.2d 121, 123 (D.C.Cir. 1941) (skin graft from 15 year old without parental consent held actionable malpractice since not in best interest of donor); *Howard* v. *Fulton-DeKalb Hospital Auth.*, 42 U.S.L.W. 2322 (Ga.Super.Ct., Dec. 25, 1973) (kidney transplant from 15 year old mentally retarded daughter to mother); *Foster* v. *Harrison*, No. 68674 (Eq., Mass.Sup.Jud.Ct., Nov. 27, 1957); *Huskey* v. *Harrison*, No. 68666 (Eq., Mass.Sup.Jud.Ct., Aug. 30, 1957); *Masden* v. *Harrison*, No. 68651 (Eq., Mass.Sup.Jud.Ct., June 12, 1957), cited in Berman, "The Legal Problems of Organ Transplantation," 13 Vill.L. Rev. 751, 756 n.17 (1968) (kidney transplant between minor twins permitted since donor would suffer grave emotional impact if not allowed to donate). The single reported decision rejecting an application for authorization to consent to a kidney transplant is *In re Richardson*, 254 So.2d 185 (La.Ct.App.), *cert.* den. 284 So.2d 338 (Sup.Ct. 1973). In *Richardson, supra,* the court refused to sanction a kidney transplant from a 17 year old incompetent to his 32 year old sister. *Id.* at 187. The decision was based on a finding that the transplant would not be in the incompetent's best interest. *Id.* See generally, Comment, "Kidney Donation From Minors and Incompetents," 35 La. L. Rev. 551 (1975); Annot., "Power of Court or Guardian to Make Non-Charitable Gifts or Allowance Out of Funds of Incompetent Ward," 24 A.L.R. 3d 863, 871.

[26]See *In re Trott, supra,* at 440-42; *Marsh* v. *Scott,* 2 N.J.Super. 240, 246 (Ch.Div. 1948); *Hart* v. *Brown, supra,* 29 Conn.Sup. at 375-376, 289 A.2d at 390-91; *Howard* v. *Fulton-DeKalb Hospital Auth., supra,* 42 U.S.L.W. at 2322; *Strunk* v. *Strunk, supra,* 445 S.W.2d at 148. See generally, Annotation, "Power of Court or Guardian to Make Non-Charitable Gifts or Allowances Out of Funds of Incompetent Ward," 24 A.L.R. 2d 863 (1969).

[27]This Court has construed *parens patriae* to impose "a duty on the sovereignty to protect such persons with disabilities who have no rightful protector." *Johnson* v. *State*, 18 N.J. 422, 430 (1955), *cert.* den. 350 U.S. 942 (1956). See generally, *Hawaii* v. *Standard Oil Co. of California*, 405 U.S. 251, 257-260 (1972); *State* v. *Tuddles*, 38 N.J. 565, 571 (1972); *State in the Interest of L.N.*, 109 N.J.Super. 278 (App.Div.), aff'd o.b. 57 N.J. 165 (1970), *cert.* den. 402 U.S. 1009 (1971); Katz, "The Legal Control of Psychosurgery," 21 Med.Tr. Tech. Q. 407, 427-428 (1975). See also *Freeholders of Burlington Cty.* v. *McCorkle*, 98 N.J.Super. 451

(Law Div. 1968); Note, "Compulsory Medical Treatment and the Free Exercise of Religion," 42 Ind. L. J. 386, 390-393 (1969); Note, "The Right to Die," 18 U.Fla.L.Rev. 591, 592-597 (1966).

[28]See, *e.g., Simon* v. *Graham Bakery,* 17 N.J. 525 (1955); *Hagopian* v. *Fuchs,* 66 N.J.Super. 374 (App.Div. 1961); *Marsh* v. *Newark Heating and Ventilating Mach. Co.,* 57 N.J.L. 36 (Sup.Ct. 1894).

[29]The State's regulation of the physician-patient relationship is manifested in the law of malpractice. See, *e.g., Schueler* v. *Strelinger,* 43 N.J. 300 (1964). Statutory licensing provisions in the field of health care are designed to guarantee the health of those in the community. See N.J.S.A. 45:9-1, *et seq.*

[30]The police power of the State constitutes the residual governmental authority not delegated to the Federal Government and not reserved by the people. The police power encompasses a State's interest in protecting the health, safety and welfare of its citizens. See, *e.g., Jacobsen* v. *Massachusetts,* 197 U.S. 11, 25 (1905); *South Burlington Cty. NAACP* v. *Mount Laurel Tp.,* 67 N.J. 151 (1975); *Rothman* v. *Rothman,* 65 N.J. 219 (1974); *P.T. & L. Construction Co.* v. *Comm'r Dept. Transportation,* 60 N.J. 308 (1972); *Pied Piper Ice Cream Inc.* v. *Essex Cty. Park Comm.,* 132 N.J.Super. 480 (App.Div. 1975); *Stephens* v. *Bongart,* 15 N.J.Misc. 80, 82 (J.D.R.C. 1937). *Parens patriae* is a role that the State assumes to protect the well-being of its people. Katz, "The Legal Control of Psychosurgery," 21 Med. Tr. Tech. Q. 407, 427-428 (1975); see, *e.g., Hawaii* v. *Standard Oil Co. of California,* 405 U.S. 251, 257-260 (1972); *State* v. *Tuddles,* 38 N.J. 565, 571 (1972); *State in the Interest of L.N.,* 109 N.J.Super. 278 (App.Div.), aff'd o.b. 57 N.J. 165 (1970), *cert.* den. 402 U.S. 1009 (1971). See also *Freeholders of Burlington Cty.* v. *McCorkle,* 98 N.J.Super. 451 (Law Div. 1968); Note, "Compulsory Medical Treatment and the Free Exercise of Religion," 42 Ind. L. J. 386, 390-393 (1969); Note, "The Right to Die," 18 U.Fla.L.Rev. 591, 592-597 (1966). Under the theory of *parens patriae* the State has a duty to protect individuals with disabilities who are otherwise without a rightful protector. *Johnson* v. *State,* 18 N.J. 422, 430 (1955). Karen Quinlan, an incompetent adult, clearly is entitled to the aegis of the State in the defense of her life.

One of the leading *parens patriae* cases in the field of medical treatment to support life is *Application of President and Director of Georgetown College, Inc.,* 331 F.2d 1000 (D.C.Cir.), rehearing *en banc* den., 331 F.2d 1010 (D.C.Cir.), *cert.* den. 377 U.S. 978 (1964). In *Georgetown,* a trial judge's order authorizing a hospital to administer blood transfusions was upheld. The patient and her husband had refused to consent to the transfusions for religious reasons. Their objections were found insufficient to override the sovereign *parens patriae* interest. *Georgetown's* rationale has been followed in many jurisdictions, including New Jersey.

[31]See, *Wisconsin* v. *Yoder,* 406 U.S. 205 (1972); *Sherbert* v. *Verner,* 374 U.S. 398 (1963); *Braunfeld* v. *Brown,* 366 U.S. 599 (1960); *Cantwell*

v. *Connecticut*, 310 U.S. 296 (1940); Sharpe & Hargest, "Lifesaving Treatment for Unwilling Patients," 36 Fordham L. Rev. 695, 704 (1968); Note, "The Right to Die," 7 Hous. L. Rev. 654, 662-64 (1970); Note, "Compulsory Medical Treatment and the Free Exercise of Religion," 42 Ind. L. J., note 27, *supra* at 396-404; Note, "Compulsory Medical Treatment: The State's Interest Reevaluated," 51 Minn. L. Rev. 293, 297 (1966). See *e.g., Jacobsen* v. *Massachusetts*, 197 U.S. 11, 25 (1905) (compulsory smallpox vaccination); *Mormon Church* v. *United States*, 136 U.S. 1 (1890) (polygamy); *Reynolds* v. *United States*, 98 U.S. 145 (1878) (polygamy); *Hill* v. *State* 28 Ala.App. 404, 88 So.2d 880, (Ct.App.), *cert.* den. 264 Ala. 697, 88 So.2d 887 (Sup.Ct. 1956) (snake handling); *Cude* v. *State*, 237 Ark. 927, 377 S.W.2d 816 (1964) (compulsory smallpox vaccination); *Lawson* v. *Commonwealth*, 291 Ky. 437, 164 S.W.2d 972 (1942) (snake handling); *State* v. *Massey*, 229 N.C. 734, 51 S.E.2d 179 (Sup. Ct.), app. dism'd *sub nom Bunn* v. *North Carolina*, 336 U.S. 942 (1949) (snake handling); *Harden* v. *State*, 188 Tenn. 17, 216 S.W.2d 708 (Sup. Ct. 1948) (snake handling). But see *People* v. *Woody*, 61 Cal.2d 716, 40 Cal. Rptr. 69, 394 P.2d 813 (Sup.Ct. 1964) (peyote).

[32]See generally, Survey, "Euthanasia: Criminal, Tort, Constitutional and Legislative Considerations," 48 Notre Dame Law. 1202, 1237-1252 (1973).

[33]*In re Maida Yetter,* 62 D.C.2d 619, 623 (Pa. Dist. Ct. 1973); Unreported Florida decision discussed in Trubo, *An Act of Mercy: Euthanasia Today* (1973) at pp. 27-28. See *In re Brooks' Estate*, 32 Ill. 2d 361, 205 N.E.2d 435 (Sup.Ct. 1965).

[34]Gurney, "Is There A Right To Die?—A Study of the Law of Euthanasia," 3 Cumb.-Sam. L. Rev. 235, 245 (1972); Kutner, "Due Process of Euthanasia: The Living Will, a Proposal," 44 Ind. L. J. 539, 543-45 (1969); Note, "The Right to Die," 7 Hous. L. Rev. 654, 669-70 (1970); Note, "Compulsory Medical Treatment: The State's Interest Reevaluated," 51 Minn. L. Rev. 293 (1966); Note, "Is There a Right to a Natural Death?" 9 New Eng. L. Rev. 293, 304-10 (1974); Note, "Death with Dignity: A Recommendation for Statutory Change," 22 U.Fla.L. Rev. 368, 375-76 (1970).

[35]Kutner, "Due Process of Euthanasia: The Living Will, a Proposal," 44 Ind. L.J. 539, 545 (1969).

Note, "Compulsory Medical Treatment: The State's Interest Re-evaluated," 51 Minn. L. Rev., 293, 296-97 (1966); Note, 9 New Eng. L. Rev., note 34, *supra* at 306-10; Note, 22 U.Fla.L.Rev., note 34, *supra* at 375-77; Note, "The Right to Die," 18 U.Fla.L.Rev. 591, 603-05 (1966).

[36]*Moose Lodge No. 107* v. *Irvis*, 407 U.S. 163 (1972); *Reitman* v. *Mulkey*, 387 U.S. 369 (1967); *Baker* v. *Carr*, 369 U.S. 186 (1962); *Burton* v. *Wilmington Parking Auth.*, 365 U.S. 715 (1961); *Barrows* v. *Jackson*, 346 U.S. 249 (1953); *Terry* v. *Adams*, 345 U.S. 461 (1953); *Shelley* v. *Kramer*, 334 U.S. 1 (1948).

[37]*E.g., Bell* v. *Maryland*, 378 U.S. 226, 309-12 (1964); (Goldberg, J.,

concurring); Survey, "Euthanasia: Criminal, Tort, Constitutional and Legislative Considerations," 48 Notre Dame Law. 1202, 1227-31, 1251-52 (1973). *Cf.* Foreman, "The Physician's Liability for the Practice of Euthanasia," 27 Baylor L. Rev. 54, 61 (1975).

[38]Flexibility and some discretion is permissible in legislation designed to enable an individual to meet the exigencies of a possible terminal illness. The Uniform Anatomical Gift Act (U.A.G.A.) N.J.S.A. 26:6-57 *et seq.*, for example, authorizes *inter vivos* disposition of human organs. Conceivably, a legislature might devise a statutory scheme by which terminal patients could direct the withholding or withdrawal of extraordinary medical treatment. Such legislation would satisfy the desires of those who support the "living will" concept. Kutner, "The Living Will: Coping with the Historical Event of Death," 27 Baylor L. Rev. 39 (1975); Sackett, "Euthanasia: Why No Legislation," 27 Baylor L. Rev. 3 (1975); Teel, "The Physician's Dilemma, A Doctor's View," 27 Baylor L. Rev. 6, 9 (1975).

Both the "living will" proposals and the U.A.G.A. seek to obviate the possibility of fraud and to emphasize the gravity of the "testator's" choice. The high degree of memorialization embodied in these formal documents accomplishes these ends. The nature of the decision necessary to establish the criteria for validating these quasi-testamentory dispositions is inherently legislative.

One alternative suggestion has focused on the possibility of employing established fiduciary relationships to shift the responsibility for termination of care to a trustee who would be bound by a comatose patient-settlor's instructions. Note, "The Qualified Right to Refuse Medical Treatment and Its Application in a Trust for the Terminally Ill," 13 J.Fam.L. 153 (1973). See also Kutner, "The Living Will: Coping with the Historical Event of Death," 27 Baylor L. Rev. 39 (1975); Kutner, 44 Ind. L. J., note 34, *supra* at 550-554; Sackett, "Euthanasia: Why No Legislation," 27 Baylor L. Rev. 3, 5 (1975); Teel, "The Physician's Dilemma, a Doctor's View," 27 Baylor L. Rev. 6, 9 (1975). *Cf.* Fried, "The Need for a Philosophical Anthropology," 48 Ind. L. J. 527 (1973); Wasmuth, "The Concept of Death," 30 Ohio St. L. J. 32, 57-60 (1969); Wasmuth & Stewart, "Medical and Legal Aspects of Organ Transplantations," 14 Cleve.-Mar. L. Rev. 442, 468 (1965); Comment, "The Tell-Tale Heart," 27 Baylor L. Rev. 157, 167 (1975); see generally, *e.g.,* Capron & Kass, note 18, *supra*; Weigel, "The Dying Patient's Rights—Do They Exist?", 16 So. Tex. L. J. 153, 168-170 (1975).

A number of legislative attempts to legalize the practice of both voluntary and involuntary euthanasia have occurred in the past four decades. In 1937 proposed legislation providing a detailed scheme for voluntary and involuntary euthanasia was unsuccessfully introduced in the Nebraska Legislature. L.B. 135, 52d Sess., Neb. Legislature (see appendix). Equally unsuccessful was a voluntary euthanasia proposal submitted to the New York Legislature in 1947. See Mannes, "Euthanasia vs. The Right to Life," 27 Baylor L. Rev. 68 (1975). Two proposals, almost identically phrased, providing for voluntary euthanasia, were killed in committee during the 1971 session of the Wisconsin Legislature. S.B. 670, Wis. Legislature (1971); S.B. 715 Wis. Legislature (1971) (see appendix). A bill providing for "death with dignity" has been introduced into the Florida Legislature each year since 1971. See H.B. 239, Fla. Legislature (1975) (see appendix).

English attempts to enact euthanasia legislation have failed in the House of Lords in 1936, 1950 and 1969. Gurney, "Is There a Right to Die?—A Study of the Law of Euthanasia," 3 Cumb.-Sam. L. Rev. 235, 251 (1972); Mannes, "Euthanasia vs. The Right to Life," 27 Baylor L. Rev. 68, 70-72 (1975). It appears that civil law jurisdictions consider motive to diminish the degree of criminal culpability attached to euthanasia. See, *e.g.,* Norwegian Penal Code, §235 (1961) (see appendix).

[39]Foreman, "The Physician's Criminal Liability for the Practice of Euthanasia," 27 Baylor L. Rev. 54 (1975); Mannes, "Euthanasia vs. The Right to Life," 27 Baylor L. Rev. 68 (1975); Meyers, The Human Body and the Law (1970), at p. 139 citing St. John-Stevas, *Life, Death and the Law* (1971), at p. 262; Note, "The Right to Die," 7 Hous. L. Rev. 654 (1970).

[40]Fletcher, *Morals and Medicine* (1954), at 172. Accord, Cantor, "A Patient's Decision to Decline Life-Saving Medical Treatment: Bodily Integrity Versus the Preservation of Life," 26 Rut. L. Rev. 228, 258-259 (1973); Gurney, "Is there a Right to Die?—A Study of the Law of Euthanasia," 3 Cumb.-Sam. L. Rev. 235 (1972). See also Fletcher, "Ethics and Euthanasia," 73 Am. J. Nursing 670 (1972).

[41]*E.G.,* Foreman, note 39, *supra* at 58: Gurney, note 40, *supra*; Morris, "Voluntary Euthanasia," 45 Wash. L. Rev. 239 (1970); Comment, "Informed Consent for the Terminal Patient," 27 Baylor L. Rev. 111, 112 (1975). See, *e.g.,* G. Fletcher, "Legal Aspects of the Decision Not to Prolong Life," 203 J.A.M.A. 119 (1968); Wechsler and Michael, "A Rationale for the Law of Homicide," Pt. 1, 37 Colum. L. Rev. 701, 739-40 (1937). See generally, *Euthanasia and the Right to Death* (Downing ed. 1969).

[42]Sackett, "Euthanasia: Why No Legislation," 27 Baylor L. Rev. 3, 3-4 (1975); Sharp and Crofts, "Death with Dignity and the Physician's Liability," 27 Baylor L. Rev. 86, 93 (1975); Comment, "Informed Consent for the Terminal Patient," 27 Baylor L. Rev. 111, 121 (1975); see Annas & Healy, "The Patient Rights Advocate: Redefining the Doctor-Patient Relationship in the Hospital Context," 27 Vand. L. Rev. 243, 243-45 (1974); G. Fletcher, "Prolonging Life," 42 Wash. L. Rev. 999 (1967); Morris, note 41, *supra* at 240; Potter, "The Paradoxical Preservation of a Principle," 13 Vill. L. Rev. 784 (1968).

[43]Elkinton, "The Dying Patient, The Doctor and the Law," 13 Vill. L. Rev. 740 (1968); Foreman, note 39, *supra* at 57; Gurney, note 40, *supra*; Halley & Harvey, "The Definitional Dilemma of Death," 37 J. Kan. B. A. 179, 179-80 (1968); Hirsh, "Brain Death," 21 Med. Tr. Tech. Q. 377, 380 (1975); Meyers, "The Legal Aspects of Medical Euthanasia," 23 Bio Science 467, 468-70 (1973); Note, 5 Cal. W. L. Rev. 110, 115 (1968). See Horan, "Euthanasia, Medical Treatment and the Mongoloid

Child: Death as a Treatment of Choice?" 27 Baylor L. Rev. 76, 82-83 (1975); Potter, Note 42, *supra* at 785-86. See also Editorial, "Officiously to Keep Alive," 214 J.A.M.A. 905 (1970), citing "Discussion of the British Euthanasia Bill," 63 Proc. Roy. Soc. Med. 659 (1970).

[44]Note, 7 Hous. L. Rev., note 34, *supra*; see Bellegie, "Medical Technology as It Exists Today," 27 Baylor L. Rev. 31 (1975).

[45]Foreman, note 39, *supra* at 55-56.

[46]Bonnet, "Bill of Rights of the Dying Patient," 27 Baylor L. Rev. 27, 29-30 (1975); Cassell, "Permission to Die," 23 Bio-Science 475, 476-77 (1973); Elkinton, note 43, *supra* at 742-44; Gurney, note 40, *supra* at 248; Kutner, "The Living Will: Coping with the Historical Event of Death," 27 Baylor L. Rev. 39, 48 (1975); Meyers, "Legal Aspects," note 43, *supra* at 469-70; Pope Pius XII, "The Prolongation of Life," 4 *Pope Speaks* 393 (1958); Sharp & Crofts, note 42, *supra* at 107-08; Wassmer, "Between Life and Death: Ethical and Moral Advances," 13 Vill. L. Rev. 759, 781-83 (1968); Weigel, "The Dying Patient's Rights—Do They Exist?" 16 So. Tex. L. J. 153, 164 (1975).

[47]Elkinton, note 43, *supra* at 743; Elliot, The Gods of Life (1974); Flew, "The Principle of Euthanasia," in Euthanasia and the Right to Death (Downing ed. 1972), at 30-48; Meyers, note 43, *supra* at 139; Pope Pius XII, note 46, *supra*; Wassmer, note 46, *supra* at 762-67; but see Martin, "Euthanasia: The Three-In-One Issue," 27 Baylor L. Rev. 62, 67 (1975).

[48]Note, 5 Cal.-W. L.Rev., note 43, *supra* at 114.

[49]Foreman, note 39, *supra* at 55; Horan, note 43, *supra* at 79.

[50]Foreman, note 39, *supra* at 54-55, 60-61; Gurney, note 40, *supra* at 239; Note, "Scarce Medical Resources," 69 Colum. L. Rev. 620, 624-25 (1969); Note, 7 Hous. L. Rev., note 39, *supra* at 656-57. See Horan, note 43, *supra* at 78.

[51]G. Fletcher, 42 Wash. L. Rev., note 42, *supra* at 999-1001. See Horan, note 43, *supra* at 78-79; Weigel, note 38, *supra* at 165-67; Comment, "The Criteria for Determining Death in Vital Organ Transplants—A Medico-Legal Dilemma," 38 Mo. L. Rev. 220, 231 (1973). *Cf.* Kutner, 27 Baylor L. Rev., note 46, *supra* at 50; Randall & Randall, "The Developing Field of Human Organ Transplantation," 50 Gon. L. Rev. 20, 37 (1969). See generally, Williams, The Scarcity of Human Life and the Criminal Law (1957), at 311-50.

[52]Cantor, note 40, *supra* at 258-62; Elkinton, note 43, *supra* at 744; Foreman, note 39, *supra* at 56-57; Wassmer, note 46, *supra* at 765-67; Weigel, note 38, *supra* at 16; Williams, note 51, *supra* at 326; Note, 27 Baylor L. Rev. 121, 125-27 (1975); Note, 69 Colum. L. Rev., note 50, *supra* at 625-27; Note, 7 Hous. L. Rev., note 39, *supra* at 658-60. See G. Fletcher, 42 Wash. L. Rev., note 42, *supra* at 1804-14; G. Fletcher, in Euthanasia and the Right to Death (Downing Ed. 1972), at p. 71-84. *Cf.* Note, "The Time of Death—A Legal, Ethical and Medical Dilemma,"

18 Cath. Law. 243, 248 (1972); Note, 45 Chi.-Kent L. Rev. 202, 203 (1968). See also Crane, "Physician's Attitudes Toward the Treatment of Critically Ill Patients," 23 Bio-Science 471, 472-73 (1973). But see Gurney, note 40, *supra* at 238, 247; Kamisar, "Some Non-Religious Views Against Proposed 'Mercy-Killing' Legislation," 42 Minn. L. Rev. 969, 974 (1958).

[53]*People* v. *Roberts*, 211 Mich. 187, 178 N.W. 690 (Sup.Ct. 1920); *Turner* v. *State*, 119 Tenn. 663, 108 S.W. 1139 (Sup.Ct. 1908). *Cf. People* v. *Conley*, 64 Cal. 2d. 310, 49 Cal. Rptr. 815, 411 P.2d 911 (Sup.Ct. 1966); *Blackburn* v. *State*, 23 Ohio St. 146, 162-164 (Sup.Ct. 1872); Gurney Note 40, *supra* at 239-40.

SENATE, No. 3314

STATE OF NEW JERSEY

INTRODUCED JULY 31, 1975

By Senators GREENBERG and McGAHN

Referred to Committee on Institutions, Health and Welfare

AN ACT concerning standards for the determination of death and supplementing Title 26 of the Revised Statutes.

1 BE IT ENACTED *by the Senate and General Assembly of the State of*
2 *New Jersey:*
1 1. As used in this act:
2   a. "Person" means an integrated, whole, living human being, and
3 shall not include any part or parts of a human body which may
4 continue to function following a determination, pursuant to this
5 act, of an irreversible cessation of spontaneous or vital bodily
6 functions of such human being.
7   b. "Ordinary standards of medical practice" means such stan-
8 dards as require that, in the performance of professional acts, an

9 individual possess and exercise the degree of skill, knowledge and
10 care ordinarily possessed by members of the medical community at
11 the time of such determination.

12   c. "Spontaneous" means the absence of any artificial means of
13 support.

14   d. "Artificial means of support" means any medical technique,
15 including administration of chemotherapy, any therapeutic device,
16 instrument or machine, or other medical process which is engaged
17 or administered for the purpose of aiding, assisting or sustaining
18 vital bodily functions, or any technique, device, instrument
19 machine or process which may effect an accurate determination of
20 whether such bodily functions are spontaneous.

21   e. "Vital brain functions" means discernible central nervous
22 system activity in the absence of negating effects produced by the
23 presence in the body of any drug or depressant or by the existence
24 of hypothermia or of a similar condition or conditions.

1   2. A person shall be considered dead if in the announced opinion
2 of a physician, based on ordinary standards of medical practice,
3 he has undergone an irreversible cessation of spontaneous respira-
4 tory and circulatory functions. In the event that artificial means of
5 support preclude a determination that these functions have ceased,
6 a person shall be considered dead if in the announced opinion of a
7 physician, based on ordinary standards of medical practice, he has
8 undergone an irreversible cessation of vital brain functions. Death
9 will have occurred at the time when the relevant functions ceased.

1   3. This act shall take effect immediately.

STATEMENT

The purpose of this bill is to provide general standards for the
determination of death in line with current medical thinking. It is
intended to supplant the common law definition which was based
entirely on circulatory and respiratory functions by providing that
where a final determination by these standards is precluded because
of the use of resuscitative and supportive means, the irreversible
cessation of brain functioning may be used to make the determination. Such a definition is of particular pertinence in the organ
transplant situation where time is a crucial element.

H.B. 239

FLORIDA LEGISLATURE (1975)

A bill to be entitled an act relating to medical treatment providing for termination of life-sustaining treatment of a terminally ill or injured patient in certain circumstances providing immunity of physicians, medical institutions and certain employees of such institutions from civil and criminal liability under certain circumstances; exempting persons complying with this act from the provision of Section 782.08 Florida Statute; providing for revocation of a document authorizing termination of life-sustaining medical treatment; providing an effective date.

BE IT ENACTED *by the Legislature of the State of Florida:*

1. As used in this act, "terminal illness" or "injury" means any illness or injury which would result in a natural expiration of life regardless of the use or discontinuance of medical treatment to sustain the life processes. Any person 18 years or older and competent may at any time execute a document directing that medical treatment designed solely to sustain the life processes to be discontinued. However, such document should not take effect until two licensed physicians declare by written sworn document said person is terminally ill or injured.

2. A physician who relies on a document executed in accordance with the provision of Section 1 to refuse medical treatment or who makes a determination of terminal illness or injury shall be presumed to be acting in good faith and, unless negligent, shall be immune from civil or criminal liability that otherwise might be incurred.

3. Any medical institution employing a physician who relies upon a document executed in accordance with the provisions of Section 1, to make a determination of terminal illness or injury and any employee of such institution acting in good faith and upon the instruction of the physician in charge of treatment, unless negligent, shall be immune from civil or criminal liability that otherwise might be incurred because of termination of medical treatment or services resulting in the death of a patient who executed a document in accordance with the provisions of Section 1.

4. No person participating in good faith in the execution of a statement or document required by the provisions of this act shall be deemed to be in violation of Section 782.08, Florida. [Florida self-murder statute].

5. A person who has executed a document to refuse medical treatment shall have the power to revoke such document at any time by oral or written statement.

6. This act shall take effect upon becoming a law.

NEBRASKA LEGISLATURE (1937)

* * *

2. In each county of the State there shall be a referee in euthanasia who shall be the judge of the District Court that is presiding as the Domestic Relations Judge. Such referee in euthanasia shall have the powers and duties as hereinafter set out.

3. Any adult of sound mind, suffering from an incurable and fatal disease or any person helpless and suffering from the infirmities of old age may file a written application with the referee in euthanasia which application shall be verified and set out the following facts:

a. That the applicant is suffering from an incurable and fatal disease and that the process of death is liable to be protracted and painful; that the applicant has his affairs in order, that his next of kin has been notified of his intention to file such application and the names, degrees of kinship and addresses of such next of kin shall be set out in said application. That the fact of such fatal and incurable disease has been verified through two medical practitioners and their names and addresses shall be set out and that the applicant knows of no valid reason why he or she should not be granted a permit to be euthanitized. Such application must be accompanied by medical certificates from two reputable physicians of no relation to the applicant and who will benefit in no financial way from the applicant's death, verifying the fact that the applicant is suffering from an incurable and fatal disease or diseases.

4. In the case of a mentally incompetent adult such application may be made by next of kin and such application shall be made in the manner hereinbefore set out and verified by the person making the application.

5. The parents or parent of a minor suffering from an incurable or fatal disease or diseases or if neither parent be living, his duly appointed guardian, may file an application asking for euthanasia for such minor person and such application shall be verified by the parents or guardian seeking the license and shall contain such facts and be accompanied by such affidavits as provided in Section 3 hereof. Provided, however, if such minor child is of an age of fourteen years or older and is mentally competent, such application shall not be considered unless signed by said minor person and verified that he has read the application, understands its contents and desires the euthanasia.

1. Each person shall have the right to die with dignity and to refuse and deny the use or application by any person of artificial, extraordinary, extreme or radical medical or physical means or procedures calculated to prolong his life.

2. Any person with the same formalities as required for the execution of a will may execute a document exercising such right and refusing or denying the use or application by any person of artificial, extraordinary, extreme or radical medical or physical means or procedures calculated to prolong his life.

3. If any person who is a minor or adult who is physically or mentally unable to execute, or is otherwise incapacitated from executing such document, it may be executed in the same form on his behalf,

    (a) by either parent of the minor
    (b) by his spouse,
    (c) if his spouse is unwilling or unable to act, by his child 18 years or older,
    (d) if he has more than one child 18 or over by a majority of such children, or if he has no spouse 18 older by either of the parents or
    (e) if he has no parent living by his nearest living relative.

4. Every document executed under this section shall be filed with a register of deeds in the county of residence of the person to be effected.

5. Any person, hospital or other medical institution which acts or refrains from acting in reliance on, or in compliance with the document shall be immune from liability otherwise arising out of such failure to use or apply artificial extraordinary, extreme or radical medical or surgical means or procedures calculated to prolong such person's life.

NORWEGIAN PENAL CODE §235 (1961)

If somebody is killed or seriously injured in body or health with his own consent, or if anybody kills a hopelessly sick person out of mercy, or is an accessory thereto the punishment may be reduced below the minimum provided, and to a milder form of punishment.

In The

SUPREME COURT OF NEW JERSEY

September Term, 1975

Docket No. A-116

IN THE MATTER OF KAREN ANN QUINLAN,
AN ALLEGED INCOMPETENT

ON APPEAL FROM JUDGMENT OF THE SUPERIOR COURT OF
NEW JERSEY, CHANCERY DIVISION (MORRIS COUNTY)
SAT BELOW: HONORABLE ROBERT MUIR, JR., J.S.C.

BRIEF ON BEHALF OF DEFENDANTS-RESPONDENTS, DR. ARSHAD JAVED AND DR. ROBERT J. MORSE

Porzio, Bromberg & Newman,
Attorneys for Defendants-Respondents,
Dr. Arshad Javed and
Dr. Robert J. Morse,
One Washington Street,
Morristown, New Jersey 07960.

Ralph Porzio,
Of Counsel.

E. Neal Zimmermann,
Ralph Porzio,
On the Brief.

Procedural History

On September 12, 1975, plaintiff filed a Complaint with the Clerk of the Superior Court seeking an adjudication that Karen Quinlan is mentally incompetent and appointing plaintiff as guardian "with the express power of authorizing the discontinuance of all extraordinary means of sustaining the vital processes" of Karen Quinlan.*

On September 15, 1975, the Hon. Robert Muir, Jr., J.S.C., issued an Order appointing Daniel Coburn, Esq. as Guardian Ad Litem of Karen Quinlan.

On September 17, 1975, plaintiff filed a Supplemental Complaint naming Hon. Donald F. Collester, Jr., the Morris County Prosecutor, Dr. Robert Morse, Dr. Arshad Javed and St. Clare's Hospital in Denville as defendants. This Supplemental Complaint sought an injunction against the Prosecutor from initiating a criminal prosecution arising out of any relief that might be granted by this Court and likewise sought an injunction against the physicians and the hospital from interfering in any such relief.

Judge Muir, apparently because of the nature of the case, fixed an early Pre-Trial Conference date, namely, September 22, 1975. For the same reason, and apparently with consent of all counsel, the necessity of filing answers or proceeding with formal discovery was dispensed with.

During the course of the Pre-Trial Conference, the Attorney General of New Jersey made application to have the State of New Jersey intervene as a party defendant. This application was granted.

---

* Since all briefs in this expedited proceeding are being filed contemporaneously, page references to appellant's appendix cannot be provided. In the event any pertinent material is omitted from all appendices, these will be supplied in a reply brief.

Subsequent to the Pre-Trial Conference, counsel for the plaintiff filed and served on October 2, 1975, "Factual and Legal Contentions of the Plaintiff."

Trial was held before Judge Muir on October 20, 21, 22, 23 and 27. On October 23, 1975, the Trial Judge, with consent of all counsel, entered an Order amending Paragraph 2 of the Pre-Trial Order dated September 22, 1975, to include the stipulation that Karen Quinlan was legally and medically alive.

On November 10, 1975, the Trial Judge rendered his written Opinion and a Judgment based upon that Opinion was consented to as to form by all counsel on the same day. A supplemental written Opinion, confined solely to the rights or duties of the parents and the guardian of the person with respect to the care of Karen Quinlan, was entered on November 12, 1975.

A Notice of Appeal to the Appellate Division of the Superior Court was filed by the plaintiff-appellant on November 17, 1975. Apparently on the same day or upon receipt of the Notice of Appeal, the Supreme Court, on its own motion, certified this case to it for review.

Statement of Facts

The trial began with a stipulation by all counsel that Karen Ann Quinlan is incompetent within the scope of the rules of court on guardianship (T44-1 to 14).

Testimony began with the calling of Dr. Robert Morse, a board-eligible neurologist, as plaintiff's first witness (T54-23 to 25). Dr. Morse, the treating physician of Karen, first saw her on a consulting basis on April 18, 1975, at Newton Memorial Hospital at the request of Dr. McGee (T55-9 to 19). On April 25, 1975, Dr. Morse was requested to accept Karen on his service at St. Clare's Hospital in Denville; he agreed to do so and Karen was transferred that day (T55-23 to T56-7).

Dr. Morse testified that he had great difficulty obtaining information about the events leading up to her admission to Newton, i.e., the initial history (T56-13 to 25), also called etiology (T64-6). In neurology the history is very important (T56-18), even more important than the examination itself (T58-18 to 22). On numerous occasions, Dr. Morse indicated that the lack of history severely limited both the diagnosis and prognosis in this case (T80-22 to T81-15; T139-2 to 6).

Dr. Morse first ran a cranial nerve test which showed that she had intact pupillary responses and intact ocular vestibular responses, indicating that certain primary centers of the brain were intact (T60-16 to 18). His impression was that she was in a state of decortication and in a coma (T60-5 to 6). She was on a respirator at Newton (T61-15).

At St. Clare's Dr. Morse ran an electroencephalograph (EEG) on Karen which was abnormal but showed some activity and was consistent with her clinical state (T62-24 to T63-2). A brain scan and angiogram were run and both were normal, indicating no tumor or obstruction (T63-7 to T65-5). A lumbar puncture was also normal, indicating no infection (T65-7 to 20). Another test ruled out lead poisoning (T67-12 to 17).

Dr. Morse testified that Karen has been in a state of coma since he began treating her. Coma is a lack of consciousness (T69-23 to T70-2). There are two types of coma, sleep-like unresponsiveness and awake unresponsiveness (T70-13 to 17). Karen was originally in a sleep-like unresponsive condition but soon developed "sleep-wake" cycles (T70-22 to T71-1). In the awake unresponsive periods her eyes are open, she blinks and does things of that sort, but is totally unaware of people around her (T72-1 to 15).

Dr. Morse testified that Karen is in a persistent vegetative state (T73-9 to 12). She has the capacity for arousability but no capacity for behavior or awareness (T73-19 to 25). He has never had any inkling that Karen recognized him (T74-9). He described the "locked-in" syndrome where a patient can understand your questions and respond with her eyes and testified that Karen was not in this condition (T74-12 to T76-11).

Karen is presently being supported by oral feedings through a small nasal gastro tube. Intravenous feeding alone would not sustain her because of the high caloric intake (T76-20 to T77-7). She is moved every couple of hours to prevent decubiti (bed sores) from forming (T77-8 to 19). Her urine and blood routinely are examined for infection (T77-23 to 24). Karen is in the intensive care unit where there are nurses 24 hours a day (T78-19 to T79-2).

Karen has an "insult," i.e., an offending agent which interrupts the integrity of the central nervous system (T74-25 to T75-2). The decortization she evidences indicates that the insult might be to the cerebral hemorrhage, subcortical white matter and certain parts of the diencephalon and the brain stem (T79-20 to T80-1). The major insult is probably in the cranial hemisphere and subcortical white matter (T80-3 to 5). When asked if the damage is irreparable, he replied:

> "Well, my personal feeling is that no doctor ever likes to arrive at a position where, no doctor can ever say that someone is definitely irreversible, but after six months and watching the, her recovery, one has to be very, very pessimistic that she could lead some sort of functional existence. I don't know what level she'll return to." (T79-4 to 19)

Her only improvement has been the change from sleep-like to awake-like unresponsiveness, and Dr. Morse did not know of any course of treatment that would lead to improvement or cure of her condition (T80-15 to 23).

Dr. Morse has seen other patients in chronic vegetative state, but never one also on a respirator (T83-19 to T84-1). A patient does not have to be in a coma to be in a chronic vegetative state (T85-14).

Dr. Morse testified Karen requires a respirator to force air in and out of her lungs (T86-10). He did not know how long she could live without the respirator (T87-10 to 14). There are inherent risks in the use of the respirator on Karen but they are outweighed by its benefits (T89-12 to 18). The greatest danger to Karen is that of infection, especially as long as she stays in the intensive care unit (T88-4 to 14; T111-11 to 20).

The fact that an individual is connected to a respirator does *not* mean that she is not breathing on her own. Whenever the assist light is on, the patient is breathing on her own and when the light is off, the respirator is taking over (T90-16 to T91-1).

The course of treatment for Karen was initially approved by the Quinlan family (T91-6 to 10). Dr. Morse said he would never do anything for Karen without the family's permission (T91-11 to 18). He tried without success to place her in a chronic care facility (T92-9 to 13). After this the Quinlans raised the question of extraordinary means of care (T93-2 to 4). Dr. Morse showed the EEG's to the family and told them that Karen was not "brain dead" (T93-6). The Quinlans requested that Karen be removed from the respirator (T94-24 to T95-1). Dr. Morse refused because there was no reported case in medical history which would justify such an action under these circumstances (T95-4 to 10).

On cross-examination by Mr. Coburn, Dr. Morse testified that the etiology of this condition is a critical factor and that he is making no determination as to the hope for recovery (T98-11 to 16).

Karen's first urine test revealed there was quinine, together with a combination of drugs, all within the therapeutic range in her urine (T99-10 to T100-2). The drugs were aspirin, barbituates and valium (T100-3 to 11). The quinine could have come from quinine water used in mixed drinks (T100-12 to 22). Dr. Morse tetified that coma can be induced by the consumption of drugs (T100-23 to 25).

Karen's condition had its origin in anoxia, the lack of oxygen for one reason or another (T101-21 to 25). There was no evidence of physical violence to her (T102-1 to 9). Dr. Morse's first impression was that Karen's condition was possibly caused by drug overdose (T102-10 to 13).

While a respirator was considered an extraordinary means by the Quinlans, Dr. Morse testified "really, it is an ordinary means in one aspect and it depends on how you look at it. It depends on your background and what you feel" (T106-12 to 23).

Dr. Morse testified that it is possible that a person such as Karen can respond to a voice she recognized even though her eyes are not capable of focusing or recognizing (T108-16 to 19). He did not know what plateau of recovery she could reach but, absent an Act of God, he did not see how she could lead a functional cognitive life. In other words, she would not be able to say "Mr. Coburn, I am glad that you are my guardian" (T110-9 to 20).

When asked if the respirator is an extraordinary medical device, he replied that he could not answer the question, that he could not circumscribe or pigeonhole the concept in that manner (T112-10 to 22). The respirator serves also to ward off infections by keeping her lungs full (T114-15 to 22).

Karen has intact blood pressure and has control over her body temperature (T116-10).

Dr. Morse was familiar with the criteria of the Harvard Ad Hoc Committee. He testified Karen was not "brain dead" and did not meet *any* of its criteria of brain death

93

(T116-17 to 21). He further testified that he could say this with medical certainty (T116-24).

On cross-examination by Mr. Hyland, Dr. Morse testified that if this court authorized the guardian to discontinue the respirator, he would not honor the request unless his medical colleagues showed him cases where such was a step taken under similar circumstances (T117-3 to 17). Current accepted medical practices would not permit shortening her life by removing the respirator (T118-6 to 18).

Dr. Morse also clarified that Karen was admitted to Newton Memorial Hospital on April 15, 1975, at 2:00 A.M. and that he just saw her on April 18, 1975, at 10:00 P.M. (T118-19 to 25).

On cross-examination by Mr. Collester, Dr. Morse testified that the brain stem controls vital functions, including respiration (T122-14 to 20). Karen has some brain stem function for respiration control (T122-23 to T123-5). She also has other senses which one normally associates with being alive, such as pain, movement, feeling, as well as reaction to light and sound (T123-5 to T124-17), and not all of these senses have their origin in the brain stem (T124-18 to 22).

She does have cerebral function as evidenced by the brain waves shown on her EEG (T124-22 to T125-4). The EEG measures cerebral activity (T129-20 to 22). Four or five EEG's were done on Karen, about one per month (T130-5 to 19). "Brain death" would mean a flat EEG (T132-7 to 21), which Karen does not have (T130-24 to T131-1).

Decortication means the lesions in the brain are most probably below the cerebral cortex in the white matter of the brain (T133-4 to 23). Her pupillary responses indicated that this was probably not a structural lesion (T136-23 to T137-4). However, he could not diagnose exactly what the insult is (T138-12).

94

Dr. Morse testified that since her history is inadequate, his prognosis cannot be definitive (T139-2 to 6).

There is a possibility for some form of recovery (T139-7 to 9). If there is a destructive lesion, the likelihood of coming back is less than if there is a metabolic insult (T139-17 to 21).

Mr. Collester concluded:

> "Q. With this problem that you have, that is to say the lack of adequate history, the inability of the patient to communicate with you, is it correct to say that there is a possibility of recovery and the level of recovery would be unknown to you?
>
> "A. That's correct. That's absolutely correct." (T139-22 to T140-2)

On cross examination by Mr. Porzio, Dr. Morse stated that he was initially brought in as a consultant to evaluate Karen (T140-13 to 18). He asked Dr. Javed for his assistance before allowing Karen to be transferred to St. Clare's (T141-10 to 25). Dr. Javed is a pulmonary internist, i.e., he specializes in the use of the respirator (T141-1 to 7).

Karen has grimacing, chewing-like movements. She has blood pressure, has bowel movements, has corneal reflexes and can blink her eyes (T143-24 to T144-12). Her caloric tests were intact from the beginning, indicating integrity of the brain stem (T144-13 to 18).

Mr. Porzio then marked for identification three charts of the brain (T145-22), which were later introduced into evidence as DD-1, A, B and C (T258-3).

The term lesion indicates the location of the anatomical substraight (sic) of the symptom complex in that instance (T146-16 to 22). With high certainty, Dr. Morse could locate Karen's lesion in the cortex more clearly than with some involvement of the brain stem (T147-2 to 10). In his opinion Karen's lesion was metabolic rather than destructive (T151-4 to 18). A metabolic insult could be caused by factors such as low blood sugar, adrenal insufficiency, shock, loss of blood in the brain, anoxia, exposure to heavy metals or drugs and the like (T151-12 to 16).

Dr. Morse testified that Karen certainly has a chance for improvement (T153-6 to 8) but he felt she would never lead a cognitive existence (T153-20). The possibility of removing the repirator was raised by the Quinlans suddenly rather than gradually (T154-12 to 22). He would have considered removing the respirator if there were some medical tradition for doing so, absent brain death (T155-23 to T156-6). The issue was never whether Karen was brain dead (T156-6). He thought perhaps the Church might have some medical support for such a decision (T156-1 to 2). He made a remark in his notes to check into the feasibility of removal (T157-6 to 17).

Dr. Morse called several neurologists about this. He then telephoned Mrs. Quinlan and told her that while he empathized with her, he could not break with medical tradition (T158-4 to 11). He then attended a meeting with the hospital administrator, the hospital attorney, and the Quinlans where he and Dr. Javed indicated that they would not remove the respirator (T159-7 to T160-20).

On cross-examination by Mr. Einhorn, Dr. Morse testified that the criteria for brain death enunciated by the Harvard Ad Hoc Committee were response to pain, pupillary reflexs, corneal reflexs, maintenance of blood pressure and a flat EEG (T162-3 to 12). He stated that the Harvard Criteria are accepted medical determinations and standards of ordinary medical practice (T163-9 to 16).

Counsel then stipulated into evidence P-1, the medical records from Newton Memorial Hospital and P-2, the medical records from St. Clare's Hospital (T164-14).

Mr. Armstrong next called Dr. Arshad Javed, a board-certified pulmonary internist (T169-8) and a consulting physician for Karen Quinlan (T169-10 to 12). Dr. Javed first saw Karen about April 27, 1975, at St. Clare's. At that time she was on the respirator. She was not breathing on her own and was totally dependent on the respirator. Since she was not initiating the breathing, she was not "assisting" the respirator at that time (T169-20 to T170-11).

His examination was limited since a pulmonary examination requires considerable cooperation from the patient (T171-4 to 10). However, she was not cyanotic, i.e., she did not have unoxydated hemoglobin in the system which produces blue discoloration of the fingernails and lips through a lack of oxygen (T171-10 to 21).

His examination with a stethoscope revealed normal breath sounds (T172-8 to T173-2). There are three blood gas tests: PH measures acidity in the blood, PO-2 measures oxygen and PCO-2 measures carbon dioxide excreted in the blood (T173-3 to 24). These tests showed no abnormality while Karen was on the respirator (T176-13 to 16).

Dr. Javed stated that a respirator is a mechanical device meant to deliver a given volume of air at a certain rate. Every so often it will also expand the lungs with a relatively large volume of air called a "sigh volume" which prevents the collection of excretions in those parts of the lung which do not expand with the normal tidal volume (T176-23 to T177-7).

Karen is on a volume cycle respirator (T177-25). At times she is totally dependent on it and at other times it only assists her own breathing (T178-6 to 10). When she is in her awake cycle she is able to initiate her own breathing and the machine merely assists her (T178-11 to 16). When she initiates the breathing, she "triggers" the machine (T179-24 to 25).

Weaning is an attempt to take the patient off the respirator (T180-5). Before weaning is attempted, the patient must have a stable respiratory pattern, and there were certain parameters of Karen's respiratory pattern which Dr. Javed could not even measure because of her inability to cooperate (T180-8 to 17). Nevertheless, weaning was tried several times. Karen would start with a slow respiratory rate but gradually the rate increased and her tidal volume dipped (T180-21 to T181-4). During these attempts to wean, she was off the respirator for a little more than a half hour at most (T181-5 to 13).

Dr. Javed testified that Karen's respiratory problem is just a secondary manifestation of her basic neurological problem. He is very much satisfied with the weaning attempts, but since there was no neurological improvement, there was no reason to keep trying (T182-5 to 11). He did not know how long her bodily functions could be maintained if she were removed from the respirator (T182-18 to 21). She is capable of spontaneous respiration both on and off the respirator (T182-24 to T183-3).

As a consultant his basic responsibility was to the attending physician (T184-8 to 13). He attended a meeting in the hospital administrator's office with the Quinlans in which there was a general discussion concerning taking Karen off the respirator. Dr. Javed told the Quinlans that he felt she was unable to come off the respirator and that he would not discontinue that treatment (T188-1 to 19).

On cross-examination by Mr. Coburn, Dr. Javed testified that when he originally saw Karen, she was totally dependent on the respirator and that today she is something less than totally dependent on it (T191-14 to 19). Even though she might have spontaneous breathing, this might only provide low oxygen and could cause further brain damage (T192-5 to 9). Most patients who go on the respirator are not totally apneic, i.e., they do have some spontaneous ventilation, however inadequate (T192-12 to

16). A patient lying in one position with a poor pulmonary mechanism for clearing her lung excretion runs a high risk of pneumonia and lung infections without the respirator (T192-21 to T193-2).

Soon after Karen came to St. Clare's and began to have more awake cycles, her condition changed from total dependence to the present condition (T193-3 to 9). Today her condition with regard to dependency remains the status quo (T194-1 to 9). If her neurological condition improves, her respiratory condition will probably also improve (T194-16 to T195-1).

One of Dr. Javed's fears in turning off the respirator is that the condition of anoxia, lack of oxygen, would worsen (T197-13 to 17). The brain is the first portion of a person's body to be affected by a lack of oxygen (T198-7 to 12).

Dr. Javed testified that he has not been paid for his services and that he does not expect to be paid (T200-2 to 8). Dr. Morse testified on this point, "I'm in the same situation as Dr. Javed. We have not asked for remuneration" (T202-9).

On cross-examination by Mr. Hyland, Dr. Javed testified that in his opinion an order by this court directing the removal of Karen from the respirator would be a violation of the traditional practices and medical practices in his field of specialty (T200-20 to 24).

Dr. Julius Korein, a board-eligible neurologist and electroencephalographist, was called by Mr. Armstrong (T208-14). Dr. Korein is professor of neurology at New York University and does research on brain function (T210-1 to 16). In 1968 he participated in a study in which the researchers reviewed patients in a coma and attempted to predict traditional death through neurological examinations (T214-10 to T215-7). The object was to define brain death, cerebral death, irreversible coma and the like (T215-8 to 11).

Dr. Korein saw Karen on October 10, 1975, at St. Clare's from 10:45 to 12:30 A.M. (T221-2 to 4). He obtained the medical history from Drs. Morse and Javed, from the hospital records and from the police report (T221-5 to 12). He described Karen as a young catechtic, meaning an emaciated woman with flexion contractures of the upper extremities and of the knees with her ankles plantar flexed or down in a ballet pose (T224-9 to 18). Her eyes were closed and she was not triggering the respirator since the light on the machine at that time was not on (T229-21 to 23).

When Dr. Korein made a loud clap, Karen would blink and occasionally trigger the respirator. When he made repeated claps or stuck her with a pin or touched her face, she would have an arousal reaction similar to being awakened by a loud noise when drowsy (T230-14 to 25). She often had disconjugate eye movements, meaning they moved separately, and she had lip smacking, chewing movements (T231-12 to 16). She had grimacing, grinding-teeth movements and one could hear her teeth click (T232-2 to 3). She sometimes gave a huge yawn (T232-7).

Dr. Korein described these phenomena as a "highly complex pattern reflex" (T232-16). Highly complex reflex means a higher level of the neuraxis of the central nervous system is involved than is the case with simple reflexes (T232-17 to T233-7). Pattern reflexes means stereotyped as opposed to directed movement (T233-13 to 25).

Dr. Korein did three parts of an EEG which were moderately abnormal indicating bilateral cerebral dysfunction, i.e., something wrong with the cerebrum and the cerebral hemispheres (T235-17 to 19).

P-3, a photograph of a young woman in a similar posture for ten years, was admitted into evidence to clarify Karen's posture for purposes of the record (T236-24).

Dr. Korein testified that Karen's states of sleep are not normal because the machine is breathing for her (T237-

18 to T238-16). However, when stimulated she would trigger the respirator, the rate would rise and the breathing would be irregular (T238-17 to 24). Dr. Morse told him that she had gone as long as fifty minutes that night without triggering (T239-13).

An ice water calorics test of the vestibular function of the brain stem was abnormal, indicating high brain stem dysfunction (T240-15 to T242-16). Karen could move her arms a little bit but in reaction to stimuli and not in a voluntary sense (T243-10 to 17). She had corneal reflexes bilaterally. Her pupils were large and responded sluggishly to light, indicating abnormality (T244-18 to 22).

From the history available to him, Dr. Korein concluded that the patient had a period of anoxia (T246-2 to 4). The police report indicated she was "blue, pulseless and apnea," the last term meaning not breathing. She was that way for at least fifteen minutes prior to the police arriving during which time she received mouth-to-mouth resuscitation of some sort (T246-10 to 24). When the ambulance arrived, and she was given oxygen, she turned pink (T246-25 to T247-1).

When Karen arrived at Newton Memorial Hospital, she had a temperature of 100°, her pupils were unreactive and she was unresponsive even to deep pain (T250-21 to 25). The first impression in the hospital notes was "Overdose, unknown substance, with decorticate brain activity" (T251-3 to 5). The blood test indicated low oxygen and the toxicology reports were positive for quinine, valium and librium (T251-10 to 17). Within her first ten days at St. Clare's she developed some vocalization (T252-19 to 21). One test indicated her muscle tissue is breaking down continuously as part of a deterioration process (T254-3 to 12).

Dr. Korein's impression was that the lesion was located in the high brain stem, the top above the pons and the midbrain. This is called the diencephalon region and a single lesion there could cause all the damage (T254-13 to 23). The second possibility is severe bilateral cerebral involvement especially if there was anoxia or hypoxia as indicated by the history (T254-24 to T255-5).

The general term for Karen's condition is persistent or chronic vegetative state in which the bilateral cortex is wiped out (T255-6 to 14). In such a condition a patient has an altered state of consciousness, no communication, no ability for purposeful activity or high cerebral activity and no speech (T255-15 to 25). The "locked-in" syndrome would be further down the brain stem where motor activity is impaired but consciousness is not impaired and the patient can communicate with her eyes (T256-7 to 17). Karen does not have the "locked-in" syndrome (T256-18).

Dr. Korein then went into a long explanation of the central nervous system and its nomenclature, utilizing exhibit DD-1, a chart of the brain (T258-15 to T264-22). During this discussion, while describing brain death, he was interrupted by Mr. Armstrong and asked:

"Q. Excuse me, Doctor. Are we dealing with brain death here?

"A. No, absolutely not. Miss Quinlan is not brain dead." (T261-19 to 21)

He testified that in his opinion the art of medicine cannot repair the cerebral damage sustained by Karen and that there is no course of treatment which will lead to improvement of her condition (T265-15 to 25). He testified that he had seen upwards of fifty patients on a respirator (T266-19 to T267-1). He did not know whether she could breathe on her own without the respirator "for minutes, hours, days, even years" but low oxygen would certainly cause more damage (T267-7 to 16).

Dr. Korein was asked if there is any medical significance in his specialty for the words "extraordinary" and "ordinary" care or treatment and he responded:

102

"A. They have meaning but I mean the meaning is not precise or well defined. And I could give examples." (T269-1 to 8)

He gave an example of a complete exchange of all the blood in a patient's system (T270-5 to 20). He stated that "extraordinary procedures have to do with the utilization of medical personnel, medical technology and time. And they should be used in all situations where the outcome has a reasonable possibility of success" (T271-13 to 17). He further testified:

"Q. Doctor, in your medical opinion is the medical care and treatment presently being administered to Karen ordinary or extraordinary?
"A. It is extraordinary." (T273-15 to 21)

On cross-examination by Mr. Coburn, Dr. Korein outlined the Harvard Criteria defining "brain death" and authorizing the discontinuance of a respirator. Dr. Korein said the Harvard Criteria is "probably one of the most widely accepted standards" in medicine on this issue (T274-10 to T275-3). Karen does not meet the Harvard Criteria or even any one facet of it (T275-6 to 9). Karen is at a cognitive functional level above brain death (T282-5 to 9).

Dr. Korein testified that medical history is much more important in the acute stage of Karen's condition than in the present chronic stage (T286-6 to T287-6). He has seen patients in a persistent vegetative state for five years, although without breathing problems (T292-3 to 12).

On cross examination by Mr. Hyland, Dr. Korein testified that he had no test to divide treatment into categories of "ordinary" and "extraordinary" (T296-5 to 12). Factors include the extent of effort and health, care, time, personnel and energy involved (T296-25 to T297-2). It is ordinary care to use a respirator and round-the-clock nurses in an acute stage but use for prolonged periods becomes extraordinary (T298-3 to 11). Where there is irreparable damage and no thought content, prolonged use of a respirator becomes extraordinary for Dr. Korein (T299-10 to 13). However, he admitted neurology is one of the more developing and changing fields in medical science and what would have been characterized forty years ago as extraordinary is commonplace today (T300-12 to 20).

On cross-examination by Mr. Collester, Dr. Korein testified that some additional tests might produce a more authoritative diagnosis or prognosis, but the increment would be very small compared to the danger to the patient (T301-17 to T303-7).

Dr. Korein testified that his own research had developed his own criteria for brain death and that Karen meets none of these criteria also (T307-2 to 12).

Karen is neither brain dead nor cerebrally dead (T312-9 to 11).

He testified that if he were the treating physician, he would want more medical history than the police report and that such history is about ninety percent of a diagnosis (T309-2 to 20).

The term extraordinary care is couched in terms of medical resources and capability (T316-6 to 8). There is an implicit value judgment here and people may differ on such value judgments (T317-20 to 24). Every physician makes value judgments in the practice of medicine (T318-2).

On cross-examination by Mr. Porzio, Dr. Korein testified that Karen probably needs the respirator to survive (T321-9 to 15). His distinction between ordinary and extraordinary care is not subject to precise definition and in subject to change, depending on developments in the field as they relate to the patient (T322-3 to 9). He further testified:

"Q. Dr. Korein, you will admit, will you not, that when we use the terms 'extraordinary means, ordinary means' that we have one meaning to the layman and one meaning to those in the medical profession. Isn't that so?

"A. They may be subject to many interpretations, yes." (T325-15 to 19)

In reaching his decisions, value judgments are intricately related to the medical factors; they cannot be separated (T325-3 to 10).

On cross examination by Mr. Einhorn he admitted that quality of life is an implied factor in the decision as to extraordinary means (T325-13 to 23). Value judgments made by physicians are made within the confines of certain accepted medical standards (T327-11 to 14). Dr. Korein believed there are standards in the profession as to ordinary and extraordinary care which are "accepted but not spoken of" (T327-15 to 24). There is an unwritten law or code (T327-25 to T328-4).

In giving the following example, Dr. Korein qualified it by stating that "I really can't speak for every physician obviously. So I don't want to distort my colleagues." In this context he gave the example of a patient dying of cancer, in agony. In this case he would instruct the nurse not to resuscitate him if he stops breathing (T328-14 to T329-4).

Dr. Korein testified that there are several dozen different sets of criteria of brain death. All are basically similar and acceptable and Karen does not meet any of these criteria (T331-18 to T332-1).

On recross by Mr. Collester, the following exchange took place as to this "unwritten rule":

"Q. Would it be fair to state that there's considerable debate within the medical profession as to this type of thing?

"A. There is a term that perhaps I should introduce—

"Q. Can you answer my question?

"A. Not directly.

"Q. All right. Go ahead, doctor. What term do you want to introduce?

"A. It's called judicious neglect. There are situations where physicians will say: Don't treat this patient anymore, that it does not serve either the patient, the family or society in any meaningful way to continue treatment with this patient.

"Q. And that determination, of course, depends upon the individual physician in part?

"A. And the family.

"Q. And the family, both. Right?

"A. Oh, yes." (T332-22 to 333-14)

Mr. Armstrong next called Joseph Quinlan, husband of Julia Quinlan and father of Karen (T334-1 to 23). He is a member of the Roman Catholic faith and belongs to Our Lady of the Lake parish in Mount Arlington. All his children, including Karen, were raised as Catholics and attended Catholic elementary and high schools (T335-6 to T337-6). Karen's baptismal certificate, P-5, was introduced into evidence (T336-5).

In late August after meetings with Dr. Morse and Dr. Javed he decided to start this lawsuit (T340-4 to 22). Mr. Quinlan testified Dr. Morse told him that Karen would eventually die; it was a matter of time (T341-15 to 22). After a number of meetings with the doctors and others, he became convinced it was God's will (T341-23 to 25). He first decided to take this step, then consulted his pastor, Father Thomas Trapasso, who helped him with his conscience and made it definite (T344-18 to 21).

Mr. Quinlan testified Dr. Javed advised them to discontinue the respirator and Dr. Morse did not advise them either way (T345-6 to 17). At a meeting with the family and two priests he requested that the machine be discontinued (T345-18 to T346-22). The hospital drew a release which he and his wife signed (T347-1 to 12) but the doctors did not discontinue treatment of Karen (T347-1 to 2).

On cross-examination by Mr. Coburn, Mr. Quinlan stated Karen never told him her religious beliefs on this subject (T348-21 to 23). After he made his decision he learned that it coincided with his religion's teachings (T349-15 to 19). As a parent he felt he had a right to enforce Karen's right of self-determination (T348-2) and to make the religious decision on her behalf (T354-5 to 10). Mr. Quinlan stated that in his view "extraordinary means" are any artificial means used to extend her life beyond her normal time, but not anything being used for her comfort (T355-22 to T356-4).

Mr. Quinlan made his decision after prayer and based on the belief that Karen's condition was absolutely hopeless (T357-3 to 25). If he felt there were any trace of hope he would not be seeking this legal relief (T358-7 to 23). He wants Karen put back in her "natural state" and let the Lord decide how long she shall live (T361-1 to 8).

Mr. Quinlan testified that Karen had not been living at home for five or six months prior to her admission to Newton Memorial Hospital (T363-2 to 4). He was not paying the hospital bills. He had applied to Medicaid since Karen was of age, did not live at home and had no income (T363-11 to 16). If appointed guardian, he would authorize the physicians to discontinue the respirator (T364-6 to 10).

On cross-examination by Mr. Collester, Mr. Quinlan testified that after he executed the release, the doctors told him that they could not turn off the machine (T377-1 to 25). He stated that the pain and helplessness he and his family felt over Karen caused him to start this lawsuit (T379-1 to 19).

107

On cross-examination by Mr. Porzio, Mr. Quinlan testified that in the early months he strongly believed Karen could recover (T379-24 to T380-2). However, at one point Dr. Morse showed him the EEG's and told him not to be optimistic (T380-8 to 19). Mr. Quinlan gradually decided to discontinue the respirator (T380-20 to T382-19) and then went to Father Trapasso who told him that his decision was in conformance with the Church's teachings (T382-16 to T383-12).

After Mr. Quinlan spoke to Dr. Morse, the doctor indicated that he had to look into this and check it out (T383-25 to T384-5). Dr. Morse mentioned that he had a moral problem with the decision and wanted to call in his old professor, Dr. Morris Bender (T384-5 to 9). He later attended a meeting where Dr. Morse and Dr. Javed informed the family that they could not discontinue the respirator because it was contrary to medical tradition (T387-19 to 22).

While Mr. Quinlan thought Dr. Javed had advised them to discontinue the respirator, he admitted that his recollection on this point could very well be mistaken (T392-4 to 18). Dr. Javed had previously told him that it was rather risky to attempt weaning Karen from the machine again (T392-19 to T393-9). Before the last meeting, Dr. Javed testified that she would probably die off the respirator (T393-5 to 13). However, Mr. Quinlan did not want Karen to die, only to return to her natural state and let the Lord decide (T393-14 to 20).

Mr. Armstrong next called Father Thomas J. Trapasso, a Catholic priest and pastor of the Quinlan's parish (T398-9 to T399-10). His understanding of the Catholic position on this issue is that extraordinary means are not required to prolong life (T402-2 to 6).

Mrs. Quinlan works in the parish rectory and Father Trapasso had an on-going discussion with her as to Karen's problem (T402-13 to 24). He only spoke to Mr.

Quinlan after a meeting with Dr. Javed about weaning Karen off the respirator (T407-5 to 24). He wanted to explain the Church's position slowly and gently to him (T408-2 to 24). In mid-July, Mr. Quinlan told him he had decided and Father Trapasso reassured him (T409-7 to T410-14).

On cross-examination by Mr. Coburn, Father Trapasso admitted that this was an optional Catholic tenet and that nothing was required of Mr. Quinlan (T411-1 to 6). On November 24, 1957, Pope Pius XII delivered an *allocutio* to a group of anesthesiologists on the removal of respirators (T412--21 to T413-5), but this was Catholic tradition, morality and theology prior thereto (T412-17 to 19). Father Trapasso stated that he brought up the Church's position to Mr. Quinlan (T414-18 to 24).

On cross-examination by Mr. Baime, Father Trapasso stated that the Catholic Church does not require the termination of the use of extraordinary means (T417-7 to 17).

On cross-examination by Mr. Collester, Father Trapasso stated that he never discussed this teaching with Karen (T419-1 to 4).

An *allocutio* is less authoritative than a papal bull or a papal encyclical (T420-6 to 21). The *allocutio* is subject to interpretation and the word "extraordinary" is relative (T421-22 to T422-3). The final decision must come from medical procedures and all the circumstances of the patient (T423-22 to T424-1). The positions of Dr. Morse and Dr. Javed are not inconsistent with the position of the Church (T425-8 to 14).

Father Trapasso testified that Karen's soul is still in her body and that, theologically, it is the soul which distinguishes a corpse from a living human being (T427-17 to T428-6).

On cross-examination by Mr. Porzio, Father Trapasso testified that this papal *allocutio* was not covered by the doctrine of papal infallibility (T429-19 to T430-18). To his knowledge, the Pope had not further defined the terms "extraordinary means" or "hopeless" since the 1957 address (T433-12 to T434-3).

A document, "The Pope Speaks," was marked into evidence as DD-2 (T435-24), and stipulated to contain a true copy of the 1957 address (T436-11). It contained the following question by a physician and the answer of Pius XII:

"Q. Has death already occurred after grave trauma of the brain, which has provoked deep unconsciousness and central breathing paralysis, the fatal consequences of which have nevertheless been retarded by artificial respiration? Or does it occur, according to the present opinion of doctors, only when there is complete arrest of circulation, despite prolonged artificial respiration?

"A. Where verification of the fact in particular cases is concerned, the answer cannot be discussed from any religious and moral principle, and under this aspect does not fall within the competence of the church. Until an answer be given, the question must remain open. *But consideration of a general nature allows us to believe that human life continues for as long as its vital functions distinguish from the simple life of organs manifest themselves spontaneously or even with the help of artificial processes.* A great number of these cases *are the object of insoluble doubt* and must be dealt with according to the presumptions of law and of fact of which we have spoken." (T436-14 to T437-23) (emphasis added)

Mr. Armstrong next called Father Paschal Caccavalle, a Catholic priest and chaplain at St. Clare's Hospital (T440-6 to 22). He attended a meeting with Dr. Morse, the Quinlans and a nurse in a conference room near the intensive care unit (T441-10 to 17). He was asked the Church's position and explained that there was no obligation to continue extraordinary means (T441-18 to T442-1). He also attended the meeting in the administrator's office with the Quinlans and the doctors (T443-2 to 9).

On cross-examination by Mr. Coburn, he testified he advised Mr. Quinlan that the obligation to use the respirator had ceased and that he had a choice or option on the matter (T444-9 to 18). On cross-examination by Mr. Collester, he testified thae the phrase "quality of life" is not in the Pope's statement (T445-12 to 25).

Mr. Armstrong next called Julia Ann Quinlan, wife of the plaintiff and mother of three children, including Karen Quinlan (T466-18 to T467-2). Mrs. Quinlan is a Roman Catholic and a member of Father Trapasso's parish. She raised all her children as Catholics (T467-3 to T468-10).

Mrs. Quinlan reached the decision to discontinue the respirator before the rest of the family (T468-14 to T469-19). Father Trapasso told her to be patient and wait until the entire family agreed (T470-1 to 23) and he advised her of the Church's position (T473-11 to 19). After she felt her husband had decided, the family discussed the matter (T473-18 to 24).

Mrs. Quinlan then described three instances when she discussed similar problems with Karen. The first instance involved her Aunt Eleanor who was dying of cancer about three years ago. The second instance was in January, 1974, when the father of a girl friend was dying. The third instance was in February, 1975, when a family friend was dying of cancer (T475-22 to T477-5).

When Aunt Eleanor was dying Karen told Mrs. Quinlan that she would never want to be kept alive by "any extraordinary means" (T484-8 to 20). Mrs. Quinlan could not remember if those were her exact words. She described Karen as active and full of life and as loving life (T484-21 to T485-11). The other two occasions were similar to the first instance (T486-1 to 14).

On cross-examination by Mr. Baime, Mrs. Quinlan testified that Aunt Eleanor had breast cancer, was suffering great pain and knew full well that she was dying (T487-1 to T488-2).

With regard to the third instance, Mr. Birch, the family friend, was also suffering from cancer and was in pain (T490-1 to 14). Mrs. Quinlan was sure that Karen used the words "extraordinary means" (T491-20 to T492-2).

Mary Ellen Quinlan, the sister, was called by Mr. Armstrong and testified that she supports her parents' position in this lawsuit (T495-3 to 12). Her religious beliefs and education as a Catholic were stipulated (T494-7 to T495-2). She had discussed the use of extraordinary means with Karen (T495-23 to 25). Karen's views were "about the same thing" as her mother had said but she added that Karen had said she would not want to be kept alive because she had seen part of the respective families die, too, during the ordeal (T496-18 to T497-4).

A similar stipulation was entered with regard to the religious training and beliefs of John Quinlan, the brother, as well as his support of the lawsuit (T498-1 to 9).

As this point the Court allowed Mr. Porzio to call Dr. Javed out of order. He testified that he never made a decision that Karen should come off the respirator and that he absolutely did not speak to Mr. Quinlan of any such decision (T499-14 to 25). Any decision would be Dr. Morse's as attending physician and not his (T500-1 to 12). Dr. Javed never told Dr. Morse that he had decided that she should come off the respirator and Dr. Morse never made such a statement to him (T500-13 to 20). Dr. Javed only discussed weaning Karen with the Quinlans, which was confirmed by his notes (T500-22 to T503-13). Such weaning attempts are standard medical practice in this field (T503-14 to 16).

Julia Quinlan was then recalled by Mr. Armstrong and testified that it was her impression that Dr. Javed recom-

mended discontinuance of the respirator (T505-7 to 10).
When Dr. Morse arrived later, Dr. Javed said it was not
his decision (T505-23 to T506-4). At a subsequent meeting with the doctors both the Quinlans and Dr. Morse
signed the release and it was her impression everyone felt
that this was the best thing to do (T507-18 to T509-9).
The release, P-6, was admitted in evidence (T508-20).

On cross-examination by Mr. Porzio, Mrs. Quinlan was
shown the release, and admitted she was mistaken about
Dr. Morse signing it (T509-21 to T510-10). She also
stated that she might have been wrong about Dr. Javed
being at the last meeting (T511-9 to 17).

Mr. Armstrong's last witness was Lori Gaffney, a
friend of Karen's (T516-18). She had a discussion with
Karen when they were taking her girl friend to the hospital to see her dying father during which time Karen
told her that she would not "want to be kept alive by
such extraordinary means." Lori also discussed Mr. Birch
with Karen and was told that she would never want to
be kept alive by machines (T517-17 to T518-14).

Mr. Coburn's first witness was Dr. Eugene Loeser, a
board-certified neurologist (T547-9 to 19). Dr. Loeser,
saw Karen at 8:00 A.M. of October 2, 1975, together with
Dr. Stuart Cook, Dr. Fred Plum and Dr. Henry Liss
(T549-4 to 14). The four doctors examined Karen jointly
(T550-2 to 5). Karen had a tracheostomy and was attached via it to the respirator (T550-13 to 18). She was
on her back with her eyes open at times and closed at
times. Her arms were tightly drawn on her chest and
tightly flexed. Her wrists and fingers were tightly flexed
and inverted. Her legs were in an extreme state of
flexion. None of the flexion in these limbs could be overcome (T550-23 to T551-7). Her muscle tone was extremely rigid (T551-22).

In Dr. Loeser's opinion her care at St. Clare's was
"exceptionally excellent." Considering the time she was

in a coma, she was well-nourished and had remarkably few scars from bed sores (T552-5 to 16). Dr. Morse and Dr. Javed presented the doctors with the medical history (T553-14).

Dr. Loeser stated that at times Karen was in an awake state. Her eyes moved spontaneously and had "the doll's head movement." Karen made periodic high-pitched sounds, especially when stimulated. Her deep tendon reflexes could not be elicited. There were sucking movements of her mouth when stimulated and body movement when startled. There was no indication of awareness of her surroundings on a conscious level. Her pupils reacted normally to light (T554-4 to T555-14).

The doctors disconnected the respirator for 3 minutes and 45 seconds but she received some oxygen from the catheter during this time (T555-15 to T556-24). During this time also a blood gas test was done and the blood gases were within normal limits (T558-1 to 24). An EEG was also performed which was normal, considering the presence of drugs needed to perform the test (T560-3 to T561-19).

Dr. Loeser outlined the Harvard Criteria for "brain death" (T561-24 to T563-5). He stated that Karen met none of the criteria and to a medical certainty was not "brain dead" (T564-4 to 11).

Dr. Loeser testified that Karen was living at a reflex level with primitive function of the brain stem centers rather than of the cortex of the brain itself (T568-1 to 4). He saw no hope for improvement of the cognitive functions, with some possibility of improvement of the non-cognitive functions (T568-14 to T579-6).

On cross-examination by Mr. Baime, Dr. Loeser testified that during the examination she was triggering the respirator at all times (T572-1 to 4). On cross-examination by Mr. Collester, he testified that there was fear of infection both on and off the respirator (T572-17 to 24).

114

On cross-examination by Mr. Porzio, he testified that if she were taken off the respirator her life could be shortened (T573-2 to 5). On cross-examination by Mr. Einhorn, he testified that the Harvard Criteria are accepted in ordinary medical practice to determine whether a person's cardio-pulmonary functions are being artificially maintained (T573-8 to 15).

On cross-examination by Mr. Armstrong, Dr. Loeser testified that Karen did not have "the locked in syndrome" (T575-2 to 5). Dr. Loeser then acknowledged the following quotation from his report:

> "It is my opinion that the progress (sic) for recovery is nil. Based on the severity of the findings described the known poor prognosis for this vegetative state and the already long duration of a relative status quo with no indication of recovery of higher cerebral function.

> "I do not feel that I should speculate on the causative etiology of this condition. I think, however, that we see the end stage of brain dysfunction regardless of the original causative factor.

> "I do not feel that Miss Quinlan is dead. I do believe she has irreversible brain damage as described above." (T576-14 to T577-15)

At this point, on motion of Mr. Porzio, the portion of the pretrial order on stipulations was amended as follows without objection:

> "Under any legal standard recognized by the State of New Jersey and also under standard medical practice, Karen Ann Quinlan is presently alive."

Mr. Coburn next called Dr. Fred Plum, chief neurologist at the New York Hospital and Chairman of the department at Cornell Medical School as well as president-elect of the American Neurological Association. Dr. Plum is the author of over one hundred scientific papers and three books, one of which deals with the subject matter of this case (T582-7 to T583-11).

When he saw Karen she was emaciated. She turned spontaneously from side to side and made intermittent sterotype moans. Each startle evoked the same primitive response. She had continuous brief periods of sleeping and waking. She had spontaneous eye movements and intact pupil responses. She had rigid muscles. She would cry if pinched and her temperature was normal (T587-13 to T588-8).

Dr. Plum testified that the brain supplies both internal vegetative regulation and highly developed, uniquely human functions. "Brain death necessarily must mean the death of both these functions of the brain, vegetative and the sapient" (T589-1 to 25). The presence of vegetative function means the brain is not biologically dead (T589-25 to T590-4).

Dr. Plum testified that Karen absolutely has brain vegetative function under any criteria (T590-18 to T591-13). She is absolutely not brain dead (T592-1 to 5). Under all the Harvard Criteria she has brain life (T592-6 to 15).

Dr. Plum defined the persistent vegetative state as a condition where the subject has the capacity to maintain the vegetative parts of the neurological function but no longer has any cognitive function (T597-9 to 25). He concluded that Karen is in a persistent vegetative state (T598-1 to 4).

On cross-examination by Mr. Armstrong, Dr. Plum testified that most patients with brain injuries this severe die fairly early in their illness and that he had personally examined twenty-five to thirty such patients (T600-2 to 12). In his opinion Karen's brain damage is irreparable (T601-15 to 17). Karen does not have the "locked in" syndrome (T604-16 to 19).

Dr. Sidney Diamond, a board-eligible neurologist and professor of neurology at Mt. Sinai School of Medicine was called by Mr. Baime (T605-4 to T606-9). Dr. Diamond saw Karen on October 15, 1975 (T607-25). He reviewed the medical history given to him (T608-11 to T610-12). Dr. Morse's notes of April 18 indicated that she was already showing signs of decerebration (T610-11). This means there was a figurative parting of the cortex and higher cerebral functions from the brain stem functions which she had (T611-1 to 10). He reviewed various previous tests by Dr. Morse and Dr. Javed and expressed confidence in their findings of normality (T611-13 to 17).

Dr. Diamond described Karen as being emaciated and in a grotesque position of flexion contractures. Her eyes were open and moved together in random. She frequently would tighten up even more than she was already. There were sounds made by her without stimulation. She would blink if a hand were waved in front of her, but she was not scanning for information. She had pupillary light reflexes. Clapping or touching would set off blinking and spasms (T612-2 to T614-9). She was triggering the respirator (T615-9). She does not meet the Harvard Criteria (T615-4 to 9).

Dr. Diamond testified with reference to the respirator:

> "You could not find a physician who would not have provided that support when she was first admitted or the period during which a determination of cause was being carried out. No physician to my knowledge will ever interrupt a device which is performing a life-saving measure at any time at all." (T618-18 to 23)

When the Harvard Criteria are met, the respirator is being turned off on a dead person, a person without life, and the doctor can ethically and legally terminate supportive measures (T618-24 to T619-8). Dr. Diamond stated:

117

"I do not think based on my examination and experience that anybody would interrupt this device, the use of this device now on the patient." (T619-9 to 12)

He testified that we do not know whether this respirator is an extraorinary measure in this case now because there is no way of knowing if she can survive without it (T619-21 to 24). He further testified that the actions of Dr. Morse and Dr. Javed were perfectly consistent with the standards of medical practice (T621-1 to 18).

The last witness, Dr. Stuart Cook, Chairman of Neurosciences at New Jersey Medical School, was called by Mr. Coburn as the final witness. He examined Karen with Dr. Plum and Dr. Loeser and he testified as to the clinical results of that examination substantially as they had testified.

In Dr. Cook's opinion Karen received excellent care which resulted in her remaining in rather remarkable condition considering her illness (T628-10 to 15). Karen exits in a state variously described in the literature as a persistent vegetative state, a pallic state, a kenetic muckosum (sic) or a coma vigil (sic) (T634-5 to 9). In his opinion Karen is clearly not brain dead (T635-2). She probably has anoxic damage to the brain, i.e., lack of oxygen (T635-4 to 14), but he cannot do more than guess (T637-1 to 8).

Dr. Cook expressed the view that Karen has suffered irreversible brain damage and the chances for any useful sapient or discriminative return of function are extremely remote (T639-5 to 8). However, it is "very hard in medicine to say anything with absolute certainty" (T639-14 to 15). The pessimistic opinion is also tempered by the confusion around the precipitating events. Another qualification is the fact that there have been patients in a comatose state for more than a year who have made some useful recovery. Finally, there is always the possibility of a medical breakthrough and research advances (T640-4 to 15). While there is almost no chance Karen will ever return to any significant level of psychological function, Dr. Cook could not give an opinion as to where she might progress along the psychological function scale (T640-16 to T641-4).

ARGUMENT

POINT I

Karen Ann Quinlan is both medically alive and legally alive.

The important issues raised by this appeal cannot be discussed by respondent doctors until the medical condition of Karen Ann Quinlan has been clearly delineated. While the hearing below was highly publicized in the media as a case which would decide the definition of death, that issue was not litigated.

Indeed, the Pretrial Order of September 22, 1975, sets forth questions relating to the definition of death and whether or not Karen Ann Quinlan was legally dead as two of the legal and factual issues at trial. However, in his trial Brief dated October 10, 1975, plaintiff shifted his ground and stated:

> Plaintiff Believes That Karen Ann Quinlan Is Not At Present Dead According to Any Legal Standard Recognized By The State of New Jersey (Pb Trial-29).

At trial, plaintiff's subsequent belief proved to be correct. Seven physicians who had examined Karen testified. These physicians consisted of six neurologists and one pulmonary internist. Each and every one of the neurologists testified that Karen was not "brain dead" under any present medically recognized definition of "brain death". Dr. Morse (T116-17 to 21), Dr. Korein (T331-18 to 332-1), Dr. Loeser (T564-4 to 11), Dr. Plum (T592-1 to 5), Dr. Diamond (T618-24 to 619-12) and Dr. Cook (T635-2) were unanimous in their opinion that Karen was medically alive. Dr. Javed, the pulmonary internist currently treating Karen, was not asked the question directly since "brain death" is not within his field of specialty. However, he did testify that removal of Karen from the respirator would be a violation of the medical traditions and medical practices of his speciality (T200-20 to 24).

On the fourth day of trial, the Pretrial Order was amended by Judge Muir, with the consent of all counsel, to include the following stipulation:

> Under any legal standard recognized by the State of New Jersey and also under standard medical practice, Karen Ann Quinlan is presently alive. (T581-14)

Finally, Judge Muir ruled in his written opinion that Karen is alive under both the legal and the medical definitions of death (Slip op. at 26).

Thus, Karen is a living human being today. Nevertheless, plaintiff is seeking authority from this court to take steps which would result in the termination of her life. The respondent doctors respectfully submit that this court must examine plaintiff's petition in that context and must determine whether plaintiff has presented sufficient evidence to justify such an extraordinary, literally unprecedented, judicial step. It is further submitted that an examination of the record below will reveal that no such evidence was presented and that Judge Muir properly refused to overrule the sound judgment of the treating physicians that the present treatment of their patient should continue.

Although there is no dispute as to Karen's medical and legal status as a living human being in this case, some comment on the issue of the definition of death is perhaps in order. On October 22, 1975, counsel for St. Clare's Hospital wrote to Judge Muir requesting that the Pretrial Order be amended to include the following Count for a Declaratory Judgment:

Whether the use of the criteria developed and enunciated by the Ad Hoc Committee of the Harvard Medical School on or about August 5, 1968, as well as similar criteria, by a physician to assist him in the determination of the death of a patient whose cardio-pulmonary functions are being artificially sustained, is in accordance with ordinary and standard medical practice (Letter of Theodore E. B. Einhorn, Esquire, to the Honorable Robert Muir, Jr., J.S.C., dated October 22, 1975).

Counsel subsequently amended his request to limit the issue to the facts in this case. (Letter of Theodore E. B. Einhorn, Esquire, to the Honorable Robert Muir, Jr., J.S.C., dated October 30, 1975). Counsel for the defendant physicians submitted two letter Briefs in opposition to the application. (Letters of Ralph Porzio, Esquire, to the Honorable Robert Muir, Jr., J.S.C., dated October 28, 1975, and November 4, 1975).

In his written opinion Judge Muir ruled that a Declaratory Judgment on the above issue should not be made on the facts of this case since it is undisputed that Karen is alive and that such an adjudication must await an actual controversy. Moreover, Judge Muir added that the definition of death is a factual question to be decided on the basis of expert medical testimony as to generally prevailing accepted medical standards and that this is not a question of law. Judge Muir wrote:

Additionally, just as the matter of the nature and extent of care and treatment of a patient and therefore the patient's removal from a respirator is a medical decision based upon ordinary practice, so, too, is the decision whether a patient is dead and by what medical criteria. Whether Karen Quinlan one day becomes brain dead and therefore should be removed from the respirator is a decision that will have to be based upon the extant medical criteria at the time (Slip op. at 35).

Respondent physicians wholeheartedly support Judge Muir's decision on this point and contend that the rapid advances in medical research and technology mandate that this court not attempt to define death as a matter of law.

When the question of what constitutes death does arise in a case, that issue must be decided as a question of fact based upon expert medical testimony at that time. To do otherwise would be to restrict the law to a definition of death which may be medically acceptable today and yet be totally out of line with medical standards two years from now.

The current case law relies heavily upon the following definition of death given in *Black's Law Dictionary*, 488 (Rev. 4th ed. 1968):

> The cessation of life; the ceasing to exist; *defined by physicians as* a total stoppage of the circulation of the blood, and a cessation of the animal and vital functions consequent thereon, such as respiration, pulsation, etc. (Emphasis added)

Clearly, the author was not attempting to define death as a legal matter, but rather to set forth his understanding of the then existing state of medical knowledge on the subject, which would be the ultimate arbiter of such questions.

Many courts have directly cited the above definition in support of their decisions. Comment, "The Criteria for Determining Death in Vital Organ Transplants—A Medico-Legal Dilemma", 38 *Mo. L. Rev.* 220, 229 (1973). See, *e.g.*, *Smith* v. *Smith,* 229 Ark. 622, 317 S.W. 2d 275 (Sup.

Ct. 1958); *In re Estate of Schmidt*, 261 Cal. App. 2d 262, 67 Cal. Rptr. 847 (Dt. Ct. App. 1968); *Thomas v. Anderson*, 96 Cal. App. 371, 215 P. 2d 478 (Dt. Ct. App. 1950); *Schmidt v. Pierce*, 344 S.W. 2d 120 (Mo. Sup. Ct. 1961). Other courts have relied heavily upon expert medical opinion, based upon either personal observation or upon the recounting of events by witnesses, to reach a determination of the time of death without defining the concept. See, *e.g., In re Davenport's Estates*, 79 Idaho 548, 323 P. 2d 611 (1958); *Gray v. Sawyer*, 247 S.W. 2d 496 (Ky. Ct. App. 1952); *Taylor v. Cawood*, 211 S.W. 47 (Mo. Sup. Ct. 1919). In any event, the definition certainly is not a legal issue, but rather a factual issue to be determined on the basis of standard medical practices at a given time.

The courts of this state apparently have not had occasion to rule on the legal definition of death. However, *Fernandez v. Baruch*, 52 N. J. 127, 130-131 (1968) is instructive on the issue. In that case a defendant doctor was charged with medical malpractice in connection with the suicide of one of his patients. This court held that plaintiff did not create a jury issue on liability because his medical expert testified as to *his* personal opinion on the proper steps to be taken rather than as to accepted medical practices or prevailing standards under the circumstances. Since there was no testimony establishing the proper medical standards, there was no fact issue for the jury. *Fernandez* stands for the proposition that medical questions, such as the definition of death, are issues of fact to be resolved with the aid of expert medical testimony. Moreover, *Carbone v. Warburton*, 11 N. J. 418, 426 (1953) makes clear that such medical questions must be decided as issues of fact within the ambit of "the present state of scientific knowledge."

The only attempt by the New Jersey Legislature to define the time of death is embodied in the Uniform Anatomical Gift Act, N.J.S.A. 26:6-63(b) which provides in part:

The time of death shall be determined by a physician who attends the donor at his death, or, if none, the physician who certifies death.

Thus, our own Legislature has recognized the need to maintain flexibility in the definition of death and to rely upon the sound judgment of the treating physician or certifying physician based upon ordinary medical practices at the time of death.

The question of "brain death" amply demonstrates the need for flexibility in the concept of death dependent upon the current state of scientific knowledge. There was much testimony below concerning the criteria for "brain death" set forth by the Harvard *Ad Hoc* Committee. See *Ad Hoc* Committee of the Harvard Medical School to Examine the Definition of Brain Death, Report: A Definition of "Irreversible Coma", 208 *J.A.M.A.* 85 (1968). [Hereinafter cited as Harvard *Ad Hoc* Committee Report]. The Committee, all members of the faculty of Harvard University, consisted of ten physicians, an historian, a lawyer and a theologian. See Capron and Kass, "A Statutory Definition of the Standards for Determining Human Death: An Appraisal and Proposal", 121 *U. Pa. L. Rev.* 87, 89 n. 9 (1972). The Committee sought to set forth the criteria for the presence of "brain death" in instances of irreversible coma which would justify discontinuance of life-supportive measures, such as the respirator in the instant case. (See Slip op. at 11).

It may safely be said that twenty years ago there was no consensus in the medical community as to the concept of brain death. Yet, several physicians testified at trial that the Harvard *Ad Hoc* Committee Criteria are the standards of ordinary medical practice today (See *e.g.* testimony of Dr. Morse, T163-9 to 16). On the other hand, Dr. Korein testified below that there are several dozen *basically similar* tests of "brain death" (T331-18 to 332-1) and the trial court noted that the question is "the subject of a plethora of written material." See Slip Op. at 26A, n. 8; see, *e.g.*, Task Force on Death and Dying of the Institute of Society, Ethics, and the Life Sciences, Report: "Refinements in the Criteria for the Determination of Death": An Appraisal, 221 *J.A.M.A.* 48 (1972) which takes issue with some aspects of the Harvard *Ad Hoc* Committee Criteria.

While the respondent physicians certainly do not refute that the Harvard *Ad Hoc* Committee Criteria are the standard of accepted medical practice today, it is equally clear that continuing medical research into this question will leave the issue somewhat in a state of flux. Surely, it may be said that no hard and fast legal guidelines on the definition of death ought to be laid down under these circumstances.

There have been several legislative enactments which have granted credence to the concept of "brain death." See, *e.g.*, *Alas. Stat.* § 09.65.120; *Calif. Health & Safety Code* § 7180, 7181; *Kan. Stat. Ann.* § 77-202; *Md. Code Ann. art.* 43, § 54(f); *N.M. Stat. Ann.* § 1-2-2:2. *Okla. Stat. Ann.* § 1-301(9) (Pub. L. 1975, c. 91, §1, April 28, 1975); *Va. Code* § 32-364.3:1 *W. Va. Code Ann.* §16-19-1.

These statutes accord recognition to the concept of "brain death" but do not set forth criteria for determining when "brain death" occurs. Rather, the statutes are couched in general terms such as "the absence of spontaneous brain functions" and leave the specifics to the opinion of the treating physician based upon ordinary standards of medical practice. See, *e.g.*, New Jersey State Senate Bill No. 3314 introduced July 31, 1975, which refers to "irreversible cessation of vital brain functions" in the opinion of the physician based on ordinary standards of medical practice. (Trial Brief of State of New Jersey at DHa1).

Such legislation surely is helpful to the physician who wishes to undertake an organ transplant from a patient whom he considers to be "brain dead." Nevertheless, when any "brain death" issue is actually litigated, regardless of the cause of action involved, the ultimate question will remain, what are the prevailing standard, accepted medical practices at that time to determine what constitutes "brain death"?

In this respect, these statutes add little to the common law. The definition of death must remain flexible and must reflect current accepted medical thinking on the subject. Regardless of legislation, it will remain a fact question to be determined by prevailing medical opinion at the time in question.

Because of the foregoing, respondent physicians contend that the trial court properly exercised its discretion in refusing to consider the merits of the defendant hospital's amendment to the Pretrial Order seeking a Declaratory Judgment on the Harvard *Ad Hoc* Committee Criteria. Since Karen Ann Quinlan is conceded to be alive, the applicable definition of death is not an issue in this case and the controversy is not ripe for adjudication. See *Hildebrant* v. *Bailey,* 65 N. J. Super. 274, 279 (App. Div. 1961). It is unwise and unnecessary to deal with hypothetical questions in the abstract. See *N. J. Sports & Exposition Authority* v. *McCrane,* 61 N. J. 1, 27-28 (1972).

In *Hildebrant* the court quoted with approval the following passage from *American Federation of Labor* v. *Reilly,* 113 Colo. 90, 155 P. 2d 145, 151-152 (Sup. Ct. 1945):

> We cannot here decide any of the various questions raised, however desirable it might be to have them settled, unless we are now willing to answer questions "which have not yet arisen and which may never arise" and reply to mere "speculative inquiries." We cannot thus permit the courts to be converted into legal aid bureaus.

Hildebrant v. *Bailey, supra,* 65 N. J. Super. at 285.

If and when the issue does arise, respondent physicians submit that the court should exercise its discretion and limit that issue to the facts of that case and not make it the subject of a Declaratory Judgment which would tend to fossilize the law in one position when medicine is constantly refining and re-evaluating the definition of death.

POINT II

Karen Ann Quinlan has not given her informed consent to the discontinuance of the respirator.

At the outset of the hearing below all counsel stipulated that Karen Ann Quinlan is incompetent within the scope of the statutes and court rules on guardianship (T44-1 to 14). See N.J.S.A. 3A:6-36; Rule 4:83-1, *et seq.* On the basis of the medical testimony below it should also be undisputed that Karen has been incompetent since she arrived at Newton Memorial Hospital on April 15, 1975.

The incompetency of Karen eliminates many difficult issues from this case, as did the stipulation that she is medically and legally alive. The courts of this state have never specifically ruled on the effect of an informed refusal of treatment given by a competent adult patient. Resolution of this issue must await another day because the facts of this case clearly do not put that question before this court.

In *State* v. *Perricone,* 37 N. J. 463, *cert.* den. 371 U. S. 890 (1962) this court ruled that a judge could order a blood transfusion for a minor, over the religious objections of the parents, to attempt to save the minor's life. Similarly, in *Raleigh-Fitkin-Paul Morgan Mem. Hosp.* v. *Anderson,* 42 N. J. 421, *cert.* den. 377 U. S. 985 (1964) the principle was extended to require such a transfusion on a woman in the 32nd week of her pregnancy, in spite of religious objections, in order to protect the life of the child. In *Muhlenberg Hosp.* v. *Patterson,* 128 N. J. Super. 498 (L. Div. 1974) a transfusion was ordered for a child where the potential harm was serious injury rather than death. See *In re Sampson,* 29 N. Y. 2d 900, 328 N. Y. S. 2d 686, 278 N. E. 2d 918 (1972), affirming 37 A. D. 2d 668, 323 N. Y. S. 2d 253 (1971), affirming 65 Misc. 2d 658, 317 N. Y. S. 2d 641 (1970) (ordering treatment of a minor for Von Recklinghausen's disease); *In re Karwath,* 199 N. W. 2d 147 (Iowa Sup. Ct. 1972) (ordering removal of tonsils and adenoids); but see *In re Green,* 448 Pa. 338, 292 A. 2d 387 (1972). See generally, Annotation, "Power of Court or Other Public Agency to Order Medical Treatment Over Parental Objections for Child whose Life is Not Immediately Endangered," 52 *A.L.R.* 3d 1118.

In *John F. Kennedy Mem. Hosp.* v. *Heston,* 58 N. J. 576 (1971) an adult woman was involved in an automobile accident and was taken to a hospital. The woman maintained that she had expressed her refusal to accept blood, but the evidence showed her to be in shock, disoriented and incoherent at the time. This court upheld an order for a blood transfusion needed to save her life in spite of her religious objections to such a transfusion. See generally, Annotation, "Power of Courts or Other Public Agencies, in the Absence of Statutory Authority, to Order Compulsory Medical Care for Adult," 9 *A.L.R.* 3d 1391.

In the case of competent adults without minor dependents, courts in other jurisdictions have upheld the adult's right to exercise an informed refusal of treatment. See *In re Osborne,* 294 A. 2d 372 (D. C. Ct. App. 1972); *In re Brooks,* 32 Ill. 2d 361, 205 N. E. 2d 435 (Sup. Ct. 1965); *Erickson* v. *Dilgard,* 44 Misc. 2d 27, 252 N. Y. S. 2d 705 (Sup. Ct. 1962). Other jurisdictions have ordered such treatment under similar circumstances. See, *e.g., United States* v. *George,* 239 F. Supp. 752 (D. Conn. 1965); *Application of President and Directors of Georgetown Col-*

lege, Inc., 118 U. S. App. D. C. 80, 331 F. 2d 1000, rehearing den. 331 F. 2d 1010 (D. C. Cir.) *(en banc)*, *cert.* den. 337 U. S. 978 (1964).

The *Heston* decision indicates that this state probably falls into the category of jurisdictions which would order life-saving medical treatment in spite of an *informed refusal* by a patient. However, the competency of the patient to make such a decision was questionable in *Heston*, and resolution of the precise question of the effect of an informed refusal by a competent adult must await another day since the facts of this case do not present that issue.

Under the doctrine of informed consent a physician must make disclosure to a patient of those risks and advantages of a proposed course of treatment which a reasonable physician would have disclosed under the circumstances. See *Kaplan* v. *Haines,* 96 N. J. Super. 242 (App. Div. 1967), *aff'd* o.b. 51 N. J. 404 (1968); *Natanson* v. *Kline,* 186 Kan. 393, 350 P. 2d 1093 (Sup. Ct. 1960); *cf. Parker* v. *Goldstein,* 78 N. J. Super. 472 (App. Div.), *certif.* den. 40 N. J. 225 (1963).

A physician who treats a patient in spite of an informed refusal of treatment by the patient commits a battery, see *Bednarik* v. *Bednarik,* 18 N. J. Misc. 633, 16 A. 2d 80 (Ch. 1940), unless there is an emergency and the patient is unconscious. See *Schloendorff* v. *Society of New York Hosp.,* 211 N. Y. 125, 105 N. E. 92 (1914) (Cardozo, J.). The theory of informed consent is that the patient should have the various pros and cons of a proposed course of treatment explained to her in order that she may make a rational, informed decision about what shall be done with her person.

Judge Muir correctly ruled below that Karen Ann Quinlan cannot be said to have made an informed refusal of continuance of the respirator which presently supports her life. Certain hearsay statements of hers were admitted into evidence under Rule 63(12), a hearsay exception for statements of declarant's then existing state of mind. Respondent physicians maintain that these statements should not have been admitted at all because they were opinions expressed with reference to a different situation, namely, terminal patients in great pain, and because Karen's state of mind on a hypothetical discussion of death was not relevant to the issue as to what she would actually wish when faced with death. Nevertheless, after admitting the statements, Judge Muir properly discounted the weight of these statements because of the above factors and held that plaintiff had not proved that Karen would elect her own removal from the respirator today.

Little need be said of the inherent unreliability of such hearsay. See Morgan, "Hearsay Dangers and the Application of the Hearsay Concept", 62 *Harv. L. Rev.* 177 (1948). In this state in administrative adjudications, hearsay may be used to corroborate competent proof, but a finding of fact cannot be based upon hearsay alone. Administrative decisions which affect substantial rights of the parties must be based on a residuum of competent evidence on the record. See *Weston* v. *State,* 60 N. J. 36, 51 (1972). Yet, the trial court below was asked to authorize the death of Karen Ann Quinlan on the *sole* basis of hearsay which would not even have supported an administrative fact finding. The court below was entirely correct in giving little weight to the hearsay declarations of Karen Ann Quinlan on an issue of her life and death, especially in view of Judge Muir's astute observation that these statements were not made in the context of a "personal confrontation" with death (Slip op. at 40).

There has recently been some legal commentary concerning "living wills" whereby a person would make an informed rational decision in advance as to the circumstances under which he would refuse treatment. See, *e.g.,*

Kutner, "The Living Will: Coping with the Historical Event of Death", 27 *Baylor L. Rev.* 39 (1975); Kutner, "Due Process of Euthanasia: The Living Will, a Proposal", 44 *Ind. L. J.* 539 (1968). Yet even these proposals, however doubtful their validity, would require that this "living will" be reduced to writing, be notarized and be witnessed by at least two individuals who would affirm that the maker was of sound mind and acted of his own free will. Compare N.J.S.A. 3A:3-2 which sets forth the formalities needed to devise and bequeath property under a will. One commentator suggests that the "living will" take the form of a written contract between the prospective patient and his physician. Comment, "Antidysthanasia Contracts: A Proposal for Legalizing Death with Dignity", 5 *Pac. L. J.* 738 (1974).

Karen's informal hearsay statements must be weighed in the light of the standards which proponents of "living wills" would themselves require to insure that the individual is taking this fatal step with full knowledge and understanding of its import and consequences.

On the other hand, Judge Muir held that there is a presumption that one chooses to go on living (Slip op. at 40). See generally *John F. Kennedy Mem. Hosp.* v. *Heston, supra,* 58 N. J. at 581 where Chief Justice Weintraub notes that even those who express a desire to die may hold contrary subconscious views. This presumption that one favors life finds support in the case of *In re Osborne, supra,* 294 A. 2d at 374-75, where the court distinguishes the careful, informed refusal in that case from a situation such as the instant case:

> Thus, where the patient is comatose, or suffering impairment of capacity for choice, *it may be better to give weight to the known instinct for survival which can, in a critical situation, alter previously held convictions.* In such cases it cannot be determined with certainty that a deliberate and intelligent choice has been made. (Emphasis added)

See generally *Application of President and Directors of Georgetown Coll., supra,* 331 F. 2d 1008, where Judge Wright implies that a guardian must assume that his ward wishes to continue living.

In light of all the foregoing, respondent physicians respectfully submit that the trial court below was correct in its finding of fact that Karen Ann did not give her informed consent to removal from her of the respirator under these circumstances. While this court certainly has the power to make new findings of fact, see Brochin and Sandler, "Appellate Review of Facts in New Jersey, Jury and Non-Jury Cases," 12 *Rut. L. Rev.* 482, 483 (1958), it is equally clear that great deference should be given to the trial court's findings of fact. See *Grossman* v. *Grossman,* 142 N. J. Eq. 714 (E. & A. 1948); *Gawales* v. *Gawales,* 140 N. J. Eq. 421 (E. & A. 1947); *Brodzinsky* v. *Pulek,* 75 N. J. Super. 40 (App. Div. 1962).

POINT III

The trial court was correct in refusing to exercise its substituted judgment to authorize Karen Ann Quinlan's death.

A. While the trial court had jurisdiction over the matter, it lacked the power to grant the relief sought by plaintiff.

New Jersey recognizes the doctrine of substituted judgment. Under that concept a court of equity has jurisdiction as representative of the sovereign under the *parens patriae* doctrine to intervene in the affairs of an incompetent person to advance that individual's best interests. Such intervention has been permitted for the incompetent's personal well-being, *cf. State* v. *Perricone, supra,* as well as for management and administration of his estate. See *In re Trott,* 118 N. J. Super. 436, 440 (Ch. Div. 1972).

132

Two aspects of this doctrine deserve comment. First, the substituted judgment must be that of the court of equity and not that of the relatives of the incompetent. The doctrine "represents a delegation to the Chancellor of the Crown's right as parens patriae to interfere in particular cases for the benefit of such persons as are incapable of protecting themselves." 27 *Am. Jur.* 2d, Equity §69, p. 592 quoted in *Strunk* v. *Strunk,* 445 S.W. 2d 145, 147 (Ky. Ct. App. 1969).

The second, somewhat connected, point is that the doctrine may only be exercised to further the best interests of the incompetent. See *Ex parte Whitbread,* 35 Eng. Rep. 878, 879 (Ch. 1816). Similarly, this state's adherence to that requirement was expressed by Judge Allcorn as follows:

> The sole person in interest here is the incompetent. The exclusive concern of the court in this proceeding is the benefit and advantage of the incompetent and her estate.

In re Trott, supra, 118 N. J. Super. at 443, n. 1.

The two reported cases which authorize interference by a court in the personal affairs of the incompetent confirm this second requirement. In *Strunk* v. *Strunk, supra,* the Kentucky Court of Appeals authorized a kidney transplant from a mentally retarded adult to his competent brother. The trial court heard testimony from the incompetent's psychiatrist and its findings were summarized by the Court of Appeals as follows:

> The court found that the operation was necessary, that under the peculiar circumstances of this case it would not only be beneficial to [the brother] but also beneficial to [the incompetent] because [the incompetent] was greatly dependent on [the brother], emotionally and psychologically, and that his well being would be jeopardized more severely

by the loss of his brother than by the removal of the kidney. 445 S.W. 2d at 146.

In *Hart* v. *Brown,* 29 Conn. Sup. 368, 289 A. 2d 386 (Super. Ct. 1972) a trial court considered the question of a kidney transplant from one seven-year old twin to the other twin. The court heard psychiatric testimony of the harm which would result to the infant from her sister's death and medical testimony that there was almost no risk involved for the infant. Moreover, within the limits of her capacity to understand, the infant indicated a desire to donate her kidney to her sister. The court approved the transplant, noting that there would be benefit to the infant kidney donor from the operation.

Thus, while the trial court had jurisdiction to inquire into what would be in the best interests of Karen Ann Quinlan, it did not have the power under that doctrine to cause the discontinuance of the life-supportive respirator which would result in her death. Since there was unanimous medical testimony that Karen is alive, the court simply lacked the power to say that it was in Karen's best interests to be dead.

Certainly, there is no legal authority for the proposition that an incompetent is better off dead than alive. Plaintiff cites no legal authority for such an extraordinary statement. In both *Strunk* v. *Strunk, supra,* 445 S.W. 2d at 148-49 and *Hart* v. *Brown, supra,* 289 A. 2d at 289, those courts went to great lengths to explain that the risk of danger to a kidney transplant donor was extremely minimal. There is no doubt that if the kidney removal from the incompetent or infant in *Strunk* or *Hart* would have probably resulted in his or her death, the decisions would have gone the other way.

Undisputed it is that Karen Ann Quinlan is legally and medically alive today. As a matter of law it must be said that it is in Karen Ann Quinlan's own best interests to remain alive rather than to be allowed to die.

Consequently, the trial court lacked the power under the doctrine of substituted judgment to cause the termination of her life by disconnecting her life-supportive respirator. As Judge Muir wrote below:

> It is also noted the concept of the Court's power over a person suffering under a disability is to *protect* and aid the best interests. As pointed out, the *Hart* and *Strunk* cases deal with protection as it relates to the future life of the infants or incompetent. Here the authorization sought, if granted, would result in Karen's death. The natural processes of her body are not shown to be sufficiently strong to sustain her by themselves. The authorization, therefore, would be to permit Karen Quinlan to die. This is not protection. It is not something to her best interests, in a temporal sense, and it is in a temporal sense that I must operate whether I believe in life after death or not. The single most important temporal quality Karen Ann Quinlan has is life. This Court will not authorize that life to be taken from her." (Slip op. at 31-32) (emphasis in original)

Moreover, any claim of authority to terminate the life of an individual "in her own best interest" would certainly be violative of the Due Process Clause of the Fourteenth Amendment. Karen Ann Quinlan has committed no crime. It is only her status as an incompetent which brought about this action. Regardless of the procedural niceties surrounding a hearing authorizing her death, the end result of allowing her to expire by withholding life-supportive treatment would amount to a substantive violation of the Due Process Clause. Cf. *Roe* v. *Wade,* 410 U.S. 113, 35 L. Ed. 2d 147 (1972); *Jackson* v. *Indiana,* 406 U. S. 715, 32 L. Ed. 435, 447 (1972); Epstein, "Substantive Due Process by Any Other Name: The Abortion Cases," 1973 Sup. Ct. Rev. 159; Comment, "New Equal

Protection—Substantive Due Process Resurrected under a New Name," 2 *Ford Urb. L.J.* 311 (1975); Note, 6 *Seton Hall L. Rev.*, 568 (1975).

B. Assuming *arguendo* that the doctrine of substituted judgment could empower a court to terminate a person's life, such an inquiry would entail questions of quality of life which courts should not entertain.

Even if the doctrine of substituted judgment could under certain circumstances be authority for the termination of a human being's life, respondent physicians contend that sound principles of judicial restraint should deter courts from undertaking such an inquiry. For once a person is conceded to be legally and medically alive, the plaintiff in such a case would really be contending that the quality of this person's life is so low that she would be better off dead. The very nature of such a quality-of-life inquiry opens a veritable Pandora's box of complex problems.

Plaintiff proposes that the standard of "extraordinary means" to sustain life should govern who is to continue living and who is to die. Yet even Dr. Korein, who gave credence to the term, admitted that its meaning is not precise or well-defined (T269-1 to 8) and that there is an implicit value judgment involved in the term concerning which people may differ (T317-20 to 24). Dr. Morse testified that he could not "pigeonhole" treatment into "ordinary" and "extraordinary" categories (T112-10 to 22). See St. Martin, "Euthanasia: The Three-In-One Issue," 27 *Baylor L. Rev.* 62, 63 (1975); Gurney, "Is There A Right to Die?—A Study of the Law of Euthanasia," 3 *Cum. Sam. L. Rev.* 235, 247-248 (1972) for a discussion of the difficulties with these categories. See generally, Kamisar, "Some Non-religious Views Against Proposed 'Mercy Killing' Legislation," 42 *Minn. L. Rev.* 969 (1959). Surely questions of life and death should not hang in the balance on distinctions so nebulous.

If "ordinary" and "extraordinary" treatment measures are an inadequate test of who should continue to live and who should die, what shall be the test? How shall a court analyze the quality of life of an individual? Even if that quality could be measured, how shall a court decide that it is so low the individual would be better off dead? Even to undertake such an inquiry is a perilous step fraught with profound ramifications. Who will be safe in our society if a court in a civil suit has the power to say that it is in one's own best interests that she should die?

Once one enters the arena of quality-of-life, almost insurmountable difficulties arise as to what should be the standard or standards, and who shall fix that standard or those standards, in arriving at a judgment that one person of low quality, who is conceded to be medically and legally alive, shall continue to live and, on the other hand, another person of low quality who is conceded to be medically and legally alive, shall die?

Conceded it is that there are many gradations of low quality of life. The complexities that must necessarily arise in this life-death issue call for answers to these questions: Where shall the line be drawn? Who shall draw the line? What shall be the standards? Who shall determine the standards?

Finally, where does hope fit into this scheme of things? As Judge Muir points out:

> None of the doctors testified there was *no* hope. The hope for recovery is remote but no doctor talks in the absolute. Certainly he cannot and be credible in light of the advancements medical science has known and the inexactitudes of medical science (Slip op. at 29) (Emphasis in original).

Simply put, where there is life, there is hope. To decide that a patient's quality of life is so low that she would be better off dead is to negate the existence of hope.

In summary, this Court should refrain from embarking upon a quality-of-life inquiry concerning Karen Ann Quinlan's life. Such an inquiry would involve value judgments about the worth of an individual's life which no other person, much less the state, should undertake. It would be an inquiry without standards or guidelines other than the personal values of the inquirer. Moreover, such an inquiry would deny the existence of hope for the incompetent as well as repudiate the sanctity-of-life principle regardless of quality.

C. The trial court ruled correctly on the merits.

Respondent physicians contend, as argued above, that the trial court should not even have considered the merits of plaintiff's application for relief. Nevertheless, having reached the merits, Judge Muir exercised the discretion inherent in his equitable role and properly refused to grant the relief sought.

Any discussion of Judge Muir's decision must begin with a reiteration of two crucial findings of fact which he made, namely, (a) Karen Ann Quinlan is legally and medically alive and (b) she did not give her informed consent to the removal of the respirator. Given those two facts, the court below was asked to decide that, nevertheless, Karen would be better off dead than alive. Thus, the relief sought below was judicial euthanasia for Karen. Whether that euthanasia be active or passive is merely a matter of semantics and not a matter of substance since the court below was asked to take steps which would have certainly resulted in Karen's death. See *John F. Kennedy Mem. Hosp.* v. *Heston, supra,* 58 N. J. at 581-582; Cantor, "A Patient's Decision to Decline Life-Saving Medical Treatment: Bodily Integrity Versus the Preservation of Life", 26 *Rut. L. Rev.* 228, 259 (1973).

The decision-making process in such a case must balance the possible interest of the incompetent in death, if any, against the interest in life which the incompetent as a member of our society is presumed to have. One possible interest of the incompetent in dying, namely, pain, was discounted by the trial judge in his finding that there was no evidence to indicate that Karen is in pain. Respondent physicians know of no other interest of Karen's which would justify permitting her to die.

On the other hand, Karen must be presumed to place the same high value on life as the rest of our society does. At this point it may be instructive to examine some of our society's values on the subject of life to assist in the balancing process.

Our country's first expression of nationhood, the Declaration of Independence, tells us that it it self-evident that life is one of man's unalienable Rights and that Government is instituted to secure this Right. Likewise, this state's own Constitution refers to life as one of our natural and unalienable rights. *N. J. Const.* Art. I, § 1 (1947). Our Federal Constitution provides that neither the federal government nor the states may deprive an individual of life without due process of law. *U. S. Const.*, Amendments 5, 14.

At one time in our state attempted suicide was a crime. See *John F. Kennedy Mem. Hosp.* v. *Heston, supra,* 58 N. J. at 580. Capital punishment in this state was reserved for the most heinous crimes of murder in the first degree, N.J.S.A. 2A:113-4, assault with intent to kill high executive officers of the government, N.J.S.A. 2A:148-6, kidnapping for ransom, N.J.S.A. 2A:118-1, and treason, N.J.S.A. 2A:148-1. Of course, since *Furman* v. *Georgia,* 408 U. S. 238, 33 L. Ed. 2d 346 (1972) no capital punishment executions have taken place because the United States Supreme Court has held that the penalty, as then administered, constituted cruel and unusual punishment. In *Furman* Justice Brennan wrote in his concurring opinion:

Death is a unique punishment in the United States. In a society that so strongly affirms the sanctity of life, not surprisingly the common view is that death is the ultimate sanction. The material feeling appears all about us.

* * *

The only explanation for the uniqueness of death is its extreme severity. Death is today an unusually severe punishment, unusual in its pain, in its finality and in its enormity. No other existing punishment is comparable to death in terms of physical and mental suffering. 33 L. Ed. 2d at 376-77.

Another indicator of our society's interest in life are the standards for civil commitment to a mental institution which require a finding that the individual is dangerous to himself or to others to warrant commitment. See *State* v. *Krol*, 68 N. J. 236, 252 (1975). See also N.J.S.A. 30:4-26.3(a) authorizing temporary hospitalization of one who attempts suicide.

The blood transfusion cases, *State* v. *Perricone, supra, Raleigh Fitkin-Paul Morgan Mem. Hosp.* v. *Anderson, supra,* and *John F. Kennedy Mem. Hosp.* v. *Heston, supra,* all amply demonstrate the high value which our society places upon life itself and the steps which individuals and the state will take to preserve the life of another.

Another indication of society's view of life is the decision in *Roe* v. *Wade,* 410 U. S. 113, 35 L. Ed. 2d 147 (1972) which permits a state entirely to proscribe abortions during the final trimester of a pregnancy when the potential life first becomes viable. At that time the fetal life has evolved to a point where the state may protect the life of the fetus regardless of the mother's wishes, unless her life or health is in danger.

Finally, *Gleitman* v. *Cosgrove,* 49 N. J. 22 (1967) is also informative on our society's views on the value of life. In *Gleitman*, a physician was charged with failing to counsel a patient as to the effects of her German measles during her pregnancy. Plaintiff alleged that if she been counseled she would have sought an abortion. One of the counts was on behalf of the infant who was born with certain defects as a result of the German measles. Justice Proctor, writing for this Court, held that there were no damages cognizable at law to the infant since the alternatives would have been no life at all. 49 N. J. at 28.

In other words, Justice Proctor was saying that as a matter of law it cannot be said that one would be better off dead than alive, regardless of the quality of life involved in being alive. See also *Zepeda* v. *Zepeda*, Ill. App. 2d 240, 190 N. E. 2d 849 (App. Ct. 1963), *cert.* den. 379 U. S. 945, 13 L. Ed. 2d 545 (1964) and *Williams* v. *State of New York*, 18 N. Y. 2d 481, 276 N. Y. S. 2d 885, 223 N. E. 2d 343 (Ct. App. 1966) denying damages on public policy grounds in "wrongful life" actions by illegitimate children.

All of the foregoing sets forth some of the legal indicia of the high value which our society places on life and which value Karen Ann Quinlan must also be presumed to hold. However, this Court should not be confined to such legal indicia in analyzing the value of life in our society; it should not be asked to leave its common sense outside the courtroom. Certainly, this court may take notice of the traditional celebration upon the birth of an individual as well as the traditional mourning which surrounds a death. No citation of authority can equal the court's own knowledge of the value which our society places on the sanctity of life.

And what of Karen Ann Quinlan? What can be said of her? There was abundant medical testimony below that it was unusual for a person to remain in Karen's condition this long, much less with the assistance of a respirator. Yet, in spite of her alleged prior statements, it is undisputed that she is alive today. Surely, it can be said that, notwithstanding her lack of cognitive function, Karen is demonstrating a ferocious will to live, a powerful instinct for survival. Perhaps in a non-verbal way Karen herself is telling us that she wants to live.

Indeed, Karen's mother describes her as an active person who loves life and who was full of life prior to her illness. It cannot be said that Karen would be better off without that life. Plaintiff has failed to carry his burden of proving that it would be in Karen's best interests to be dead rather than alive.

Judge Muir also correctly noted that the decision on whether to remove the respirator cannot be isolated and detached from the treatment which she has received to this date from Dr. Morse and from his recommendations for future treatment. Dr. Morse testified that he refused to discontinue the respirator because there was no reported case in medical history which would justify such an action under these circumstances (T95-4 to 10). All other neurologists concurred in Dr. Morse's conclusion that Karen is not "brain dead" and Dr. Diamond went even further when he said with reference to the respirator:

> You could not find a physician who would not have provided that support when she was first admitted or the period during which a determination of cause was being carried out. No physician to my knowledge will ever interrupt a device which is performing a life-saving measure at any time at all. (T618-18 to 23).
>
> *   *   *
>
> I do not think based on my examination and experience that anybody would interrupt this device, the use of this device now on this patient. (T619-9 to 12).

The members of the Harvard *Ad Hoc* Committee, it should be noted, addressed themselves *directly* to the issue as to when a respirator should be discontinued in their report outlining the criteria for "brain death" when they wrote:

> The patient's condition can be determined only by a physician. When the patient is hopelessly damaged as defined above, the family and all colleagues who have participated in major decisions concerning the patient, and all nurses involved, should be so informed. Death is to be declared and *then* the respirator turned off. The decision to do this and the responsibility for it are to be taken by the physician-in-charge, in consultation with one or more physicians who have been directly involved in the case. It is unsound and undesirable to force the family to make the decision. (Emphasis in original)

Harvard *Ad Hoc* Committee Report, supra, 205 *J.A.M.A.* at 86.

In other words, the Committee anticipated the very issue presented in this case. It concluded the respirator should not be turned off where the patient could not be declared "brain dead" under its criteria.

All neurologists testified that the Harvard Criteria constitute standard medical practices under these circumstances. As may be easily seen, the treatment by Dr. Javed and Dr. Morse was perfectly consistent with the Harvard Criteria. Karen's "brain death" could not be declared and so the respirator could not be discontinued.

Given the fact that the treatment by Dr. Javed and Dr. Morse of Karen is in accordance with standard, accepted medical practice, the decision of the trial judge became somewhat easier. The shared values of our society mandated that his decision on the discontinuance of the respirator had to be made in the context of sound medical opinion and judgment on the subject. Judge Muir wisely perceived the nexus:

> "The judicial conscience and morality involved in considering whether the court should authorize Karen Quinlan's removal from the respirator are inextricably involved with the nature of medical science and the role of the physician in our society and his duty to his patient." (Slip op. at 27)

Judge Muir next analyzed the role of the physician in our society and noted that our society has chosen to entrust to the medical profession the responsibility for determining when death occurs and what treatment shall be administered to the living (Slip op. at 31, 35). This is a value judgment which is virtually unanimously accepted in our society and so may be said to be a part of its conscience and morality. Judge Muir concluded that courts should not be willing to take steps in the medical treatment of an individual which his or her own physician would not take and which would amount to a deviation from accepted medical practices (Slip op. at 31).

Karen's treating physicians have testified that the respirator should not be discontinued. They further stated to discontinue the respirator would be violative of the traditions of their profession. Their decision is in accordance with the Harvard Criteria which were unanimously recognized by the expert witnesses as constituting accepted medical practice in this field. Under the circumstances, Judge Muir could not have ruled otherwise without repudiating the consensus of medical knowledge on this subject. This he refused to do.

Any discussion of the role of the physician in our society in this context must begin with the *Hippocratic Oath,* the traditional ethical guide of the medical profession. The *Oath* provides, *inter alia,* that the physician will not prescribe deadly medicine or drugs if asked, nor will he counsel others to do so. See *Roe* v. *Wade, supra,*

35 L. Ed. 2d at 165. Thus, the physician's credo is to heal his patient if he can, but, at the very least, he should avoid doing harm in the course of his treatment. No court of equity should require a physician to act in derogation of this sacred and time-honored oath.

In his Opinion Judge Muir made reference to the higher standards and duties which the medical profession imposes upon itself through this Oath (Slip op. at 28). He cites an article entitled "The Role of the Physician in the Prolongation of Life" by Dr. Franklin H. Epstein of Harvard Medical School (Slip op. at 28, Footnote 9). See Volume II, pages 103-109 of a series bearing the title "Controversy in Internal Medicine II" edited by Dr. Franz J. Ingelfinger, Editor of the prestigious *The New England Journal of Medicine,* and others, W. B. Saunders Company, Philadelphia (1974).

Written with wisdom and insight by Dr. Epstein, Professor of Medicine at Harvard Medical School, associated with Beth Israel Hospital in Boston, as well as being Director of the Harvard Medical Unit and Thorndike Memorial Laboratory, Boston City Hospital, this article is both perceptive and farsighted.

When taken in conjunction with his patient's privacy rights, the physician's right to practice medicine has been said to be one of constitutional dimensions. See *Y.W.C.A. of Princeton* v. *Kugler,* 342 F. Supp. 1048 (D. N. J.) vacated 475 F. 2d 1398 (3 Cir. 1972) ; cf. *Roe* v. *Wade, supra,* 35 L. Ed. 2d at 183. Indeed, once a physician has begun a course of treatment, it is questionable whether even a competent adult may require him to continue treatment in a manner which is violative of his Oath. In *United States* v. *George, supra,* 239 F. Supp. at 754, the court wrote:

> "Here, however, the doctor's conscience and professional oath must also be respected. In the present case the patient voluntarily submitted himself to

and insisted upon medical care. Simultaneously he sought to dictate to treating physicians a course of treatment amounting to medical malpractice. To require these doctors to ignore the mandates of their own conscience, even in the name of free religious exercise, cannot be justified under these circumstances. The patient may knowingly decline treatment, but he may not demand mistreatment. See *Application of President & Directors of Georgetown College, supra,* 331 F. 2d at 1010."

In this state, the role of the physician in our social system is set forth in *Bennan* v. *Parsonnet,* 83 N. J. L. 21 (Sup. Ct. 1912). In *Bennan,* the court notes that a physician has the duty to consult with his patient about proposed treatment and to exercise sound medical judgment on his behalf. In other words, there is a special relationship between a physician and his patient under the law.

At least one other state has referred to this special relationship as a "fiducial" relationship. See *Cobbs* v. *Grant,* 8 Cal. 3d 229, 104 Cal. Rptr. 505, 502 P. 2d 1 (Sup. Ct. 1972); *Emmett* v. *Eastern Dispensary & Casualty Hospital,* 396 F. 2d 931 (D. C. Cir. 1967).

Respondent physicians respectfully submit that such a denomination is an unfortunate use of words which distorts the realities of the physician-patient relationship. An analysis of fiduciary duties as they relate to physicians will show this to be so.

The term "fiduciary" carries with it special connotations and duties in the law. A fiduciary generally owes a duty of ordinary care to his principal, see *Restatement (Second) Agency,* §379, p. 177 (1958), while the physician may owe a higher duty of care based upon his specialty. See *Clark* v. *Wichman,* 72 N. J. Super. 486, 493 (App. Div. 1962). Moreover, a fiduciary owes a duty of full disclosure to his principal. See *Restatement (Second) Agency,*

§381, p. 182 (1958). But the law of "informed consent" makes clear that the physician does *not* have the duty of full disclosure under *all* circumstances. Specifically, he should not make full disclosure whenever in his judgment it would be detrimental to the health of the patient to do so. See *Kaplan* v. *Haines,* 96 N. J. Super. 242 (App. Div. 1967), aff'd. o.b. 51 N. J. 404 (1968) quoting with approval *Natanson* v. *Kline,* 186 Kan. 393, 350 P. 2d 1093 (Sup. Ct. 1960).

While it is clear that physicians have a special relationship in the law to their patients, the term "fiduciary" relationship is not dispositive of the interplay and merely confuses the issue. Certainly, on the facts of this case, it may be said that these physicians had a legal duty to continue the treatment which they began until the demise or recovery of Karen Ann Quinlan and that they could have been held liable for damages if they abandoned that treatment. See *Lathrope* v. *Flood,* 6 Cal. Unrep. Cas. 637, 63 P. 1007, rev'd on other grounds, 135 Cal. 458, 67 P. 683 (Cal. Sup. Ct. 1901); *Barbour* v. *Marten,* 62 Me. 536 (Supreme Jud. Ct. 1837).

The *Bennan* case is also enlightening on the issues in the instant case since the court there speaks of the duties of a physician with reference to an unconscious patient. In such a case, the court pointed out:

> ". . . the law will by implication constitute such surgeon the representative *pro hac vice* of his patient and will, within the scope to which such implication applies, cast upon him the responsibility of so acting in the interest of his patient that the latter shall receive the full benefit of that professional judgment and skill to which he is entitled." *Bennan* v. *Parsonnet, supra,* 83 N. J. L. at 25.

Thus, in the instant case there is an added responsibility upon the defendant physicians to act in the best interest of the unconscious Karen Ann Quinlan. Since the law

147

imposes this added responsibility, there is all the more reason for courts to adhere to the *bona fide* medical judgment of the physicians exercised in compliance with that responsibility.

In the final analysis, the responsibilities and duties of a physician in our modern society are articulated in *Schueler* v. *Strelinger*, 43 N. J. 330 (1964). *Schueler* is the leading medical malpractice decision in this state. It has been cited with approval in numerous other jurisdictions as one of the most important malpractice cases in the nation. The following passage from *Schueler* definitively delineates the modern role of the physician as seen through the eyes of the law:

> "The law recognizes that medicine is not an exact science. Consequently, it does not make the physician a guarantor of the cure of his patient. When he takes a case it imposes upon him the duty to exercise in the treatment of his patient the degree of care, knowledge and skill ordinarily possessed and exercised in similar situations by the average member of the profession practicing in his field. Failure to have and to use such skill and care toward the patient as a result of which injury or damage results constitutes negligence.

> "The fact that a good result may occur with poor treatment, and that good treatment will not necessarily prevent a poor result must be recognized. So, if the doctor has brought the requisite degree of care and skill to his patient, he is not liable simply because of failure to cure or for bad results that may follow. Nor in such case is he liable for an honest mistake in diagnosis or in judgment as to the course of treatment taken. A physician must be allowed a wide range in the reasonable exercise of judgment. He is not guilty of malpractice so long as he employs such judgment, and that judgment does not represent a departure from the re-

quirements of accepted medical practice, or does not result in failure to do something accepted medical practices obligates him to do, or in the doing of something he should not do measured by the standard above stated. *Carbone* v. *Warburton,* 11 N. J. 418, 424 (1953); *Clark* v. *Wichman,* 72 N. J. Super. 486 (App. Div. 1962); *Stottlemire* v. *Cawood,* 213 F. Supp. 897 (D.D.C. 1963)."

Schueler v. *Strelinger, supra,* 43 N. J. at 344-345. See *Fernandez* v. *Baruch,* 52 N. J. 127 (1968); *Tramutola* v. *Bortone,* 118 N. J. Super. 503 (App. Div. 1972).

The *Schueler* formulation of the physician's role is applicable to the instant case and dispositive of the controversy. If in the opinion of the attending physicians the respirator should be continued on Karen Ann Quinlan, their medical judgment should be followed by the courts unless plaintiff can show that such treatment is a deviation from accepted medical practices. This is a role which both our society and our law have devolved upon the medical profession.

This is also a role from which Dr. Morse and Dr. Javed have not shrunk; they have willingly accepted the responsibility which society has entrusted to them. They have made a decision that in their medical opinion Karen is alive and treatment should continue. Plaintiff has failed to carry his burden of proving that their judgment in this case is a deviation from medical standards. Consequently, plaintiff should not prevail in his request to have this court authorize the selective discontinuance of certain treatment of his daughter. In *John F. Kennedy Mem. Hosp.* v. *Heston, supra,* 58 N. J. at 582, Chief Justice Weintraub observed:

"Hospitals exist to aid the sick and the injured. The medical and nursing professions are consecrated to preserving life. That is their professional

149

creed. To them, a failure to use a simple, established procedure in these circumstances of this case would be malpractice, however the law may characterize that failure because of the patient's private convictions. A surgeon should not be asked to operate under the strain of knowing that a transfusion may not be administered even though medically required to save his patient."

Similarly, in the instant case, Dr. Javed and Dr. Morse should not be asked by this court to continue their treatment with the exception of the use of the respirator when they know full well that the respirator is needed to save Karen's life. This court must not be said to lend judicial sanction to an act of medical malpractice.

Finally, some consideration should be given in this regard to plaintiff's own words on the subject. In his *Factual and Legal Contentions of the Plaintiff*, p. 5, submitted to the trial court below, plaintiff makes the following significant statement in reference to the medical treatment of Karen Ann Quinlan:

> "(3) Where actual or potential personal autonomy and bodily integrity are absent, the state can neither command nor prohibit the artificial maintenance of bodily functions, rather it must leave freedom of choice in such matters to the individuals more closely concerned with them.
>
> "(a) *The State should defer to sound medical judgment with regard to the continuance of treatment.*" (emphasis added)

Respondent physicians fully agree with subsection (a) above. They ask no more and no less from this Honorable Court.

POINT IV

The constitutional arguments advanced by plaintiff do not require this court to direct discontinuance of the respirator.

A. Plaintiff lacks standing to assert these alleged constitutional rights.

As was discussed *supra*, Judge Muir made a finding of fact that Karen Ann Quinlan did not express a desire prior to her incompetency that the respirator now sustaining her life should be discontinued under the circumstances of this case. The trial judge's finding of fact on this issue merits great deference by an appellate court in its review of the decision below.

Under these circumstances, Karen's parents lack standing to assert her constitutional rights of privacy and religious freedom. This must be so since it is not known what Karen's wishes on this subject would be if she were competent. As *parens patriae*, the state, through the courts, has the constitutional right to protect and to preserve the lives of its incompetent citizens.

As a general rule, a litigant may only assert his own constitutional rights or immunities and may not assert the constitutional rights or immunities of another individual. See *McGowan* v. *Maryland,* 366 U. S. 420, 6 L. Ed. 2d 393 (1961); *O'Malley* v. *Brierly,* 477 F. 2d 785 (3 Cir. 1973); see also *Alderman* v. *United States,* 394 U. S. 165, 22 L. Ed. 2d 176 (1969) (Fourth Amendment rights). There is a narrowly drawn exception to that rule which permits a litigant to raise the constitutional rights of third parties if it would be difficult or impossible for the aggrieved individual to raise those rights for herself. See *Corey* v. *City of Dallas,* 492 F. 2d 496 (5 Cir. 1974).

However, there is certainly an implicit prerequisite to the application of this exception to the general rule on standing. Specifically, the third party must be able to maintain that the rights which he asserts are, in fact, identical with the wishes of the incompetent. As Judge Muir noted below, the dilemma always exists as to "whether it is the conscious beings relief or the unconscious beings welfare that governs the parental motivation." (Slip op. at 31).

Judge Muir found as a fact that we do not know Karen's wishes in this matter. As to the claim of the free exercise of religion, the evidence is abundantly clear that the concept of "extraordinary means" was not a binding tenet of her religion. Compare *John F. Kennedy Mem. Hosp.* v. *Heston, supra,* and *State* v. *Perricone, supra,* where blood transfusions were strictly forbidden by the patient's religion. Moreover, there is no proof on the record that Karen was even aware of this optional doctrine of faith, much less proof that she subscribed to it. Indeed, the evidence shows that neither of her parents, both devout Catholics, were aware of this permissive doctrine until Karen's condition arose.

As to the freedom of self-determination claim by plaintiff, respondent physicians point out the inconsistency in a third party asserting a self-determination claim for another individual, at least absent conclusive evidence of that individual's wishes. It must be remembered that Karen Ann Quinlan is an emancipated person, of full age, who had not even lived in the Quinlan household for a period of time.

B. Assuming *arguendo* that plaintiff can assert these rights, a sufficient state interest exists to preserve Karen Ann Quinlan's life.

If this Court overturns the trial court's finding of fact that Karen Ann Quinlan's wishes in this matter are unascertainable and if this Court determines that her father has standing to assert her rights, respondent physicians contend that the Constitution does not mandate this Court to allow Karen to die when medical science is capable of preserving her life.

Neither the constitutional right of privacy nor the constitutional right of free exercise of religion is absolute. Unlike the freedom of religious belief, which is absolute, see *Cantwell* v. *Connecticut,* 310 U. S. 296, 84 L. Ed. 1213, 1218 (1940), both the right to privacy and the right to free exercise of religion may be infringed where there is a sufficient state interest to justify the intrusion. See *State* v. *Saunders,* 130 N. J. Super. 234 (L. Div. 1974); *John F. Kennedy Mem. Hosp.* v. *Heston, supra; Cooke* v. *Tranburg,* 43 N. J. 514 (1964).

Respondent physicians maintain that *Heston* is dispositive of the freedom of privacy and freedom of exercise of religion claims in the instant case. In *Heston,* Chief Justice Weintraub pointed out that there is no constitutional right to die. 58 N. J. at 580. He found that the state's interest in the preservation of life and in permitting the hospital and physicians to fulfill their sacred obligation to preserve life constituted a compelling state interest, sufficient to warrant the administration of life-saving blood to a patient who had been hospitalized in an emergency. Likewise, in the instant case, the same state interests are present and are sufficient to justify any infringement of constitutional liberties needed to preserve Karen Ann Quinlan's life.

The words "compelling state interest" have a formidable ring to them. Consequently, a brief discussion of some of the cases where such an interest was found by the courts of this state should be of assistance.

In *Hamilton* v. *N. J. Real Estate Commission,* 117 N. J. Super. 345 (App. Div. 1971) all applicants for a real estate salesman's broker's license were required to be fingerprinted. The Court ruled that the public interest in the integrity of salesmen and brokers justified the invasion of privacy. In *Kochman* v. *Keansburg Bd. of Ed.,* 124 N. J. Super. 203 (Ch. Div. 1973), the Court classified the protection of school children from abnormal teachers as a compelling state interest justifying the requirement of a psychiatric examination upon evidence of abnormality. In *State* v. *Saunders, supra,* it was argued that the statute on fornication was an unconstitutional infringement on the right to privacy. The trial court found a compelling state interest in the prevention of the birth of illegitimate children and in the prevention of venereal disease. It is urged that the interests of the state in the preservation of life and in permitting physicians to practice medicine in accordance with their Oath are at least as great as, if not far greater than, the state interests found to be compelling in the *Hamilton, Kochman* and *Saunders* cases.

Respondent physicians contend that a compelling state interest to continue to preserve Karen Ann Quinlan's life does exist within the meaning of that test.

C. The Eighth Amendment of the United States Constitution against the imposition of cruel and unusual punishment has no application to this case.

The language and the thrust of the Eighth Amendment proscribing cruel and unusual punishment is directed to governmental action, whether it be by the executive, legislative or the judicial branch. It is not concerned with pain, anguish or suffering brought about by the vicissitudes of life. It speaks in terms of "excessive bail." It speaks in terms of "excessive punishment."

The leading and most recent case under this amendment is *Furman* v. *Georgia,* 408 U. S. 238, 33 L. Ed. 2d 346, reh. den. 409 U. S. 902, 34 L. Ed. 2d 164 (1972).

Mr. Justice Brennan in his concurring Opinion deals with punishment by the state directed toward human conduct. In a nutshell, the decision is concerned with "[T]he infliction of severe punishment by the state." 408 U. S. 238, 271, 274, 277, 279.

As Judge Muir pointed out, all of the concurring and dissenting Opinions in *Furman* are in accord that the proscription is directed to "state imposed criminal sanctions." (Slip op. at 41).

POINT V

The trial court properly delineated the role of the guardian of the person of Karen Ann Quinlan.

In his written opinion below, Judge Muir set forth the role of the guardian of the person of Karen Ann Quinlan and of her parents with regard to her continued treatment. Both the decision as to the respirator and future decisions as to further treatment are *medical decisions*. The parents may concur in those decisions (Slip op. at 31), and the guardian may give his counsel, advice and concurrence (Slip op. at 43), but the basic decisions are medical ones. Thus, the roles of both the guardian and the parents are sharply limited and are subordinate to the medical judgment of the treating physicians.

On November 10, 1975, after distributing his written opinion, Judge Muir conducted a short hearing with counsel and the Quinlans to expand upon his decision with regard to the guardian. [Hereinafter referred to as Supplemental Transcript ST-1 *et seq.*]. On November 12, 1975, Judge Muir wrote a letter to all parties on this subject further clarifying his views.

At the hearing Judge Muir stated that these are "medical decisions[s] to be made by Dr. Morse in concert with the ordinary standards of medical care." (ST3-1 to 4). The guardian may only concur with the physician's decisions. The guardian *cannot initiate* a course of treatment. Mr. Coburn is not to replace Dr. Morse (ST6-8 to 25). As Judge Muir wrote in the aforementioned letter:

> Mr. Coburn's appointment is designed to deal with those instances wherein Dr. Morse, in the process of administering care and treatment to Karen Quinlan, feels that there should be concurrence on the extent or nature of the care or treatment. If Mr. and Mrs. Quinlan are unable to give concurrence, then Mr. Coburn will be consulted for his concurrence.

Thus, the crucial issue here is not *who* is the guardian, but rather whether Judge Muir properly conceived of the role of the guardian. Respondent physicians urge that the trial court's delineation of the duties of the physicians and of the guardian and of the parents of Karen Quinlan is absolutely correct. These are *medical decisions* and must remain so. The practice of medicine is properly left to the medical profession.

It is well-settled law that in choosing a guardian, a court should select that individual whose service would be in the best interests of the infant or incompetent. See *In re Roll*, 117 N. J. Super. 122 (App. Div. 1971); *Strohsahl* v. *Equitable Life Assurance Society of U. S.*, 71 N. J. Super. 300 (Ch. Div. 1962).

Judge Muir decided below that the Quinlans' anguish over their daughter's condition would have a detrimental effect on their decision-making processes with regard to the continued treatment of their daughter. He, therefore, found that it would be more appropriate and in Karen's best interests if someone else were appointed guardian of the person. This was a correct application of the best interests test.

CONCLUSION

For the reasons stated above, the judgment of the trial court should be affirmed.

Respectfully submitted,

PORZIO, BROMBERG & NEWMAN,
Attorneys for Defendants-Respondents,
Dr. Arshad Javed and Dr. Robert J.
Morse.

RALPH PORZIO,
Of Counsel.

E. NEAL ZIMMERMANN,
RALPH PORZIO,
On the Brief.

In The

SUPREME COURT OF NEW JERSEY

September Term, 1975

Docket No. 12,041

IN THE MATTER OF KAREN ANN QUINLAN, AN ALLEGED INCOMPETENT

ON APPEAL FROM A FINAL JUDGMENT OF THE SUPERIOR COURT, CHANCERY DIVISION—SAT BELOW: HONORABLE ROBERT MUIR, JR., J.S.C.

BRIEF ON BEHALF OF THE PROSECUTOR OF MORRIS COUNTY

Donald G. Collester, Jr.
Prosecutor of Morris County
Attorney for the
State of New Jersey
Hall of Records
Morristown, New Jersey 07960

Donald G. Collester, Jr.
Prosecutor of Morris County
Of Counsel and on the Brief

STATEMENT OF PROCEDURAL HISTORY

Appellant Joseph Quinlan filed an application for appointment as the guardian of the person and property of his 21 year old daughter, Karen Ann Quinlan, an incompetent. The allegation set forth was that Karen Quinlan's "vital processes are artificially sustained via the extraordinary means of a mechanical MA-1 Respirator". The relief sought was his appointment as guardian with the authorization to discontinue "all extraordinary means of sustaining the vital processes" of Karen Ann Quinlan.

Thereafter, an amended pleading was filed in the form of a Complaint and Order to Show Cause to restrain the Morris County Prosecutor, St. Clare's Hospital and the attending and treating physicians of Karen Ann Quinlan from interfering with the authorization and relief sought and, furthermore, to enjoin the Prosecutor of Morris County from instituting any prosecution for homicide upon exercise of the extraordinary power sought.

The Court thereafter appointed a guardian ad litem, and, at a pretrial conference, the Attorney General of the State of New Jersey intervened as a party to the action.

Trial was held commencing October 20, 1975, and a decision was rendered by the Chancery Division Judge on November 10, 1975 denying the relief sought by the plaintiff in terms of any power to terminate the respirator, appointing him guardian of the property of his daughter but denying his request to be appointed guardian of her person. Rather, the guardian ad litem, Daniel R. Coburn, Esq., was appointed as guardian of the person of Karen Ann Quinlan. Subsequent to his acceptance of this appointment, Mr. Coburn thereafter resigned as guardian and was replaced by Thomas R. Curtin, Esq. as guardian of the person of Karen Ann Quinlan.

Plaintiff Joseph Quinlan appeals from the determination of the Chancery Division denying the relief sought of terminating the respirator assisting his daughter and from that portion of the Order denying his petition to be appointed guardian of the person of Karen Ann Quinlan. This Court has exercised its authority to directly certify the matter for argument.

160

STATEMENT OF FACTS

The facts are elaborately detailed in the Chancery Division opinion of Judge Muir. Therefore, counsel will endeavor only to highlight certain aspects of the testimony and evidence adduced at the trial.

As to certain factual matters there is no controversy. All counsel agree that Karen Ann Quinlan was born on April 24, 1954, that she is one of the three children of Joseph and Julia Quinlan, that she presently is in a coma described as a persistent vegetative state, and is a patient in the Intensive Care Unit of St. Clare's Hospital, where she is being treated by Dr. Robert Morse, a neurologist and Dr. Arshad Javed, a pulmonary internist.

While the precise etiology of her condition is unknown, there is agreement that it commenced in the early morning hours of April 15, 1975, when she was rushed by friends from her apartment to the Newton Memorial Hospital emergency room. The initial impression of the nature of her condition was pulmonary. Mouth-to-mouth resuscitation had been applied by her friends, and other respiratory assistance was given by police and emergency ambulance personnel. Shortly after she arrived at Newton Memorial Hospital, she was placed on a respirator to assist her breathing.

The following evening, April 16, 1975, Karen Quinlan was first seen by her present treating neurologist, Dr. Morse. His clinical evaluation at that time was that Karen Quinlan was in a state of decortitation and required continuation of the respirator for assistance in breathing. Some ten days later she was transferred to St. Clare's Hospital in Denville, New Jersey, where she has remained under the care of Dr. Morse with the assistance of Dr. Javed. To this day the precise cause of her condition remains a subject of speculation, but the condition itself remains in essence the same.

At the time of the initiation of this action, plaintiff maintained that Karen Quinlan was medically and legally dead, but subsequently it was conceded that she is alive by any standard recognized by the State of New Jersey. Furthermore, as shall be indicated *infra.*, Karen Quinlan is alive by any generally accepted medical or legal definition of death.

All parties stipulate to the incompetency of Karen Quinlan (T44-11 to 14) and thereby admit that a guardian is required over both her person and her property. The central issue of this case is not the propriety of guardianship but rather the extraordinary and awesome power sought by the plaintiff, *viz*, the power to terminate the respirator and thereby precipitate the death of Karen Quinlan.

161

Also not in dispute is the sincerity or motive of the plaintiff and the entire Quinlan family. All counsel have conceded that no ulterior motive exists. Moreover, the sincerity of plaintiff based upon his deep religious beliefs is not in any way attacked or brought into question.

In addition to the concession that Karen Quinlan is not dead, which is confirmed by all medical testimony at the time of trial, there also appears to be unanimity on the point that Karen Quinlan requires the use of the respirator at this point to maintain her life although attempts to "wean" her off the respirator have been made and no doubt will continue to be made in the future. Similarly, there is agreement among the medical experts that there is a great pessimism as to any recovery to a significant level of cognitive function (T640; T110-11 to 17; T265-15 to 17; T568-18 to 21; T601-15 to 17; T619-12 to 14). Furthermore, it cannot be specified with precision as to how long the life of Karen Quinlan will continue. As stated by Dr. Morse, she could live for months or die tonight. (T110-6 to 8).

Dr. Morse testified that at one point in the late summer or early fall of 1975 Mr. Quinlan approached him and requested that the respirator be removed. (T117-9 to 17). The doctor stated that after he had thought the matter over and discussed it with at least one colleague, he determined that he could not and would not discontinue the respirator since Karen Quinlan did not meet any medical criteria whereby she should be declared to be dead. (T117-1 to 118-18). He attempted to ascertain whether there was some medical tradition that would permit him to take this action, and he concluded there was none. He further determined together with Dr. Javed that removal of Karen Quinlan from the respirator would violate traditional standards of medical practice (T158-2 to 11; T200-20 to 24), and it is for this reason that both treating physicians did not concur with the request of the plaintiff. It was shortly after the doctors communicated their decision to the family that this action was instituted.

Aside from the two treating physicians, five eminent neurologists examined Karen Quinlan subsequent to the initiation of this action and thereafter testified as to their findings and conclusions.

Dr. Julius Korein testified as the plaintiff's expert. Based upon his clinical examination as well as his review of hospital records and consultation with treating physicians, Dr. Korein concluded that Karen Quinlan had suffered irreparable cerebral damage (T265-10 to 24) but that she was not "brain dead" within the accepted medical meaning of that phrase as set forth in a 1968 report of the Ad Hoc Committee of the Harvard Medical School to examine the definition of death. (T261-20 to 21).

162

Indeed, she does not meet any facet of brain death (T275-8 to 9), and she also cannot be considered "cerebrally dead". (T312-9 to 11).

Dr. Korein further defined "extraordinary" medical treatment in terms of utilization of medical resources in circumstances dependent upon a reasonable possibility of success of treatment. (T271-13 to 17). He testified that in his opinion the medical treatment being administered to Karen Quinlan was "extraordinary". (T273-19 to 22). However, he admitted that such a determination by him involved a value judgment, that value judgments of physicians may differ and that others within the same field of medical expertise could reach an opposite conclusion as to what is "extraordinary" treatment (T273-15; T299-10 to 16; T317-20 to 318-3). He also spoke in terms of "unwritten or unspoken standards" for continued treatment as well as "judicious neglect" (T327-15 to 24; T333-5 to 9). However, he did not define these concepts within the context of the case at bar, and, in any event, he indicated that such "judicious neglect" must be made with the concurrence of *both* the treating physician and the next of kin. (T333-10 to 14).

Dr. Eugene Loesser testified on behalf of the guardian that Karen Quinlan was not brain dead although she was living at the reflex level of an infant. (T567-9 to 12). He indicated that the chances of improvement to the extent of cognitive function were nil although improvement was possible so that she could recover respiratory function without the use of a respirator. (T508-24 to 569-9). He also asserted that the Harvard Ad Hoc criteria was the generally accepted definition of death and that Karen Quinlan did not meet any of its tests. (T573-9 to 15).

Dr. Fred Plum, an eminent neurologist and author of the phrase "persistent vegetative state", testified also on behalf of the guardian. He reaffirmed the testimony of the earlier witnesses that Karen Quinlan has certain vegetative functions (T594-9 to 11) and that her prognosis in terms of recovery of sapient behavior is remote. (T601-1 to 5). However, he also asserted that she is absolutely not brain dead. (T592-1 to 5).

Dr. Stuart Cook also testified that Karen Quinlan has suffered irreversible brain damage and that the chances for any useful sapient or discriminate return of function is extremely remote (T639-6 to 9), but he asserted that it was very difficult to say with absolute certainty, especially with a lack of clear history, that there would not be the possibility of recovery. (T639-9 to 24). He stated that in certain instances patients in a coma had made useful recoveries, that there is always a remote possibility of a medical breakthrough but that the chances of return to any significant level of psychological function in this instance is virtually infinitesimal. (T640-1 to 22).

Of special significance was the testimony of Dr. Sydney Diamond, who testified on behalf of the State. Dr. Diamond concurred with the testimony of the other experts that Karen Quinlan was not brain dead. (T615-7). He further stated that the initial and continued use of the respirator under the circumstances presented in the Quinlan case was in conformity with standard medical practice (T621-1 to 5). The doctor stated that:

> "You could not find a physician who would not have provided that support when she was first admitted or the period during which a determination of cause was being carried out. No physician to my knowledge will ever interrupt a device which is performing a life-saving measure at any time at all.

> "When respirators are disconnected in case of cerebral death—and I have attended many such decision-making things, sometimes providing the last piece of evidence to fit the Harvard criteria—the plug is being pulled, as it is said, or the respirator is being turned off a dead person, a person without life. The respirator is not being used in those circumstances at that time to maintain physical existence. The life is over and then the physician is ethically and so far legally permitted to terminate those supportive measures." (T618-18 to 619-8).

As to his opinion on the issue of the medical-ethical propriety of terminating the respirator in the instant case, the doctor responded:

> "I do not think based on my examination and experience that anybody would interrupt this device, the use of this device now on the patient." (T619-9 to 11).

Dr. Diamond admitted there were limits insofar as certain types of treatment modalities with a patient such as Karen Quinlan, and he gave as an example certain surgical procedures. (T619-12 to 23). Nonetheless, he reaffirmed that because Karen Quinlan needs the respirator to live, it is his opinion that medical ethics require its continuance. (T621-1 to 5).

Moreover, as if responding directly to the unwritten or unspoken standards of "judicial neglect" mentioned by Dr. Korein, Dr. Diamond stated that:

> "Many physicians wish that there were different standards, but as physicians they can't and they are constrained to act in accordance with the standards. If new standards are set in cases like this I also think it is

164

beyond the physician's competence, beyond all physicians' competence to deal with the problems relating to quality of life by themselves. They deal with physical reality and can advise considerations of what should constitute conditions which, in which life support systems might be withheld, but they cannot make this determination by themselves. Dr. Morse and Dr. Bender have acted in my opinion, and all the other physicians concerned, acted and advised in a manner that is perfectly consistent with the standards of medical practice.'' (T621-5 to 18).

Point I

THE TRIAL COURT DID NOT ERR IN DENYING THE RELIEF SOUGHT BY PLAINTIFF-APPELLANT BECAUSE KAREN QUINLAN IS ALIVE BY ALL LEGAL AND MEDICAL STANDARDS

As indicated in the Statement of Facts, *supra*, the plaintiff conceded prior to trial that Karen Quinlan is not dead by any legal standards recognized by the State of New Jersey; and the testimony of all medical witnesses at the time of trial verified that Karen Quinlan is not dead by any medical standard.

Traditionally, the law defined death in terms of the complete cessation of respiratory and circulatory functions. See, *e.g., Taylor* v. *Cawood,* 211 *S.W.* 47 (*Mo.* 1919). Indeed, in certain specific cases the concept of "brain death", *viz,* where the brain no longer functions and has no possibility of functioning again, was rejected as a definition or test of death. See, *Douglas* v. *Southwestern Life Insurance Co.,* 374 *S.W.* 2d 788 (*Tex. Civ. App.* 1964); *Smith* v. *Smith,* 220 *Ark.* 579, 317 *S.W.* 2d 275 (1953). However, it is fair to state that the more modern view appears to be an acceptance of "the irreversible cessation of brain function" as an appropriate standard for the determination of death. See, *State* v. *Brown,* 491 *P.2d* 1193 (*Or.Ct.App.* 1971); *People* v. *Saldona,* 121 *Ca.Rptr.* 243 (*Cal. Ct. of App.* 1975), and *People* v. *Lyons,* 15 *Crim.L.Rep.* 2240 (*Cal.Sup.Ct.* 1974). Furthermore, brain death has been adopted by statute as an appropriate test in five states, and there is presently pending in the New Jersey State Legislature Senate Bill 3314, which would introduce this concept to the statutory law of New Jersey.

The most generally accepted medical criteria for brain death was the work product of the Ad Hoc Committee of the Harvard Medical School

165

to examine the definition of brain death. Its findings were published in the *Journal of the American Medical Association* (*J.A.M.A.*), in an article entitled "A Definition of Irreversible Coma" 205 *J.A.M.A.* 337 (1968). Briefly, the characteristics of irreversible coma and brain death as defined by the Committee were as follows:

(1) "Unreceptivity and unresponsitivity to externally applied stimuli and inner need;

(2) No movements or breathing;

(3) No reflexes including ocular movement;

(4) A flat or isoelectric electroencephalagram;

All of the above tests are to be repeated at least 24 hours later with no change before determination can be made of brain death.

Admittedly, other authorities disagree with the criteria of the Harvard Ad Hoc Committee, but it is interesting to note that the criticisms are that the Harvard Ad Hoc criteria are incomplete and that a greater showing of lack of brain response is necessary. See, "Irreversibly Comatose Individual", 33 *Cambridge L.J.* 130 (1974) and "Standards for Determining Death" 121 *U.Pa.L.Rev.* 87.

As indicated *supra* all of the medical witnesses who testified indicated that Karen Quinlan did not possess one aspect of the criteria for brain death. Moreover, it is apparent that even other medical definitions of death other than the Harvard Ad Hoc Committee criteria, Karen Quinlan is still alive. (T330-21 to T332-1).

Because she is still alive medically as well as legally, the determination of her physicians to continue treatment and continue use of the respirator must be respected, especially since it is in accord with standard medical practice. Furthermore, as is shown by comparison of the testimony of Drs. Korein and Diamond, there is considerable debate within the medical community on the subject of continued treatment or "judicious neglect" of moribund patients. See articles by Sackett & Epstein in *Medical Economics*, April 2, 1973. See also Ramsey, P., *The Patient as Person,* 101-112 (1970) and Ross, E.K., *On Death and Dying,* (1969).

Human life is unique, and its uniqueness may not be sidestepped by arguments based upon some concept of "the quality of life". As asserted by one eminent physician, it is unfair to place such a standard for non-treatment upon the medical community.

"It is sometimes suggested that the 'quality of life' should be entered into an equation in which length of life multiplied by 'quality' would equal a number that would guide the doctor's conduct. The only judge of

166

the quality of his life, however, is the living patient. If his alternative is death, it would be arrogant indeed for an outsider, a physician, employed by the patient to fight for his life, to judge its quality so poor as not to merit the effort. If we say that for the physician-as-judge, life itself is less important than its quality, that it must be life where a man can appreciate a poem, or read the Sunday *Times*, or love his wife, or recognize her, or perceive the difference between light and dark, or heat and cold, then we put ourselves in the position of saying that there is a human life that is not worth living. That is not the doctor's prerogative." Epstein, "The Role of the Physician in the Prolongation of Life", *Controversy in Internal Medicine II* 103, 106 (1974).

The doctor's contractual duty is toward his patient, not the family or next of kin, and as such he must make the decision for treatment when the patient is still alive. As stated by Dr. Epstein,

"Physicians belong to an ancient profession, standing apart from all others in its primary concern and respect for human life and its enmity to death. In the long run, that attitude of the profession may be as important for society as any miracle that modern technical medicine can perform.

"Attitudes toward the prolongation of life are invested with a peculiar emotional ambivalence that springs from the horror most people have of contact with the ill, or with any reminder of their own vulnerability. The nightmare that men might live forever as vegetables springs from this irrational horror. It should be relegated to science fiction. The world will never be peopled with cripples and corpses. The fact is that for all our miracles, life cannot be prolonged indefinitely. For all our talk and our science, we do only a little. Death comes at last. The comatose patient treated with antibiotics falls victim a few weeks later to a resistant organism, or to a heart attack. Patients die, and always will, despite the best efforts of doctors. But the little we can do has an importance that transcends the patient, for it carries a message to all our patients and to the world: *Human beings are important. Humanity is to be preserved"*. *Id.* at 109, (emphasis supplied).

This Court is being asked to reverse a trial court and thereby make a decision that will shorten the life of a human being, albeit a person in a persistent vegetative state with irreparable brain damage resulting in deprivation of cognitive function. There is no legal authority or medical standards which would permit such action. Moreover, the Court is also being asked to make an *ad hoc* decision without the benefit of proper proof. For example, what in fact is meant by "extraordinary means"? Even the plaintiff-appellant appeared to be uncertain since he wanted removal of the respirator, believed the intravenous and the catheter to be in the same category but would expect the physician to treat his daughter with antibiotics if she developed an infection. (T355-1 to 356-9).

If some exception to legal and medical tradition is to be made, it is submitted that clarity of rule making and moral consensus is best promoted by legislative action. It is submitted that judicial decision-making on this record would leave existing doctrine in an ill-defined and unsettled condition for the foreseeable future. See Capron and Kass, "A Statutory Definition of the Standards for Determining Human Death", 121 *U.Pa.L.Rev.* 87 (1972).

It is significant to point out that there has been considerable legislative attention to these problems. Since 1937 state legislators have pondered various proposals to legalize euthanasia in one form or another. See *Note*, 48 *Notre Dame Lawyer*, 1202, 1245 (1973). Some bills introduced would permit premature death of the terminally ill with the consent of the person who is going to die by providing that there should be a right to refuse "unnatural or surgical means or procedures" to prolong life. See, *e.g.,* Senate Bill 715, Wisconsin Legislature (1971). Other bills enable a merciful end to physical suffering even though the patient is unconscious or incapable of giving consent. See, *Legislative Note,* 22 *U.Fla.L.Rev.* 368 (1970). For example, legislation has been proposed to permit the next of kin with a committee of doctors to approve the withholding of life-sustaining measures or even to expedite death with a drug overdose. 48 *Notre Dame Lawyer, supra* at 1245; see also Morris, "Voluntary Euthanasia" 45 *Wash.L.Rev.* 239, 269 (1970). Notably, none of the legislative proposals have been enacted.

Legislative consideration has also been given to the so-called "living will" concept, for bills have been introduced both in Florida and Massachusetts. Therefore, legislative consideration of these problems is not without precedent, and it is submitted that the legislative forum is most appropriate toward the proper airing of moral concerns and the establishment of a general rule setting forth guidelines and standards to be interpreted by subsequent judicial decisions.

Point II

THE TRIAL COURT DID NOT ERR IN DENYING THE RELIEF SOUGHT, SINCE THAT RELIEF WOULD CONSTITUTE A VIOLATION OF THE LAWS OF THIS STATE GOVERNING HOMICIDE.

N.J.S. 2A:113-1, 113-2, and 113-5 encompass the statutory law of New Jersey concerning homicide, which is divided into the categories of murder and manslaughter. This legislative scheme modified the common law by setting forth gradations of guilt for homicide; however, the common law definition persists that murder is defined as the unlawful killing of one person by another with either expressed or implied malice. *State* v. *Brown* 22 *N.J.* 405, 411 (1956); see also *Schlosser, Criminal Laws of New Jersey*, sec. 57:8, p.89 (1970). "Malice" has been defined, in turn, as an intention to cause the death of, or grievous bodily injury to, any person with knowledge that the act in question will probably cause death or grievous bodily harm. *State* v. *Gardner,* 51 *N.J.* 444, 457-58 (1968). As a general rule, all homicide is malicious and amounts to murder, except where justified by the command or permission of the law, excused on account of accident or self-preservation, or alleviated into manslaughter. *State* v. *Brown,* 22 *N.J.* 410 (1956). In the instant case, the relief sought by plaintiff does not possess legal justification or excuse, as would remove this act of terminating life from the category of murder under existing law.

No one disputes that petitioner's motive arises from compassion, but compassion of itself cannot form the basis for an applicable general rule of law, excluding an act from the applicability of the law of homicide. The law is well settled that if a killing is done willfully, the crime of murder exists irrespective of the motive of the defendant. *State* v. *Ehlers,* 98 *N.J.L.* 235, 240 (*E. & A.* 1922); *State* v. *Beard,* 16 *N.J.* 60-61 (1954); see also *State* v. *Jaggers,* 71 *N.J.L.* 231 (*E. & A.* 1904). The law does not recognize a "good motive" to terminate life. *Ibid.* As stated in *State* v. *Ehlers, supra,* 98 *N.J.L.* 236 at 240:

> "(Proof) of motive is not an essential element in a conviction of murder in the first degree. If the proved facts establish that the defendant did the killing willfully; that is, with intent to kill (which is presumed from the proof of killing, until the contrary appears, *State* v. *Zellers,* 7 *N.J.L.* 220; *Brown* v. *State,* 66 *Id.* 666, and as a result of premeditation and deliberation,

169

thereby implying pre-consideration and determination, there is murder in the first degree, no matter what defendant's motive may have been, nor, although he in fact had no motive (using the word in its usual sense of self-serving reason) whatsoever. . . This is so because the State has a deep interest and concern in the preservation in the life of each of its citizens, and (except in case of self-defense), does not either commit or permit to any individual, no matter how kindly the motive, either the right or the privilege of destroying such a life, except in punishment for crime and in the manner prescribed by law. . .''.

Since motive is irrelevant, no matter how kindly, and because murder is defined as the unlawful killing of a human being, it must follow that, with present statutory and common law, the termination of the life of a human being under circumstances such as suggested here, constitutes euthanasia and violates the law of homicide. As stated in *People* v. *Conley*, 411 *P.2d* 911, 918 (1966):

"One who commits euthanasia bears no ill will against his victim and believes his act is morally justified, but he nonetheless acts with malice if he is able to comprehend that society prohibits his act regardless of his personal belief."

In the case of *People* v. *Rodericks*, 178 *N.W.* 690 *(Sup.Ct.Mich.* 1920), the defendant-husband pleaded guilty to murder based upon his having placed a quantity of poison within easy reach of his dying wife. Upon appeal, the Court rejected the assertion that the conduct of the husband did not constitute homicide. In this case, as in other cases, it was held that the motive of the defendant, however humanitarian, did not constitute a defense to the crime. Furthermore, some legal writers have gone so far as to say that a physician who withholds life-preserving treatment "commits criminal homicide by omission". Kamisar, *Some Non-Religious Views Against Proposed Mercy Killing Legislation*, 42 *Minn. L.Rev.* 969, 982 (1958); *Informed Consent and the Dying Patient*, 83 *Yale L.J.* 1632 (1974); see also *Annotation:* "Homicide: *Failure to* Provide Medical or Surgical Attention" 100 *ALR* 2d 483 (1965).

The fact that the victim is in a terminal condition is, likewise, no defense to a homicide charge. *Perkins; Criminal Law* 31 *(2d Ed.* 1969); *State* v. *Francis*, 152 *S.C.* 17, 149 *S.E.* 348 (1929). To hasten death, absent legal justification or excuse, is to commit a homicide.

"In the eyes of the criminal law, if a person hastens death, such person is considered the cause of the death.

Though a person may be at the threshold of death, if the spark is extinguished by a wrongful act, it is sufficient for a conviction." *State* v. *Mally*, 366 *P.2d* 838, 873 (*Sup.Ct.Mont.* 1961).

Furthermore, applicability of the law of homicide to the relief sought is not obviated by statements attributed to Karen Quinlan to the effect that she would not desire to be kept alive by "extraordinary means". (T484-12 to T486-12). Aside from questions as to admissibility or probability of such statements, they are irrelevant to the applicability of the law of homicide to the factual complex *sub judice*. That is, the rationale for the statements is a form of advance consent to euthanasia, but consent of the victim is not a defense to a criminal homicide. "He who kills another upon his desire or command is, in the judgment of the law as much a murderer as if he had done it merely of his own head." *Turner* v. *State*, 119 *Tenn.* 663, 671, 108 *S.W.* 1139, 1141 (*Sup.Ct. Tenn.*, 1908) *cf.*, *John F. Kennedy Memorial Hospital* v. *Heston*, 58 *N.J.* 576 (1971). The point is summarized by a recent law note as follows:

> "(T)hose special factors which may be said to distinguish euthanasia from more reprehensible forms of killing—humanitarian motive, possible consent of the victim, the victim's hopeless condition—are irrelevant in the eyes of the law. The common law makes no exception for euthanasia, but jealousy guards the life of every individual, however grotesque it may be. One who acts to shorten such a life, for any reason whatsoever, is guilty in the first degree.
>
> "A similar liability is imposed on one who aids another in the commission of euthanasia, or who is part of a successful conspiracy to commit euthanasia ... thus, a family has decided that a dying relative's suffering should be put to an end, and therefore agree to persuade medical personnel to perform the act, would be guilty of a conspiracy to commit murder should the result be accomplished." *Survey, Euthanasia: "Criminal, Tort, Constitutional and Legislative Considerations"*, 48 *Notre Dame Lawyer* 1202, 1205-06 (1973).

Moreover, for anyone to argue that termination of the support systems or the failure to render treatment necessary to sustain life does not constitute a homicide because there is no "act", is to assert a distinction without a difference. Initially, it is difficult to conceive how action to turn off a mechanical respirator so as to terminate a person's life can be anything but an "act". Once life-supporting equipment has begun to operate on a patient, it is fallacious to assert that cessation of that treatment is a mere "omission" and not an "act" in the legal sense of the word. To turn a switch to the "off" position, there is obviously physical movement and positive action. See *Restatement, Torts, 2d,* sec. 2, p.5 (1965); Prosser, *The Law of Torts* 355 (1964).

Even accepting the "omission-action" dichotomy as valid, does not assist appellant because the law also attaches criminal liability in instances where there is duty to act, and an omission to perform that duty is a direct cause of death. *People* v. *Beardsley,* 150 *Mich.* 206, 113 *N.W.* 1128, 1129 (*Sup.Ct.Mich.*, 1907); see generally, Kircheimer, *"Criminal Omissions",* 55 *Harv. L.Rev.* 615 (1942) and Hughes, *"Criminal Omissions",* 67 *Yale L.J.* 590 (1958). In the precise context of the withholding of necessary medical treatment to preserve life, it has been held that failure to provide or maintain such treatment subjects the person with the duty to the law of homicide, where the act amounts to willfulness and the lack of treatment is a proximate or contributing cause of death. See cases collected in 100 *A.L.R. 2d, supra* at 487.

In the case at bar, the duty to act is clear as to both the next of kin and the physicians and hospital in behalf of the patient. See *John F. Kennedy Memorial Hospital* v. *Heston, supra,* 58 *N.J.* 576; *State* v. *Perricone,* 37 *N.J.* 463 (1962); *cf., State* v. *Watson,* 77 *N.J.L.* 299 (*Sup.Ct.* 1909). Furthermore, it is important to underscore that the fact that the physicians and the hospital have not sought and do not seek to abandon their treatment of Karen Quinlan, and they also concur that their duty to treat exists because she is alive. Therefore, to grant the relief sought by the appellant would not only conflict with the medical opinion and ethics of the treating physicians and hospital, as well as of a substantial body of medical ethical opinion, but it would also carve out an exception to the law of homicide and, thereby, lessen the deterrent effect of that law, as well as place upon the State the untenable burden of proving "impure motive".

It is, therefore, the position adopted by this respondent that because Karen Quinlan is alive by legal and medical standards, any intentional termination or shortening of her life would be contrary to the existing law of homicide.

Point III

THE TRIAL COURT DID NOT ERR IN DENYING THE RELIEF SOUGHT BECAUSE THERE IS A PARAMOUNT INTEREST TO PRESERVE AND PROTECT LIFE, AND, ASSUMING ARGUENDO THAT THERE IS A RIGHT TO DIE, THERE IS AN ABSENCE OF THE REQUISITE INFORMED CONSENT.

The preservation of life has been adjudged to be of paramount importance to the courts of the State of New Jersey even in the face of a claim of a constitutional right to withhold treatment. *John F. Kennedy Memorial Hospital* v. *Heston,* 58 *N.J.* 576 (1971); *State* v. *Perricone,* 37 *N.J.* 463, *cert. den.,* 371 *U.S.* 890 (1962); *Hoerner* v. *Bertinago, 67 N.J. Super.* 517 *(J.D.R.C.,* 1961); *Raleigh Fitkin—Paul Morgan Memorial Hospital* v. *Anderson,* 42 *N.J.* 421, *cert. den.,* 377 *U S.* 985 (1964); *Muhlenberg Hospital* v. *Patterson,* 128 *N.J. Super.* 498, 520 *(Law Div.* 1974). The right to life is considered inalienable. *Gleitman* v. *Cosgrove,* 49 *N.J.* 22 (1967).

The most significant precedent is *John F. Kennedy Memorial Hospital* v. *Heston, supra,* 58 *N.J.* 576. In that case a 22 year old woman was severely injured in an automobile accident and rendered unconscious. Taken to the hospital, she was examined, and it was determined she would die unless operated upon for a ruptured spleen. The medical opinion was also that she would expire unless whole blood was administered to her during and after the operation. Both the patient and her parents were Jehovah's Witnesses, and it is a tenet of that religious faith that blood transfusions are forbidden. Although there was a subsequent claim by the patient that she refused consent to a transfusion, the Court found that the matter was far from clear since she was in a state of shock. In any event, her mother refused consent, necessitating an application by the hospital to a Superior Court Judge for the appointment of a guardian with authority to consent to the blood transfusion to preserve the life of the patient. The appointment was made, the operation was performed, blood was administered, and Miss Heston survived.

Subsequently, this Court accepted the case in order to resolve the important public interest question presented. It balanced the interest of the State in protecting life against the constitutional argument set forth by the defendants, and, in an opinion by the former Chief Justice, it was held that the State's interest in preserving life was paramount.

Initially, the opinion dealt with the argument raised by the appellant that a distinction existed between suicide, which was conceded to be against public policy, and passive submission to death. In language particularly applicable to the case at bar, the Court stated the following:

> "Appellant suggests there is a difference between passively submitting to death and actively seeking it. The distinction may be merely verbal, as it would be if an adult sought death by starvation instead of a drug. *If the State may interrupt one mode of self-destruction, it may with equal authority interfere with the other. It is arguably different when an individual, overtaken by illness, decides to let it run a fatal course. But unless the medical option itself is laden with the risk of death or serious infirmity, the State's interest in sustaining life in such circumstances is hardly distinguishable from its interest in the case of suicide." John F. Kennedy Memorial Hospital* v. *Heston, supra,* 58 *N.J.* at 581-82 (emphasis supplied).

As in *Heston,* the Court is not confronted with "deadly options". No exploratory surgery or other procedure with a probability or even possibility of resultant death is contemplated or suggested. Rather, what is sought to be protected is the continuance of medical care and treatment rendered in accordance with standard medical practice.

Another significant factual similarity between *Heston* and the case *sub judice* is that in *Heston,* the Court did not find that the patient's refusal of treatment was sufficiently clear to merit acceptance, and the Court then went on to reject the substituted judgment of the parent who wished to refuse life-saving treatment. In the instant case, Karen Quinlan is, of course, incapable of any consent to discontinue use of the respirator. Moreover, as noted by the trial court, her statements to her mother, sister, and friend made in context of discussing the plight of others, are hardly sufficiently probative of the issue in this case. Such statements were obviously speculative and are, at best, only arguably admissible. See *Rule* 63 (12)(a) of the *New Jersey Rules of Evidence; In re Spiegelglass,* 48 *N.J.Super.* 265 (App.Div. 1958). Therefore, the rationale set forth in *Heston* would appear to be indistinguishable and compel the rejection of the substituted judgment of the parent. Compare, *Collins* v. *Davis,* 254 *N.Y.S. 2d* 666 (*Sup. Ct.* 1964) in which surgery was performed upon an unconscious husband after the wife refused consent to the procedure.

Since Karen Quinlan is an incompetent, cases dealing with refusal of treatment of children are apposite since the law deems a child incapable of such consent. But see, *In re Green,* 292 *A2d* 387 (*Pa.* 1972), 307 *A2d*

279 (1973). The law is clear that medical treatment will be provided to children in the face of a refusal to consent by a parent. *State* v. *Perricone, supra,* 37 *N.J.* 463; *Application of President and Directors of Georgetown College, Inc., supra,* 331 *F2d* at 1008; see also, "The Right To Die", 7 *Houston L. Rev.* 664 (1970).

In cases of adults the courts find an important distinction between an instance where a patient is alert and capable of making an intelligent decision as opposed to a situation where the patient is comatose and someone else is making the decision for him. The standard is that of "certainty" that the patient gives consent and that his consent be informed. *In re Osborne,* 294 *A2d* 372 (*D.C. Ct. of App.* 1972); *In re Memser,* 51 *N.Y. Misc.* 2d 616, 273 *N.Y.S.2d* 624 (*Sup.Ct.* 1964); see also *In re Green, supra,* 292 *A2d* 387, 307 *A2d* 279 (in which the Pennsylvania Supreme Court remanded in order to get the opinion of a 12 year old boy as to whether he concurred with his parents' refusal to consent to a spinal operation in a situation where his life was not endangered by the condition).

The *Osborne* decision held that a competent 34 year old Jehovah's Witness who was not in a condition of *in extremis* could refuse to accept whole blood and thereby run the risk of death. The same result was reached under similar fact by the Illinois Supreme Court in *In re Brooks,* 32 *Ill.2d* 361, 205 *NE2d* 435 (*Sup.Ct.* 1965). Although both the results and the reasoning of these decisions are contrary to *Heston,* (58 *N.J.* at 584), it is important to note that the decisions of refusal of medical care were made by informed competent adults. The point was stressed in *Osborne.*

> . . ."Whenever possible, it is better for the judge to make a first-hand appraisal of the patient's personal desires and ability for rational choice. In this way, the Court can always know, to the extent possible, *that the judgment is that of the individual concerned and not that of those who believe, however well-intentioned, that they speak for the person whose life is in the balance. Thus, where the patient is comatose, or suffering impairment of capacity for choice, it may be better to give weight to the known instinct for survival which can, in a critical situation, alter previously held convictions. In such cases, it cannot be determined with certainty that a deliberate and intelligent choice has been made."* (Emphasis supplied.) (294 *A.2d* at 374).

Similarly, even with respect to legal writers who urge some form of passive or active euthanasia or anti-dysthanasia, stress has been placed upon the fact that it is the patient alone who may give his or her informed consent to termination of treatment, which act will result in death. "Informed Consent and the Dying Patient," 83 *Yale L.R.* 1632, 1650 (1974); "The Right To Die", 10 *Calif. Western L. Rev.* 613 (1974). The refusal to permit substituted judgment of next of kin to terminate life supporting treatment is obviously based in part upon the fact that "the consequence of error is so irreparable", Kamisar, *supra*, 42 *Minn. L. Rev.* 969, 982, as well as the pre-eminence given to the sanctity of life as expressed by *Heston* (58 *N.J.* at 580) and other authorities.

> "Because of society's interest in the life of the individual, because of the law's traditional view of the sanctity of human life, and because life can be saved without too great a curtailment of the religious liberty of those patients who refuse treatment on religious grounds, the law should not give its protection to the individual decision to choose death.

> Society has an interest in the life of the individual. In the *Georgetown* case, the patient was the mother of a seven month old child and it is apparent that others than herself would have suffered had she died. Once it is admitted that there is sufficient interest in the life of a particular patient to deny him a legal right to refuse life-saving treatment, then the decision must be the same for all patients. That is, the criterion of the 'social worth' of the patient would lead the Courts into insolvable problems. Any distinction based on 'social worth' in this area is repugnant to the basic ideal of equality: if the mother of several children is to be saved, then so must the childless individual."

> "Unauthorized Rendition of Lifesaving Treatment", 53 *Calif. L. Rev.* 860, 872 (1964).

It follows that while under the dictates of *Heston,* a person may not choose death by terminating life supporting treatment, those contrary decisions of other jurisdictions and contrary statements of legal commentations require in any event the informed consent of the patient to either the refusal of initiation of life-supporting measures or the termination of life-supporting measures previously initiated. Because Karen Quinlan is alive and there is an absence of a sufficient manifestation of informed consent, the relief sought is contradicted by legal authorities. Therefore, the trial court properly denied the application for the extraordinary power sought.

THE CONSTITUTIONAL DOCTRINES RELIED UPON BY APPELLANT ARE INAPPLICABLE TO THE CASE SUB JUDICE AND, IN ANY EVENT, ARE OUTWEIGHED BY THE OBLIGATION OF THE STATE TO PROTECT AND PRESERVE LIFE.

Against the interest of the State to protect and preserve life, the appellant has raised constitutional arguments relating to free exercise of religious beliefs and the right to privacy. He asserts that these constitutional principles are applicable to the instant case and that, by a balancing of interest test, the State interest in life is outweighed by the Quinlan family's constitutional rights. However, it is submitted that the law is to the contrary; that is, these constitutional principles are inapplicable to the case *sub judice*, and the assertion of such rights are in any case overbalanced by the State's responsibility to protect and preserve life.

Former Chief Justice Weintraub succinctly summed up the existing state of the law when he asserted that, "It seems correct to say that there is no constitutional right to choose to die". *John F. Kennedy Memorial Hospital* v. *Heston, supra,* 58 *N.J.* at 580. Applied to allegations of constitutional rights based on religion, the Court further stated that:

> "Nor is constitutional right established by adding that one's religious faith ordains his death. Religious beliefs are absolute, but conduct in pursuance of religious beliefs is not wholly immune from governmental restraint."
> *Ibid. See also, Mountain Lakes* v. *Maas,* 56 *N.J.Super* 245 (*App.Div.* 1959), *aff'd.,* 31 *N.J.* 537 (1960), *cert. den.* 363 *U.S.* 843 (1960) (Involving compulsory vaccination for children); *Reynolds* v. *United States,* 98 *U.S.* 145 (1878) (Polygamy); *Sherbert* v. *Verner,* 374 *U.S.* 298, 83 *S.Ct.* 1790, 10 *L.ed.* 965 (1973) (Refusal to work on Saturday Sabbath relating to State Unemployment Compensation). See also, "Compulsory Medical Treatment and the Free Exercise of Religion", 42 *Ind. L.J.* 386, 390-93 (1969).

In the instant case much is made of the fact that the Quinlans are Catholics and that "extraordinary" medical measures need not be employed to prolong life. Passing for the moment the inherent difficulties in defining the term "extraordinary" in the context of life and death, it is submitted the religious beliefs of Mr. or Mrs. Quinlan on the subject of termination of "extraordinary" means sustaining life is not relevant, although arguably the religious attitude of Karen Quinlan *may* have some bearing. See *John F. Kennedy Memorial Hospital* v. *Heston, supra,* 58 *N.J.* at 580.

However, the proofs adduced at the time of trial are insufficient to establish more than the simple facts that she was born and baptized a Catholic, attended Catholic affiliated schools and was a member of the same Church as her parents (T339-7 to 15). Moreover, there is no testimony which would indicate that Karen Quinlan ever had knowledge of the *allocutio* of November 24, 1957 by Pope Pius XII on the prolongation of life, much less that she would have elected to die under these circumstances for the reason that termination of the respirator would not constitute a sin (T419-1 to 22). However, although there is no proof as to the degree or depth of faith of Karen Quinlan or even her knowledge of the *allocutio,* the Court is being asked to *assume* her total acceptance of the dogma and her election to die and enter a hereafter in which the Court must assume that she also believed.

Since there is a paucity of proof as to the depth and direction of Karen Quinlan's religious beliefs, appellant bases his argument upon the assertion that the constitutional doctrines of freedom of religion and the free exercise of religion are not strictly personal but also are "familial" in nature. The implications of the acceptance of this argument under the factual complex *sub judice* are devastating. Stripped of constitutional rhetoric, it means that because Karen Quinlan is a Catholic (whether practicing or not) and is in a persistent vegetative state, her family may terminate her life based upon a theological statement permissive in nature and about which Karen Quinlan may or may not have known and accepted.

Appellant has cited as authority the cases of *Meyer* v. *Nebraska,* 252 *U.S.* 390 (1923) and *Pierce* v. *Society of Sisters,* 268 *U.S.* 510 (1925), which dealt with the balancing of the *parens patriae* duty and power of the State in education against the asserted constitutional right of parents to educate their children as they see fit in the framework of their religion. See also, *Wisconsin* v. *Yoder,* 406 *U.S.* 205 (1972). These cases are obviously inapplicable to a factual context in which an adult child's life is sought to be ended because of the acceptance by other members of the family of a permissive religious doctrine.

First, it is submitted that the constitutional rights of freedom of religious belief and exercise are personal to Karen Quinlan and may not be asserted on her behalf except by the legal guardian of her person as appointed by the Court. See, *State* v. *Bibbo,* 83 *N.J.Super.* 36, 39 (*App.*

Div. 1964); *In re Green, supra,* 292 *A.2d* 387. Furthermore, even assuming that appellant had the status of lawful guardian of the person of Karen Quinlan, case law indicates that he could not assert the constitutional arguments based upon religion as a basis for terminating the respirator and thereby ending her life. It was made clear by the United States Supreme Court in *Prince* v. *Massachusetts, supra,* 321 *U.S.* 158, that no one has a right, constitutional or otherwise, to be a martyr or make his child a martyr. As previously indicated, religious beliefs are absolute, but conduct or practices pursuant to such beliefs are not immune from governmental restraint. *John F. Kennedy Memorial Hospital* v. *Heston, supra,* 58 *N.J.* at 580. Parents do *not* have the power to discontinue or prohibit life-saving treatment or efforts, whether the child be an adult or a minor. *Ibid;* see also, *Application of President and Directors of Georgetown College, supra,* 331 *F.2d* at 1008; *Collins* v. *Davis, supra,* 254 *N.Y.S.*2d 666.

Appellant has relied upon the case of *In re Estate of Brooks,* 32 *Ill.* 2d 361, 205 *N.E.2d* 361, 205 *N.E.2d* 435 (*Sup.Ct.* 1955), a decision of the Supreme Court of Illinois which this Court declined to follow in *Heston.* 58 *N.J.* 584. In *Brooks* it was held that the appointment of a guardian to authorize a transfusion of whole blood without notice to the patient or her husband interfered with their basic constitutional rights after the doctor and the hospital had been previously notified directly that, as Jehovah's Witnesses, neither patient nor husband would consent to a blood transfusion. The decision of the Illinois Supreme Court was based upon its finding that there was "no clear and present danger" warranting interference with the religious beliefs of the patient. However, this Court took issue with that rationale in *Heston.* Quoting from Chief Justice Weintraub:

> "It has been suggested that the 'clear and present danger' test, appropriate with respect to free speech, is not the applicable criterion here, and that the relevant question is whether there is a 'compelling State interest' justifying the State's refusal to permit the patient to refuse vital aid. 44 *Texas L. Rev.* 190 (1965). We think the latter test is the correct one..." 58 *N.J.* at 584.

Petitioner also makes an argument for the relief sought based upon the doctrine of right of privacy. This concept, recent in nature as a constitutional doctrine, has been interpreted to reach beyond the factual setting of the right of the individual to be secure in his own home and left alone within the meaning of the Fourth Amendment. *Stanley* v. *Georgia,* 394 *U.S.* 557 (1969); *Homestead* v. *United States,* 277 *U.S.* 438 (1928).

179

This emerging right of privacy was first recognized in *Griswold* v. *Connecticut*, 381 *U.S.* 479, 14 *L.ed* 510 (1965) and followed in *Roe* v. *Wade*, 410 *U.S.* 113, 35 *L.ed.* 147 (1973) and *Eisenstadt* v. *Baird*, 405 *U.S.* 438, 31 *L.ed. 2d* 349 (1972).

In *Griswold* the United States Supreme Court invalidated a Connecticut statute which barred the use of contraceptives by married couples and the distribution of birth control devices and information. Though the decision was based on the right of privacy, it is important to underscore that the Court in *Griswold* did not find a compelling State interest to outweigh the privacy rights of the petitioners. The Court said:

> "Although the Connecticut birth control law obviously encroaches upon a fundamental personal liberty, the State does not show that the law serves any 'subordinating [State] interest which is compelling' or that it is 'necessary ... to the accomplishment of a permissible State policy'. The State, at most, argues that there is some rational relation between this statute in what is admittedly a legitimate subject to State concern—the discouraging of extra-marital relations. It says that preventing the use of birth-control devices by married persons helps prevent the indulgence by some in such extra-marital relations. The rationality of this justification is dubious, particularly in light of the admitted widespread availability to all persons in the State of Connecticut, unmarried as well as married, of birth-control devices for the prevention of disease, as distinguished from the prevention of conception, see *Tilston* v. *Ullman*, 129 *Conn.* 84, 26 *A2d.* 582. But, in any event, it is clear that the State interest in safeguarding marital fidelity can be served by a more discriminately tailored statute, which does not, like the present one, sweep unnecessarily broadly, reaching far beyond the evil sort to be dealt with and intruding upon the privacy of all married couples." 14 *L.ed. 2d* at p.523.

In *Roe* v. *Wade, supra*, 410 *U.S.* 113, the United States Supreme Court invalidated a Texas statute which made it a crime to procure or attempt to procure an abortion except where it was medically advised for the purpose of saving the life of the mother. The Supreme Court held the statute unconstitutional on the ground that it violated a pregnant woman's right of privacy and her right to control her body through the second trimester of pregnancy.

The decisions in both *Griswold* and *Roe* indicate that although privacy is a fundamental right and can be found in the First, Fourth, and Ninth Amendments, it is no more an absolute prerogative than religious freedom or the exercise thereof. See, Cantor, "A Patient's Decision to Decline Life-Saving Medical Treatment: Bodily Integrity Versus the Preservation of Life", 26 *Rutgers Law Review* 228, 241 (1973). Indeed, neither *Griswold* nor *Roe* speak in absolute terms. On the contrary, the decision in *Griswold* rested upon the absence of a compelling State interest to uphold the legislation invading the privacy of citizens of Connecticut, and *Roe* recognized the right of states to define life and to extend legal sanctions at least in the third trimester of pregnancy to protect the lives of their citizens. Courts have recognized in fact certain compelling interests overriding the right to control one's own body. As stated by one authority,

> ". . [T]he constitutional standard used to test the validity of judicially compelled treatment will remain substantially the same whether the patient relies upon the free exercise clause or penumbral guarantees of privacy. That is, to justify an invasion of bodily integrity the State will have to demonstrate that a compelling State interest exists and that it outweighs countervailing interest in individual rights. As previously noted, this entails careful assessment of the asserted State interests and the extent of harm posed to them by upholding the individual privacy and self-determination". *Cantor, supra,* 26 *Rutgers Law Review* at 242.

As indicated in the above discussion, New Jersey along with a majority of jurisdictions has held that there is no constitutional right to choose to die even if one's religious faith ordains his death. Furthermore, even if the right to privacy envisions or permits one to elect death, Karen Quinlan is incapable of doing so because of her present condition. As previously stated, under such circumstances, courts will opt for survival. *In re Osborne,* 294 *A.2d* 372, 374-75 (*D.C. Ct. App.* 1972).

Therefore, in these circumstances it is submitted that the State's interest in preserving life and upholding the sanctity of life outweighs the "familial" constitutional rights asserted by the appellant.

Finally, appellant also has cited the cruel and unusual punishment section of the Eighth Amendment of the United States Constitution and argues that to maintain the operation of the respirator on Karen Quinlan and thereby continue her life inflicts cruel and unusual punishment upon her family. Aside from the obvious issue of standing to assert the doctrine, the argument must fail because this is a civil and not a criminal proceeding. See *Furman* v. *Georgia*, 408 *U.S.* 238, 33 *L.ed 2d.* 164 (1972). Moreover, it can hardly be said that the maintenance of life preserving devices upon a comatose patient is either cruel or unusual.

CONCLUSION

While this Court properly restricts itself to the case at bar, there must be some concern of the consequences of the relief sought since it will open a door leading to problems unknown at present to our law and court system. Other cases equally difficult and heartrending will be presented for determination to this and other courts with similar medical, moral and religious problems without the benefit of legislative guidelines or medical agreement.

What really is at issue is not only the question of whether a respirator should be turned off or treatment continued. The crucial concern is the effect of the ultimate decision upon the sanctity of life and its paramount position as enunciated by judicial decisions of this State such as *John F. Kennedy Memorial Hospital* v. *Heston*. To carve out an exception to the sanctity of life may well lessen its ultimate importance.

Therefore, with the greatest of compassion for the Quinlans and sorrow for the eldest daughter, it is respectfully submitted that the determination of the court below should be affirmed.

Respectfully submitted,

/s/

_____

Donald G. Collester, Jr.
Prosecutor of Morris County

182

In The

SUPREME COURT OF NEW JERSEY

September Term, 1975

Docket No. A-116

IN THE MATTER OF KAREN ANN QUINLAN, AN ALLEGED INCOMPETENT

On Appeal from Judgment in the Superior Court,
Chancery Division, Morris County

Sat Below: Muir, J.S.C.

SUPPLEMENTAL BRIEF ON BEHALF OF DEFENDANT-RESPONDENT ST. CLARE'S HOSPITAL

Theodore E. B. Einhorn
*Attorney for Defendant-
Respondent St. Clare's Hospital*

183

PROCEDURAL HISTORY OF THE CASE

On September 12, 1975, plaintiff filed a Complaint seeking a Judgment declaring Karen Quinlan to be mentally incompetent and granting to plaintiff letters of Guardianship ". . .with the express power of authorizing the discontinuance of all extraordinary means of sustaining the vital processes of his daughter, Karen Ann Quinlan." In addition, an Affidavit of plaintiff was filed in support of this application. Affidavits' of Dr. Robert J. Morse and Dr. Arshad Javed were also filed in support of this application.

On September 17, plaintiff filed a Supplemental Complaint and Supporting Affidavit of plaintiff joining the Prosecutor of Morris County, Dr. Robert Morse, Dr. Arshad Javed and St. Clare's Hospital and sought various types of injunctive relief against the Prosecutor, Dr. Morse, Dr. Javed and St. Clare's Hospital in addition to the original relief sought.

During the course of the non-jury trial held before Judge Muir, the Pretrial Order was amended to allow the Prosecutor to seek a Declaratory Judgment as to the effect of a Judgment granting relief to the plaintiff on the criminal laws of the State of New Jersey, particularly N.J.S.A. 2A:113-1 and 2 and to allow the Attorney for St. Clare's Hospital to seek a Declaratory Judgment declaring that the use of certain criteria by physicians in the determination of death was in accordance with ordinary medical practice.

The Judgment of Judge Muir declared Miss Quinlan to be an incompetent and appointed plaintiff as the Guardian of her property and Mr. Daniel R. Coburn as the Guardian of her person. The Judgment also denied plaintiff's request concerning the authorization to discontinue the respirator as well as the other relief sought by plaintiff and the Prosecutor and Attorney for St. Clare's Hospital.

Plaintiff appeals from the Judgment of Judge Muir and the Supreme Court certified the appeal to the Supreme Court on its own Motion. Plaintiff has also filed a Notice of Motion returnable before Judge Muir on December 12, 1975, to stay that portion of the Judgment appointing Mr. Coburn as Guardian of the person of Miss Quinlan and seeking the appointment of a person other than Mr. Coburn to act as Guardian of the person.

184

STATEMENT OF FACTS

Karen Ann Quinlan (hereafter Miss Quinlan) is a 21 year old woman who is the daughter of plaintiff and his wife, Julia Ann Quinlan. The Quinlan family are members of the Roman Catholic Church and Miss Quinlan was baptized as a Roman Catholic (T335-24 to T337-6).

On April 15, 1975, Miss Quinlan was admitted to Newton Memorial Hospital in an unresponsive state (T250-21 thru 25) and has remained in a coma (T69-23 to T70-2). The history of the events which preceded her admission to the Hospital was fragmentary or sketchy at best (T56-13 and 14). While at Newton Memorial Hospital, a tracheostomy was performed and Miss Quinlan was placed on a respirator in the intensive care unit (T68-17 and T183-18 thru 20). Dr. Robert Morse, a Neurologist, examined Miss Quinlan on April 18, 1975, (T55-10 to 19) and she was transferred to St. Clare's Hospital on April 25, 1975, (T56-13 thru 14). On admission to St. Clare's Hospital, plaintiff executed an authorization for treatment (Included in Exhibit P2). Miss Quinlan was placed in the Intensive Care Unit (I.C.U.) where she still is a patient. Since her entry to I.C.U. Miss Quinlan has been on a MA-1 Respirator (T83-24 and 25).

While initially Miss Quinlan was in a sleep-like unresponsive coma, she now remains in a coma, but one which has states of wakeful unresponsiveness as well as periods of sleep-like unresponsiveness (T70-11 to T72-25 and T80-16 to T82-2). Attempts were made to "*wean*" Miss Quinlan from the respirator by Dr. Javed, a Pulmonary Internist, but these attempts were unsuccessful (T180-3 to T182-17).

Miss Quinlan is alive (T116-24 thru 26, T295-1 thru 5).

During the later part of July, 1975, the plaintiff and Mrs. Quinlan requested Dr. Morse to discontinue the respirator (T154-15 to T157-17). On July 31, 1975, the plaintiff and Mrs. Quinlan executed an authorization concerning the discontinuance of the respirator (Exhibit P6).

Dr. Morse advised the plaintiff and Mrs. Quinlan that he would not accede to their request (T158-2 thru 11). This denial was reaffirmed at a meeting with Hospital officials and the plaintiff and Mrs Quinlan by Drs. Morse and Javed (T160-6 thru 10) and the request was not acceded to by the Hospital (T160-11 thru 16 and T374-7 thru 16).

At the trial, Dr. Morse testified that Miss Quinlan was in a chronic persistent vegetative state (T73-9 thru 12). Dr. Morse also testified that

185

his investigation did not disclose any other cases in which a respirator has been disconnected (T117-10 thru 17) and to do so would be a deviation from medical tradition (T118-6 thru 18).

Dr. Morse further testified that while he believes Miss Quinlan would not reach a level of recovery where she could function on a cognitive basis (T110-11 thru 20) he could not rule out a possibility of some form of recovery (T139-22 to T140-2 and T152-13 to T153-21).

Dr. Korein, a Neurologist, testified on behalf of plaintiff. He stated that Miss Quinlan was not "brain dead". He also testified that, in his opinion, medical treatment which was being administered to Miss Quinlan was "extraordinary", (T273-19 thru 22) but he also testified that others might disagree with this opinion (T299-14 thru 16). Dr. Korein also testified that Miss Quinlan needs the respirator to survive (T321-9 thru 14).

Dr. Sydney Diamond, a Neurologist, testified that the continued use of the respirator would not be an extraordinary measure (T619-21 thru 23) and to discontinue it would be a deviation from standard medical practice (T621-1 thru 18). He also stated that it was necessary to continue Miss Quinlan on the respirator (T619-23 and 24).

Dr. Eugene Loeser, a Neurologist, testified that while in his opinion the possibility of Miss Quinlan recovering to some form of cognitive functioning was remote, he could not rule out such a possibility due to the lack of a definitive history (T568-15 to T569-13).

At the trial, the Papal Allocutio of November 24, 1957, entitled "The Prolongation of Life" was admitted into evidence (Exhibit DD2). Father Trapasso, the family priest, testified as to the counselling he had given to the Quinlan family (T407-5 to T410-14) and that these particular tenets of the Church were optional (T411-2 thru 6). Father Caccavalle, the Chaplain at St. Clare's also testified as to the responses he had given to the Quinlan family when asked as to the position of the Roman Catholic Church if the respirator were discontinued (T442-1 to T443-1).

Mrs. Quinlan testified that Miss Quinlan had told her, while discussing the tragic last dying days of an Aunt, that she (Miss Quinlan) did not want her life extended by the use of extraordinary means (T484-8 to T485-11) and Miss Quinlan had expressed similar feelings while discussing the last days of a family friend (T486-4 thru 20). Similar testimony as to Miss Quinlan's expressed feelings was given by Miss Lori A. Gaffney, a friend of Miss Quinlan (T516-25 to T518-18).

LEGAL ARGUMENT

Point One

The Decision by the Treating Physician Not To Terminate the Respirator Is a Medical Decision Which Is In Accordance with Standards of Ordinary Medical Practice and as such, Should Not Be Interfered With by a Court.

Traditionally, the New Jersey Courts and the Legislature have strenuously respected the patient-physician relationship. Instances of this have been the court-ordered confirmation of the medical profession's doctrine of confidentiality of communications between Patient and physician in *Hague* vs. *Williams*, 37 N.J. 328 (1962) and the legislation codifying this rule in N.J.S.A. 2A:84A-22.2. As further evidence the Court's attention is directed to N.J.S.A. 26:6-63(b) where the Legislature designated the treating physician as the individual to determine the time of death on proposed organ transplants.

In keeping with this respect for the relationship between the patient and the doctor and the status of the practice of medicine, the Courts have limited their review of the type of treatment prescribed by the physician to whether it was in accordance with ordinary medical practice and not to what the Court, in an exercise of its own judgment, determined to be proper medical treatment, *Scheuler* vs. *Strelinger*, 43 N.J. 330 (1964). As stated in that case:

> "The law recognizes that medicine is not an exact science. Consequently, it does not make the physician a guarantor of the cure of his patient. *When he takes a case it imposes upon him the duty to exercise in the treatment of his patient the degree of care, knowledge and skill ordinarily possessed and exercised in similar situations by the average member of the profession practicing in his field.* Failure to have and to use such skill and care toward the patient as a result of which injury or damage results constitutes negligence." (Emphasis supplied). (43 N.J. at 344).

In addition, this Court has recognized the role of hospitals and the medical profession by stating:

> "Hospitals exist to aid the sick and the injured. The medical and nursing professions are consecrated to preserving life. That is their professional creed. To them,

187

a failure to use a simple, established procedure in the circumstances of this case would be malpractice, however, the law may characterize that failure because of the patient's private convictions." *John F. Kennedy Memorial Hospital* vs. *Heston*, 58 N.J. 576 at 582 (1971).

Notwithstanding these strong expressions of judicial and legislative policy, plaintiff seeks relief which would inject the Court into the patient-physician relationship and override the medical treatment decided on by the treating physician—a course of treatment which is in accordance with ordinary medical practice as well as medical tradition and ethics.

It is clear that the decision to continue the respirator is one relating to the medical care and treatment of the patient—it relates to whether or not the patient should live.

Dr. Morse, the treating physician, testified that to terminate the respirator would be in violation of medical tradition and ethics (T118-6 thru 18). Dr. Diamond testified that he agreed and that to terminate the respirator would be in violation of medical tradition and also would be in violation of standard medical practice (T621-1 thru 18). Dr. Diamond simply and succinctly stated ". . .All the evidence points to the fact that she continues to need it. . ." (T619-23 and 24).

Therefore, the Court was faced with the situation where the treating physician, in the exercise of his duty and obligation to his patient to render ordinary medical care, decided that the continued use of the respirator was the proper medical treatment to be rendered to the patient, and on the other hand, with a request by plaintiff to terminate this medical treatment, even though such a termination would have been a violation of medical ethics and the standard of ordinary medical care.

The Court's decision to allow Dr. Morse to continue the medical care he prescribed was correct—especially when to do otherwise would be to violate medical ethics and standards of ordinary medical practice.

In addition to the Court's decision following the judicial and legislative philosophy of a reluctance to intrude into the patient-physician relationship and to practice medicine, the testimony at the trial clearly supports the decision of Dr. Morse as being in accordance with medical tradition and ethics as well as being in accordance with ordinary medical practice.

Realistically, the medical outlook for Miss Quinlan is dim, at best. However, as the result of failure to have a complete and accurate history, none of the doctors could testify that there was no hope of recovery for Miss Quinlan.

188

To have granted the relief sought by plaintiff, would, in fact, be a decision by the Court that it should assume the role of physician and prescribe the treatment which should be given or not be given to the patient. The fact that the medical prognosis for Miss Quinlan is very pessimistic, but not entirely without hope, cannot be the basis for such a ruling. To grant relief on such a basis only compounds and intensifies the medical nature of the decision being made by the Court. Such a decision would require further medical decisions to be made by the Court—what should be done if Miss Quinlan contracts pneumonia or develops an infection?

There is no basis on the record below to hold that the decision reached by the treating physician should not be respected and upheld. A decision to terminate the respirator would constitute a violation of the duty of medical care which the patient is entitled, by law, to receive from Dr. Morse.

Point Two

The Extraordinary Relief Sought by Plaintiff Cannot Be Granted Based on the Statements Made by the Patient Prior to Her Illness Nor the Substituted Judgment of Plaintiff as Guardian

Plaintiff's application was based, in part, upon the fact that his daughter had made certain statements prior to her illness, and also upon the fact that he had determined the discontinuance would be in her best interests. However, neither can validly support the extraordinary relief sought.

The decision in New Jersey closest to the fact situation here is that of *John F. Kennedy Memorial Hospital* vs. *Heston*, 58 N.J. 576 at 582 (1971). In *Heston* this Court was faced with an application of a Hospital to order a patient to accept a blood transfusion which would be needed for a life-saving operation. The patient was a Jehovah's Witness whose religious faith prevented her from accepting transfusion of whole blood. At the time, the patient, a 22 year old adult was not lucid, and her mother opposed the transfusion. This Court granted the relief sought and stated:

"It seems correct to say there is no constitutional right to choose to die. . ." (58 N.J. at 580),

and then went on to state:

"Appellant suggests there is a difference between passively submitting to death and actively seeking it.

189

The distinction may be merely verbal, as it would be if an adult sought death by starvation instead of a drug. If the State may interrupt one mode of self-destruction, it may with equal authority interfere with the other. It is arguably different when an individual, overtaken by illness decides to let it run a fatal course. But unless the medical option itself is laden with the risk of death or of serious infirmity, the State's interest in sustaining life in such circumstances is hardly distinguishable from its interest in the case of suicide." (58 N.J. at 581-582.)

While there are certain differences between the fact situations of *Heston* and the instant case, the public policy enunciated in *Heston* to preserve life is so clear as to deny the relief sought especially when the request is not made by the patient herself.

Even those decisions which honor the request of a patient not to accept certain types of treatment do not aid plaintiff in this application because of the fact that plaintiff cannot speak for herself now at this grave moment of decision. In *In re Osborne,* 294 A. 2d. 372 (D.C. Ct. of App. 1972) the Court denied the application of a hospital to order a patient (Jehovah's Witness) to accept a blood transfusion since the patient was competent and sincerely held the religious convictions preventing the requested blood transfusion. However the Court did state:

". . .Whenever possible it is better for the judge to make a first-hand appraisal of the patient's personal desires and ability for rational choice. In this way the Court can always know, to the extent possible, that the judgment is that of the individual concerned and not that of those who believe, however well-intentioned, that they speak for the person whose life is in the balance. *Thus, where the patient is comatose, or suffering impairment of capacity for choice, it may be better to give weight to the known instinct for survival which can, in a critical situation alter previously held convictions. In such cases it cannot be determined with certainty that a deliberate and intelligent choice has been made.* (Emphasis supplied.) (294 A. 2d. at 374.)

Therefore, even if the *Osborne* case was the law in New Jersey, the plaintiff's application would fail since she is in a comatose state and cannot speak for herself. Under these circumstances "the known instinct for survival" should prevail and it should be deemed that the patient does not reject the life-sustaining treatment. While the fact that Miss Quinlan had previously made statements concerning the discontinuance of "extraordinary means" may have given the Court below pause for consideration, such statements cannot be given the weight of a presently held conviction, assuming such a request could be honored in New Jersey. How is the Court to know whether the declarant has changed her mind since making the statement? Was the statement made purely in the context of the effect of such measures on someone else and not the declarant? And most important, now that the question is the declarant's own life, would she still affirm these feelings if it meant her own death?

Mr. Kutner, the leading proponent of the concept of the "Living Will" has stated that such a document should be reviewed if there are subsequent circumstances which indicate a contrary intention on the part of the patient. Kutner, *The Living Will—Coping with the Historical Event of Death,* 27 *Baylor L. Rev.* 1, at 48 (1975). And assuming that these prior statements are in the nature of an informal "Living Will", how can the Court be satisfied that such statements would represent the patient's decision made after a lucid and conscious review of her present illness.

In addition, can the Court be satisfied that circumstances have not occurred which would indicate a change of mind on the part of the patient.

Therefore, these statements, without a present confirming statement, cannot serve as a basis for plaintiff's request even if such a request could be honored in New Jersey.

As an alternative basis for relief, plaintiff seeks to invoke the doctrine of "Substituted Judgment", and to allow the plaintiff, as the guardian, to act on behalf of his ward since she cannot act for herself, and ask the Court to discontinue the respirator. While this doctrine has only been used in New Jersey in reference to the business affairs of the incompetent, *In re Trott*, 118 N.J. Super., 436, at pp. 440-441 (Ch. Div. 1972), there are out-of-state cases which have allowed a guardian to make decisions which affect the physical integrity of his ward (transplant of kidneys from ward to a close relative). In those cases, the Courts made specific findings that its use would be for the ward's benefit—both physical and mental. *Strunk* vs. *Strunk*, 445 S.W. 2d. 145, (Ky. Ct. App. 1969) and *Hart* vs. *Brown*, 299 Conn. Sup. 368, 289 A. 2d. 386 (1972).

Again, it is clear that plaintiff cannot prevail on the basis of "Substituted Judgment". Such a final and fatal decision cannot and should not be made by a guardian.

". . .A guardian should not be permitted to make

191

such a declaration [Living Will] on behalf of his ward
nor a parent on behalf of his child. . ." Kutner, *The
Living Will—Coping with the Historical Event of
Death*, 27 *Baylor L. Rev.* 1, at 48 (1975).

The basis for the use of this doctrine is that the guardian should be
allowed to act since the Court is satisfied that the ward, as a reasonably
prudent man, would have acted similarly. While the use of this doctrine
can be justifiably resorted to in business situations or situations where
the physical and mental well-being of the ward will be improved, there is
no basis for its use where it will cause the ward to die.

Therefore, the law and the evidence support the decision of the
Court below in rejecting the arguments raised by the plaintiff in this
Point.

Point Three

There Is No Constitutional Basis To Grant
the Relief Sought by Plaintiff.

At the trial, plaintiff contended that since the Quinlan family were
Roman Catholics, a denial of the relief sought would be a violation of the
constitutional rights under the First Amendment of the free and unfet-
tered exercise of their religion.

The law in New Jersey is to the contrary.

This Court in *Heston, supra,* stated:

> "Nor is constitutional right established by adding
> that one's religious faith ordains his death. Religious
> beliefs are absolute, but conduct in pursuance of relig-
> ious beliefs is not wholly immune from governmental
> restraint. . . .(cases cited)", 58 N.J. at 580.

This Court in the *Heston* case went on to quote with approval a portion of the decision in *Reynolds* vs. *United States*, 98 U.S. 145, 25 L. Ed.
244 (1878) where the United States Supreme Court stated:

> ". . . Laws are made for the government of actions,
> and while they cannot interfere with mere religious be-
> lief and opinions, they may with practices. . . ." (25
> L. Ed. at p. 250).

This distinction between religious beliefs (wholly exempt from governmental regulation) and religious practices (subject to governmental
regulation) was followed in *Application of President and Directors of*

Georgetown Col., 331 F.2d 1000 (U.S. Ct. of App., D.C. 1964), petition for rehearing denied *en banc*, 331 F.2d 1010 (1964) where the trial court overruled the objection of a Jehovah's Witness to receiving a whole blood transfusion. The Court stated:

> "If self-homicide is a crime, there is no exception to the law's command for those who believe the crime to be divinely ordained. The Mormon cases in the Supreme Court establish that there is no religious exception to criminal laws and state *obiter* the very example that a religiously inspired suicide attempt would be within the law's authority to prevent. (Cases cited). (331 F.2d at 1009).

Therefore, no matter how sincerely and devoutly held the religious convictions of the Quinlan family, such convictions and beliefs where translated into practice and acts are subject to governmental regulation and under the doctrine of the *Heston, supra,* case, the interest of the State in preserving life must prevail.

The recent decision of the United States Supreme Court in *Wisconsin* v. *Yoder*, 406 U.S. 205, 32 L. Ed. 2d. 15 (1972) does not assist the plaintiff. In that case, the Court declared unconstitutional a Wisconsin statute which required compulsory school attendance through age 16, as it applied to a particular Amish religious sect. The Court in its decision noted:

> "In sum, the unchallenged testimony of acknowledged experts in education and religious history, almost 300 years of consistent practice, and strong evidence of a sustained faith pervading and regulating respondents' entire mode of life support the claim that enforcement of the State's requirement of compulsory formal education after the eighth grade would gravely endanger if not destroy the free exercise of respondents' religious beliefs." (32 L. Ed. 2d. at 27).

and also:

> "This case, of course, is not one in which any harm to the physical or mental health of the child or to the public safety, peace, order, or welfare has been demonstrated or may be properly inferred. The record is to the contrary and any reliance on that theory would find no support in the evidence." (32 L. Ed. 2d. at 33-34).

The testimony at the trial as to the tenets and teachings of the Roman Catholic Church (T411-2 thru 6) would not justify a finding as made in *Yoder, supra* at 27, that the failure of the Court to grant relief sought by plaintiff would ". . .endanger, if not destroy, the free exercise" of plaintiff's religious beliefs. In addition, again contrary to the finding made in *Yoder, supra* at 33-34, the evidence at the trial clearly established that rather than promote "the physical and mental health of the child", the effect would be the opposite.

And, finally, there is no evidence of the religious beliefs presently held by Miss Quinlan.

As further justification for the relief sought, plaintiff contended that, inherently, the family had the right to make this decision and also that the right of privacy included the right of the family and Miss Quinlan to discontinue the respirator.

The cases which support the constitutional right of a family, as a family unit, to make familial decisions, dealt with situations where it was eminently clear that the decisions were traditionally made by a family and served the best interests of a family and its members. See *Meyers* vs. *Nebraska*, 262 U.S. 390, 76 L. Ed. 1042, (1923) upholding the constitutional right of a family to determine which subjects a child should select in public school and *Pierce* vs. *Society of Sisters,* 268 U.S. 510, 69 L. Ed. 1070 (1925) upholding the constitutional right of a family to determine where to enroll a child in school.

The constitutional right of a family to make certain decisions as to its children does not extend to decisions which would have the fateful implications which have been testified to in this case. The constitutional rights enunciated in the *Meyer* and *Pierce, supra,* cases were to be exercised to improve the family unit—not to have the result requested.

The right of privacy as enunciated and developed by the United States Supreme Court is not based on a particular article or section of the Federal Constitution, but is drawn and developed from a review and consideration of the entire document as a whole. *Griswold* vs. *Connecticut*, 381 U.S. 479, 14 L. Ed. 2d 510 (1965). However, the United States Supreme Court has also recognized that:

> ". . . The Court's decisions recognizing a right of privacy also acknowledges that some state regulation in areas protected by that right is inappropriate. . . ." *Roe* vs. *Wade*, 410 U.S. 113 at 153, 35 L. Ed. 2d. 147 at 177 (1972).

Therefore, the Right of Privacy, if such a right exists in the context used here, is not an absolute one and the state has the right to regulate such a "right". As previously noted in the *J.F.K.* case, *supra,* the State of New Jersey has a strong public policy to preserve life and this policy would prevail over the assertion of such a right, if such a right exists at all. In addition, the Court is unable to determine what the wishes of Miss Quinlan are as to the exercise of this alleged constitutional right.

Plaintiff also contends that to refuse his application would be a violation of prohibitions against "cruel and unusual punishment" of the Eighth Amendment. However, it is clear that the prohibitions in the Eighth Amendment against "cruel and unusual punishment" were directed ". . .specifically at the exercise of legislative power". *Furman* vs. *Georgia*, 408 U.S. 238 at 263, 33 L. Ed. 2d. 246 at 363 (1972).

In conclusion, there are no constitutional rights which would support the request of plaintiff and assuming such rights to exist, Miss Quinlan is unable to make a decision as to whether she wishes to exercise these "rights" in making this fateful and final decision.

CONCLUSION

The tragic situation of Miss Quinlan and her family cannot be disputed. The sympathy and compassion of St. Clare's Hospital is extended to the entire Quinlan family.

However, it is respectfully submitted that for the foregoing reasons the decision of the Court below should be affirmed.

Respectfully submitted,

THEODORE E. B. EINHORN
Attorney for Defendant-Respondent
St. Clare's Hospital

In The

SUPREME COURT OF NEW JERSEY

September Term, 1975

Docket No. A-116

IN THE MATTER OF KAREN ANN QUINLAN, AN ALLEGED INCOMPETENT

ON APPEAL FROM JUDGMENT OF THE SUPERIOR COURT OF
NEW JERSEY, CHANCERY DIVISION (MORRIS COUNTY)
SAT BELOW: HONORABLE ROBERT MUIR, JR., J.S.C.

BRIEF FOR NEW JERSEY CATHOLIC CONFERENCE, AMICUS CURIAE

Edward J. Leadem,
106 Bull Run Road,
Trenton, New Jersey 08638.
*Attorney for New Jersey Catholic
Conference, Amicus Curiae.*

BRIEF FOR NEW JERSEY CATHOLIC CONFERENCE
AMICUS CURIAE

Introductory Statement

The procedural history and the opinion of the Court below are set forth in the brief and appendix of the appellant. This *amicus* accepts them for the purposes of its own brief. The facts of record in this case and the issues raised on appeal are set forth in the brief of appellants and this *amicus* accepts them for purposes of its own brief.

On December 19, 1975 this *amicus* filed a Motion for Leave to File a Brief *Amicus Curiae*, with supporting affidavit.

On December 31, 1975 this Court granted the application of the New Jersey Catholic Conference for Leave to File a Brief *Amicus Curiae*.

The Interest of this Amicus

The New Jersey Catholic Conference is an organization approved by the Catholic Bishops of New Jersey as an instrument in the promotion of interdiocesan cooperation and coordination of Catholic representation on statewide issues in the State of New Jersey.

It is organized to give witness to spiritual values in public affairs and to provide corporate Catholic service to the statewide community.

On November 1, 1975 Bishop Lawrence B. Casey of the Diocese of Paterson issued a Statement in which the position of the Bishop of Paterson on the use of extraordinary means to sustain the life of Karen Ann Quinlan, is set forth.

The Statement of Bishop Casey reflects the uniform position of all the Catholic Bishops of New Jersey and, since there is an overlap in the disciplines of theology, law and medicine as applied to the facts in the instant case, this *Amicus* sets forth the full Statement of Bishop Lawrence B. Casey on the application of the Church's teaching in the case of Karen Ann Quinlan.

198

STATEMENT OF BISHOP LAWRENCE B. CASEY
CONCERNING KAREN ANN QUINLAN

The Position of The Bishop of Paterson on the Use of Extraordinary Means To Sustain the Life of Karen Ann Quinlan

"It is in the face of death that the riddle of human existence becomes most acute."[1] These words of the Second Vatican Council have a special meaning to the family of Karen Ann Quinlan and, indeed, to a host of people who have come to know about her tragic condition. Her parents have made a painful and difficult decision, to request the discontinuance of the means sustaining the continuation of her life; it is a decision which elicits the sympathy and concern of many people and which now demands the attention of the courts. It has been with the competent advice of their pastor, the Rev. Thomas J. Trapasso, that the family has made this decision, and it is incumbent upon me, as Bishop of Paterson, to comment on the moral correctness of that decision in the light of the Catholic Church's teaching.

I.

BASIC ASSUMPTIONS

1. The Bishop of Paterson has the authority and competence to present the Church's teachings in this matter.

The local bishop has both the responsibility and the right to witness to the divine and Catholic faith by proclaiming the teaching of the Church as it is held and taught by Peter's successors and his fellow bishops; and he has a similar responsibility and right to apply that teaching in a particular instance as a matter of faith and morals to be held and practiced by the people he serves.[2]

A primary office of the bishop as pastor of souls in the diocese committed to his care by the Church's supreme authority is to be within the territory of his competence the principal dispenser of the mysteries of God and the one called upon to teach them with the authority of Christ.[3]

It is with this authority and competence that I, as Bishop of Paterson, accept the responsibility and right to apply the teachings of the Catholic Church to the request for permission to discontinue the use of a respirator as an extraordinary means of sustaining the life of Karen Ann Quinlan, which request is made by her loving parents and our beloved brother and sister in Christ, Joseph and Julia Quinlan, faithful members of the Parish of Our Lady of the Lake, Mount Arlington, New Jersey, within the Diocese of Paterson.

2.   Karen Ann Quinlan is alive.

The verification of the fact of death in a particular case cannot be deduced from any religious or moral principle, and, under this aspect, does not fall within the competence of the Church.[4] Therefore, we appeal to the traditional medical standards for determining death; by these standards, Karen Ann Quinlan is assumed to be alive. The same assumption is deduced from the proposed standards of the "Ad Hoc Committee of the Harvard Medical School to Examine the Definition of Brain Death", in their report issued in 1968.[5] In this case, then, from the viewpoint of the Church, the "brain death" issue is a secondary one.

3.   What is being requested by Joseph and Julia Quinlan
      is not euthanasia.

Karen Ann Quinlan's parents have requested the termination of a medical procedure which is an extraordinary means of treatment. The Ethical and Religious Directives for Catholic Health Care Facilities, approved in November 1971 at the annual meeting of the National Conference of Catholic Bishops, states: "The failure to supply the ordinary means of preserving life is equivalent to euthanasia."[6] It also states: "Neither the physician nor the patient is obliged to use extraordinary means."[7] Since the Bishops in these directives forbid **all** forms of euthanasia, they thus teach that non-use of extraordinary means does not constitute euthanasia. Pope Pius XII in discussing the case of a patient in deep unconsciousness, a case, moreover, considered hopeless in the opinion of the competent doctor, said that the discontinuance of a respirator as an extraordinary means is not to be considered euthanasia in any way. "There is not involved here a case of direct disposal of the life of a patient, nor of euthanasia in any way; this would never be licit."[8]

Euthanasia or "mercy killing" may be described as the deliberate and direct causing of the painless death of a human being who is helpless or who, for whatever reason, is deemed unable to live a so-called meaningful life. The Church teaches that: "Euthanasia is immoral and unlawful because it is intrinsically evil and entails a direct violation of man's right to life and of God's supreme dominion over His creatures."[9] A person does have the ethical right to die peacefully and doctors and family do have the ethical right to allow such a death to happen in accord with the presumed will of the patient, when there is no reasonable hope for some recovery. However, there is never a right to take the life of a patient or to comply with a family or patient's request that the patient be allowed to take his own life. This would be contrary to divine law and contrary to the obligation of the state and society in general to uphold and defend the right to life from direct attack.

4. The possibility of God's intervention in the recovery
    of health is not and cannot be precluded.

God's intervention in human life takes many forms. He can do all things. He can and does work through His creation, and, in particular, through the knowledge and expertise of His people. These are interventions in accord with nature. For this reason we pray for those who undergo surgery and medical treatment. He can and does also work beyond the powers of nature, in which cases He does not need the intervention of man-made machines. He can restore life and health without them.

II.
GENERAL TEACHING OF THE CHURCH ON THE PRESERVATION OF LIFE

Human life is God's great and first gift to each of us. We must love life and work to preserve it. When there is hope for returning a person from the threshold of death to a measure of recovery we should work to preserve God's gift of life.[10]

The Church further teaches that human life does not end with death. "The Church has been taught by divine revelation, and herself firmly teaches, that man has been created by God for a blissful purpose beyond the reach of earthly misery," and, further, "God has called man and still calls him so that with his entire being he might be joined to Him in an endless sharing of a divine life beyond all corruption."[11]

As for the methods to be used in preserving human life, Pope Pius XII has laid down the principle: "Natural reason and Christian morals say that man (and whoever is entrusted with the task of taking care of his fellowman) has the right and the duty in case of serious illness to take the necessary treatment for the preservation of life and health." The Holy Father states further: "But normally one is held to use only ordinary means—according to circumstances of persons, places, times, and culture—that is to say, means that do not involve any grave burden for oneself or another."[12]

The distinction between "ordinary" and "extraordinary" means has been expressed in the 1974 document entitled "Respect Life", prepared by the Family Life Division of the United States Catholic Conference, and issued in the name of the National Conference of Catholic Bishops' Committee for Population and Pro-Life Activities:

• Distinguishing between "ordinary" and "extraordinary" means has become commonplace in discussing the obligation to prolong life when a person is irremediably ill and death is certain.

• Citing Pope Pius XII for his assertion of the principle, moralists and ethicians hold that we must take all ordinary means to preserve life, even if there is little hope of recovery. We are not obliged to use extraordinary means to prolong life when recovery is no longer possible, although we may do so.

• Ordinary means are described as "all medicines, treatments and operations which offer a reasonable hope of benefit for the patient and can be obtained and used without excessive pain, expense, or other inconveniences."

• By extraordinary means are meant "all medicines, treatments and operations which cannot be obtained or used without excessive pain, expense, or other inconveniences, or which, if used, would not offer a reasonable hope of benefit."[13]

The "Respect Life" document quoting the Rev. Gerald Kelly[14] does qualify the elements of pain and expense, but accepts the over-all criteria as working principles for the determination as to which means are ordinary and which means are extraordinary.

Pope Pius XII in his address of November 24, 1957 to anesthesiologists, quoted above, dealt with a specific question stated as follows: "Does the anesthesiologist have the right, or is he bound, in all cases of deep unconsciousness, even in those that are considered to be completely hopeless in the opinion of the competent doctor, to use modern artificial respiration apparatus, even against the will of the family?"[15]

In answering the question the Holy Father makes several points:

1. In ordinary cases the doctor has the right to act in this manner, but is not bound to do so unless this is the only way of fulfilling another certain moral duty.

2. The doctor, however, has no right independent of the patient. He can act only if the patient explicitly or implicitly, directly or indirectly gives him the permission.

3. The treatment as described in the question constitutes extraordinary means of preserving life and so there is no obligation to use them nor to give the doctor permission to use them.

4. The rights and duties of the family depend on the presumed will of the unconscious patient if he or she is of legal age, and the family, too, is bound to use only ordinary means.

5. This case is not to be considered euthanasia in any way; that would never be licit. The interruption of attempts at resuscitation, even when it causes the arrest of circulation, is not more than an indirect cause of the cessation of life, and we must apply in this case the principle of double effect.

III.

APPLICATION OF THE CHURCH'S TEACHING TO THE CASE OF KAREN ANN QUINLAN

Competent medical testimony has established that Karen Ann Quinlan has no reasonable hope of recovery from her comatose state by the use of any available medical procedures. The continuance of mechanical (cardiorespiratory) supportive measures to sustain continuation of her body functions and her life constitute extraordinary means of treatment. *Therefore, the decision of Joseph and Julia Quinlan to request the discontinuance of this treatment is, according to the teachings of the Catholic Church, a morally correct decision.*

IV.

THE INTERRELATIONSHIP OF THE THREE DISCIPLINES OF THEOLOGY, LAW AND MEDICINE

The right to a natural death is one outstanding area in which the disciplines of theology, medicine and law overlap; or, to put it in another way, it is an area in which these three disciplines convene.

Medicine with its combination of advanced technology and professional ethics is both able and inclined to prolong biological life. Law with its felt obligation to protect the life and freedom of the individual seeks to assure each person's right to live out his human life until its natural and inevitable conclusion. Theology with its acknowledgment of man's dissatisfaction with biological life as the ultimate source of joy, proclaims the individual's call to an endless sharing in a divine life beyond all

203

corruption. It also defends the sacredness of human life and defends it from all direct attacks.

These disciplines do not conflict with one another, but are necessarily conjoined in the application of their principles in a particular instance such as that of Karen Ann Quinlan. Each must in some way acknowledge the other without denying its own competence. The civil law is not expected to assert a belief in eternal life; nor, on the other hand, is it expected to ignore the right of the individual to profess it, and to form and pursue his conscience in accord with that belief. Medical science is not authorized to directly cause natural death; nor, however, is it expected to prevent it when it is inevitable and all hope of a return to an even partial exercise of human life is irreparably lost. Religion is not expected to define biological death; nor, on its part, is it expected to relinquish its responsibility to assist man in the formation and pursuit of a correct conscience as to the acceptance of natural death when science has confirmed its inevitability beyond any hope other than that of preserving biological life in a merely vegetative state.

The common concern of the three disciplines as they focus on the situation of Karen Ann Quinlan is that of life and death. This fact demonstrates the need for theology, medicine and law to develop an even greater interrelationship in an open, continuing and growing dialogue on the profound issues arising from the Biological Revolution, a designation aptly applied to the age in which we live.

V.
CONCERNS FOR THE FUTURE—KAREN ANN QUINLAN'S CASE AS A PRECEDENT

Since many are concerned that the decision in the case of Karen Ann Quinlan will establish a precedent, it is necessary to look beyond the immediate decision regarding this young woman.

What may be the overriding issue in this case is whether society is prepared to distinguish in law and in practice between the non-obligation to use extraordinary means of treatment in cases that are determined by competent medical authority to be hopeless, and euthanasia, so-called mercy killing. Can society understand and accept the distinction between the right to die a natural death peacefully, and the call for a right to take another's life or the life of oneself even for reasons of compassion?

The first alternative may in fact represent the status quo at least in some practicing medical circles, and it does not in itself undermine society's reverence for life. The other alternative—euthanasia, again, even when advocated by compassionately motivated people—does undermine society's reverence for life. This has been the admirable and traditional position of both the state and the medical profession in our country. The taking of life even for allegedly noble motives is a first step toward barbarism. The horrifying euthanasia statutes of Nazi Germany earlier in this very century bear witness to this.

In the present public discussion of the case of Karen Ann Quinlan it has been brought out that responsible people involved in medical care, patients and families have exercised the freedom to terminate or withhold certain treatments as extraordinary means in cases judged to be terminal, i.e., cases which hold no realistic hope for some recovery, in accord with the expressed or implied intentions of the patients themselves. To whatever extent this has been happening it has been without sanction in civil law. Those involved in such actions, however, have ethical and theological literature to guide them in their judgments and actions. Furthermore, such actions have not in themselves undermined society's reverence for the lives of sick and dying people.

It is both possible and necessary for society to have laws and ethical standards which provide freedom for decisions, in accord with the expressed or implied intentions of the patient, to terminate or withhold extraordinary treatment in cases which are judged to be hopeless by competent medical authorities, without at the same time leaving an opening for euthanasia. Indeed, to accomplish this, it may simply be required that courts and legislative bodies recognize the present standards and practices of many people engaged in medical care who have been doing what the parents of Karen Ann Quinlan are requesting authorization to have done for their beloved daughter.

In all of this we pray for God's guidance of our society in its efforts to appreciate the precious gift of human life, and for His blessings upon the family of Karen Ann Quinlan and of all those in similar circumstances who must make their judgments based on mutual love. Finally, we pray for Karen herself that the Lord Who has brought her into the hearts and minds of more people than perhaps she ever dreamed, will bestow on her the happiness which is the goal and purpose of all mankind.

†**Lawrence B. Casey**
Bishop of Paterson

November 1, 1975
Feast of All Saints
Paterson, New Jersey

FRANK J. RODIMER
Chancellor

205

— FOOTNOTES TO BISHOP CASEY'S STATEMENT —

[1]Con. Vat. II, "The Church Today", par. 18. (This and following translations are in *The Documents of Vatican II*, ed. W. Abbott, The American Press, 1966.)

[2]Con. Vat. II, "The Church", par. 25.

[3]cf. Con. Vat. II, "The Bishops' Pastoral Office in the Church", par. 15, and "The Church", par. 25.

[4]Address of Pope Pius XII to an international Congress of Anesthesiologists, Nov. 24, 1957. AAS XXXXIX (1957). (Translation from original French, *The Pope Speaks,* Spring, 1958, Vol. IV, n.4, pp. 393-398).

[5]cf. discussion of Report "A Definition of Irreversible Coma" in "The Eerie Need to Redefine Death", *America,* Sept. 27, 1975, p. 164.

[6]Article 28, "Ethical and Religious Directives for Catholic Health Facilities", Department of Health Affairs, United States Catholic Conference, Washington, D.C. 20005. 1971.

[7]*idem.*

[8]Address of Pope Pius XII, *supra.*

[9]"Euthanasia", *New Catholic Encyclopedia,* Vol. V, p. 639, Washington, D.C., 1967.

[10]cf. Chancery Statement, Diocese of Paterson, Sept. 16, 1975, reported in "The Beacon", Paterson diocesan newspaper, Vol. IX, n.34, p.21. September 18, 1975.

[11]Con. Vat. II, "The Church Today", par. 18.

[12]Address of Pope Pius XII, *supra.*

[13]"Respect Life", Family Life Division, United States Catholic Conference, Washington, D.C. 20005. 1974, p.33.

[14]"The Duty to Preserve Life", *Theological Studies* 12:550. 1951.

[15]Address of Pope Pius XII, *supra.*

CONCLUSION

There are profound ethical considerations involved in the instant case.

The Bishop of Paterson has the authority and competence to present the Church's teaching in this matter, as a matter of faith and morals to be held and practiced by the people he serves.

All of the Catholic Bishops of New Jersey have adopted the position of Bishop Casey as contained in his Statement, as the uniform position of said Catholic Bishops in the State of New Jersey.

For these reasons, this *Amicus* respectfully urges this Court to accept the Statement of Bishop Casey as setting forth the application of the teaching of the Catholic Church to the request of the parents of Karen Ann Quinlan for permission to discontinue the use of a respirator as an extraordinary means of sustaining the life of Karen Ann Quinlan.

Respectfully submitted,

EDWARD J. LEADEM
*Attorney for New Jersey Catholic
Conference, Amicus Curiae*

Dated: January 12, 1976.

In The

SUPREME COURT OF NEW JERSEY

September Term, 1975

Docket No. A-116

IN THE MATTER OF KAREN ANN QUINLAN,
AN ALLEGED INCOMPETENT

TRANSCRIPT OF PROCEEDINGS

Trenton, New Jersey
January 26, 1976

BEFORE:

RICHARD J. HUGHES, *Chief Justice of the State of New Jersey*
ROBERT L. CLIFFORD, *Associate Justice*
WORRALL F. MOUNTAIN, *Associate Justice*
MORRIS PASHMAN, *Associate Justice*
SIDNEY M. SCHREIBER, *Associate Justice*
MARK A. SULLIVAN, *Associate Justice*
MILTON B. CONFORD, *J.S.C. t/a*

APPEARANCES:

PAUL W. ARMSTRONG, ESQ., *801 Lindsley Drive, Morristown, New Jersey, on behalf of Appellant Joseph Quinlan.*

JAMES M. CROWLEY, ESQ., *of the New York Bar, on behalf of Appellant Joseph Quinlan.*

DANIEL R. COBURN, ESQ., *20 Park Place, Morristown, New Jersey, 07960, on behalf of Guardian Ad Litem Thomas R. Curtin, Esq.*

WILLIAM F. HYLAND, ESQ., *Attorney General of the State of New Jersey, State House Annex, Trenton, New Jersey 08625, on behalf of Respondent State of New Jersey and Office of the Attorney General.*

DONALD G. COLLESTER, JR., ESQ., *Morris County Prosecutor, Morristown, New Jersey, on behalf of the State of New Jersey.*

ROBERT PORZIO, ESQ., *Porzio, Bromberg & Newman, One Washington Street, Morristown, New Jersey 07960, on behalf of Robert J. Morse, M.D., and Arshad Javed, M.D.*

THEODORE E.B. EINHORN, ESQ., *Morristown, New Jersey, on behalf of St. Clare's Hospital.*

PROCEEDINGS

CHIEF JUSTICE HUGHES: The Court will hear argument in the case A116, *In the Matter of Karen Quinlan.*
Mr. Armstrong?

ORAL ARGUMENT OF PAUL W. ARMSTRONG, ESQ., ON BEHALF OF APPELLANT JOSEPH QUINLAN

MR. ARMSTRONG: Honorable Chief Justice and Associate Justices of the New Jersey Supreme Court, learned counsel, and the members of the Quinlan family:

I am privileged to stand before this highest tribunal of our State on behalf of the Quinlan family. While through the technical vehicle of procedure, these arguments are advanced on behalf of Joseph Quinlan only, it is in fact the right of the entire Quinlan family, including Ann, Karen Ann, that we set forth, for it is the love, faith, and courage unique to a father and mother, a sister and brother, the love, faith, and courage unique to the Quinlan family that brings us here today.

Preliminarily I would at this point respectfully move for the admission of Mr. James M. Crowley of the New York Bar, *pro hoc vici,* for the purpose of arguing on behalf of the Quinlan family as he has ably done in the lower courts and in the brief filed in the instant proceedings.

THE COURT: The Court will be glad to hear him.

MR. ARMSTRONG: Thank you, Your Honor.

The arguments to be advanced on behalf of the Appellant have been divided as follows: I will set forth on behalf of the Quinlan family the guardian aspect of the argument, the probative weight to be accorded to Karen Ann's prior statements, and the privacy argument.

THE COURT: As a preliminary matter, Mr. Armstrong, do you concede that this young woman is alive? I notice that in the pretrial, the amendment to the pretrial order was simply to the effect that you conceded that under existing definitions, legal definitions of death, that she was alive. Now are you yielding on the argument that we should not amend, or should amend, the definition of death?

211

MR. ARMSTRONG: As far as we're concerned, Mr. Justice, the definition of death is irrelevant to the argument that we're setting forth.

THE COURT: In other words, you agree that this woman is alive?

MR. ARMSTRONG: That's correct.

THE COURT: And you are not asking this Court to change the common law definition of death?

MR. ARMSTRONG: That's correct.

THE COURT: Even though she's in a persistent vegetative state, as I understand?

MR. ARMSTRONG: That is correct.

THE COURT: And even though she may not ever regain—or the evidence, as I understand, is to the effect that she will not regain any cognitive powers?

MR. ARMSTRONG: That's correct.
Nor will she recover from this state.

THE COURT: So that you state therefore that somebody who will be, in effect, a vegetable the rest of her existence, if you want to put it that way, is not dead.

MR. ARMSTRONG: That's correct.

THE COURT: You say, "nor will she recover"?

MR. ARMSTRONG: That's correct.

THE COURT: There is nothing in the record to support that definitive conclusion. Pessimism runs rampant. There are other observations made, but who is there who unequivocally says what you just said—unequivocally states it, not dances around it?

MR. ARMSTRONG: Well let me see if we understand what I just said. What I said—I don't think I made myself clear—she is terminally ill; that she is in a persistent vegetative state; and that she will die within a year. This is adduced from Dr. Morse's testimony, that she will—

THE COURT: This is your inference. He didn't say that.

MR. ARMSTRONG: Yes, he did.

THE COURT: The way you're saying it?

THE COURT: Did the trial judge find that as a matter of fact?

MR. ARMSTRONG: No, he didn't find any in—in relation to the period of time that she—how long she would live.

THE COURT: That's right.

212

THE COURT: Well I think he did.

Didn't he find, on page 72 of your appendix, that her condition is categorized as irreversible and the chance of returning to discriminate functioning remote? Most assuredly there is implicit in that, is there not, a further finding with respect to how long she will live? That is, in terms of it likewise being a remote proposition?

MR. ARMSTRONG: That's not necessarily so. What he was addressing himself to there, Justice, was the fact that she is in a persistent vegetative state, that she will remain in a coma for an extended period of time. What I am talking about is death. Dr. Morse advised through his testimony that she will die within a year. She may die tomorrow; she may die within a month; but the outside perimeter is a year that we're talking about.

THE COURT: But clearly your position is that the definition of death is not part of your case.

MR. ARMSTRONG: That's correct.

THE COURT: Specifically, Mr. Armstrong, what do you ask this Court to do?

MR. ARMSTRONG: We ask this Court on behalf of the Quinlan family that an individual who is terminally ill in a persistent vegetative state, that they can request the suspension of futile medical measures in order to allow the natural processes of the body to take place. That's what we're advancing.

THE COURT: I don't understand that answer at all.

MR. ARMSTRONG: What we're saying is: Look, if I'm terminally ill—

THE COURT: Are you asking this Court to direct something?

MR. ARMSTRONG: No, Your Honor. What we're asking is to determine whether or not an individual exercising his constitutional right to make that decision, whether or not that would be licit. We're not asking this Court to enjoin anyone to do anything against those particular beliefs which they might hold.

THE COURT: In other words, you're seeking a declaratory judgment.

MR. ARMSTRONG: With reference to the Homicide Statute as advanced by the Prosecutor.

THE COURT: No. In addition to that, aren't you seeking—what you just stated seems to me to be nothing more than asking for a declaratory judgment.

MR. ARMSTRONG: That's correct.

THE COURT: May I see if I understand you? Are you asking the Court to declare that a request by your client of the doctors to terminate this apparatus is a non-actionable thing? That is, it would meet no civil or criminal adverse consequences? Is that what you're asking?

MR. ARMSTRONG: We're asking, first, that the Court determine whether or not an individual can exercise, pursuant to his constitutional rights, this type of decision. If the Court deems it licit, I feel that—

THE COURT: Now wait. You're not getting to what concerns me, nor do I think to what concerns Justice Sullivan. It would seem to me that there's nothing to prevent your clients from talking to the doctors about terminating this situation. Now you're asking the Court to declare that if they do ask the doctors to terminate this situation, no adverse criminal or civil consequences will attach. Is that what you're asking?

MR. ARMSTRONG: That's correct. That's one aspect of it. I think—

THE COURT: And what else are you—you're asking the Court to declare that—and are you asking for the Court to declare anything else?

MR. ARMSTRONG: Only to recognize that the individuals have a constitutional right to make this type of decision.

THE COURT: Well that's just an abstract statement. We're concerned in terms of an order. You're not asking the Court to order the doctors to terminate the apparatus?

MR. ARMSTRONG: Absolutely not. We're not asking this Court to order the doctors to do anything which they may feel contrary to their beliefs.

THE COURT: You're simply asking the Court to declare that if your client asked the doctors to terminate life, there will be no civil or criminal consequences to attach to that?

MR. ARMSTRONG: That's correct.

THE COURT: Well it goes beyond that, because they have asked, and the doctor has taken the position, that he will not medically authorize that action. Aren't you really asking us to overrule the doctor's decision?

MR. ARMSTRONG: No. What we're asking, and I believe a fair categorization of the doctor's testimony, is that while he feels that he may be incapable of doing it, there are others who would not feel incapable of doing it. What essentially we are asking for is that if the physicians don't feel that they are capable of doing this, in this instance Dr. Morse and Dr. Javed, that they not interfere with a physician who would be wont to grant the request of the Quinlan family.

THE COURT: To a physician, another physician other than the two treating Miss Quinlan?

MR. ARMSTRONG: That's correct.

THE COURT: What will you do, bring in a third who will say that he agrees with what you want him to do? Is that what you're saying to us?

MR. ARMSTRONG: We will do what is normally done in a physician-patient relationship. That is, if the doctor and the patient are at loggerheads, this particular physician, we would request that these particular physicians resign and ask to bring in another physician.

THE COURT: And have him exercise the discretion which comports with your way of thinking.

MR. ARMSTRONG: That's correct.

THE COURT: Well has your client asked, or requested these doctors to get off the case?

MR. ARMSTRONG: No, he has not—they have not.

THE COURT: Well I don't follow you then. If your doctors—if you haven't asked the doctors to get off the case, why are you here at all?

MR. ARMSTRONG: Well we're here I think, Your Honor, I think a fair characterization of the doctor's testimony is they are not standing before this Court and saying: No, we're not going to do this, unequivocally. They are saying: Please give us some guidance, like everyone else that's appearing before you. We don't know. Help us to determine whether or not there's going to be any legal ramifications of our action. We would like to do it. However, there are no standards for us to follow.

THE COURT: Where did they say that?

THE COURT: They don't say that, do they?

THE COURT: Where did the doctors say they'd "like to do it"?

MR. ARMSTRONG: I think Dr. Diamond in his testimony advised, as pointed out in the Prosecutor's brief, that there are individuals who may wish to follow this. However—

THE COURT: I thought for a moment you were talking about the treating physicians. I understood you to say that these treating physicians were in a position of having asserted that they would like to do it, but felt constrained because of a variety of things, not the least of which was good medical practice by Mr. Armstrong.

MR. ARMSTRONG: I think I can cite you to Dr. Morse's testimony, if I may just take a moment to—

THE COURT: The legal position of both Dr. Morse and Dr. Javed is quite to the contrary, is it not?

MR. ARMSTRONG: I don't perceive Dr. Morse's and Dr. Javed's testimony or position as to be totally contrary. I think they are asking, like all of us, for guidance from the Court.

THE COURT: Now would you come back and point to Dr. Morse's testimony?

MR. ARMSTRONG: Yes.

I think it would be transcript 118—118-12, in response to a question. May I read it?

THE COURT: Read it, would you please?

MR. ARMSTRONG: I'll read the question:

> "Q. In other words, you are saying that according to accepted medical practice that Karen's medical condition at the present time would not meet the medical standards for permitting her life to be shortened by the removal of the respirator or whatever else would be essential to the continuation of life?"

This is the Doctor's response:

> "A. Well, I would have to qualify my response to that. Remember, I think Mr. Einhorn stated that, you know, perhaps some other criteria will have to be positively laid out, that the medical profession along with the legal profession can make some sort of judgment as to how to handle a chronic case, especially with all these new modalities of support. Right now she does not meet the criteria. That's correct."

THE COURT: Now wait a minute. That's your—that portion that you read me suggests to you that Dr. Morse would like to remove the life-sustaining members?

MR. ARMSTRONG: I believe so. It's an extraordinary—

THE COURT: I'll have to read it again. I did not derive that meaning at all.

MR. ARMSTRONG: Okay. Would you like the question also, Mr. Justice?

THE COURT: The answer, I suspect, is somewhat more significant, but suppose you tell me the question for his answer.

MR. ARMSTRONG: All right. The question is:

> "Q. In other words, you are saying that according to

216

the accepted medical practice that Karen's condition at the present time would not meet the medical standards for permitting her life to be shortened by the removal of the respirator or whatever else would be essential to a continuation of her life."

Dr. Morse's response was—

THE COURT: You read me the response, didn't you?

MR. ARMSTRONG: I'm about to read it now, yes.

THE COURT: I thought you did.

MR. ARMSTRONG: No, that was the question.

THE COURT: Well didn't you read the answer before?

MR. ARMSTRONG: Sure. Yes.

THE COURT: I recall the answer, and I confess at this time that reading the question does not shed any more light on what I thought the answer was, than I originally thought.

THE COURT: Mr. Armstrong, is it not fundamentally correct that in order for you to survive in this action, would it prevail that in the final analysis you want us to declare that the Quinlans have a constitutional right to make this decision? Must we not hold in that fashion in order for you to prevail in this case?

MR. ARMSTRONG: There is another vehicle.

THE COURT: What is it?

MR. ARMSTRONG: If you determine that in the common law best interests of Karen, looking to her set-forth ideals, values, and outlook towards life, that it would be in her best interests to terminate the life-support system at this point, the Court doesn't even have to address itself to the constitutional arguments.

THE COURT: Absent that, however, we must direct our attention to the constitutional right of the Quinlans to make this decision, the decision being to terminate the life of Karen. Isn't that true?

MR. ARMSTRONG: I—there's an additional element, Mr. Justice, and that is that we're asserting on behalf of Karen her individual right to make this decision, as manifest in her prior statement. So we've got—it's coming under a two-prong attack: Both the family's, and Karen's, right.

THE COURT: Yes. Well let's not get into the evidential problem of Karen's statements in her lifetime. That's something else. But just staying with my question: Now other than that fact, again it is correct that

217

we will be confronted with that question, the question from your standpoint being the constitutional right of the Quinlans to make this decision, this decision being to terminate the life of Karen. That is the problem that you're giving us. That's the question, and that's something that hopefully a decision will be forthcoming on that score.

MR. ARMSTRONG: That's correct.

THE COURT: Mr. Armstrong, I gather from your last few answers to questions, that in answer to my previous question you're asking for more than simply the Court's declaration that no adverse consequences will attach to the Quinlans by their making this request. You are also asking the Court to say that no adverse consequences will attach to the physicians if they accede to the Quinlan's request?

MR. ARMSTRONG: Absolutely.

THE COURT: Then in effect you're asking the Court to make a determination that in this case it is legal and without any actionable consequences for the physicians to make a determination and to carry out the determination that the life-sustaining apparatus should be turned off in this case?

MR. ARMSTRONG: No. I'm saying that it's licit for the family, in concert with the physicians, to make this decision. What I'm—I think that perhaps what we're at loggerheads about is I don't think the physician—

THE COURT: Well are you not also asking for a determination that if the physicians accede to the parents' request it will be without any adverse consequences to those physicians?

MR. ARMSTRONG: Yes, to that; but I think perhaps that what I misinterpreted was—is that this is a physician's decision.

THE COURT: I understand.

MR. ARMSTRONG: We contend that it is not.

THE COURT: In other words, you're saying that under these facts and circumstances if the physician elects to terminate at the request of the parent there will be no civil, adverse civil or criminal consequences attaching to the physician?

MR. ARMSTRONG: That's correct.

THE COURT: All right.

THE COURT: That has to be implied in your prayer for relief. You did not ask for that, did you?

MR. ARMSTRONG: That's correct. It is implied that this is a declaratory judgment action along those lines.

218

THE COURT: Wait a minute. Just a moment. You asked for three things. I take it that you put a lot of thought into them because they seem to go in logical sequence, the first being a prayer for judgment that Karen Ann be declared mentally incompetent, and that the plaintiff be given letters of guardianship with the express power of authorizing a discontinuance of what you there referred to as "all extraordinary means of sustaining the body processes."

MR. ARMSTRONG: That's correct.

THE COURT: And then in the event that's granted, you want the Prosecutor Mr. Collester to refrain from interference with or criminal prosecution arising out of any relief which the Court might grant. And then in the event that both of those are granted, then you want the doctors to be enjoined from interference with any relief. Now is that the sum and substance of what you seek?

MR. ARMSTRONG: That's correct.

THE COURT: All right. Nothing else?

MR. ARMSTRONG: Nothing else.

THE COURT: Mr. Armstrong, I chose to—I prefer in looking at this matter above and beyond the Quinlan case, and with that thought in mind, am I correct that you are advocating a position which envisions the exercise of a constitutional right in all cases of illnesses, terminal or otherwise; that this decision is something which should belong to the parents, close friends, relatives, whoever it is? That, again, this is a concept—a constitutional right—which you are advocating not just in the Quinlan case but in any other similar situation where illnesses are involved?

MR. ARMSTRONG: I can't—I can't address myself to any other circumstances, Your Honor. What I would like to do is distill it to the purest form and set forth what we're asking for in response to your question.

THE COURT: Well let's assume that in any other case that it is conceded that it is terminal, whether it be one year or six months or two years, whatever. Your position, I guess to be consistent, would have to be that there is this constitutional right to make this decision in any one of those situations?

MR. ARMSTRONG: I would not be wont to address myself to circumstances that I am not fully apprised of. What I would submit to the Court is that—

THE COURT: No. I've given you the facts. I've said that it is a terminal illness. I assume that.

MR. ARMSTRONG: I would have to throw into that assumption, again, the imposition of futile medical measures, the medical measures which serve no purpose whatsoever exclusive of drawing out the natural death process, which is the circumstances that are before the Court today.

CHIEF JUSTICE HUGHES: Mr. Armstrong, along the way of simplicity that you mentioned, I agree that that's the way to attack this problem, and passing the question of competency of Miss Quinlan and the rights of guardianship and mandatory features of instructions to that guardian and so forth, doesn't it come down to this, the long and short of it being: That you ask the Court to declare the law to be, there having been no precedent in any part of the common law that I can figure, that the Court is to declare now that if the doctors stop this procedure and cause death, that it will not result in any civil or criminal sanctions as to such doctors or indeed as to such family members?

MR. ARMSTRONG: That's correct.

CHIEF JUSTICE HUGHES: So that in effect you're asking the Court, as a court, to make new law.

MR. ARMSTRONG: On these facts, that's correct.

CHIEF JUSTICE HUGHES: On these facts. And that absent any constitutional compulsion to make that new law.

MR. ARMSTRONG: Yes. You can do that through the common law best interests doctrine.

CHIEF JUSTICE HUGHES: To make new law, without legislation? Wouldn't the Court be legislating, in that case?

MR. ARMSTRONG: No, Your Honor. It would be doing, or reflecting the majesty of the evolution of common law as it has since it's inception in England. It's simply addressing itself and drawing an analog from existing court cases to circumstances which, because of these particular instances, technological innovations have brought before the Court. I genuinely think that the Court is fully competent to address itself to these types of problems.

THE COURT: Well, Mr. Armstrong, suppose instead of Karen Ann Quinlan being in a deplorable condition in which she is, she were conscious, had cognitive powers, but was on the verge of death from some terminal illness and said, herself, to the doctors and to the hospital that she did not want artificial means of this kind to be employed. What is the law as to that?

MR. ARMSTRONG: Given that circumstance, we would advise that an individual, if death is imminent and the medical measures proposed are futile, they do no more than ford—they offer no hope of cure or any treatment known, then we most assuredly would assert that she *a fortiori* has a constitutional right to come before the Court.

THE COURT: All right, that's what I thought you would state. Now you are then carrying forward this constitutional right and reposing it in her guardian, or next-of-kin—

MR. ARMSTRONG: That's correct.

THE COURT: —and suggesting that the right may be exercised vicariously in that manner?

MR. ARMSTRONG: That's absolutely correct.

THE COURT: Isn't that really the burden of your argument here?

MR. ARMSTRONG: Essentially—

THE COURT: At least one thrust of it?

MR. ARMSTRONG: That's one thrust. It is the stronger thrust, granted. It's a two-prong individual right that of course the family has the right to make this decision where its incompetent member can't advise the court as to their own wishes. Most assuredly.

THE COURT: Are you then asking this Court to reverse its position that it took in the *Heston* case?

MR. ARMSTRONG: Well, what we're asking you to do is to follow the second set of dicta as set forth in the *Heston* case—*i.e.* that it seems, if an individual who is terminally ill wishes to allow or to follow in essence its natural course—

THE COURT: Well didn't Chief Justice Weintraub in that case say that it seems correct to say, I believe his words were, "It seems correct to say that one has no constitutional right to die"?

MR. ARMSTRONG: He did say that. However—

THE COURT: Would you ask this Court to disagree with that statement, that proposition?

MR. ARMSTRONG: With that general proposition, most assuredly. Applying it to these particular circumstances we find a differentiation in fact. The treatment was commonly employed everywhere, a simple blood transfusion. The prognosis was that with it she could recover.

THE COURT: Do you think *Heston* gives you any support, really?

MR. ARMSTRONG: Pardon me?

THE COURT: Do you think *Heston* really gives you or anybody else in this case much support?

221

MR. ARMSTRONG: Not really, Your Honor.

THE COURT: Everybody has cited *Heston* incidentally.

MR. ARMSTRONG: That's correct.

THE COURT: All the adversaries as well as you.

MR. ARMSTRONG: That's correct.

THE COURT: The minute I read that I'm in trouble. That means it's valueless.

MR. ARMSTRONG: That's correct.

THE COURT: Mr. Armstrong, the implicit argument against the position that you just outlined is that it would open the door to the exercise of determinations by physicians and families terminating life in situations not as acute as this where the continued life of the individual is just a nuisance to the family, and that a precedent of this kind would be an open door toward shutting off life in many situations where life should not be shut off, and that therefore it is sacred in the light of the general public good for the Court not to take affirmative action in this kind of situation. What would be your response to that, to that objection?

MR. ARMSTRONG: My response to that would be that an individual would be sacrificed for an uncontested general principle. My answer to the broader aspects of that question is this: It is that we submit that a terminally ill individual, pushing it very closely to these facts only, wherein the circumstances wherein the terminally ill is unable to do so, which are also the facts here, his family had the constitutionally protected right to terminate the administration of futile medical measures, another aspect that must be addressed only in these type circumstances. The only thing we advance are those three: That where we've got a terminally ill individual who is comatose, that the family who knows this individual best can exercise on her behalf that judgment to terminate futile medical measures which do no more than ford the death process and—

THE COURT: You have me a little confused at this point, and I hate to bring you back over again, but I'm not exactly sure what you want.

You seem to say that this is a medical question, and at the same time you say that the family and the doctor should make the decision. Well here the doctor has said "no." Now what do you want us to do?

MR. ARMSTRONG: It's a medical question, to this point: The nature of the decision to be made by a physician is this, that he can give you a diagnosis; he can ask you as the individual what do you wish to do with your body, especially in the circumstances where you are terminally ill and the treatment that he advances is of no value to you. The physician can say: Mr. Justice, what would you do? Not: I am going to employ this type of medical treatment regardless of what your particular views may be on the subject.

THE COURT: Mr. Armstrong, we agree that the right of privacy does not approach the constitutional right, as such. Is that correct?

MR. ARMSTRONG: I followed you—

THE COURT: That the right of privacy does not approach constitutional dimensions. Is that correct? The right of privacy does not approach constitutional dimensions?

MR. ARMSTRONG: No. I would advise, then, that that's not correct in our position.

THE COURT: And where, in the Constitution, is the right of privacy set forth?

MR. ARMSTRONG: The right of privacy is essentially in three categories: One is the penumbral theory set forth by Justice Douglas in the *Griswold* decision. That is, specific guarantees of rights have emanations which, of necessity, give life to those—

THE COURT: I'm satisfied that there is an inalienable right of privacy and I understand how it was handled in *Roe* v. *Wade*, the abortion case, and others; but basically there is no constitutional provision that speaks of "right of privacy," as such.

MR. ARMSTRONG: It's not specifically delineated.

THE COURT: All right. Now—right—now that being so, you would be satisfied, so to speak, that the right to make this decision would be predicated—might be predicated upon this right of privacy although the phrase, as such, does not appear in the Constitution?

MR. ARMSTRONG: Sure enough. Fair statement.

THE COURT: Fair statement?

MR. ARMSTRONG: Yes.

THE COURT: Therefore, if that is so and it does not approach constitutional dimensions, is not the exercise of that right a form of euthanasia?

MR. ARMSTRONG: I didn't follow you on that last step where you advised that it's not a constitutional dimension.

THE COURT: Well we agree that the right of privacy does not appear in the United States Constitution?

MR. ARMSTRONG: Fine.

223

THE COURT: It just doesn't.

Now we know the various cases which have reached out and interpreted the right of privacy and have suggested that that right emanates from certain provisions of the Constitution and so forth. But, as such, the best minds—the constitutional minds—agree that there is no constitutional basis for saying that one has that right of privacy.

MR. ARMSTRONG: I don't—no. I would have to disagree. What they say is that this—well, it's specifically delineated and most assuredly it is a constitutionally guaranteed right of privacy; and it's enunciated on three theories: The penumbral, the Ninth Amendment, and the Fourteenth Amendment due process concept of liberty.

THE COURT: Are the rights, or part of the right of a person to determine his own liberties—is it not as set forth in the Fourteenth Amendment to the Constitution?

MR. ARMSTRONG: He has liberties. I don't know if he has the right to determine them in the absence of—

THE COURT: Well isn't that the basis of *Roe* against *Wade*, that it's a constitutional right?

MR. ARMSTRONG: Oh, surely, but not to determine it by himself.

THE COURT: In other words, you're saying that if you had a competent person who decided he did not want medical attention, that he doesn't have a constitutional right to refuse medical attention?

MR. ARMSTRONG: No, I'm saying—no, no, no. Yes, he would.

THE COURT: And that that isn't his right of liberty?

MR. ARMSTRONG: That is a right of liberty that is his.

THE COURT: And isn't that really what you're relying upon here?

MR. ARMSTRONG: That's one of them. The theory, the whole concept again, Mr. Justice, of privacy is enunciated in essentially these three theories. Whichever theory you use to hang your hat on to demonstrate the existence of privacy is equally as valid.

THE COURT: Then why is it not comparable to the exercise of this right—call it whatever you'd like at the moment—why is it not comparable to euthanasia, whether you want to classify it as active euthanasia or passive euthanasia, and I can give you a lot of other synonyms that are being thrown around in these cases all of which as far as I am concerned in the final analysis add up to the same thing; why is it not the practice of euthanasia when one exercises the right to terminate his life?

MR. ARMSTRONG: Well essentially we follow the definitions set forth in Bishop Casey's statement that has been filed by the New Jersey

Catholic Conference and adopted by all the Bishops in the State of New Jersey.

What we're talking about is allowing the natural bodily process of an individual to follow its course in the presence of futile medical measures. Merely removing these futile medical measures and allowing the body to follow its natural process is not the act of taking a human life in the sense of injecting with an air bubble or injecting with an overdose of morphine. That's the—

THE COURT: Do you truly believe that these nuances will help to justify us in taking a position that the manner in which this life is terminated in the way you've just described it is something upon which we can intelligently base a decision?

MR. ARMSTRONG: Oh, surely, given this: "Terminal illness, futile medical measures." That's as far as it goes. No further than that.

THE COURT: Well how do you characterize, how do you safely characterize the medical measures as "futile"? They serve—

MR. ARMSTRONG: I'm sorry?

THE COURT: You started to say they serve no purpose except to keep the person alive.

MR. ARMSTRONG: Except to thwart the death process.

THE COURT: Except to keep her alive.

MR. ARMSTRONG: It's a matter of interpretation. She's 75 pounds and was once 130 pounds.

THE COURT: I understand that, but the—and this is, you're quite consistent. It's what you responded also to Justice Sullivan when you asked him to assume that the measures are doing no good. Well, yes, they're doing no good if you insist that to do good must be to work improvement and eventual cure. I think that's what you mean?

MR. ARMSTRONG: Surely.

THE COURT: Rather than simply to sustain an ongoing life.

MR. ARMSTRONG: Rather than to allow a physical entity to debilitate to the circumstances that Karen Ann is in now. I think we've got to throw that into the input, too, because maintaining a status quo, we couldn't call it futile.

THE COURT: Well isn't it maintaining a status quo now?

MR. ARMSTRONG: What it's doing is allowing her to debilitate to the point where she will ultimately die within—

THE COURT: Is there continued debilitation, given the life-sustaining

225

devices that are now and have been working? Or has there now been reached and been sustained for some time a plateau so that there is no further debilitation nor has there been for some time?

MR. ARMSTRONG: There is a plateau, yes. However, as pointed out in the doctors' testimony, Dr. Green's and Dr. Morse's—

THE COURT: Can I interrupt you? You started to say something that interested me very much, and you trailed off. You said, "She will die within—"

MR. ARMSTRONG: The physicians, in response to the direct question, Your Honor, advised—only one would really give us an outside time, and that would be less than a year, and that's Dr. Morse, the treating physician.

THE COURT: What was your answer going to be—

MR. ARMSTRONG: The one I was just about to develop?

THE COURT: Well, when you got down to the "within."

MR. ARMSTRONG: I don't think I'm following you as to what the question was that I was responding to when I gave you that particular answer?

CHIEF JUSTICE HUGHES: You previously said it might be a day, it might be a month, it would be a year at the outside per Dr. Morse's testimony.

MR. ARMSTRONG: That's correct.

THE COURT: And he's the only one who undertook to make such a prediction.

MR. ARMSTRONG: Most of them advised honestly, Mr. Justice, that they don't know. They are sure that she will die within a period of months.

THE COURT: I'm sure others may have questions on this point, but I'm going to forget this one. I have looked and I have searched the record and now I've asked the Clerk to search the record, and I fail to come up with the hospital record of Newton Memorial Hospital. Am I correct that it was marked in evidence?

MR. ARMSTRONG: That's correct.

THE COURT: Where is it?

MR. ARMSTRONG: I have copies and I have advised the Court that I would be happy to convey the copies to them. As a matter of fact, when we came down to file the briefs, I so advised Mr. Townsend of the fact when he pointed it out to me.

226

THE COURT: Then I can get one?

MR. ARMSTRONG: Absolutely. We have copies right here.

THE COURT: What is your response, Mr. Armstrong, to those who argue that there is always the possibility of that miracle drug or the miracle remedy which may come to pass between the date that one decides that the person should die and the date that the person perhaps would normally have died with the supportive measures? What is your response to the fact—that we should not concern ourselves with that possibility?

MR. ARMSTRONG: As a broad general principle, that's fine. However that was investigated thoroughly for close to nine months by the family in concert with Drs. Morse and Javed to find out the existence of any research, of any developments at all that could alleviate the particular irreparable brain damage suffered by Karen. It was found that there is none, nor was any advanced—

THE COURT: Miracles don't come about that way. They just wake up one morning and someone says we have a Salk vaccine. They didn't give "warnings" beforehand. There it was. There it was. Why is it so impossible that this could come to pass?

MR. ARMSTRONG: Basically, Mr. Justice, those miracles come about as a result of Ford Foundation grants for about $1½ million. There are no grants doing research along these lines to alleviate irreparable brain damage. There simply is no one doing research along those lines.

THE COURT: What if someone where to accidently just come upon something even though they weren't doing research in this particular area, just accidentally came across something which does the trick?

MR. ARMSTRONG: Well then we'd all be better off for it.

THE COURT: Including Miss Quinlan?

MR. ARMSTRONG: Most importantly Miss Quinlan.

THE COURT: Now what is your response to Justice Pashman's question?

MR. ARMSTRONG: Well I can only gauge it on the possibility. It's a possibility but not a probability.

THE COURT: And if there is a possibility and if there is this doubt engendered by that possibility, should we not if at all possible resolve all doubts in favor of life, in favor of the continuation of life as to the very last moment?

MR. ARMSTRONG: That is something that should go into the equation when the individual or the individual's family is to make this

227

constitutionally protected decision. Certainly if there is something in the offing along those lines the individual must take that into consideration; or if the physician knows about it he should advise the family or the individual of the existence of some research along that line and allow him to assess the probability of it being able to alleviate the situation within which that particular individual finds himself.

THE COURT: Mr. Armstrong, I suspect that philosophically behind your position is something that has not been proven, although you might have attempted to prove it at the trial, and that is the assumption that many physicians without any argument about it every day make decisions to stop giving life-sustaining help to people who are hopelessly ill. Was there an attempt made to prove that? Was there evidence to that effect at the trial?

MR. ARMSTRONG: I think the thrust of the evidence advanced by Dr. Korein is that the requested relief is within the context of medical tradition.

THE COURT: And is being done?

MR. ARMSTRONG: Surely.

THE COURT: Well that would be—you see, to me that might be influential if it were proven. I've heard that this is so. I've heard that physicians frequently as a matter of daily routine without talking about it make personal decisions in the interest of all concerned not to kill somebody, not to give them a tablet which would kill them, but to stop giving life-sustaining artificial sustenance where it is totally helpless and where the patient is going to suffer more from being kept alive than being terminated—

MR. ARMSTRONG: That's also my understanding.

THE COURT: —and I suppose what you are really arguing here is that the Court should assume that if Karen were able to make the request herself and made it and the physician acceded to that request, he would not be subject to any penalties.

MR. ARMSTRONG: That's one of the thrusts.

The other is that if you deem that you haven't sufficient evidence to persuade you that Karen has made that decision, then that you should do the same just interposing the family as the decision-maker and all that would follow.

THE COURT: It wouldn't be subject to any penalties if the Prosecutor didn't find out about it. The one to ask is the Prosecutor, whether in fact he knows, whether it's a matter of common knowledge to him and a source of investigation on his part that he's overlooking. I'm sure he's going to say "no."

228

THE COURT: And, Mr. Armstrong, isn't it a fact that if such proofs were developed, proofs that it is common practice for doctors to suspend life-supporting measures and to do other things that you've referred to in order to hasten death, that proofs like this might result in indictments of some form?

MR. ARMSTRONG: Absolutely, Mr. Justice.

THE COURT: Of course they would. Therefore, isn't it naive on our part to expect that anyone will ever prove that this is a common practice despite the fact that down deep we all know it is?

MR. ARMSTRONG: It's very difficult to get a witness to testify to that effect under the glare of litigation, Mr. Justice.

THE COURT: Well of course they won't because he's testifying to a crime.

THE COURT: Because they're afraid.

MR. ARMSTRONG: Absolutely.

THE COURT: Well that's not so, is it, Mr. Armstrong? That Dr. Heisetz's book, *The Right to Die*, he gives a number of examples of exactly that situation. It's set out there in print and published for everyone to read.

MR. ARMSTRONG: That's correct, Your Honor, but during my request I could understand the quest of Diogenes in looking for an honest man to come before this Court and testify to the effect that he had done so. It's easy for them to say in the inner recesses of their office that, yes, this is done, or this is done quite often. "Would you testify to that effect?" is something different.

THE COURT: He gave express examples in which he participated, as I recall his book. Had you read his book?

MR. ARMSTRONG: Yes, I have.

THE COURT: But you do agree that it is common practice in most hospitals that labels are assigned in certain cases, "d.n.c.—do not code," "d.n.r.—do not resuscitate." Is that right?

MR. ARMSTRONG: What you're referring to, Justice, is the concept of judicious neglect.

THE COURT: I mean—but that is correct, is it not?

MR. ARMSTRONG: Yes.
    Advanced by Dr. Korein.

THE COURT: Yes. And that's what it is, yes. You want to—we're in another phase now. We move from euthanasia—active, passive—judicious neglect, right on down the line, and this transparent wall of semantic brick takes hold and that's all we really are playing with here, because in the final analysis they all add up to the same thing. Don't they?

MR. ARMSTRONG: Well it depends on what they all are. I mean if we—I can only—

THE COURT: The termination of life. That's what it adds up to.

MR. ARMSTRONG: Within specific circumstances.

THE COURT: Sure, I know. I know. That's the end result, except we got there through one of various routes that I just enumerated, and I can give you a long list of them above and beyond those.

THE COURT: In view of the momentous consequences of what you're asking the Court to do, although theoretically you are right that the Court does develop common law by applying its notion of justice, in view of the momentous consequences of a decision such as you request here, isn't public policy in its most fundamental aspect here involved so that it would be more appropriate for the legislature to take the first step rather than the Court?

MR. ARMSTRONG: Well this Court, in *Heston*, addressed itself to the other side of the coin. What I'm saying is that if the Court can address itself to one side of the coin, it can address itself to the concomitant side of the coin.

THE COURT: Well in *Heston* the Court addressed itself to the conservative concept that a person does not have a right to terminate life. I say "conservative" because of the fact that for a long time it's been a crime to attempt suicide. But what you're asking the Court to do is not conservative. I think you'd agree with that. You're asking the Court in the name of the development of the common law to make a very momentous and profound determination of public policy. Is not the making of that public policy judgment more appropriate for the legislature than for a common law court?

MR. ARMSTRONG: No.

THE COURT: All right. You've answered my question.

CHIEF JUSTICE HUGHES: Mr. Armstrong, would it simplify our thinking on this approach if we were to consider a parallel case where, let us say, some patient, Karen, were brought in terribly burned, suffering terrible pain, obviously terminally ill and the doctor, in his judgment, decided not to apply the life-support respirator and mechanism as a matter of judgment. Would he be any more or less amenable to criminal or civil sanctions in that case, as opposed to a case, let us say,

230

where he happened to be away for the weekend and his assistant applied the life-sustaining mechanisms and the doctor disagreed when he came back on Monday with that procedure—the fact that he has to do the affirmative act of stopping something that has been started—is that any different, logically, than declining to start something?

MR. ARMSTRONG: I think if I could pull us back to this factual situation and say—because here we have had the administration of medical treatment, the respirator. If he makes the decision beforehand in his judgment and I'm going to say in concert with the patient or his family, that it wouldn't work, it would be the same thing. However, if once you've applied the machine and you see it's futile, *a fortiori*, that particular decision should be protected because you haven't ruled out the possibility. You've applied it, and you've demonstrated to yourself within the realm of your science—here, medicine—that this machine does nothing. It offers no hope of cure. It's just thwarting and dragging out the natural processes of the body.

CHIEF JUSTICE HUGHES: So that you'd say there is no difference. Is that the idea?

MR. ARMSTRONG: In our circumstance.

In the burn case, I don't think you advised me as to whether or not the individual had anything to do with that decision.

CHIEF JUSTICE HUGHES: Well supposing it's a perception of Dr. Morse upon first seeing Karen that there was no utility whatsoever, aside from prolonging her life for a month or two, in applying the life-sustaining treatment. Would he be any less amenable to criminal or civil sanctions then, or would he be in the realm of the Hypocratic Oath responsibility to his professional duties, rather than amenability to the law?

MR. ARMSTRONG: I think he's got to at least come in contact with the individual or his family. They should make that decision. If it's a purely emergent decision, I think that the physicians are, pursuant to the Hypocratic Oath, bound to apply those life-sustaining measures.

THE COURT: No matter their futility?

MR. ARMSTRONG: Well if it's totally futile and there's—well, I think—

CHIEF JUSTICE HUGHES: I'm talking about a totally futile case where it is obvious from the doctor's experience and medical knowledge that this patient is either going to die tomorrow or three months from tomorrow, after suffering very bitter pain. If he makes that medical decision, can you conceive that he would be responsible to the law?

MR. ARMSTRONG: If he didn't do it in consort with either the family or the individual, I think he should be.

231

THE COURT: Mr. Armstrong, you began by saying that we should not consider any other definition of death. I'd like to just look at that with you for a moment. Despite the fact that you don't believe we ought to involve ourselves in it from your standpoint, why is it inappropriate for us to reconsider what has become the traditional concept of death? We all agree, I'm sure, that the traditional concept was and is the cessation of cardiovascular activity in that sense and this all came about by case law; there's no statute. Isn't that true?

MR. ARMSTRONG: That's correct.

THE COURT: And therefore this so-called "definition of death" today is a result of case law.

Now, if that is so, why is it inappropriate for us to re-examine that concept and determine whether or not there is an area of brain death concept or cerebrum brain death concept and something along those lines, something for us to evaluate and perhaps promulgate in the same way as the traditional form of death to which I referred was originally promulgated?

MR. ARMSTRONG: I would submit, Mr. Justice Pashman, that there's really no end to its application to the facts of the instant proceeding.

THE COURT: No, but that would really make your case. What Mr. Justice Pashman is suggesting would really make your case, would it not, Mr. Armstrong?

MR. ARMSTRONG: She doesn't—

THE COURT: If this Court were to determine that this young woman in fact was legally dead, then that changes the entire picture of this case, does it not?

MR. ARMSTRONG: Surely. But, pursuant to those standards, she doesn't fall within the purview of those standards.

THE COURT: Of what standards?

MR. ARMSTRONG: Of the Harvard Ad Hoc Committee.

THE COURT: Well I know, but are those the only standards?

MR. ARMSTRONG: To any of the standards.

THE COURT: The cerebrum—brain? Uh-uh. There's a concept—

THE COURT: The concept of the functions of a person? Why couldn't this Court come along and say, look, that person is really not alive.

MR. ARMSTRONG: Well it flies in—

THE COURT: There's just a vegetable. It's like any vegetable.

THE COURT: I didn't say the brain death concept. The cerebrum brain concept is a different concept, and I'm not so sure that if that concept were applied—I'm not sure that you do not necessarily come to the conclusion that Karen Quinlan is dead.

MR. ARMSTRONG: Within that realm, Justice Pashman, I've got to be frank and honest with you. Based upon the information from my expert, it's my understanding that she would not fall within the purview of that particular test.

CHIEF JUSTICE HUGHES: Mr. Armstrong, in order to save a reasonable amount of time for Mr. Crowley, would you mind—you've been interrupted quite much, I know, by questions but that's in order to have the Court inform itself in this important case.

MR. ARMSTRONG: I think I'd like to, if I may, address myself to perhaps the most tragic and painful aspect of the unfortunate decision rendered by the lower court—and genuinely. That is, the appointment of a person other than Joseph Quinlan as the guardian of his daughter. Common law and the statutes in New Jersey mandate the appointment of Karen's father as her guardian unless it has been proved to the court, unless it has been proved to the court that such an appointment would not be in Karen's best interests. The Appellant has abundantly, I submit, and without controversion demonstrated both his fitness to serve as guardian and most importantly his intention not to act in any manner in which the court deems not to be in Karen's best interests.

CHIEF JUSTICE HUGHES: Well is that important, assuming that he doesn't go further and say I want to be guardian and I want you to instruct me or declare that I may do so-and-so?

MR. ARMSTRONG: It's important to this effect, that if the court didn't authorize it for Mr. Quinlan, he certainly wouldn't do it. He came to this court to ask them guidance and what they did was they denied in law what he is in fact, the father and guardian of his daughter Karen Ann. That's one aspect of the decision we can't understand.

CHIEF JUSTICE HUGHES: But from the early days of the common law when things were a little different in England, the courts did not want the guardian of the property—the next of kin who might inherit, let's say, and not applying it to this case but the basis of the rule—wanted the guardian of the person to be a different person for the safety of the particular incompetent, so that obviously the Judge had a right in his discretion, didn't he, to appoint one other than the next-of-kin as guardian of the person?

MR. ARMSTRONG: Well I think—I think I can point out the rule to be followed by the Judge in exercising that discretion, if I may. It's *In the Matter of Benjamin Role*, wherein the Appellate Division of the Superior Court clearly stated, and if I may read:

233

> "The Statute and rule gives a preference to the next-of-kin as opposed to other persons, and that such preference must be recognized unless it is shown to the court's satisfaction that the appointment of next-of-kin would be affirmatively contrary to the best interests of the incompetent, which hasn't been done, or his estate in the sense of being deleterious thereto in some significant way."

It would appear that the present framework of statute and rule, Mr. Chief Justice, was designed to eliminate the former practice under which the court commonly appointed a friend of the court.

THE COURT: Well you shade the issue a little bit, Mr. Armstrong, when you suggest that Mr. Quinlan came to the court seeking guidance. He didn't. He came to the court seeking three things which I recited before, each of which was denied by the trial court. And I suppose the position of the trial court was that it was inconsistent to put the parent in the position of having to abide by a decision of the trial court that went contrary to the specific and express requests of the parent himself. I don't see—

Frankly I think I share the Chief Justice's expressed confusion as to why this is so crucial.

MR. ARMSTRONG: Why is it crucial?

THE COURT: Yes.

MR. ARMSTRONG: Why is it crucial to deny a man the rights he has for his daughter?

THE COURT: You can put it in whatever dramatic terms you want. The fact remains that the man came in and sought to withdraw life-sustaining devices; and the trial court said: No, you cannot do it. And presumably, by prosecution of this appeal, he in good conscience wishes to pursue the relief that originally he sought, which is still contrary to that which the court below has declared. Now should not the court below in its wisdom appoint someone who is—whose thought in the matter is in keeping with the instruction of the trial court?

MR. ARMSTRONG: Because there has been demonstrated evidence during the course of that trial that Mr. Quinlan would do nothing unless the court authorized it.

THE COURT: I don't doubt that for a moment. But it's a matter of my own personal response to it. I'm certain from what I divine from this record that that is so, but I fail to see how the trial court can be charged with an abuse of its discretion in the appointment that he made—

234

MR. ARMSTRONG: Let's look, let's look—

THE COURT: Given the facts, that you have somebody coming not seeking guidance—I repeat, he didn't do that.

MR. ARMSTRONG: I disagree wholeheartedly, as much as I can, with you—

THE COURT: Look at the complaint.

MR. ARMSTRONG: Pardon?

THE COURT: Look at the complaint.

MR. ARMSTRONG: Well I drafted the complaint. I understand what the complaint is.

THE COURT: The complaint says in the first paragraph that he seeks authorization to withdraw the life-sustaining devices. That isn't seeking guidance.

MR. ARMSTRONG: Of course it is. That's a technical procedure. That's the way I speak, that you speak, but Mr. Quinlan came to me and said, "Give me guidance." He came to the court and said, "Give me guidance."

THE COURT: He came to the court and said: Give me a right to do that which the court eventually said the law will not allow.

MR. ARMSTRONG: I think we are involved in a semantic quagmire.

THE COURT: I think not. I think we are involved in something very basic, and I think Judge Muir perceived it, and I perceive it.

MR. ARMSTRONG: Well I think, let's—I think we ought to look at the order, then, and what was in it. Let's look at the supplementary order concerning the appointment of the guardian. What does the guardian do? The guardian does nothing. The primary function of the family and the primary aspects of the physician-patient relationship still remains with the family. If for some reason which is totally impossible and impractical in these situations the family is unavailable, then the doctor would seek the consent of the guardian. Now that certainly isn't a straightforward guardianship approach that was applied by the lower court.

THE COURT: Are you concerned that in the event that this is turned down that if the situation becomes even more hopeless and the position is on the borderline of making a decision to terminate and he consulted with the guardian, the guardian would say, "no"; whereas if the father were the guardian the father might say, "yes"? Is that the contingency that concerns you?

MR. ARMSTRONG: The contingency is that—

THE COURT: If that contingency does not concern you, I should think maybe it would, but if it doesn't, then what difference does it make who the guardian is?

MR. ARMSTRONG: I think I've got a little bit of adrenalin flowing, Mr. Justice, and I don't really think I followed your reasoning. If you'll rephrase—

THE COURT: Well I was suspecting that the reason that you're concerned about Mr. Quinlan being made the guardian is that perhaps in the future when this situation gets even worse than it is now, the physician may go to whoever is in charge to make a final determination to turn it off and if it were the guardian, the guardian might say "no", but the father might say "yes." I suspected that that was your concern in being insistent upon the father being made the guardian. Now, if that is not your concern, then what difference does it make who the guardian is?

MR. ARMSTRONG: Well what you've done, you've interposed an artificial decision-maker who really has no power to make a decision. That's what—

THE COURT: An artificial decision-maker. Then you are concerned about the contingency that I've just referred to.

MR. ARMSTRONG: No. I think if we look at Judge Muir's supplemental opinion, that this particular artificial decision-maker has no decision-making power exclusive of some hypothetical situation wherein the parents are unavailable.

THE COURT: Well then tell me: What specifically is your concern as to who is the guardian from this point on?
What difference does it make?

MR. ARMSTRONG: Well it makes an awful lot of difference to a father to have—

THE COURT: Do you mean as a matter of pride? As a matter of—

MR. ARMSTRONG: As a matter of honor, a matter of honor and a matter of truth.

THE COURT: All right.

THE COURT: Mr. Armstrong, before you leave us, I'm getting into something which I believe is a little more substantial, at least from my viewpoint. Is it correct that the trial judge found that this was, as he put it, "a medical decision and not a judicial one"? Is that correct?

MR. ARMSTRONG: That's correct.

THE COURT: And you, I take it, take very serious exception to that conclusion, do you not?

MR. ARMSTRONG: Unequivocally.

THE COURT: All right. Now that being so, do you envision perhaps a possibility of a decision being the result or the end product of a combination of the medical profession or specific doctors arriving at a conclusion utilizing judicial guidelines concerning the definition of death? Does this concept at all appeal to you or appear to you as something worthy of this Court's consideration?

MR. ARMSTRONG: What we advance, Mr. Justice Pashman, is that it is the roll and function of the physician to advise an individual of his diagnosis, what's wrong with him.

THE COURT: He does that.

MR. ARMSTRONG: What is his prognosis, what are his chances of recovery.

THE COURT: And we have the prognosis here that the brain damage is irreversible and we all understand what the prognosis is.

Yes, go on from there.

MR. ARMSTRONG: From there I'm saying that further I can advise that the physician should advise as to the nature of treatments that are available, what the options are.

THE COURT: Yes, sir?

MR. ARMSTRONG: Then that decision should be made by either the individual or his family.

THE COURT: That is your basic concept and that's what you're urging. I understand that.

I'm suggesting to you, however, that if the Court should consider a revision of the definition of death, if we should, may I respectfully suggest to you and ask you for your comments concerning the possibility of a decision forthcoming from a group of people—meaning just more than one or two—and in different professions involved, namely the medical profession again guided by judicial suggestions or guidelines or whatever we might promulgate. Is this possibility at all worth any comment on your part? And is it possible for the Court to consider that?

MR. ARMSTRONG: I think, if I understand you correctly, that perhaps you mean setting up another element of decision-making in circumstances like this?

THE COURT: We would set up guidelines. We might redefine death. Could not the medical profession then utilize those guidelines—

MR. ARMSTRONG: Absolutely.

THE COURT: —in arriving at its decision?

MR. ARMSTRONG: Absolutely.

THE COURT: What's wrong with that?

MR. ARMSTRONG: It just doesn't apply in the instant circumstances, Mr. Justice.

I think at this point I would like to have Mr. Crowley address himself to the First Amendment arguments and the "best interest" concept.

CHIEF JUSTICE HUGHES: Thank you very much, Mr. Armstrong. Mr. Crowley?

ORAL ARGUMENT OF JAMES M. CROWLEY, ESQ., ON BEHALF OF APPELLANT JOSEPH QUINLAN

MR. CROWLEY: Mr. Chief Justice, Honorable Justices, permit me to thank you for extending me the privilege of speaking before this Court on behalf of the Quinlan family.

We submit that the Quinlans' decision has a valid claim to constitutional protection not only because it is an exercise of the right of privacy, but also because it is an effectuation of their religious beliefs. Now when such a claim is made, the Court must apply the threefold tasks laid down in *Wisconsin* versus *Yoder*. First, is the proposed action motivated by sincerely held religious belief? Second, is the proposed action intimately related to daily living? And third, are the beliefs in question shared by an organized group?

When the religious nature of a proposed course of action is revealed, the Court must then determine whether any secular state interest is sufficiently compelling to prohibit the proposed action. Joseph Quinlan's claim meets all three *Yoder* tests, and the lower court, we submit, erred in not finding that such a claim was rooted in religious beliefs.

First, the evidence shows him to be a sincerely religious man who as part of his religion believes in the sanctity of life and the perfection of this life in the next and the futility of clinging to this life when hope is gone, in man's ability to know God's will within himself and to carry it out, and in the role of the family in promoting the spiritual good of its members.

Second, it is clear that for a religious person nothing is more intimately related to daily life than a consideration of and a preparation for the end of it.

Third, the testimony of Mr. Quinlan's pastor and the hospital chaplain, the Papal Allocution admitted into evidence and the official teaching of the Catholic Church contained in the Statement of Bishop Casey, which all the Roman Catholic Bishops of this State have seconded and which they as friends of this Court have laid before you, make it clear that the course of action chosen by Mr. Quinlan is actively supported by his Church and is a concrete effectuation of its teachings.

THE COURT: May I stop you?

It is my understanding that the position of the Catholic Church on this subject is neutral. In other words, it neither advocates nor refuses to advocate the termination of life in a situation of this kind and leaves it to the judgment of those directly concerned.

MR. CROWLEY: This, Your Honor, we submit was the error into which the lower court fell when having considered the evidence it then engaged in what we submit is a constitutionally impermissible weighing of religious belief—that is, an examination of the underlying religious principles and the importance of those principles to the totality of Catholic beliefs.

THE COURT: Are you saying that the teaching is that Mr. Quinlan and his family have the right to make this decision, as opposed to the doctor? Is that what the Church is passing—

MR. CROWLEY: That is how the teaching of the Catholic Church is effectuated—

THE COURT: And they say it's Mr. Quinlan's prerogative to make this determination?

MR. CROWLEY: It's the prerogative of the individual and the family to make life-influencing decisions for themselves and their members.

THE COURT: I see.

THE COURT: Mr. Crowley, don't you agree constitutionally though, that in order to evoke the protection of the First Amendment, that it is very well settled that there must be a burden—an underlying burden—that there must be a burden on the free exercise of that person's religion? Isn't that what the cases hold?

MR. CROWLEY: I submit, Your Honor, that there is a burden; but the stronger test is that the exercise—the claimed exercise—has to be a manifest abuse of some societal interest.

THE COURT: Now pursuing the fact, and pursuing the facts that there must be a burden, may I suggest to you that none of the positions taken by any of the parties here religiously indicate that the Church requires termination, just as Judge Conford noted. In fact, the Church does not "require" termination of any extraordinary means. That's correct, isn't it? Do we agree so far? That it does not require? That this is optional with the individual involved? Is that correct?

MR. CROWLEY: Again, Your Honor, we must consider the nature of the religious right claimed. And again I feel that this is an error into which the lower court fell into, because by—

THE COURT: Mr. Crowley, I would prefer if you responded to my question.

MR. CROWLEY: Well I'm saying, Your Honor, that because the Petitioner was not thrust into mortal sin by the denial of his request, or saying that another member of the Catholic religion could not come in similar circumstances to a different decision, is an impermissible weighing of that belief and it is not to say that Mr. Quinlan is not exercising his religious belief, which is that he is the one to make the choice, in this case. And denying him the choice is placing a burden on his exercise of the right to privacy and on the exercise of his religion.

THE COURT: It's the choice of Karen, is it not?

MR. CROWLEY: We claim that the family right—

THE COURT: In other words, that's irrespective of her desires—

MR. CROWLEY: In this case, as a matter of fact—this position as a matter of fact is one in which the family is making the decision, taking into account her desires.

THE COURT: And you agree that the option in this case is available to Roman Catholics without religious sanction or prohibition. That is a truism, is it not?

MR. CROWLEY: A truism in the true sense of the word. It is irrelevant, Your Honor—

THE COURT: Well, if that's so then, sir, does it not follow that the refusal to terminate treatment is therefore not considered sinful or violative of religious dogma? That's correct, is it not?

MR. CROWLEY: I pose an example—

THE COURT: You don't want to say "yes" or "no" to that.

CHIEF JUSTICE HUGHES: You're entitled to answer as you wish, Mr. Crowley. Go ahead.

THE COURT: You still don't want to say "yes" or "no," as I say.

MR. CROWLEY: May I pose my example?

THE COURT: Go ahead.

MR. CROWLEY: If Joseph Quinlan, before having married and raised a family, had decided to enter the priesthood and chose celibacy, and the State denied him that choice, I think it is abundantly clear that the State's denial would be an infringement on the free exercise of his religion, if he had chosen celibacy for the Kingdom of God, even though the majority of Catholics do not. And it's entirely optional. It's a matter of internal religious belief and conviction, and it's a matter of acting out God's will in one's life, and that's what's being claimed here. What another person may choose is irrelevant.

THE COURT: Well, Mr. Crowley, the reason I started this interrogation about the position of the Church being neutral, is that in the Jehovah's Witnesses cases you have a situation where the position of the religious adherent is not neutral, but there is an affirmative policy in his religion not to accept treatment. Nevertheless, if the interests of society are sufficiently contrary to the exercise of that religious belief, the courts have had no hesitancy in sustaining the interests of society as against the positive religious beliefs of the Jehovah's Witnesses.

MR. CROWLEY: Fair enough.

THE COURT: Now that being so, why shouldn't that principle apply even more forcefully to a case where the alleged religious interest is, as in this case, neutral and not affirmative.

MR. CROWLEY: Because, Your Honor, I conceive the wall of separation between church and state as being one in which whatever goes on on the church side of the wall is not to be interfered with from the state side of the wall. No matter for what reason it goes on, if the church is playing ball on its side of the wall, as long as the ball doesn't go over to the other side and harm some societal interest, then the church should be left alone and people should be left alone with their religious beliefs. Once it impinges on the legitimate societal interests, then the state can step in and—

THE COURT: All right. Now doesn't that then beg the—you would then concede, on the basis of the Jehovah's Witnesses cases, that if the Court's construction of the interests of society in this case are such that the declaratory judgment here sought should be denied, it should make no difference what the religious beliefs of the Applicant are?

MR. CROWLEY: Fair enough.

THE COURT: All right. Well then the issue before us really is: What are the interests of society? And the religious preferences of your client are really irrelevant. Is that not so?

MR. CROWLEY: They are not so irrelevant that he is not entitled to claim an explicitly constitutionally protected right.

THE COURT: Well there's nothing to prevent him from claiming them, but should the Court give any weight to them if the Court's conception of the interest of society is contrary?

CHIEF JUSTICE HUGHES: When the Court overrules a Jehovah's Witness's religious objection, say, to a transfusion and sees a recovery, either certain or certainly probable—

241

MR. CROWLEY: Those cases have found that.

CHIEF JUSTICE HUGHES: Doesn't this same thing apply? Would you think the Court should overrule the Jehovah's Witness's religious objection if it were conceded, as in this case, that it was almost hopeless or demonstrably hopeless? I mean isn't that where the societal interest comes alive, so to speak?

MR. CROWLEY: The societal interest, I believe, is found in a combination of three factors: The nature and the prognosis of the ailment; the nature of the condition, or rather the nature of the treatment; and in the societal responsibilities of the person who is refusing treatment. The nature of the religious beliefs, where it's important for the religion, should have nothing to do with it.

THE COURT: Well then, is what you are saying really that Catholic freedom of individual choice in this matter is a make-weight which the Court should put into the scales on the side of your client, but not itself be determinative?

MR. CROWLEY: I think it is constitutionally sufficient in itself, because the State has demonstrated no compelling interest, in our view, in forbidding the proposed activity. The catalogued fear—they have made appeals in this thrust and the lower court has heeded those appeals, but there has been no demonstration that in this case a specific societal interest is being harmed.

THE COURT: All right.

MR. CROWLEY: Finally, Your Honors, it is the Appellant's contention that it is the traditional common law principles which provide a legally sufficient basis for granting his request. Indeed, the common law has long recognized through the concept of legal guardianship that the rights of incompetent persons are best exercised by those closest to such persons. The right to receive or refuse medical treatment is surely one possessed by incompetent no less than competent persons, and is properly exercised by a guardian in the best interests of the incompetent. Now a determination, we submit to Your Honors, in the best interests of an incompetent requires an examination of the totality of that person's goals, desires, and values. Acting in such person's best interests means effectuating those values.

The Quinlans know, and the evidence has shown, that chief among Karen's values are her love of life, her vitality, her respect for life, and its spiritual goal, her pride, and the love which she bears for her family. These values have coalesced in the formation of her desire to forego futile medical treatment of the type she presently receives. The State, as supreme guardian, can give specific authorization, when requested, but should not disturb the reasonable decisions of an individual guardian.

Appellant's decision to effectuate what we contend is a legally permissible course of action which has been demonstrated in accord with the values and thus with the best interests of his incompetent adult daughter, is by its very nature not unreasonable; and the lower court erred in refusing to authorize it.

I want to thank the Court for its attention to our review of these sad and weighty matters which bring us before you today. Based upon the arguments advanced on behalf of the Appellant and his daughter, Karen, we respectfully request that this Court reverse the decision of the lower court and grant the prayer of the Appellant. Further, we respectfully request reservation of some time for rebuttal.

CHIEF JUSTICE HUGHES: Thank you, Mr. Crowley.

Next is Mr. Coburn for Mr. Thomas R. Curtin, guardian ad litem.

ORAL ARGUMENT OF DANIEL R. COBURN, ESQ., ON BEHALF OF THOMAS R. CURTIN, ESQ., GUARDIAN AD LITEM

MR. COBURN: May it please the Court:

My name is Daniel R. Coburn. As the Court is aware, I am the attorney for the Guardian in the case at the present time.

CHIEF JUSTICE HUGHES: Mr. Coburn, Justice Pashman points out that you have not filed a brief in this case. Is that correct?

MR. COBURN: Yes, Judge. I understood the order of the Court to be that unless there was something supplemental—something to be added to what was filed below in the Court's opinion, that it would not be necessary—

CHIEF JUSTICE HUGHES: So that you wish to depend on the brief submitted below?

MR. COBURN: Certainly. Other than one issue in the brief that had nothing to do with the case at this time, and certainly the appointment of me as the guardian has nothing to do with the case at this time.

But as to Justice Pashman, I have a response to the question as to the Court's power to adopt a definition of death, and exactly what the definition of death might be. And barring some question that I haven't prepared for, most of what I say involves matters that I have discussed with Mr. Curtin. So I'm speaking, in addition to my own opinions, also of Mr. Curtin's.

I think the Court definitely has the power, whether it's through a development of the common law definition of death, or whether it's the Court's own power, judging by what is the standard in other states where the legislature has acted, to adopt a definition of death. I think it should definitely be something other than the common law definition. I think brain death is certainly acceptable. The test of brain death—I think there is a bill in the New Jersey Legislature right now that seems to summarize what the other states have adopted as far as a decision on brain death, and all of my discussions with the doctors involved in this case, while this is certainly not a matter of record, as I recall, all the doctors seem concerned as to the definition of death. I think it's—

THE COURT: Mr. Coburn, do you see any objection to this Court considering, and ultimately perhaps defining, or redefining death, although there are those who might assume that it is a legislative function?

MR. COBURN: I don't think so.

THE COURT: In this case?

MR. COBURN: In this particular case, I don't because—

THE COURT: Everybody having agreed that it's not involved, and you are now before the highest Court of the State, and you suggest we should address that issue?

MR. COBURN: Yes.

THE COURT: Has it been briefed?

MR. COBURN: I think—excuse me?

THE COURT: Has it been exhaustively briefed, in this Court?

MR. COBURN: The question of "brain death" being accepted?

THE COURT: The question of a redefinition of death. Do you think we still ought to take it up in this case?

MR. COBURN: Yes.

THE COURT: Everybody having agreed that this incompetent is not dead by any thus-far-accepted definition, we nevertheless should make it part of the opinion?

MR. COBURN: I think so because of the tenor of the questions that have been asked—

THE COURT: Well we ask now, Mr. Coburn. You've been here, and in Appellate Court, so often that you know we asked all kinds of questions that may have absolutely nothing to do with the eventual resolution of the dispute with which we are confronted. And the reason—I don't say that facetiously at all—but the reason I am putting this to you is that this is obviously a most portentous question. We haven't had the views of anybody here on it, and you're standing there suggesting that we should make it a part of the resolution of this case. I hope you, therefore, make it part of your recommendation that we ask you all to submit further briefs on it.

MR. COBURN: Yes. I would be more than willing to, because it is my opinion that the issue is here. As I recall, I think I said it—not that I said it during the course of the trial has any weight at all—that was a request that I also made of Judge Muir at the time, that the definition of death obviously is of critical importance in this case. I think, under the common-law definition of death, any discussion at all of medical testimony given as to—I forgot what Dr. Korein's exact words were—but I think it was "cerebral," loss of cerebral function, death. He wanted even a more far-reaching definition that would probably include Karen—

THE COURT: That was the cerebrum death concept.

MR. COBURN: Right.

THE COURT: That goes to the brain death concept.

MR. COBURN: Yes.

THE COURT: Mr. Porzio spent point one of his brief devoted just to a definition of death, did he not?

MR. COBURN: I don't remember if it's point one—I know he spent—

THE COURT: It's point one, sir.

MR. COBURN: Right.

THE COURT: And it is covered. It is covered. The definition of death is covered. The definition of death is discussed and argued. Well, whether it is or it isn't let's continue with our problem.

The fact is I'm just suggesting to you, or asking you: You see no objection, from your standpoint, to having this Court consider or reconsider the definition of death in that sense, despite the fact that ultimately it might be a legislative assignment?

MR. COBURN: There is absolutely no question that it is a legislative question to start with, but we're going no place there—

THE COURT: But if the legislature does not act, as has occurred in many other instances, then it may behoove this Court to promulgate its definition. Is that correct?

MR. COBURN: That's correct.

THE COURT: We did it not too many days ago, or weeks ago in *Robinson* v. *Cahill* and many other cases.

THE COURT: Mr. Coburn, would that be appropriate in the case where all the parties in the case agree that this individual is not dead?

MR. COBURN: That's the real argument why it's not necessary in this case.

THE COURT: Everybody in this case, including the Plaintiff, concedes that this person is not dead.

MR. COBURN: That's absolutely correct.

THE COURT: Well, then, do you seriously suggest that this Court should enter into an inquiry as to whether she's dead or not, and perhaps decide that she is dead? Do you suggest, for a moment, that that would be appropriate?

MR. COBURN: Well I don't think that's what I'm talking about. As far as the brain death standard, she wouldn't meet it.

THE COURT: No. The broad question addressed to you by Justice Clifford and by Justice Pashman is whether this case, in its present posture, is an appropriate vehicle for the Court to determine what is the criteria of death.

Now your answer was in the affirmative. Do you persist in that answer in the light of the fact that in this record all the parties involved concede that this person is still alive?

MR. COBURN: As an attorney, as an attorney my answer to that question is that—well I persist because I'm a person. Whether I'm an attorney or a guardian, or an attorney for a guardian, my answer is obviously "no," that it isn't something that would be purely dicta in this particular case anyhow.

THE COURT: Would it be good judicial policy for this Court to enter into a determination as to the criteria of death, in this particular case on these facts and in the posture of the issues as they have been presented by the parties?

MR. COBURN: I can think of one justification for it, and only one. And that is, other than classical considerations, that somebody is finally deciding what death is in New Jersey.

But the practical consideration is that, as I understand Miss Quinlan's condition, one of the doctors—as I recall, Dr. Morse—indicated that her condition could deteriorate, and we might very well find ourselves in a situation where she would meet the qualifications of brain death. And of course then, we're going to be back—I assume back before Judge Muir—to make that decision. And, at that point, as I understand what happens when a person is brain dead, we're not talking about six weeks or eight weeks or two months or two years, we're talking about a decision that will have to be made in two days, three days, something along that line. And—

THE COURT: Mr. Coburn, is that the answer, though, to the last question? That Miss Quinlan is alive only in the traditional sense of death—that being the cessation of circulatory and cardiovascular activity—period? Dead, according to that standard, rather than alive? I'm

246

sorry. I meant to say that she's alive, according to that standard, but that perhaps she would be dead according to another standard, another definition. Is not that the answer to Judge Conford's concern, that all parties agree that she is alive? I say "alive," but "alive" according to the traditional standards.

MR. COBURN: Right. She would probably be alive according to the traditional standard, even if Dr. Korein's standard is applicable.

THE COURT: That's right. That's right. Isn't that a crucial point in this case?

MR. COBURN: Whether she's alive or dead?

THE COURT: Whether she's alive or dead. Isn't that a crucial point?

MR. COBURN: Oh, certainly. That's the case, as far as I was concerned right from the start, whether she was. Whatever the standard might be, if the plaintiff alleged, whether there was going to be brain death or it was going to be something even more—I used the word "advanced" in the sense of a more remote standard. That's what the issue was. As a matter of fact, I think it was—

THE COURT: You mean in the original complaint?

MR. COBURN: Yes.

THE COURT: But not the amended complaint.

MR. COBURN: No. It was removed by the supplemental complaint; that's right.

THE COURT: It is not before us today.

MR. COBURN: That's correct, although—

THE COURT: Why?

MR. COBURN: Well, that's correct.

THE COURT: Was it really removed, sir? All they said there, as I read the stipulation, was to the effect that she was "alive," in accordance with existing legal and medical definitions, period.

MR. COBURN: That's right.

THE COURT: That didn't say that we shouldn't consider whether or not it ought to be changed.

MR. COBURN: The stipulation?

THE COURT: No. I'm saying that the stipulation did not foreclose a court from considering whether or not the definition of death should be changed. Isn't that true?

MR. COBURN: I agree. At the trial I think the evidence could have—

For instance, Dr. Korein's standard, which was the closest I could see to meeting of Karen's condition, because it's senseless to proffer brain death as the standard when she obviously doesn't meet that anyhow. But where his condition, or his description of a condition, which as I recall—I know I asked the question, as I remember, and his answer pretty vividly was the situation of a person who's born without any brain at all—a child. And he described her condition as somewhat close to—I forgot exactly what word he used, but that's how he described her condition. He said it's his opinion, and probably a lot of doctors opinions, that she is not alive if you talk about a function—whether she can smell, or whether she can think, or she can feel emotions. And I assumed all the way up until the trial, to be honest, that's what I thought the—I didn't know exactly what his testimony was going to be, but that's what the Plaintiff's contention was going to be, and I think there might have been—I'm not saying the Court would accept that definition, but I think the facts could have very well met Dr. Korein's standard by all the witnesses including Dr. [Inaudible] who was a witness that I called on my behalf as guardian. I think, as I recall, Dr. Cook and Dr. Loeser also agreed that she met that criteria, if that is what the criteria for death was.

THE COURT: Well, Mr. Coburn, of course this Court isn't foreclosed from considering it. There is precious little that this Court is foreclosed from considering. The fact remains, however, that it is not an issue before this Court. You, for one, who presently seem to attach some significance to it, but perhaps only because we're forcing you to it by the questions, didn't even brief it. It isn't mentioned in this—

MR. COBURN: That's correct.

THE COURT: —splendid 59 page brief, every word of which I read. Nowhere is it touched upon. It's true Mr. Porzio touched upon it, and no one else does.

Now what is the answer to Judge Conford's question? As a matter of sound judicial policy, do you suggest that we now undertake to consider what I referred to as "this portentous question," in the context of this litigation as it gets to this Court?

MR. COBURN: I still say, yes, regardless of any—

THE COURT: How, then, is it that you failed to brief it?

MR. COBURN: It's probably dereliction.

THE COURT: I can't believe it.

THE COURT: You might tell us that sound judicial procedures should be left to us; that that's our headache, and not yours.

MR. COBURN: I'm not going to say that. I'm not going to comment at all.

THE COURT: Well, feel free to say it, because really that problem is ours.

[Laughter.]

THE COURT: Mr. Coburn, you say the issue should be addressed. Now how should we decide it? Should we say that this girl is not dead? Or that she is dead?

MR. COBURN: Depending on what standard you accept—

THE COURT: Now wait a minute. You're the advocate. You say that we should address the issue?

MR. COBURN: Yes.

THE COURT: Now in this case, should we decide that the girl is dead, or that she's alive?

MR. COBURN: I think that brain death, as far as this Court could possibly—

THE COURT: The answer to my question? Is she alive, or dead?

MR. COBURN: She's alive—alive, under brain death—and that would be as much medical testimony—

THE COURT: Now wait a minute. Now don't start—you suggested to the Court that we should determine what death is.

MR. COBURN: That's correct.

THE COURT: I now ask you as an advocate, since you want that issue determined, what is your contention? Is it your contention that this girl is dead, or alive?

MR. COBURN: Alive.

THE COURT: All right.

MR. COBURN: But in a condition that Mr. Armstrong indicated. A year is how long she may live. I don't think anyone has any idea at all, because I think all the doctors testified that, in a sense, she's a rarity that anyone has ever lived this long.

THE COURT: By the way, is it agreed by everybody that she is substantially in the same condition now as she was when the testimony was taken? Is that the general agreement?

MR. COBURN: I discussed with Mr. Curtin as to what her condition was, and he advised me—

THE COURT: The answer is yes, she's substantially in the same condition.

MR. COBURN: Right.

THE COURT: Mr. Coburn, do you agree with the general observation that has been made that physicians often withhold treatment of hopeless cases—let's call it that—in order to hasten death that way? The observation has been made, and we all sort of recognize it goes on in hospitals. Do you subscribe to that situation today as fact of life?

MR. COBURN: With one qualification, yes. That condition exists, but it seems that from the doctors I discussed this with, that the doctors placed great significance in whether somebody removed the respirator or didn't give any additional treatment, such as if a kidney transplant, for instance, might have been necessary.

THE COURT: Well, they draw a distinction in one of the cases as between not replacing the oxygen tent when it became empty, and terminating by withdrawing the plug.

MR. COBURN: Right.

THE COURT: Is that right?

MR. COBURN: Right. All the doctors seem to—yes, they seem to have a significance—

THE COURT: Right? They saw a great world of difference in that factual pattern.

MR. COBURN: That's right.
I don't think any of the doctors who testified here, as I recall, would have discontinued the respirator; but I think if questions had been pursued, I think most of them would have agreed—

THE COURT: They would have done other—

MR. COBURN: Dr. Cook, I can state as far as what his testimony indicated, that it was "benign neglect," "judicious neglect."

THE COURT: Judicious neglect, yes.

MR. COBURN: You just don't have to carry the same level of medication.

THE COURT: They just did not subscribe to the individual actively seeking death, but rather passively submitting to death?

MR. COBURN: That's correct. I don't think any of them, for instance, would let her starve to death. I don't think that was a possibility.

THE COURT: I understand.

MR. COBURN: But I think it would be, if her condition now develops—and not a condition such as infection and you had to increase the dosage of medication—but, for instance, if her kidneys stopped working. I myself weighed that possibility when I was the guardian, as to what I would possibly do if that occurred.

I might state one thing. I think Mr. Armstrong has the position of, or the function of the guardian a little bit confused, and perhaps it's that he answered the question that was asked and didn't have to carry forward, but as I understood Judge Muir's opinion, the guardian was not just supposed to do something if the parents were out of town. It was supposed to be if the doctor felt medical tradition required—or medical treatment required something to be done, and the family refused to consent to it. That is when the guardian was to be consulted. So it's a little bit more than a surrogate father. As to Mr. Quinlan's interest in being appointed the guardian in all respects, I would say this: That if Mr. Quinlan has no particular—or has no reason at all to disagree with whatever treatment the doctors might suggest, and other than the question of pride or honor—I can understand his position. The guardian has no further function, either, so I don't know why the guardian should object. I know why I myself ended up upsetting them, or I know at least why I feel I upset them, and that was a situation that was very quickly remedied. But now the present guardian, Mr. Curtin, has met with the family and apparently they have no objection to him—

THE COURT: Well, I assume they do. Mr. Armstrong said it still remains with Mr. Quinlan the matter of pride, honor, and truth, that he be appointed guardian of the person of his daughter.

MR. COBURN: As attorney for the guardian, I would strongly object to that.

THE COURT: Why?

MR. COBURN: Because a situation might very well develop where something affirmative should be done; and I'm talking purely speculation because this case, at this point, from a medical point of view, as Justice Pashman said before, who knows what will develop tomorrow? Who knows what change in her condition may occur? The doctors can't even tell us what caused her condition because there isn't enough—

THE COURT: Well, give me the situation you foresee that would put him in conflict, the sort of conflict that is resolved by his not being the guardian, and by Mr. Curtin's being the guardian?

MR. COBURN: As far as that, I think it's critical that somebody totally detached, such as Mr. Curtin, be available to make the decision that the doctor suggests. That decision might very well—

THE COURT: Give me a specific instance, will you?

251

MR. COBURN: All right. If the doctor says her kidneys have malfunctioned and it's his opinion that she ought to be put on a dialysis machine, for instance, and they speak to Mr. Quinlan. And Mr. Quinlan says: Look, enough is enough. You already have her on a respirator. I don't want—before you put her on the dialysis, then we'll never be able to get her off the dialysis machine. I'm not saying this critically, that Mr. Quinlan would say it, but I'm using this hypothetically—

THE COURT: I understand. That's what I asked you.

MR. COBURN: Mr. Quinlan says: No. I will not consent to it. And the doctor says no, I don't know which way to go on this, but I feel this should be done. Mr. Curtin, as I understand Judge Muir's opinion, at that point is to be consulted to obtain his consent. And if his consent, for instance Mr. Curtin doesn't consent either, I know from my discussions with Mr. Curtin and certainly I think any lawyers under these circumstances, would then appear in court and say to Judge Muir: Can we have some direction? Because the family doesn't want this, and I don't want it as the guardian, but it's a medical decision, and what is the court's opinion? I think Mr. Curtin and myself, both, feel very strongly that before anything is done of any significance, other than for instance changing a diet or maybe using drugs for bed sores instead of heat lamps, anything beyond that was done, that it would be with the court's direction. And if the court said: Look, you're the guardian; you go ahead and make those decisions yourself—that's fine. I think it's much better to be told to grow up and make some decisions yourself, than not to ask at all and have a decision made that might very well influence this girl's—whatever life she has left.

THE COURT: Do you think that is—I take it that what you're suggesting is based upon its being in keeping with the spirit of Judge Muir's decision? That is, in the hypothesis that you suggested, if Mr. Quinlan indeed says, enough is enough and I will not authorize you to go to put my daughter on a dialysis machine, Mr. Curtin ought to be in a position, if he sees fit, of overruling that and authorizing that?

MR. COBURN: Definitely.

THE COURT: All right.

MR. COBURN: Even though that decision—we've never really discussed what would happen in that situation, but I think even in that decision Mr. Curtin would probably ask the court for some direction.

THE COURT: Well, irrespective of what he might do, your legal position is that he would be permitted to overrule the father's decision and authorize a physician to do that which he suggests?

252

MR. COBURN: That's right. As I recall, Judge Muir said that the family's position is that they can approve—if they approve—for instance, a change in the medical treatment where there is no necessity at all to speak to Mr. Curtin because the doctors can do as the doctors feel they should, other than to make the final decision. And this qualification is not in the opinion, but it's something that I think perhaps should be stated. Unless the doctor says: Look, I feel at this point that now medical tradition supports my belief that I can discontinue the respirator, although I just don't see any doctors, in this particular case, making any decisions at all. If one thing has occurred as a result of this case, I think at least the doctors involved, and probably other doctors, are now going to be much more concerned about judicial approval than might have occurred before this.

THE COURT: Would Mr. Curtin have any hesitancy in recommending not putting the girl on a dialysis machine, if he felt that under all the circumstances the doctor's recommendation not to do it was warranted? Or would he feel compelled to advise against any life-termination situation?

MR. COBURN: Mr. Curtin, being an attorney, is sitting right next to me—

THE COURT: No, I mean—I'm asking you this for a purpose. I assume that thousands of decisions like this are made daily throughout the country. And they are made by families that have no predilection one way or the other, but use their best judgment on the basis of the situation presented to them by a physician. Now is it your point that Mr. Quinlan is not in a position of exercising a *de novo* judgment, because he's made up his mind one way?

MR. COBURN: That's partially a fact to be considered. And again it's not said critically, but he has indicated what his preferences were in this particular matter. It's very difficult to then come back and say: Well, that's my feelings—because things can be so subtle. A decision can be so subtle that you can say one thing, and appear to be complying with the court's decision. I think it's much better, even though the appointment of a guardian is obviously—in a case like this it's obviously something that's a lot more significant than I think any of us thought at the beginning. The appointment of an external guardian—

THE COURT: May I ask you a question? I'm a little concerned by a statement in Judge Muir's opinion in which he says that the decision of this matter is for the doctors.

Now do you think that he meant by that to be making a judicial declaration about whatever the doctors decide in a situation like this goes without any adverse consequences to the doctor? In other words, did he mean to say that if the doctor decided to terminate the life apparatus, that that would—that that decision would be without adverse consequences to the doctor?

MR. COBURN: It certainly reads that way, but I would—from the rest of the decision—I would have to say that that statement must be read in context with his statement about brain death being an acceptable standard. And I think—

THE COURT: And other statements to the effect that termination of the apparatus would be homicide.

MR. COBURN: That's right.

THE COURT: So where do you think the trial judge stands on this issue?

MR. COBURN: I read it to mean the following: That assuming her condition had deteriorated, or had reached a brain death criteria, at that point what was to be done was to be a medical decision. And I note—

THE COURT: Only if it reaches the brain death situation?

MR. COBURN: That's how I read it. And I hoped that's what he meant, because it created even more problems than with no criteria at all. Because you may have one doctor making a decision he feels very strongly about, using some standards other than brain death. That's why I think it's significant in this. Karen Quinlan's case is not, in the sense of brain death, a very significant case at all, because her condition is not brain dead. She—I think Dr. Plum stated he felt there were 13 criteria for brain death, because each doctor has their own opinion, and breaks it down into separate categories. And I remember I asked him the question on a pass/fail basis: Did she meet any of the qualifications, and he said "no." So I think, in that sense, her case is very easy because she doesn't approach brain death. But when you get somebody—and I don't know whether you make it a numerical system or you make it an absolute system—she meets every criteria of brain death, that situation comes up, and that's why I asked the court, regardless of any dereliction on my part or whether Mr. Porzio's brief will be sufficient for my argument, or whatever, that something be said in that line. And I realize that, even in this case, unless it's framed in, assuming that her condition deteriorated and the judge will be faced with determining brain death, is that an acceptable standard? We therefore give this statement: Regardless of how it's stated, it happens—

THE COURT: In other words, you think that there is a desirable certainty in the law, but that the certainty should be resolved by the court saying that unless there is brain death in a sense in which most medical experts say there is brain death, there it should not be regarded to be legal death?

MR. CURTIN: That's right.

THE COURT: And what would be your position, then, in the event that Karen met the brain death test where we are faced with the opposite situation? That is, the father saying: I do not want the life-sustaining device removed?

MR. CURTIN: Under—

THE COURT: Wait a minute now. Under Judge Muir's opinion, which seems to leave that decision to the physician, but perhaps only in the context of a contest between him and the father in the other direction, would you say that the physician could, nevertheless, remove the—

MR. CURTIN: Absolutely not.

THE COURT: Of course not. All right.

MR. CURTIN: One other thing that I felt should be brought to the Court's attention—or at least discussed—is on the religious argument that was made, where Mr. Quinlan is obviously a devout Catholic. Karen was baptized as a Catholic. There is no evidence to indicate that she also is not a Catholic—a devout Catholic. As I recall the testimony at the trial, and accepting as I did for purposes of the trial Mrs. Quinlan's statements as to Karen's beliefs that she would not want to be sustained by extraordinary measures, those statements were not said by Karen, for whatever weight we give them, in a religious context; and it might very well be that I would feel, yes, I don't want to be a vegetable. I don't want to be kept alive. And whatever the words that were used, I'm sure Karen said something indicating that. Those statements were, as I recall them, never made in a religious circumstance. And the fact would seem to belie that they could have, because the Quinlan family itself was not even aware of the extraordinary measure situation in Catholic dogma before this, before Karen went into the coma.

THE COURT: Well, that argument is made by them not in a religious context, but in the context of the right of privacy. That is, the right of self-determination of existence, as I understand it.

MR. COBURN: Well I—at least the conversation, the dialogue that occurred here, I know there was some mention of Mr. Quinlan being a devout Catholic; and that we were infringing—well, not "we," but Judge Muir was infringing upon his right of exercise of religion. And I might—while it's not before the Court, perhaps that argument might be valid if Mr. Quinlan were making this decision. But we have an optional rule, or an optional dogma of the Catholic Church being exercised by a person, Mr. Quinlan, who feels one way. But there is no reason to believe that Karen—despite the fact that she might make the right of self-determination argument: I don't want to be kept alive under those circumstances—there is no reason to believe that she would put it in the religious framework. And I think if she doesn't put it in the religious framework, and it's obviously a situation that can't be remedied at this point, that the religious argument just doesn't apply.

THE COURT: How about in the light of the right of privacy? Let me ask you to assume, although this is a hard thing to assume, that she is in exactly the same hopeless state that she is, but sufficiently cognitive to express a desire to have it terminated. She communicates that to the doctor. The doctor says "no." She communicates that to a lawyer. The lawyer goes to court. Should the Court grant the request under those circumstances?

MR. COBURN: That's—obviously that's a great question. As I know the cases—there were a couple of cases from Illinois, as I recall—

THE COURT: I think your adversaries are assuming that the Court's answer to that would be "yes," and they say that that being so, then constructively the parents should be able to exercise that choice.

MR. COBURN: Well, I say the answer is "no," but it becomes very hypocritical because the only distinction between Karen, in that situation, and Karen when she's told she has cancer and is going to die in three days, and just walks out of the hospital—

THE COURT: Take the Chief Justice's example that was given to us a little while ago. A person in absolute hopelessness, and bound to face constant pain and suffering for the remaining weeks or months that they have, should that person not have a right to be terminated if the person wants to?

MR. COBURN: If they are making the decision?

THE COURT: Is there any social value in condemning that individual to suffer for the few weeks or months that that person has left, in an otherwise hopeless context?

MR. COBURN: I see none.

As a result of the Quinlan case, obviously other things made the news. And there was a fellow out West who walked off a dialysis machine—walked out, went home. And I saw on television where he was dying. And I couldn't see anything—any court having any obligations there, or any—I couldn't see the prosecutor, for instance, going in and saying: Put him back in the hospital and put him on the machine.

THE COURT: That individual should have the right to make that choice?

MR. COBURN: Absolutely.

THE COURT: The only difference we have here is that the individual, the choice is being made by a friend, the parent, the guardian, and so forth.

MR. COBURN: Right. And I would also assume that the individual is capable of making the choice, such as—

THE COURT: Well we're assuming that in the hypothesis given to you.

MR. COBURN: Right.

THE COURT: Can I take it back on another thing, Mr. Coburn?

I was very interested in your asking the Court to define death, and Judge Muir when he was talking of brain death—when he was talking about brain death—used the, he said there should be applied extant recognized medical standards. I think some argument could be made, but you box yourself in if you try to come up with a precise definition, for the very reasons that some of the Justices here have elaborated on. Medical science is progressing and changing so much that what we may define today may be obsolete tomorrow, and why not? Why isn't Judge Muir's characterization of application of extant recognized medical standards of brain death a better way to handle it?

MR. COBURN: Because at least we can set the lowest common denominator. That is the only thing that *In re Karen Quinlan*, 20 years from now—I hope that is what the case is known for—that it sets the minimum common denominator. This at least is brain dead, or brain death. So that people, so that at least there is some criteria, even if that's an insufficient criteria, and medical science advances or medical decisions are made; and it should be something higher than that, but at least we have that. But right now—

THE COURT: But what we say is brain death today might not be tomorrow. And yet we might be giving a precise definition that is no longer medically acceptable, unless we keep changing it. Isn't it better to use the more flexible standard? I'm merely throwing it out.

MR. COBURN: I would just say this: That what we have now is nothing. And while the standard of brain death is probably insufficient, or will be insufficient in two years, it certainly is better than nothing. Because right now I think there's just mass confusion.

THE COURT: Don't you think that the medical profession, Mr. Coburn, would welcome—would embrace some guidelines from this Court concerning this problem?

MR. COBURN: I will answer this as to myself. I don't want to preclude on Mr. Porzio.

THE COURT: Obviously.

257

MR. COBURN: I would say yes.

THE COURT: I'll put that to Mr. Porzio later.

MR. COBURN: Yes. I say without question that at least something is there.

THE COURT: They are in the dark today.

MR. COBURN: Right. They certainly are. And I might state, in this particular case, perhaps the best thing that happened in this particular case was being a volunteer case—on all parties concerned, and I assume Mr. Armstrong's witnesses, also. We didn't get into the, "well, he's a defense witness, or he's a plaintiff's witness," because there were witnesses that testified frankly regardless of whose toes they stepped on, or whether they were pro-brain-death or anti-brain-death. I think we got a fair analysis of the problem. I don't think we had nearly as much as you could in the legislature, but I just don't see anything coming from that side.

THE COURT: Particularly as things stand on the recognition that there is civil and criminal exposure. And there are civil and criminal in these cases that would definitely scare away a doctor from exercising what would be a normal discretion, perhaps, and therefore he should welcome some guidelines.

MR. COBURN: I would say so. Even if it's an insufficient guidance, at least it's something. Because right now—

THE COURT: Something more than we have today.

MR. COBURN: Right, which is, the person is alive as long as they are breathing, and the heart is beating.

THE COURT: Well, in malpractice cases we use the flexible standard, don't we?

MR. COBURN: As I understand it, I don't—malpractice isn't one of my specialties.

Other than that, unless there are some questions from the Court, that's basically my position.

CHIEF JUSTICE HUGHES: Thank you, Mr. Coburn, very much.
Mr. Attorney General Hyland?

ORAL ARGUMENT OF WILLIAM F. HYLAND, ESQ., ON
BEHALF OF RESPONDENT STATE OF NEW JERSEY
AND OFFICE OF THE ATTORNEY GENERAL

MR. HYLAND: If it please the Court:
I think the difficulty that we have seen here today, and throughout the trial period of the case, demonstrates why, in my judgment, these

258

problems should be left, as Judge Muir suggested, to the medical profession. And being very willing to jump right into what seems to be one of the more specific controversies, I would very much oppose any effort on the part of this Court, on this record, to define death. It is not an issue in the case, by stipulation. There is no record from which this Court could go into the technical aspects of a definition of death under 1976 standards, as opposed to what we all know was so comparatively easy in the past. You would feel the pulse, put your ear or stethoscope on the chest of an individual, and if there was no heart and no pulse and no respiration, there was death. And in Black's Law Dictionary we lawyers very cleverly said that death is the opposite of life. I think it's a much more complex problem today. The medical profession has made some effort to establish measurable criteria in such studies as the Ad Hoc Committee in Harvard in 1968. And so we have, for a particular kind of an injury, a particular kind of a physical condition, brain death criteria. But that doesn't begin—

CHIEF JUSTICE HUGHES: Mr. Attorney General Hyland, let me just interrupt you and ask you to resolve a doubt that I have? The thing that bothers me here, as it bothered me in an opinion I wrote for the Court many years ago in the *Wynn* case which was reversed by this Court—but I felt then that a prosecutor could not really do an honest job unless he had discretion and unless he didn't need to be worried whether some taxpayer group, or some outside group, would get him indicted, or get him in trouble, if he had to consider in any way his own well-being, he couldn't be looked to for the honest discretion that a prosecutor should use.

Now, as I say, there was a little difference of opinion about how it came out the other end of the horn, but that theory—it's all very well to say, by way of platitude, that it's up to the doctor. But if the doctor has to worry about the personal consequences to himself, civil or criminal, how can his opinion be considered on that lofty plane of the best interest to his patient? That's what bothers me.

MR. HYLAND: Well, notwithstanding the fact, Mr. Chief Justice, that you were reversed in that case by the upper court, I think that your opinion was a very profound statement of the dilemma to which public officers and people who practice public professions are put in trying to determine what their duties are and in trying to receive protection from the criticism that may arise after the performance of those duties.

We have begun today in New Jersey, and in every other state, through the Anatomical Gift Act, to begin to provide protection for the practitioners who must make decisions under modern standards that have permitted life to be artificially prolonged far beyond the point at which the heart and lungs would have failed, except for respirators and other devices of that type. If we do anything at all, I think something

259

should be done in the legislature to make it clear that the declaration of death by a physician, under accepted medical standards and traditions, will provide him with some protection from civil and criminal responsibility, even where that declaration is not part of an organ transplant patient procedure. Because under the 1969 statute, that's the only application that it has. If organs are going to be transplanted, a physician has the right to make a declaration of death. And I suggest that in the kind of case that we're dealing with today, he probably would not make that declaration unless the Harvard criteria for brain death or some other accepted medical standard had been first met, and he had conferred with the family and had conferred with other colleagues.

CHIEF JUSTICE HUGHES: Well that kind of legislation, in effect, would give the doctor—it would give the doctor the same freedom of action that the law gives the court. For instance, a judge is entitled to decide a case without worrying too much whether the loser is going to sue him or not, and the reason for that is so he can be honest and objective in his decision.

MR. HYLAND: I think that's all well and good. But to attempt to go beyond the kind of bodily problems, health problems, that lend themselves to accurate measurements, scientific measurements, I think is very dangerous. If we are to go into the area where it's pain that might be the criteria, or the financial circumstances of the family, or age, or despair, or the psychological outlook, or whatever, I think we're getting into areas where we simply don't have the competence today to be precise enough and useful enough. And I recommend to the Court the opinion filed by then-Judge Berger in the *Georgetown Hospital* case, which has been cited in all the briefs, in which he indicated that there are points beyond which judicial powers should not be exercised.

THE COURT: But, General, based upon what you just said concerning pain and other observations that are made, really doesn't the horror of continued pseudo-life cry out for some type of handling, some type of treatment by a court, to perhaps eliminate that situation, or to diminish the impact of that situation?

MR. HYLAND: I'm not really persuaded, Justice Pashman, by that kind of emotional concern. I recognize that life has a great many burdens, a great many pains and anguish—

THE COURT: I didn't say "emotion." When I'm talking about truly a horrible existence, that's not emotion; that's a fact in given cases. The ones you referred to.

MR. HYLAND: Let me say what I would agree with, for example. In this case, when I first entered it, it was out of concern that notwithstanding the advice of the treating physician, and notwithstanding the position of the Hospital, that the family contended that there was still a right to die. And as Attorney General, under the *Parens Patriae* responsibilities that we have to look out for the disabled and the weak and the helpless, it seemed to me that my office should be involved in order to do what it could to seek that this case did not go beyond what we would consider to be reasonable, sensible bounds in the interests of protecting these incompetents of all ages and all conditions throughout this State. And I found that the treating physicians—and I recommend to Your Honors, because it is pertinent to the question that was asked earlier, at page 117 of the transcript, which involved cross-examination by me of Dr. Morse, in which I specifically asked him if my understanding was correct, that even if an order should be entered in this case authorizing the guardian to direct the discontinuance of the extraordinary support measures, that you, Dr. Morse, would resist that order? And I asked him if that was a correct statement, and he said it was. He went on to qualify it somewhat by saying that he was very much influenced by discussions that he had had, or that he might have with colleagues of his, and if they could show him some cases where what the Quinlans wanted would fit, he would honor the request; otherwise, no, he would even resist a court order. And Dr. Javed, the other treating physician, was cross-examined at page 200 of the transcript, and expressly said in response to a question from me:

> "Q. Do you have an opinion as to whether an order by this court directing the removal of Karen from the respirator would be in violation of those traditional standards, medical practices in your field of specialty?"

And his answer was:

> "A. That is how I feel, yes."

Now I ask the Court—rhetorically—but I ask the Court: How can any of us hope to come to grips, in a case like this, with a definition that will be helpful to physicians or to hospitals when these two very expert men, whose care and treatment was commended by everybody in the case, have said that it would be contrary to accepted medical practice and tradition to do what this family has requested? What do we tell these doctors, then, if we're going to tell them something that's contrary to medical tradition and practice?

THE COURT: General, assuming the patient involved is an adult of sound mind, and one who had reached a point where he has been advised that the illness is terminal, and he has three months to live; and assuming any other facts to do away with the problems of a minor, or the problems of an incompetent, assuming those facts, what is the State's position with reference to the right of such an individual to make a decision to accelerate his death?

MR. HYLAND: What you bother me with is when you say "accelerate," Justice Pashman.

THE COURT: How would you like me to say it? To "terminate" his life? To "refuse treatment"?

MR. HYLAND: To refuse treatment.

THE COURT: To passively submit, rather than actively involve himself?

MR. HYLAND: I'm not sure. I'm not sure that what I'm saying is consistent with the *Heston* case. I think you can possibly read into the *Heston* case—

THE COURT: General, as I said earlier, the *Heston* case was cited by everybody, and it has such little value—

MR. HYLAND: That doesn't make it wrong; it makes it popular. But—

THE COURT: Well I know, but you can twist it and turn it any way you want, but I would like the—

MR. HYLAND: I read into the *Heston* case the possibility that medical treatment might be—even be forced upon an individual who was competent, and who felt hopeless, and felt in a terminal stage and wanted to reject that treatment.

THE COURT: And therefore you feel—

MR. HYLAND: I think maybe *Heston* went too far, in that respect, and I don't know of any other decision in the country that's gone quite that far.

THE COURT: Other than that, though, your response to my question would be what, then? The State's position in that set of facts would be what?

MR. HYLAND: The State's position, I should really express more as an individual than as Attorney General, but let me tell you what I would have done in this case had the medical testimony been uniform that tradition would permit the discontinuance of the respirator.

I would not have objected to that. I can tell you what I would have done if the testimony in this case had been uncontroverted that Karen Quinlan had reached the point of brain death: I would not have objected to that. I think that that, then, would have been very much like the *Perricone* case that this Court decided in 1962, where a unanimous Court—and you recall that was another blood transfusion case involving a blue baby—said that the Court might have been persuaded otherwise if the plaintiff—if the Appellant had been able to show that there was controverted medical testimony about what the result would have been; or if there had been testimony indicating that the treatment was proffered and rejected—had some risks to it—it might have been different. But the implication of that decision, I think, which has not been overruled in any sense that I can find, is that the Court ought to be guided by what the medical testimony is in cases like this. And I believe it was Justice Sullivan who talked about the malpractice cases. Why, of course, whether we're talking about doctors or engineers or whatever it is, the standard is: What is ordinary care? What is the accepted practice? What is the accepted tradition of the profession?

THE COURT: Is it practical to handle this entire problem on an ad hoc basis, though, rather than try to reach out for some guidelines to generally assist the medical profession?

MR. HYLAND: I have talked to some doctors, Justice Pashman, since the *Quinlan* decision was handed down by Judge Muir, who expressed concern about it. And I said they should read it carefully, and then they should talk to their lawyers to find out what it really means, because it didn't mean at all what they thought it meant.

The renologists told me that they thought it really meant that they had to stop making kidney transplants. That just isn't so. They had totally ignored, for example, the protection that they have under the 1969 Statute, by saying that the issue in this case ought to be left to the doctors and not to the court. I don't think there was any suggestion by Judge Muir that doctors are not to bear responsibility if they practice their profession ineptly. I read in this morning's papers a survey saying that some 16,000 doctors in the country are probably incompetent, and we only get 66 of them a year. That's unfortunate.

THE COURT: Mr. Hyland, do you think that Judge Muir limited this decision that you're talking about to a situation where disposition found brain death on application of accepted medical criteria?

MR. HYLAND: No, I don't think so. I think that—

THE COURT: You don't think he said that?

MR. HYLAND: No. I think brain death might have been the accepted measurement in this kind of a case, but he did not intend to suggest that it was the measurement in some other cancer case, or coronary or stroke case.

THE COURT: Well do you think—do you think the Court can give any kind of guidance in this situation? Or should it just deal with the case before it?

MR. HYLAND: I think, Judge Conford, that this Court ought to deal with just the case before it. And if it's going to go beyond what the issues that have been briefed and presented are, then the case should be remanded to the trial court again so that the record could be amplified and so that we could address ourselves to different kinds of death situations.

THE COURT: So that even were we to ask you to brief the question of how you measure death, if I understand your position, the record in this case is insufficient from which to construct an illuminating brief?

MR. HYLAND: Absolutely insufficient.

THE COURT: Is that right?

MR. HYLAND: That's correct.

THE COURT: And if we stay with the trial court disposition, General, what have we contributed to this whole problem?

MR. HYLAND: That's something else. That's something else.

MR. HYLAND: And now that it's here, it doesn't mean that we should deal inexpertly with it.

THE COURT: I agree with you overwhelmingly about that, that it doesn't belong here. It should never have been started, but it was started, and it's here. Now, again, usually we try to contribute something towards a solution. I guess that's our primary and ultimate function here. And I suggest to you: What have we contributed to this very, very difficult problem by going along with the trial court disposition?

MR. HYLAND: I think this case has had a very constructive result, in that it has focused a great deal of attention within the legal professions and the medical profession and elsewhere and on the part of the public in general, on this problem. The problem being that medical science has reached a point in the last 20 years, particularly with heart transplants and with the development of these pulmonary devices and organ transplants and so on, so that earlier legal and legislative standards are probably insufficient. And I would hope that the attention that has been focused would engender interest—and it has—but even more interest on the part of the legislature, in looking not just at one person, and not considering the tenants of just one faith, and not dealing with just one kind of a health condition, but that the whole problem would be looked at. And that the expert advice of a number of disciplines would be invited in a much broader way than the judicial record indicates that it's possible to go after a problem like this. And I would hope that New Jersey would adopt, legislatively, a definition of brain death, for example, and perhaps that's as far as we can go at this point.

It may be another 20 years before we can accurately, responsibly, reliably measure the indicators that would tell the physicians that someone's life deserves to be terminated because it's absolutely hopeless. No doctor in this case really said that it was absolutely hopeless.

CHIEF JUSTICE HUGHES: Well perhaps, General, perhaps the medical profession is looking for some kind of a Good Samaritan concept such as this State put through with regard to a person injured along a highway. Along comes a doctor or a nurse who won't touch him because of the fear of malpractice claims and so forth. And there was an immunity created by statute to cover such a case. Now, always clinging to the good medical practice, the same as malpractice, the rule is: Could there not be some statutory way—I guess it would have to be not a court-way, a decision-way—to release a doctor of the fear of personal consequences to himself so long as he is basing that decision on good medical practice? He doesn't have that now, so I would doubt that his decision is uncolored by fear of his own personal consequences.

MR. HYLAND: Well I think the qualifier, you know, "so long as it's in accordance with good, sound medical practice," is something that makes your suggestion more acceptable than the—otherwise, I would rebel at the thought of singling out a profession and saying that in almost all circumstances, except perhaps gross negligence or whatever the legislature ended up calling it, that a practitioner would have immunity if something went awry, because I think it's important to maintain the standards of the medical profession and of other professions. And the one way we do that is by having people feel that they've got to measure up to some standard. And I think that a blanket immunity of responsibility for the consequences of medical misdeeds would be decidedly against the public interest.

CHIEF JUSTICE HUGHES: Thank you very much, General.
Now we have Prosecutor Collester.

ORAL ARGUMENT OF DONALD G. COLLESTER, ESQ., MORRIS COUNTY PROSECUTOR, FOR THE STATE OF NEW JERSEY

MR. COLLESTER: Good morning, Justices.
In response to some of the questions that have been addressed to General Hyland, and also to Mr. Coburn, I would like to offer my thought here, that I don't think it would be appropriate for this Court to engage in a discussion, in whatever opinion it writes, of death. We did not try that case. We did not adduce witnesses that otherwise may have been called. We did not really compare different types of standards. The Harvard Ad Hoc standard is one most commonly mentioned but there was also a Duquesne standard. Dr. Korein talked in terms of cerebral death—and, by the way, he also found that Karen Quinlan was not cerebrally dead. I think any definition of death would have to involve—to use a terrible word, now—input from many different types of disciplines, many different types of medical societies, as well as religious thought, and legal thought.

265

THE COURT: Supposing we have that, Mr. Collester? Assuming we did, do you agree that this Court has the power to re-examine and re-define death? And that it should, in fact, take that course, assuming that we had that horrible thing called "input"?

MR. COLLESTER: Well I don't think you have it right now. I'm sure you don't have it, first of all. Secondly, it would be my personal feeling with respect to this matter that the legislative body might be the most appropriate, insofar as it could hold hearings; that there would be, I think it would be able to spend a sufficient amount of time to hear all sides to a controversy, which I found out in the last four or five months, it's almost endless—the nature of the controversy and the nature of the persons who wish to be heard on it. So my feeling would be, and it's a personal feeling, I would tend to think that the legislature would be the appropriate place for such a determination.

Again, I wish to stress here that that's not this case, in any event. Karen Quinlan is alive. She is stipulated to be alive, by any medical standard that we deal with.

THE COURT: Well, you look at it from the point of view of possible criminal involvement as a prosecutor of the County.

MR. COLLESTER: Yes, sir.

THE COURT: Judge Muir, at one point, said that discontinuance of the machine would be a homicide. Do you think that he meant it in that broad a sense? Or that he meant it in a qualified sense?

MR. COLLESTER: He didn't really say that, Justice. If I may, he said it was a "reasonable construction." So I don't know whether he flat came out and said that it would be homicide. He said that it would be a "reasonable construction that the law of this State"—excuse me, this is at page 77 of the appendix, of his opinion—"that it's a reasonable construction that the law of this State would preclude the removal of Karen Quinlan from the respirator." He also noted that—

THE COURT: Well here's what he said:

> "An intricate discussion on semantics and form is not
> required since the substance of the sought-for authori-
> zation would result in the taking of the life of Karen
> when the law of the State indicates that such an author-
> ization would be a homicide."

I'm merely asking whether you consider that he meant that in an absolute sense, or whether it was a qualified statement that he was making.

MR. COLLESTER: That's very difficult for me to answer because also down below there is a footnote in which he, more or less, says—he poses a very interesting question. He doesn't, I don't think, really come to any absolute determination—

266

THE COURT: Because—I only posed the question, because later on, a page or two later, he talks about whether or not, if there's a brain death determined in the application of then-existing medical standards, that would be a proper exercise in medical judgment.

MR. COLLESTER: I think he does, although I don't think he talks in terms of an absolute sense, in any portion of the opinion.

CHIEF JUSTICE HUGHES: Mr. Prosecutor, would you assume something for me?

Supposing that Dr. Morse, on the night Karen Quinlan was received in that hospital, knew then all that he knows now about her condition and prognosis, and he decided, with the consent let's say of her father and mother, not to apply the life-sustaining apparatus. Would you think of prosecuting him in that case?

MR. COLLESTER: I don't think so, no.

CHIEF JUSTICE HUGHES: You wouldn't have a case, would you?

MR. COLLESTER: I wouldn't have a case at all, obviously.

CHIEF JUSTICE HUGHES: What's the essential difference between a decision not to connect the apparatus, and a decision to disconnect the apparatus? Is there any real difference, in logic?

MR. COLLESTER: Yes, I think there is. I think there is, in two parts. First of all we get into the act and omission dichotomy, which here I don't think is really applicable. It's hard to think of something more of an act than literally pulling out a plug, to use an odious phrase associated with this case.

CHIEF JUSTICE HUGHES: Well let me make it easier for you. Supposing that a fuse blew out, and the doctor said: Don't bother restoring that fuse.

MR. COLLESTER: I think he's still got the same problem, in terms of exposure.

THE COURT: Or, he didn't replace the oxygen tent.

MR. COLLESTER: I'm sorry, Justice?

THE COURT: Or he didn't replace the empty oxygen tent?

MR. COLLESTER: I think, under our law right now, there would be exposure to criminal liability—prosecution—as it exists right now, from my reading of it.

THE COURT: You just rebel at the concept, apparently, of affirmatively, as you put it, "pulling this plug," as opposed to all the other measures which will ultimately bring about the same result, and that is death.

MR. COLLESTER: No, I don't—I can see that the criminal law has as one of its basic functions a deterrent. I also think that the law of homicide, in this respect, is relatively clear.

THE COURT: Do you condone the Chief's hypothetical at the time she was brought into the hospital? You say that if the doctors determined not to use the supportive measure, you see nothing wrong?

MR. COLLESTER: I don't think, at that point—it would be my opinion that a duty had not, as yet, taken charge; that once the doctor, together with the parents, had determined that in order to preserve this woman's life, that in order to seek continuance of the life and a possible cure, that these measures had to be taken, at that point in time, once that decision had been made I believe the duty attaches, and therefore the consequences—both civil and criminal—attach thereafter.

THE COURT: I don't understand that. I thought the Chief Justice's hypothesis asks you to assume that that decision had been made already. As soon as she came—that is, upon her arrival at the hospital, a decision is made that it's a matter of absolute necessity, in order for life to be sustained, that the apparatus be attached. And I thought, further, the Chief Justice asked you to assume, if I understood the question, that he asked you the difference between that situation and the one in which the doctor makes a determination to remove the already-attached apparatus. You said there is a difference. What is it?

MR. COLLESTER: I believe there is.

THE COURT: What is it?

MR. COLLESTER: I think, first of all, that once the duty attaches is where I start to function or where at least the law starts to become involved. And perhaps I misunderstood the Chief Justice's hypothetical there slightly, because what I was referring to, if my recollection of the Chief Justice's hypothetical—it was along the lines of asserting that if the doctor knew that there was no hope, that this woman was going to die, that there was absolute—

THE COURT: No hope that she's going to live.

MR. COLLESTER: Excuse me. No hope that she was going to live, that in fact this—he discussed this matter with the parents at that time and the parents concurred with the doctor in his diagnosis, and that they discussed the matter and determined that life-supporting mechanisms would not be instituted.

THE COURT: I see. Then at that point, no duty arises?

MR. COLLESTER: That would be my feeling, sir.

THE COURT: And that's the distinguishing feature between that and the removal of the apparatus. I understand.

MR. COLLESTER: That would be my feeling, yes, sir.

Referring to the law of homicide, I do want to stress—

CHIEF JUSTICE HUGHES: Suppose, Prosecutor, that the life-giving machine—the respirator—became inoperative, sooner or later, and the question came up in discussion with Mr. and Mrs. Quinlan about a new respirator machine. Would they then be able to say: Oh, no, let's not carry this on any further?

You wouldn't have a disconnection there. You wouldn't have an affirmative act there. You would have a failure to continue, or to install the new respirator there.

MR. COLLESTER: You would have an affirmative cessation of treatment which was being afforded in accordance with standard medical practice. I think my feeling would be, under that hypothetical, Chief Justice, that it would not be permissible within the scope of the criminal law.

CHIEF JUSTICE HUGHES: The difference seems a little flimsy to me.

THE COURT: Why should that make any difference?

THE COURT: What difference does it make whether or not you hadn't applied the respirator at the start, or you had?

THE COURT: Some more shades of difference.

MR. COLLESTER: I grant you there are more shades of difference. There are quite a few in this case. I would—at the very beginning, I think it's a matter of when the duty attaches. And I think the duty would attach once the parents and the doctor concurred, or if the doctor, if there are no parents available, placed the individual on the respirator. Subsequently, if a respirator burned out, if a fuse blew, I think the treatment still must be continued. That would be my feeling about it.

THE COURT: But why does the duty attach?

That's stating the answer. You state the conclusion in your answer. In other words, why should there be a duty, under those circumstances?

MR. COLLESTER: Under what circumstances, Justice? In the very beginning?

THE COURT: Well, where? Where—at the very start when the patient comes in? Why? The respirator is applied, and then the doctor and the family, et cetera, all decide: Look, this is a hopeless situation. We're just not going to put in a new fuse. And if the fuse goes, or pull the plug, or what have you, why should there be any difference between those two examples?

MR. COLLESTER: Well I see the difference, again—and maybe I'm just saying the same thing—I see the difference as, once she's placed on the respirator, once the patient is on the respirator, once that decision has been made, I think that treatment must be continued.

THE COURT: You mean you can't change your mind.

MR. COLLESTER: I think, Justice, under our present law, no. That would be my feeling. Once it is there, once it is life-sustaining, until such time as, within the context and within standard medical practice, a physician utilizing whatever be the standard declares or pronounces her dead.

CHIEF JUSTICE HUGHES: Supposing the technology told us now by expert evidence that this life-sustaining could continue for the next 50 years? Would that make any difference to you?

Does the fact that there is a projected termination of the tragedy with an outside limit of a year—or perhaps much less time—but supposing that the technologists were able to say this is going to work, this artificial breathing, we can keep her alive for 50 years.

MR. COLLESTER: Well, I'm happy that that hypothetical is not in this case. Of course it would disturb me greatly. However, I can only assert what I believe to be the law as it exists now; and the law as it exists now would seem to indicate that it would have to be continued.

THE COURT: Suppose that instead of being in the condition that she is in, Karen Quinlan, under the circumstances, was able to communicate. And even though the respirator had—it's work had been commenced, she was able to communicate to the doctors, and they believed this to be an intelligent saying, that she wished it to cease. Would that change anything?

MR. COLLESTER: Well I think it changes a great deal. Again, it depends upon how you read the *Heston* case.

THE COURT: All right. Tell me how it changes. Now what would be your answer to that?

MR. COLLESTER: Well first of all, you would have the—I assume you are hypothesizing a direction given by the patient, who is—who is intelligent, and had the control of their senses—well, there are some cases in other jurisdictions which would so indicate that that would be appropriate.

THE COURT: And suppose that then—do you draw a distinction between that case, where there is an intelligent communication of a decision by a patient, and the case where the same effort is made vicariously by the parent or guardian?

MR. COLLESTER: Yes. In those cases which would—

THE COURT: That's where you draw the line?

270

MR. COLLESTER: Yes.

—those cases which would permit, by the way, that form of direction by the patient to the physician, specifically indicate—in the context, albeit *dicta*—that in the instances where a patient is incapable of communicating or for some reason does not communicate that the presumption should there be for life, that in fact there should be no termination of treatment, under those circumstances. I think the *Osborne* case is one that springs to mind right now.

THE COURT: But there is, in the case of the competent individual, there is that constitutional right to die, is there not?

MR. COLLESTER: I don't think it's so much a constitutional right to die, or at least the decisions are not phrased in that language.

THE COURT: It comes out of our New Jersey Supreme Court.

MR. COLLESTER: Which says there is none. There is no constitutional right to die.

THE COURT: That's right. And you responded to Justice Mountain by saying that where this individual is competent and makes the choice, and so forth—I'm suggesting to you that that person, too, is exercising his constitutional right when he says: I have a right to die, by making the choice.

MR. COLLESTER: As I indicated, there are jurisdictions which do assert that; and it depends on how you read the *Heston* case. As the General has indicated, perhaps some of the language in *Heston* is a little broad, because *Heston*, at least on my reading of it, would not appear to permit such a decision to be made even by a competent adult, in the State of New Jersey.

THE COURT: Do you think *Heston* is wrong when it says that?

MR. COLLESTER: I think certainly the case needs some evaluation in terms of the hypothetical that was just given by Justice Mountain. However, that isn't this case, once again.

THE COURT: That was very delicately done.

[Laughter.]

MR. COLLESTER: Thank you, Justice.

THE COURT: Do you think *Heston* is wrong, or not, in that respect?

MR. COLLESTER: I think the language is too broad in that respect. Perhaps—that would be my personal opinion.

THE COURT: You would go with that *Osborne* case?

MR. COLLESTER: In large part, yes, sir. Again assuming a competent adult, and assuming that all protections are available, so that this is an intelligent decision, and also assuming that the State policy with respect to suicide laws has also been changed—

THE COURT: Before you leave us, Mr. Collester, knowing your concern as to the homicidal overtones in this case, let me just take you to a different point: Recognizing the ecclesiastical assurance that there is a time to be born and there is a time to die, what observations do you have as to the Quinlans' finding substantial support in the abortion cases where the mother has the right to determine life and death, without any interference whatsoever on the part of the state, during the first trimester?

MR. COLLESTER: All right, that during the first trimester—but the *Roe* v. *Wade* case—

THE COURT: Well let's just hold the second and third, where the state becomes involved; that's another question. Just let's stay with the first trimester, please, where the mother determines life and death as to that fetus. Why don't the Quinlans have some substantial support in their position in the light of the philosophical concept enunciated by Justice Blackmun in that opinion, in *Roe* and other opinions?

MR. COLLESTER: As I read Justice Blackmun's opinion in *Roe*, he is determining, or in effect asserting, that in the first trimester there is not what we would determine, or chose to call "life" attaching to the fetus; that it is after the first trimester that the considerations that we deal with here today come into play. Now that is how I read the opinion.

THE COURT: Yes, but the mother has determined that there shall be no life thereafter, after the first trimester, if she chooses, if she opts for abortion. Then she has made that choice. Is that correct?

MR. COLLESTER: She has made that choice, yes, sir.

THE COURT: That's right. So she has determined that—well, I'm repeating myself—she has made that choice. Is that right?

THE COURT: She has not terminated any life.

MR. COLLESTER: That is correct. "She has not terminated any life," would have to be my response to it, yes, sir.

THE COURT: Is that the best you can find, by way of distinction, so far as the Quinlans are concerned?

MR. COLLESTER: The distinction is that once the person is adjudged to be alive, that thereafter the distinction—or rather the law's protections, will attach, as the *Roe* case, I think, indicates. Once the law's protections will attach, then it becomes a matter for both civil and criminal protection. That would be my opinion.

CHIEF JUSTICE HUGHES: Thank you, Mr. Prosecutor, very much. Mr. Porzio is next.

ORAL ARGUMENT OF RALPH PORZIO, ON BEHALF OF ROBERT J. MORSE, M.D., AND ARSHAD JAVED, M.D.

MR. PORZIO: If it please the Court:

My name is Ralph Porzio and I represent Dr. Javed and Dr. Morse. I think I should try to address my opening remarks to some of the pointed questions that were made by you in the last half-hour or so with reference to the definition of death.

First of all I take the position that the definition of death is not involved in this case. I take the position that there was a stipulation entered in this case, and that the stipulation provided that Karen Ann Quinlan is alive by all accepted medical standards in the State of New Jersey, and she is alive by all legal standards in the State of New Jersey.

Now if we move from there and say: Well, but even anyway, Mr. Porzio, shouldn't this Court now go into a definition of death different from the definition of which we have traditionally known? I'm trying to read your minds as to what are the questions that bother you. And my answer to that is: How? What has been the approach of this Court and every court prior to this Court, on the definition of death? It is that it is a factual question. And it is a factual question because it begs for flexibility, as one of you has said. It begs for flexibility. And just as it would be very bad for the legislature to give out a definition, in legalistic words, as to what the definition of death would be—and it might be outmoded two, five, and ten years from now—it would be very bad, I think, for this Court to put out a definition that would fossilize the whole concept of death, and not take into account the growth and development, and sometimes the very explosive changes, that are being made in medical science.

THE COURT: Well, Mr. Porzio, isn't there a legal definition of death today?

MR. PORZIO: There is a legal definition of death, to this extent, Your Honor. It is this: It is the definition based upon what the medical experts regard as the standard in the profession. Now, when it came to the definition of death statutes—and as you know from the briefs there are about eight or more—what did the legislatures of the various states say? They didn't put into a paragraph: This is the "newer" definition of death. They took the older definition. They took the involvement of cerebral function and mentioned it just in a few words; and then they said—these are not the exact words—as may be determined by the treating physician, or by the certifying physician, in accordance with accepted medical standards.

273

Now this is what they did, almost all of those eight definitions, and it is also the very same thing that is proposed by Senator Greenberg in the piece of legislation that is now pending in the Legislature of New Jersey now. And when we came to the Anatomical Gift Act—and I happened to serve on the Legislative Advisory Committee at that time, of three lawyers and three doctors—we recommended, and it was adopted, that the Section 7 of the Uniform Act be adopted in New Jersey. And so what does it say? It says, for purposes of organ transplants, it's in accordance with what the doctor says. And so I make the point to you, on the definition of death, that we do not freeze it. And when I say, "we do not freeze it," we do not freeze it either by legislative enactment, or by judicial enactment.

THE COURT: Mr. Porzio, in answer to Mr.—

THE COURT: First, your position is we don't address it. Isn't it?

THE COURT: Go ahead.

THE COURT: Mine is very simple and short. I want to make sure I understand you. Your threshhold position is that we do not address it in this case?

MR. PORZIO: Mr. Justice Clifford, this record—it would be a shame if this record were used to give a definition of death when, one, we have a stipulation—not a contention, now—

THE COURT: Your answer is, we don't address it?

MR. PORZIO: Absolutely. It's not an issue in the case.

THE COURT: All right.

MR. PORZIO: Everybody agrees that this girl is alive.

THE COURT: In answer to Justice Schreiber, when he said that there is a definition of death today, in New Jersey, I take it that the simple answer is: Yes, there is; and yes, it appears in our case law. The fact that it finds its genesis with doctors' opinions is beside the point. But it finds its place in our case law and we describe it as, we said several times, the cessation of cardiovascular and pulmonary activity. Is that right?

MR. PORZIO: Yes. And also—

THE COURT: And that's it. As things sit today, that's the definition.

MR. PORZIO: Well, also that it would include the involvement of cerebral function. Because if you had—if you had a case today, just as we had a case here, and it involves cerebral function, you then bring in the medical experts and you ask them: What are the standards in your profession now with reference to death?

And it brings us down to what I think is a very important part of this case. That is, the Harvard Ad Hoc standards—the Harvard Ad Hoc criteria, and the other criteria. One of you mentioned: Well why not use the device of deciding these cases on an ad hoc basis? Now you know, that is a possibility. But think about it for a moment. There are some grave dangers in it, because when a doctor is practicing medicine, he has to make decisions clinically every day. And the Chief Justice wisely said—I'm going back to an old opinion of his—that there should be some degree of freedom as far as the doctors are concerned. And what is the degree of freedom that they could have? That they could have a standard that they could retreat to.

And Justice Pashman wisely said: Why not make up a definition that would have "an input" from all of the other disciplines, such as ethics, and theology, and so forth? And I say to you that is precisely what was done in the case of the Harvard Ad Hoc Committee. Because while you may disagree with the representation on that Committee, there was a theologian; there was a lawyer; there was somebody else; and there were doctors. It was predominantly doctors. But you see, the Harvard Ad Hoc Committee has been paid the highest tribute. And the highest tribute is that it has been imitated; and that all of these criteria are basically the same.

Now what does this criteria say, Your Honors? It deals specifically with our case. Think of it: A comatose patient—read it and see. A comatose patient, number one. Number two, an involvement with the newer and more modern definition of death. Number three, a patient with serious brain damage. And number four, when do you discontinue the respirator? Now that's not only in the commentary, but you'll find it in—when you deal with the second facet, you'll find that it's dealt with specifically. And what does that criteria say? That criteria says, Your Honor, that when all—mind you—when "all" of these conditions and facets have been met, then you declare death, and then you turn off the respirator. And what did the experts in this case say? Every one of them? They said that the Harvard Ad Hoc criteria was accepted medical practice. Dr. Korein, who was the one outstanding expert who testified on behalf of the plaintiff in this case, said the Harvard Ad Hoc criteria is probably one of the most widely accepted medical standards in the world.

THE COURT: Mr. Porzio, do you mean to suggest that physicians do not commonly exercise discretionary judgment to stop giving life-supporting help, in many cases, short of this Harvard Ad Hoc test?

MR. PORZIO: I'd like to answer that in two ways. First of all, consider what happened in this case; and then let's get to a general—

THE COURT: No. First answer my general question, if you will.

MR. PORZIO: The general one? Okay.

THE COURT: Based upon your knowledge and experience in this area.

MR. PORZIO: Yes. I would say this: I have heard remarks. I have read remarks with reference to judicious neglect—what is called "judicious neglect." Frankly, I am opposed to it if it does not—if it is something that does not exist without standards.

THE COURT: I'm not asking you whether you're opposed to it, but I'm trying to examine the realistic de facto situation in existence. Because I think the Court should consider, in making determinations, what is the de facto commonly accepted practice. I have the impression that many decisions, in favor of not continuing life-support, are made in cases far short of this Harvard Ad Hoc situation, particularly when we consider that this Harvard Ad Hoc procedure requires that the whole thing be repeated 24 hours later. And only when those two tests are done 24 hours apart—if they do that—is that person so dead that I assume there is no problem. The issue that is raised here just simply wouldn't exist. The issue that's raised here is that, in situations short of the affirmative test of Harvard Ad Hoc, do not doctors, de facto, frequently exercise discretionary determinations to stop life-support systems in hopeless cases?

MR. PORZIO: I can't answer that in the affirmative.

THE COURT: In representing two doctors, that's a tough question for you, Mr. Porzio.

MR. PORZIO: No, not only that. It's not just that. It's that—
Well, first of all, there is nothing here in the record; and second, I can't answer that affirmatively because the question was put to me in terms of, you know, hopeless cases. And I think that that is an assumption that's been made here. I'm not so sure about that. There have been doubts raised with reference to the "hopelessness" in this case—and would the Court permit me a few minutes to go into that, because I think we've been laboring under a premise here that I'm not—at least I'll say I'm not sure about—I'm not positive, but at least I'll say I'm not sure about.

THE COURT: Before you do that, though, do I gather, Mr. Porzio, that you just simply—your answer to Judge Conford's question is simply you don't know?

MR. PORZIO: I am not ready to concede that that is a common-place practice, no.

THE COURT: Well is it a practice? Are you aware of the fact that it is a practice, common-place or not?

MR. PORZIO: I will say that, from what I hear by hearsay, that it has been done. And I think it's a very bad thing to be done, without the following standards. Because supposing a doctor gets into trouble, Your Honor. Supposing a doctor has a relative that says: Wait a minute. I found out that you did so-and-so and I don't like that. Now how do you proceed to adjudicate that case? You adjudicate it on the basis of standards.

THE COURT: Mr. Porzio, from your standpoint, can you envision any set of facts which would permit (a) the doctor to make such a choice, or (b) that the patient may avail himself of an option to terminate his life? Is there any set of facts that you can envision where your response to those questions would be: Yes, the patient may do thus-and-so, or the doctor may order withdrawal of supportive medicine?

MR. PORZIO: I mean, I suppose, if you have a situation where a person is brought into an emergency room and his brains are hanging out, and if the nurses come along and they are going to start doing different things, that he's going to come in and say: Now wait a minute here, you know, there is no use. But you see, I would much prefer to lean the other way, Mr. Justice Pashman. I would much prefer to take the view that is taken by Dr. Epstein, who is dealing with these kinds of cases every day—and, incidentally, his position is referred to in Judge Muir's opinion—and it is this: That you do not make it easy for the doctor to give up. You do not make it easy for the doctor to give up. And he recites in that article some very good reasons for doing that.

THE COURT: Mr. Porzio, before you leave us, the Chief Justice's observations about the hypothetical which envisioned the continuation of these supports for some 50 years, I think is terribly important and very dramatically put.

With that in mind, you will agree that we are living in an age of society, generally speaking, and it certainly is by virtue of innovations in medicine and supports and what-not, that bodies are being kept alive beyond their will and their knowledge by these machines. And frankly, to be horribly candid, really I think even beyond their usefulness to that same society. Recognizing that, don't you believe that this concern of perpetuating life for the 50 years that the Chief refers to—and that's being symbolical of an *ad infinitum* situation—is such that perhaps this Court, or someone somewhere, should involve itself to the end that a solution would be forthcoming to meet this problem? Or do we just blindly turn away and allow these things to continue that way, with no suggestions whatsoever?

MR. PORZIO: Well I can only cite to you what Dr. Franklin Epstein says. And that is: That we should continue these supports; that if we take the position that we are going to discontinue life, regardless of the circumstances, then it means that all lives are threatened; and in a sense I think we have to weigh factors here. I think we have to weigh very important factors.

277

THE COURT: So you say to the Chief to continue the support for years?

MR. PORZIO: Yes, I would say so. I would say so because, in the long run, we've got to look at this from the standpoint of the entire society. There may be a small percentage in our society that are going along like this, but in the interests of the whole, I think we've got to do it. I think we've got to draw the line somewhere, Justice Pashman. We've got to draw the line somewhere.

THE COURT: Mr. Porzio, I was wondering why your clients are resisting the order that the Plaintiffs seek here? It's an order which, if granted, can do them no harm. It can only give them protection. In other words, the order would not force them—either of them—to participate in life discontinuance. It would simply say that if they decided to do so, in consultation with the parents, they would have no liability. Why should they object to that?

MR. PORZIO: Well, it gets back to—it gets back to the question of the prognosis. And in giving—in talking about the prognosis, I'll only talk about what's in the record—

THE COURT: Now wait. Are you being responsive to my question? I don't think you are. Why should they object to the Court granting the relief that the plaintiffs are asking for here, since that relief would have no adverse effect upon them?

MR. PORZIO: Simply because there is a duty on their part. They are still the treating physicians. They are still the treating physicians.

THE COURT: The relief the Plaintiff seeks would not compel them to do anything they didn't want to do. It would simply say that if they did accede, in their judgment, to the Plaintiff's desire, they would have no liability.

MR. PORZIO: And the Doctors get a chance to step out of the picture?

THE COURT: Of course. The way they—of course there will be nothing compulsory against them if the Court granted the Plaintiff's relief.

CHIEF JUSTICE HUGHES: They would be relieved of the—I don't want to say this in this particular—of the ulterior purpose, or of the corrupting influence of self-interests, under such circumstances. You see, they wouldn't have to worry about any impediment to their doing of their full and honest duty as a physician in accordance with existing medical practice. And I don't suggest in any way that that was not done here. I'm talking theoretically, that a doctor ought not to have to carry this burden of wondering what a distant relative, or a prosecutor will do to him if he sees a case which is so plainly and tragically desperate, let's say, as this one is. I assume—I really am having trouble, Mr. Porzio, discerning the logical difference between the decision of a Dr. Morse, at the outset—assuming he knew then all he knows now—a decision not to force these life-giving procedures and extend this life for five or six months, with a good deal of tragedy and perhaps even pain in another case, and a decision to having started it to discontinue it. What's the logical difference so far as liability is concerned?

MR. PORZIO: Well I think we've got to look at the case from the standpoint of what the evidence discloses. There was a very difficult time here in getting a history. In fact the history is still not complete. And Dr. Morse had testified—and that's at page 139—Dr. Morse has testified that he cannot make a definitive prognosis in this case, that the history is inadequate. Now he's tried desperately to get a history.

Secondly, I think we've got to take into account that in neurology, in the field of neurology, history is more important than an examination, so that the history is very vital here. Frankly I don't think that he, leaving aside the legal issues for a moment if I may, frankly I don't think he should give up hope in this case. I mean we've got a decision right here in our records—*Bauer*—the *Bauer* case, where the patient is on the verge of death and is comatose for 11 months, and then a settlement goes through on a negligence case, and then shortly thereafter he begins to come back, and all of the talk up to that time is very pessimistic. Now in the—

CHIEF JUSTICE HUGHES: That wasn't the person that went to Lourdes, was it? You remember the old legal joke?

[Laughter.]

MR. PORZIO: Yes—but, anyway, there are some contradictions in this case as to what would be the possible level of recovery. There is also the fact that there is medical testimony in this case that the lesion is called metabolic rather than destructive; and you therefore have a better chance of recovery. I suppose the age of the patient is in her favor because in the case of *Bauer*, the boy was 16 years of age. And then there is the testimony of Dr. Stuart Cook. And Dr. Cook says that there are no absolute certainties in medicine. And he says that there has been considerable confusion surrounding the precipitating events. And that's why he's still holding hope. And also Dr. Cook points out in his testimony that patients who have been in a coma for more than a year have come back to make some useful recovery, and therefore we shouldn't do it here.

THE COURT: This is what Judge Muir was adverting to when he said there is some medical qualification on the issue of her returning to "discriminative functioning," and on whether she should be removed from the respirator.

MR. PORZIO: That's correct, sir.

THE COURT: I thought you were going to answer Judge Conford's inquiry before—and if you weren't going to answer it this way, I'm missing something—as to why your clients were resisting the application of the plaintiff, by saying that their resistance is based upon, irrespective of what the Court may say, under the present circumstances they perceived a violation of their medical duty. Isn't that what they said? They went around and said: I consulted with my colleagues and the standard that presently persists in our profession is such that I could not, irrespective of what the Court said, consent to the instruction.

MR. PORZIO: Absolutely. I was getting to that, that there exists in the profession a standard. That the standard—there are a number of standards: the one in Geneva, the one in Sydney, the one out in Duquesne, and one doctor said—I think it was Dr. Korein—that there are about two dozen of them. Now there exists standards and they are following these standards that are accepted, generally accepted, all around the world. And I mean if you're saying that they can't do that, then you're leaving up, on an individual basis, and it may depend upon the gastric juices of the particular physician.

THE COURT: I know. But isn't the existence of that standard and the desire to adhere to it the basis of their resistance to the Plaintiff's application?

MR. PORZIO: That is so. Not only—

THE COURT: Well, except—

MR. PORZIO: Wait. Wait. May I add one—

THE COURT: All he has to do is walk away from the case, Mr. Porzio.

MR. PORZIO: What's that?

THE COURT: All they've got to do is walk away from the case.

MR. PORZIO: By the way which they've tried to do, which they have tried to do and they have offered to do, I believe, on a number of occasions.

THE COURT: Well, Mr. Coburn is looking for another doctor who will agree with his views, and it sounds like you both want to do the same thing.

THE COURT: That should be easy.

MR. PORZIO: Speaking—speaking for my client—speaking for my client, these two doctors, they would be happy to get off this case at any time, except that they feel that they have a responsibility until somebody comes in here and substitutes.

Now as far as I know, Mr. and Mrs. Quinlan have not suggested to them that they get somebody else, but I'm quite sure—and I know this from talking to them—that if it wasn't for Mr. and Mrs. Quinlan, they would be happy to get off this case and let someone else step into it.

Now the other thing that I wanted to point out is that the doctors here, I think, have some responsibility. And there is, I believe, a responsibility on their part which society has given them. I believe there is a responsibility on their part which the medical profession has given them, and this has been recognized, and they are carrying out that responsibility in accordance with prevailing standards. And considering all of those factors, it would seem to me that they should be permitted to go on. They have not given up hope in this case, because they know of cases worse than this one. I mean, take the Bill Bauer case, where the patient began to come back after presumably they made a settlement, and then the scream was that it was very unfair because it grew out of an automobile accident case. And—

THE COURT: That was not worse than this one.

MR. PORZIO: What's that?

THE COURT: You're not citing *Bauer* as being worse than this one?

MR. PORZIO: No, I'm not citing it. No, I'm not.

THE COURT: It was not.

MR. PORZIO: But I'm just saying that the procedure that they went through—but there was a serious question there. I think somebody put it in terms of 5 percent as far as recovery goes. There was a serious question in that case as to whether or not there would be a recovery, if you will recall. And then what happened there was that there was some kind of a settlement made, and then later on the patient came back. If the patient had died, the value of the case, under our rules of damages, would have been, of course, much different, the other way.

Now it does seem to me, though, that we have got to recognize in this particular case that we do have a set of standards; that the Harvard Ad Hoc Committee, or facsimiles of that Committee Report, are now accepted around the world; and that the medical profession recognizes them and follows them; and, therefore, for those reasons, the doctors should continue. And the doctors, in their judgment, feel that they are not yet—they are not yet ready, from a medical standpoint, to write off this patient, because they know of other cases where a patient has come back in similar circumstances.

And for these reasons, I respectfully submit that the opinion below was correct, and that there should be an affirmance.

CHIEF JUSTICE HUGHES: Thank you very much, Mr. Porzio.

Mr. Einhorn, the problem arises as to whether you—how long do you think you would like to have?

MR. EINHORN: I'm not sure.

CHIEF JUSTICE HUGHES: Well supposing we get started, and you go to 1:00, and then we'll suspend until 2:00.

[Chief Justice Hughes addresses himself to the postponement of other cases.]

CHIEF JUSTICE HUGHES: All right. Mr. Einhorn?

ORAL ARGUMENT OF THEODORE E.B. EINHORN, ESQ., ON BEHALF OF ST. CLARE'S HOSPITAL

MR. EINHORN: May it please the Court, my name is Theodore E.B. Einhorn. I represent St. Clare's Hospital.

This being the last, so to speak, of the list, I don't know if it would pay to go through all the arguments which have been raised. I would like to address myself, if I could, to some of the points which have been raised in the colloquy.

As you all know from reading the transcript, during the course of trial I requested and was granted an amendment to the pretrial order seeking a declaratory judgment that the Harvard criteria and other similar criteria could be used by physicians to assist them in declaring a patient dead. That was modified and restricted to reflect particularly Miss Quinlan. The Judge in his opinion did not believe that the matter was ripe for declaratory judgment. However, I believe there was some colloquy back and forth between Mr. Coburn and Mr. Justice Clifford as to whether or not, if a physician was satisfied that a particular, I believe Miss Quinlan, met the criteria of death under the Harvard criteria and the parents disagreed, as I understand the colloquy, whether or not she could be declared dead. One of the—I come to a different conclusion than Mr. Coburn did. I realize that this is not an issue before you, but I do think—I think I should express my opinion on this.

One of the points raised originally in the pretrial order was as to whose determination it was as to a person being declared dead. Of course as a result of the stipulation, that point became moot; but I think that as a result of the colloquy between Mr. Coburn and Mr. Justice Clifford it would be the Hospital's position that the determination of when an individual is or is not dead should be left up to, and is the province of, the physician, except in certain circumstances where there may be some type of Hospital policy or some type of, to use that word, "input" from the Hospital. But ordinarily I would submit that the determination and the time of death is a decision to be made by the physician. I think that's evidenced by the anatomical statute where it specifically refers to the facts that the physician shall declare the time of death.

So, under those circumstances, I would respectfully disagree with

282

Mr. Coburn. And I would say—and I realize, that's one of the reasons why I asked for a declaratory judgment, as a result of the eyes of the world, so to speak, looking at these physicians—but in a hypothetical case, if I might, if we had a situation where an individual, in the opinion of the doctors, had met the criteria of the Harvard Ad Hoc Committee, or some of the other numerous criteria, and even though the parents disagreed, I would submit that the doctor would be justified under those circumstances in declaring the individual to be dead. I think if we're going to—

THE COURT: And would not have to pay heed to the request of the family to continue the apparatus that theretofore has sustained—had sustained life?

MR. EINHORN: I'm sorry, sir. I don't know if I followed the question.

THE COURT: Well I think what Mr. Coburn and I were talking about was this: Suppose in this instance the doctors determined that, given her present condition, Karen now met some acceptable definition of death and, therefore, sought to remove the sustaining device; but the parents said: No. I don't believe it. I want that to continue to be operating. That's the hypothetical that was spoken about.

MR. EINHORN: And the standard we're talking about is not the Harvard Ad Hoc Committee? Well, I would have—

THE COURT: We didn't fix one. He and I didn't fix one.

MR. EINHORN: Yes. Oh, I'm sorry. I misunderstood you, then.

The problem I have then is the *JFK* versus *Heston* case—and I've read it through probably as many times as anybody else. And every time I seem to come to a different decision. But I know that as an attorney representing a client, if they came to me and said: This is the situation, under the *Heston* case, is there a possibility of liability? I'd be very, very concerned for him and probably would give him conservative advice and say: Don't do it. I think rather than—if I might most respectfully—rather than addressing ourselves, the Court addressing itself to the question of a new definition of death, I think that the medical profession, the legal profession, and the public as a whole, might be better served if there was some redefinition or redefinement, so to speak, of some of the dicta in *Heston*, because I think—it bothers me. It scares me, so to speak, and certainly in my capacity as an attorney representing a hospital.

THE COURT: Mr. Einhorn, I'm asking you the same question I asked Mr. Porzio. Why does your client resist a judgment which could only exculpate your client and not inculpate them?

MR. EINHORN: It's the decision of my client that, from a philosophical point of view, they are opposed to the Court injecting itself into the relationship of the patient and the doctor; and the Court making a decision, so to speak, as to who shall live and who shall die.

THE COURT: Well, except that that's not what the Plaintiffs are asking for. The Plaintiffs are asking only for a determination by the Court that if they go to the doctor and ask that the apparatus be turned off, and if the doctor agrees to do that, nobody is liable. Now that leaves it still within the doctor's prerogative to refuse. It still leaves it within the hospital's prerogative to refuse to be a party to it. In other words, you can't be hurt by the judgment they seek. You can only be benefited by it.

MR. EINHORN: I think a realistic appraisal of the results of the request of the Plaintiff is that the young lady will be left to die. And I think—

THE COURT: Not with the participation of an unwilling doctor, and not with the participation of an unwilling hospital.

MR. EINHORN: Then we have the corollary, as pointed out, as evidenced in the transcript. Once this particular life-assisting mechanism is removed, what do we do? What do the doctors do? Or, from our point of view, what does the hospital do about the fact that she's now running—she now has pneumonia, or she's developed an infection? Who do we get to treat her? What are the Hospital's duties under those circumstances? Do we go to Judge Muir and say: Judge, put your mantle on now as a doctor and give us advice as to what we should do? I believe that—

THE COURT: Do you mean in the event that the doctors decide to cooperate with this, but the Hospital doesn't want to? Is that what you're talking about?

MR. EINHORN: Well in the event that the Court grant the relief sought, and if these doctors refuse to do it. Someone else comes in to do it and we have a situation where she's taken off the respirator. I believe Mr. Quinlan, as a result of colloquy during the course of the trial, indicated—

THE COURT: I understand. You're saying—

MR. EINHORN: —he wasn't objecting to—I'm sorry, sir.

THE COURT: You're saying you would be put into a quandry if they did get a doctor who would agree to do this but the Hospital still didn't want to be a party to it. You would have a quandry?

MR. EINHORN: I think we would have one. And then also I think we have the question—in my trial brief I did state that in the event that relief was granted, that we'd be immunized, so to speak, from criminal liability and from civil liability, and that a declaratory judgment be issued enjoining the prosecutor from taking any steps. So if in the event such relief was granted, that was my fallback position, so to speak.

CHIEF JUSTICE HUGHES: Mr. Einhorn, will you hold your thought on that point and continue at 2:00, please, so that we can recess until 2:00?

[Whereupon, the proceedings were recessed, to reconvene at 2:00 o'clock p.m., the same day.]

AFTERNOON SESSION

CHIEF JUSTICE HUGHES: Have you got some further argument, Mr. Einhorn?

ORAL ARGUMENT OF THEODORE E. B. EINHORN, ESQ., ON BEHALF OF ST. CLARE'S HOSPITAL—Resumed

MR. EINHORN: Lunch only generated one other thing, Mr. Chief Justice. In response to Mr. Justice Pashman—excuse me, Mr. Justice Conford's inquiry—I omitted one very important factor which I think I should have made reference to. Namely, that in addition to the Hospital's philosophical objection to the Court intervening into the relationship, there was a very real and a very—as they conceive it—a very pressing duty: Namely, the duty that Miss Quinlan was and—excuse me, is alive, and was alive at the time, as well; and the Hospital concedes its duty, its primary duty, is to give care and treatment to her as a patient, especially in view of the fact that it is the opinion of the physicians not to terminate the particular apparatus.

Thank you.

CHIEF JUSTICE HUGHES: All right. Thank you very much, Mr. Einhorn.

Now that completes our list.

Mr. Armstrong, do you have anything further?

REBUTTAL ORAL ARGUMENT OF PAUL W. ARMSTRONG, ON BEHALF OF PLAINTIFF JOSEPH QUINLAN

MR. ARMSTRONG: Just a simple rebuttal, if I might, Mr. Chief Justice, to the—

CHIEF JUSTICE HUGHES: That has a sinister sound. Does it imply an extensive—you won't reargue any of the primary matter, will you?

MR. ARMSTRONG: It's just simply in reference to the statements by Mr. Porzio concerning the importance of the history in rendering a competent diagnosis. It cannot be denied that a history most assuredly is important. And I think we've cited, on page 5 of our brief, that it's most important in the acute stage which is hours to days after the onset of a particular insult. It becomes less and less important as the illness progresses, and after nine months, it really has no import whatsoever.

Further, Mr. Porzio advanced that the doctors still harbor hope. I would set—try to draw the Court's attention to the affidavit of Dr. Javed before the glare of litigation and that is where Dr. Javed has set forth in his affidavit accompanying the complaint filed in this action, and I'll read it to you:

> "Since admission to St. Clare's Hospital, patient has required assisted mechanical ventilation, has extensive cerebral damage. Patient is fed through nasal gastric tube, has been in condition for more than four months, and there is no hope of improvement in patient's condition."

Exclusive of that, Your Honors, I would just simply like to thank you and express the gratitude of the Quinlan family for the expeditious scheduling of the hearing of this appeal.

CHIEF JUSTICE HUGHES: Mr. Armstrong, I think the members of the Court, although we haven't particularly discussed this, would want me to express a similar gratitude to all counsel who have worked so hard and briefed this matter so well. It's a puzzling and a tragic and a very difficult case and we feel very grateful to all counsel.

MR. ARMSTRONG: Thank you.

CHIEF JUSTICE HUGHES: All right. We'll reserve decision.

[Whereupon, argument in the above-entitled proceeding was concluded.]

Docket No. A-116

IN THE MATTER OF KAREN QUINLAN, AN ALLEGED INCOMPETENT

ON CERTIFICATION TO THE SUPERIOR COURT, CHANCERY DIVISION, WHOSE OPINION IS REPORTED AT 137 *N.J. Super.* 227 (1975).

OPINION
Argued January 26, 1976 — Decided March 31, 1976

MR. PAUL W. ARMSTRONG and MR. JAMES M. CROWLEY, a member of the New York Bar, argued the cause for appellant Joseph T. Quinlan (*Mr. Paul W. Armstrong, attorney*).

MR. DANIEL M. COBURN argued the cause for respondent Guardian adLitem Thomas R. Curtin.

MR. WILLIAM F. HYLAND, Attorney General of New Jersey, argued the cause for respondent State of New Jersey (*Mr. Hyland, attorney; Mr. David S. Baime* and *Mr. John DeCicco*, Deputy Attorneys General, of counsel; *Mr. Baime, Mr. DeCicco, Ms. Jane E. Deaterly, Mr. Daniel Louis Grossman,* and *Mr. Robert E. Rochford*, Deputy Attorneys General, on the brief).

MR. DONALD G. COLLESTER, JR., Morris County Prosecutor, argued the cause for respondent County of Morris.

MR. RALPH PORZIO argued the cause for respondents Arshad Javed and Robert J. Morse (*Messrs. Porzio, Bromberg* and *Newman*, attorneys; *Mr. Porzio* and *Mr. E. Neal Zimmerman*, on the brief).

MR. THEODORE E.B. EINHORN argued the cause for respondent Saint Clare's Hospital.

MR. EDWARD J. LEADEM filed a brief on behalf of *Amicus Curiae* New Jersey Catholic Conference.

— The opinion of the Court was delivered by HUGHES, C.J. —

THE LITIGATION

The central figure in this tragic case is Karen Ann Quinlan, a New Jersey resident. At the age of 22, she lies in a debilitated and allegedly moribund state at Saint Clare's Hospital in Denville, New Jersey. The litigation has to do, in final analysis, with her life,—its continuance or cessation,—and the responsibilities, rights and duties, with regard to any fateful decision concerning it, of her family, her guardian, her doctors, the hospital, the State through its law enforcement authorities, and finally the courts of justice.

The issues are before this Court following its direct certification of the action under the rule, *R*.2:12-1, prior to hearing in the Superior Court, Appellate Division, to which the appellant (hereafter "plaintiff") Joseph Quinlan, Karen's father, had appealed the adverse judgment of the Chancery Division.

Due to extensive physical damage fully described in the able opinion of the trial judge, Judge Muir, supporting that judgment, Karen allegedly was incompetent. Joseph Quinlan sought the adjudication of that incompetency. He wished to be appointed guardian of the person and property of his daughter. It was proposed by him that such letters of guardianship, if granted, should contain an express power to him as guardian to authorize the discontinuance of all extraordinary medical procedures now allegedly sustaining Karen's vital processes and hence her life, since these measures, he asserted, present no hope of her eventual recovery. A guardian *ad litem* was appointed by Judge Muir to represent the interest of the alleged incompetent.

By a supplemental complaint, in view of the extraordinary nature of the relief sought by plaintiff and the involvement therein of their several rights and responsibilities, other parties were added. These included the treating physicians and the hospital, the relief sought being that they be restrained from interfering with the carrying out of any such extraordinary authorization in the event it were to be granted by the court. Joined, as well, was the Prosecutor of Morris County (he being charged with responsibility for enforcement of the criminal law), to enjoin him from interfering with, or projecting a criminal prosecution which otherwise

288

might ensue in the event of cessation of life in Karen resulting from the exercise of such extraordinary authorization were it to be granted to the guardian.

The Attorney General of New Jersey intervened as of right pursuant to *R*.4:33-1 on behalf of the State of New Jersey, such intervention being recognized by the court in the pretrial conference order (*R*.4:25-1 *et seq*.) of September 22, 1975. Its basis, of course, was the interest of the State in the preservation of life, which has an undoubted constitutional foundation.[1]

The matter is of transcendent importance, involving questions related to the definition and existence of death, the prolongation of life through artificial means developed by medical technology undreamed of in past generations of the practice of the healing arts;[2] the impact of such durationally indeterminate and artificial life prolongation on the rights of the incompetent, her family and society in general; the bearing of constitutional right and the scope of judicial responsibility, as to the appropriate response of an equity court of justice to the extraordinary prayer for relief of the plaintiff. Involved as well is the right of the plaintiff, Joseph Quinlan, to guardianship of the person of his daughter.

Among his "factual and legal contentions" under such Pretrial Order was the following:

I. Legal and Medical Death
    (a) Under the existing legal and medical definitions of death recognized by the State of New Jersey, Karen Ann Quinlan is dead.

This contention, made in the context of Karen's profound and allegedly irreversible coma and physical debility, was discarded during trial by the following stipulated amendment to the Pretrial Order:

Under any legal standard recognized by the State of New Jersey and also under standard medical practice, Karen Ann Quinlan is presently alive.

Other amendments to the Pretrial Order made at the time of trial expanded the issues before the court. The Prosecutor of Morris County sought a declaratory judgment as to the effect any affirmation by the court of a right in a guardian to terminate life-sustaining procedures would have with regard to enforcement of the criminal laws of New Jersey with reference to homicide. Saint Clare's Hospital, in the face of trial testimony on the subject of "brain death," sought declaratory judgment

289

as to:

> Whether the use of the criteria developed and enun-
> ciated by the Ad Hoc Committee of the Harvard Medi-
> cal School on or about August 5, 1968, as well as simi-
> lar criteria, by a physician to assist in determination of
> the death of a patient whose cardio-pulmonary func-
> tions are being artificially sustained, is in accordance
> with ordinary and standard medical practice.[3]

It was further stipulated during trial that Karen was indeed incompetent and guardianship was necessary, although there exists a dispute as
to the determination later reached by the court that such guardianship
should be bifurcated, and that Mr. Quinlan should be appointed as
guardian of the trivial property but not the person of his daughter.

After certification the Attorney General filed as of right (R.2:3-4) a
cross-appeal challenging the action of the trial court in admitting evidence of prior statements made by Karen while competent as to her dis-
taste for continuance of life by extraordinary medical procedures, under
circumstances not unlike those of the present case. These quoted statements were made in the context of several conversations with regard to
others terminally ill and being subjected to like herioc measures. The
statements were advanced as evidence of what she would want done in
such a contingency as now exists. She was said to have firmly evinced her
wish, in like circumstances, not to have her life prolonged by the otherwise futile use of extraordinary means. Because we agree with the conception of the trial court that such statements, since they were remote
and impersonal, lacked significant probative weight, it is not of consequence to our opinion that we decide whether or not they were admissible
hearsay. Again, after certification, the guardian of the person of the incompetent (who had been appointed as a part of the judgment appealed
from) resigned and was succeeded by another, but that too seems irrelevant to the decision. It is, however, of interest to note the trial court's
delineation (in its supplemental opinion of November 12, 1975) of the extent of the personal guardian's authority with respect to medical care of
his ward:

> Mr. Coburn's appointment is designed to deal with
> those instances wherein Dr. Morse[4], in the process of
> administering care and treatment to Karen Quinlan,
> feels there should be concurrence on the extent or na-
> ture of the care or treatment. If Mr. and Mrs. Quin-
> lan are unable to give concurrence, then Mr. Coburn
> will be consulted for his concurrence.

Essentially then, appealing to the power of equity, and relying on claimed constitutional rights of free exercise of religion, of privacy and of protection against cruel and unusual punishment, Karen Quinlan's father sought judicial authority to withdraw the life-sustaining mechanisms temporarily preserving his daughter's life, and his appointment as guardian of her person to that end. His request was opposed by her doctors, the hospital, the Morris County Prosecutor, the State of New Jersey, and her guardian *ad litem*.

THE FACTUAL BASE

An understanding of the issues in their basic perspective suggests a brief review of the factual base developed in the testimony and documented in greater detail in the opinion of the trial judge. *In re Quinlan*, 137 *N.J. Super.* 227 (Ch. Div. 1975).

On the night of April 15, 1975, for reasons still unclear, Karen Quinlan ceased breathing for at least two 15 minute periods. She received some ineffectual mouth-to-mouth resuscitation from friends. She was taken by ambulance to Newton Memorial Hospital. There she had a temperature of 100 degrees, her pupils were unreactive and she was unresponsive even to deep pain. The history at the time of her admission to that hospital was essentially incomplete and uninformative.

Three days later, Dr. Morse examined Karen at the request of the Newton admitting physician, Dr. McGee. He found her comatose with evidence of decortication, a condition relating to derangement of the cortex of the brain causing a physical posture in which the upper extremities are flexed and the lower extremities are extended. She required a respirator to assist her breathing. Dr. Morse was unable to obtain an adequate account of the circumstances and events leading up to Karen's admission to the Newton Hospital. Such initial history or etiology is crucial in neurological diagnosis. Relying as he did upon the Newton Memorial records and his own examination, he concluded that prolonged lack of oxygen in the bloodstream, anoxia, was identified with her condition as he saw it upon first observation. When she was later transferred to Saint Clare's Hospital she was still unconscious, still on a respirator and a tracheotomy had been performed. On her arrival Dr. Morse conducted extensive and detailed examinations. An electroencephalogram (EEG) measuring electrical rhythm of the brain was performed and Dr. Morse characterized the result as "abnormal but it showed some activity and was consistent with her clinical state." Other significant neurological tests, including a brain scan, an angiogram, and a lumbar puncture were normal in result. Dr. Morse testified that Karen has been in a state of coma, lack of consciousness, since he began treating her. He explained that there are basically two types of coma, sleep-like unresponsiveness and awake unresponsiveness. Karen was originally in a sleep-like unresponsive condition but soon developed "sleep-wake" cycles, apparently a normal improvement for comatose patients occurring within three to four weeks. In the awake cycle she blinks, cries out and does things of that sort but is still totally unaware of anyone or anything around her.

Dr. Morse and other expert physicians who examined her characterized Karen as being in a "chronic persistent vegetative state." Dr. Fred Plum, one of such expert witnesses, defined this as a "subject who remains with the capacity to maintain the vegetative parts of neurological function but who *** no longer has any cognitive function."

Dr. Morse, as well as the several other medical and neurological experts who testified in this case, believed with certainty that Karen Quinlan is not "brain dead." They identified the Ad Hoc Committee of Harvard Medical School report (*infra*) as the ordinary medical standard for determining brain death, and all of them were satisfied that Karen met none of the criteria specified in that report and was therefore not "brain dead" within its contemplation.

In this respect it was indicated by Dr. Plum that the brain works in essentially two ways, the vegetative and the sapient. He testified:

> We have an internal vegetative regulation which controls body temperature which controls breathing, which controls to a considerable degree blood pressure, which controls to some degree heart rate, which controls chewing, swallowing and which controls sleeping and waking. We have a more highly developed brain which is uniquely human which controls our relation to the outside world, our capacity to talk, to see, to feel, to sing, to think. Brain death necessarily must mean the death of both of these functions of the brain, vegetative and the sapient. Therefore, the presence of any function which is regulated or governed or controlled by the deeper parts of the brain which in laymen's terms might be considered purely vegetative would mean that the brain is not biologically dead.

Because Karen's neurological condition affects her respiratory ability (the respiratory system being a brain stem function) she requires a respirator to assist her breathing. From the time of her admission to Saint Clare's Hospital Karen has been assisted by an MA-1 respirator, a sophisticated machine which delivers a given volume of air at a certain rate and periodically provides a "sigh" volume, a relatively large measured volume of air designed to purge the lungs of excretions. Attempts to "wean" her from the respirator were unsuccessful and have been abandoned.

The experts believe that Karen cannot now survive without the assistance of the respirator; that exactly how long she would live without it is unknown; that the strong likelihood is that death would follow soon after its removal, and that removal would also risk further brain damage and would curtail the assistance the respirator presently provides in warding off infection.

It seemed to be the consensus not only of the treating physicians but also of the several qualified experts who testified in the case, that removal from the respirator would not conform to medical practices, standards and traditions.

The further medical consensus was that Karen in addition to being comatose is in a chronic and persistent "vegetative" state, having no awareness of anything or anyone around her and existing at a primitive reflex level. Although she does have some brain stem function (ineffective for respiration) and has other reactions one normally associates with being alive, such as moving, reacting to light, sound and noxious stimuli, blinking her eyes, and the like, the quality of her feeling impulses is unknown. She grimaces, makes stereotyped cries and sounds and has chewing motions. Her blood pressure is normal.

Karen remains in the intensive care unit at Saint Clare's Hospital, receiving 24-hour care by a team of four nurses characterized, as was the medical attention, as "excellent." She is nourished by feeding by way of a nasal-gastro tube and is routinely examined for infection, which under these circumstances is a serious life threat. The result is that her condition is considered remarkable under the unhappy circumstances involved.

Karen is described as emaciated, having suffered a weight loss of at least 40 pounds, and undergoing a continuing deteriorative process. Her posture is described as fetal-like and grotesque; there is extreme flexion-rigidity of the arms, legs and related muscles and her joints are severely rigid and deformed.

From all of this evidence, and including the whole testimonial record, several basic findings in the physical area are mandated. Severe brain and associated damage, albeit of uncertain etiology, has left Karen in a chronic and persistent vegetative state. No form of treatment which can cure or improve that condition is known or available. As nearly as may be determined, considering the guarded area of remote uncertainties characteristic of most medical science predictions, she can *never* be restored to cognitive or sapient life. Even with regard to the vegetative level and improvement therein (if such it may be called) the prognosis is extremely poor and the extent unknown if it should in fact occur.

She is debilitated and moribund and although fairly stable at the time of argument before us (no new information having been filed in the meanwhile in expansion of the record), no physician risked the opinion that she could live more than a year and indeed she may die much earlier. Excellent medical and nursing care so far has been able to ward off the constant threat of infection, to which she is peculiarly susceptible because of the respirator, the tracheal tube and other incidents of care in her vulnerable condition. Her life accordingly is sustained by the respirator and tubal feeding, and removal from the respirator would cause her death soon, although the time cannot be stated with more precision.

The determination of the fact and time of death in past years of medical science was keyed to the action of the heart and blood circulation, in turn dependent upon pulmonary activity, and hence cessation of these functions spelled out the reality of death.[5]

Developments in medical technology have obfuscated the use of the traditional definition of death. Efforts have been made to define irreversible coma as a new criterion for death, such as by the 1968 report of the Ad Hoc Committee of the Harvard Medical School (the Committee comprising ten physicians, an historian, a lawyer and a theologian), which asserted that:

> From ancient times down to the recent past it was clear that, when the respiration and heart stopped, the brain would die in a few minutes; so the obvious criterion of no heart beat as synonymous with death was sufficiently accurate. In those times the heart was considered to be the central organ of the body; it is not surprising that its failure marked the onset of death. This is no longer valid when modern resuscitative and supportive measures are used. These improved activities can now restore "life" as judged by the ancient standards of persistent respiration and continuing heart beat. This can be the case even when there is not the remotest possibility of an individual recovering consciousness following massive brain damage. ["A Definition of Irreversible Coma," 205 *J.A.M.A.* 337, 339 (1968)].

The Ad Hoc standards, carefully delineated, included absence of response to pain or other stimuli, pupilary reflexes, corneal, pharyngeal and other reflexes, blood pressure, spontaneous respiration, as well as "flat" or isoelectric electroencephalograms and the like, with all tests repeated "at least 24 hours later with no change." In such circumstances, where all of such criteria have been met as showing "brain death," the Committee recommends with regard to the respirator:

> The patient's condition can be determined only by a physician. When the patient is hopelessly damaged as defined above, the family and all colleagues who have participated in major decisions concerning the patient, and all nurses involved, should be so informed. Death is to be declared and *then* the respirator turned off. The decision to do this and the responsibility for it are to be taken by the physician-in-charge, in consultation with one or more physicians who have been directly involved in the case. It is unsound and undesirable to force the family to make the decision. [205 *J.A.M.A.*, *supra* at 338 (emphasis in original)].

But, as indicated, it was the consensus of medical testimony in the instant case that Karen, for all her disability, met none of these criteria, nor indeed any comparable criteria extant in the medical world and representing, as does the Ad Hoc Committee report, according to the testimony in this case, prevailing and accepted medical standards.

We have adverted to the "brain death" concept and Karen's disassociation with any of its criteria, to emphasize the basis of the medical decision made by Dr. Morse. When plaintiff and his family, finally reconciled to the certainty of Karen's impending death, requested the withdrawal of life support mechanisms, he demurred. His refusal was based upon his conception of medical standards, practice and ethics described in the medical testimony, such as in the evidence given by another neurologist, Dr. Sidney Diamond, a witness for the State. Dr. Diamond asserted that no physician would have failed to provide respirator support at the outset, and none would interrupt its life-saving course thereafter, except in the case of cerebral death. In the latter case, he thought the respirator would in effect be disconnected from one already dead, entitling the physician under medical standards and, he thought, legal concepts, to terminate the supportive measures. We note Dr. Diamond's distinction of major surgical or transfusion procedures in a terminal case not involving cerebral death, such as here:

> The subject has lost human qualities. It would be incredible, and I think unlikely, that any physician would respond to a sudden hemorrhage, massive hemorrhage, or a loss of all her defensive blood cells, by giving her large quantities of blood. I think that ***

major surgical procedures would be out of the question even if they were known to be essential for continued physical existence.

This distinction is adverted to also in the testimony of Dr. Julius Korein, a neurologist called by plaintiff. Dr. Korein described a medical practice concept of "judicious neglect" under which the physician will say:

Don't treat this patient anymore, *** it does not serve either the patient, the family, or society in any meaningful way to continue treatment with this patient.

Dr. Korein also told of the unwritten and unspoken standard of medical practice implied in the foreboding initials DNR (do not resuscitate), as applied to the extraordinary terminal case:

Cancer, metastatic cancer, involving the lungs, the liver, the brain, multiple involvements, the physician may or may not write: Do not resuscitate. *** [I]t could be said to the nurse: if this man stops breathing don't resuscitate him. *** No physician that I know personally is going to try and resuscitate a man riddled with cancer and in agony and he stops breathing. They are not going to put him on a respirator. *** I think that would be the height of misuse of technology.

While the thread of logic in such distinctions may be elusive to the non-medical lay mind, in relation to the supposed imperative to sustain life at all costs, they nevertheless relate to medical decisions, such as the decision of Dr. Morse in the present case. We agree with the trial court that that decision was in accord with Dr. Morse's conception of medical standards and practice.

We turn to that branch of the factual case pertaining to the application for guardianship, as distinguished from the nature of the authorization sought by the applicant. The character and general suitability of Joseph Quinlan as guardian for his daughter, in ordinary circumstances, could not be doubted. The record bespeaks the high degree of familial love which pervaded the home of Joseph Quinlan and reached out fully to embrace Karen, although she was living elsewhere at the time of her collapse. The proofs showed him to be deeply religious, imbued with a morality so sensitive that months of tortured indecision preceded his belated conclusion (despite earlier moral judgments reached by the other family members, but unexpressed to him in order not to influence him) to seek the termination of life-supportive measures sustaining Karen. A communicant of the Roman Catholic Church, as were other family members, he first sought solace in private prayer looking with confidence, as he says, to the Creator, first for the recovery of Karen and then, if that were not possible, for guidance with respect to the awesome decision confronting him.

To confirm the moral rightness of the decision he was about to make he consulted with his parish priest and later with the Catholic chaplain of Saint Clare's Hospital. He would not, he testified, have sought termination if that act were to be morally wrong or in conflict with the tenets of the religion he so profoundly respects. He was disabused of doubt, however, when the position of the Roman Catholic Church was made known to him as it is reflected in the record in this case. While it is not usual for matters of religious dogma or concepts to enter a civil litigation (except as they may bear upon constitutional rights, or sometimes, familial matters; *cf. In re Adoption of E,* 59 *N.J.* 36 (1971)), they were rightly admitted in evidence here. The judge was bound to measure the character and motivations in all respects of Joseph Quinlan as prospective guardian; and insofar as these religious matters bore upon them, they were properly scrutinized and considered by the court.

Thus germane, we note the position of that Church as illuminated by the record before us. We have no reason to believe that it would be at all discordant with the whole of Judeo-Christian tradition, considering its central respect and reverence for the sanctity of human life. It was in this sense of relevance that we admitted as *amicus curiae* the New Jersey Catholic Conference, essentially the spokesman for the various Catholic bishops of New Jersey, organized to give witness to spiritual values in public affairs in the statewide community. The position statement of Bishop Lawrence B. Casey, reproduced in the *amicus* brief, projects these views:

(a)   The verification of the fact of death in a particular case cannot be deduced from any religious or moral principle and, under this aspect, does not fall within the competence of the church;—that dependence must be had upon traditional and medical standards, and by these standards Karen Ann Quinlan is assumed to be alive.

(b)   The request of plaintiff for authority to terminate a medical procedure characterized as "an extraordinary means of treatment" would not involve euthanasia. This upon the reasoning expressed by Pope Pius XII in his *allocutio* (address) to anesthesiologists on November 24, 1957, when he dealt with the question:

> Does the anesthesiologist have the right, or is he
> bound, in all cases of deep unconsciousness, even in
> those that are completely hopeless in the opinion of

297

the competent doctor, to use modern artificial respiration apparatus, even against the will of the family?

His answer made the following points:

1. In ordinary cases the doctor has the right to act in this manner, but is not bound to do so unless this is the only way of fulfilling another certain moral duty.

2. The doctor, however, has no right independent of the patient. He can act only if the patient explicitly or implicitly, directly or indirectly, gives him the permission.

3. The treatment as described in the question constitutes extraordinary means of preserving life and so there is no obligation to use them nor to give the doctor permission to use them.

4. The rights and the duties of the family depend on the presumed will of the unconscious patient if he or she is of legal age, and the family, too, is bound to use only ordinary means.

5. This case is not to be considered euthanasia in any way; that would never be licit. The interruption of attempts at resuscitation, even when it causes the arrest of circulation, is not more than an indirect cause of the cessation of life, and we must apply in this case the principle of double effect.

So it was that the Bishop Casey statement validated the decision of Joseph Quinlan:

Competent medical testimony has established that Karen Ann Quinlan has no reasonable hope of recovery from her comatose state by the use of any available medical procedures. The continuance of mechanical (cardiorespiratory) supportive measures to sustain continuance of her body functions and her life constitute extraordinary means of treatment. *Therefore, the decision of Joseph *** Quinlan to request the discontinuance of this treatment is, according to the teachings of the Catholic Church, a morally correct decision.* (Emphasis in original.)

And the mind and purpose of the intending guardian were undoubtedly influenced by factors included in the following reference to the interrelationship of the three disciplines of theology, law and medicine as exposed in the Casey statement:

> The right to a natural death is one outstanding area in which the disciplines of theology, medicine and law overlap; or, to put it another way, it is an area in which these three disciplines convene.
>
> Medicine with its combination of advanced technology and professional ethics is both able and inclined to prolong biological life. Law with its felt obligation to protect life and freedom of the individual seeks to assure each person's right to live out his human life until its natural and inevitable conclusion. Theology with its acknowledgment of man's dissatisfaction with biological life as the ultimate source of joy *** defends the sacredness of human life and defends it from all direct attacks.
>
> These disciplines do not conflict with one another, but are necessarily conjoined in the application of their principles in a particular instance such as that of Karen Ann Quinlan. Each must in some way acknowledge the other without denying its own competence. The civil law is not expected to assert a belief in eternal life; nor, on the other hand, is it expected to ignore the right of the individual to profess it, and to form and pursue his conscience in accord with that belief. Medical science is not authorized to directly cause natural death; nor, however, is it expected to prevent it when it is inevitable and all hope of a return to an even partial exercise of human life is irreparably lost. Religion is not expected to define biological death; nor, on its part, is it expected to relinquish its responsibility to assist man in the formation and pursuit of a correct conscience as to the acceptance of natural death when science has confirmed its inevitability beyond any hope other than that of preserving biological life in a merely vegetative state.

And the gap in the law is aptly described in the Bishop Casey statement:

> In the present public discussion of the case of Karen Ann Quinlan it has been brought out that responsible people involved in medical care, patients and families have exercised the freedom to terminate or withhold certain treatments as extraordinary means in cases judged to be terminal, i.e., cases which hold no realistic hope for some recovery, in accord with the expressed or implied intentions of the patients themselves. To

whatever extent this has been happening it has been without sanction in civil law. Those involved in such actions, however, have ethical and theological literature to guide them in their judgments and actions. Furthermore, such actions have not in themselves undermined society's reverence for the lives of sick and dying people.

It is both possible and necessary for society to have laws and ethical standards which provide freedom for decisions, in accord with the expressed or implied intentions of the patient, to terminate or withhold extraordinary treatment in cases which are judged to be hopeless by competent medical authorities, without at the same time leaving an opening for euthanasia. Indeed, to accomplish this, it may simply be required that courts and legislative bodies recognize the present standards and practices of many people engaged in medical care who have been doing what the parents of Karen Ann Quinlan are requesting authorization to have done for their beloved daughter.

Before turning to the legal and constitutional issues involved, we feel it essential to reiterate that the "Catholic view" of religious neutrality in the circumstances of this case is considered by the Court only in the aspect of its impact upon the conscience, motivation, and purpose of the intending guardian, Joseph Quinlan, and not as a precedent in terms of the civil law.

If Joseph Quinlan, for instance, were a follower and strongly influenced by the teachings of Buddha, or if, as an agnostic or atheist, his moral judgments were formed without reference to religious feelings, but were nevertheless formed and viable, we would with equal attention and high respect consider these elements, as bearing upon his character, motivations and purposes as relevant to this qualification and suitability as guardian.

It is from this factual base that the Court confronts and responds to three basic issues:

1. Was the trial court correct in denying the specific relief requested by plaintiff, *i.e.*, authorization for termination of the life-supporting apparatus, on the case presented to him? Our determination on that question is in the affirmative.

2. Was the court correct in withholding letters of guardianship from the plaintiff and appointing in his stead a stranger? On that issue our determination is in the negative.

300

3. Should this Court, in the light of the foregoing conclusions, grant declaratory relief to the plaintiff? On that question our Court's determination is in the affirmative.

This brings us to a consideration of the constitutional and legal issues underlying the foregoing determinations.

CONSTITUTIONAL AND LEGAL ISSUES

At the outset we note the dual role in which plaintiff comes before the Court. He not only raises, derivatively, what he perceives to be the constitutional and legal rights of his daughter, Karen, but he also claims certain rights independently as parent.

Although generally a litigant may assert only his own constitutional rights, we have no doubt that plaintiff has sufficient standing to advance both positions.

While no express constitutional language limits judicial activity to cases and controversies, New Jersey courts will not render advisory opinions or entertain proceedings by plaintiffs who do not have sufficient legal standing to maintain their actions. *Walker* v. *Stanhope*, 23 *N.J.* 657, 660 (1957). However, as in this case, New Jersey courts commonly grant declaratory relief. Declaratory Judgments Act, *N.J.S.A.* 2A:16-50 *et seq.* And our courts hold that where the plaintiff is not simply an interloper and the proceeding serves the public interest, standing will be found. *Walker* v. *Stanhope, supra,* 23 *N.J.* at 661-66; *Koons* v. *Atlantic City Bd. of Comm'rs*, 135 *N.J.L.* 329, 338-39 (Sup. Ct. 1946), *aff'd*, 135 *N.J.L.* 204 (E. & A. 1947). In *Crescent Park Tenants Ass'n* v. *Realty Equities Corp.*, 58 *N.J.* 98 (1971), Justice Jacobs said:

> *** [W]e have appropriately confined litigation to those situations where the litigants concerned with the subject matter evidenced a sufficient stake and real adverseness. In the overall we have given due weight to the interests of individual justice, along with the public interest, always bearing in mind that throughout our law we have been sweepingly rejecting procedural frustrations in favor of 'just and expeditious determinations on the ultimate merits.' [58 *N.J.* at 107-08 (quoting from *Tumarkin* v. *Friedman*, 17 *N.J. Super.* 20, 21 (App. Div. 1951), *certif. den.*, 9 *N.J.* 287 (1952))].

The father of Karen Quinlan is certainly no stranger to the present controversy. His interests are real and adverse and he raises questions of

301

surpassing importance. Manifestly, he has standing to assert his daughter's constitutional rights, she being incompetent to do so.

I.

The Free Exercise of Religion

We think the contention as to interference with religious beliefs or rights may be considered and dealt with without extended discussion, given the acceptance of distinctions so clear and simple in their precedential definition as to be dispositive on their face.

Simply stated, the right to religious beliefs is absolute but conduct in pursuance thereof is not wholly immune from governmental restraint. *John F. Kennedy Memorial Hosp.* v. *Heston*, 58 *N.J.* 576, 580-81 (1971). So it is that, for the sake of life, courts sometimes (but not always) order blood transfusions for Jehovah's Witnesses (whose religious beliefs abhor such procedure), *Application of President & Directors of Georgetown College, Inc.* 331 *F.*2d 1000 (D.C. Cir.), *cert. den.*, 377 *U.S.* 978, 84 *S.Ct.* 1883, 12 *L.Ed.* 2d 746 (1964); *United States* v. *George*, 239 *F. Supp.* 752 (D. Conn. 1965); *John F. Kennedy Memorial Hosp.* v. *Heston, supra*; *Powell* v. *Columbia Presbyterian Medical Center*, 49 *Misc.* 2d 215, 267 *N.Y.S.* 2d 450 (Sup. Ct. 1965); *but see In re Osborne*, 294 *A.*2d 372 (D.C. Ct. App. 1972); *In re Estate of Brooks*, 32 *Ill.* 2d 361, 205 *N.E.* 2d 435 (Sup. Ct. 1965); *Erickson* v. *Dilgard*, 44 *Misc.* 2d 27, 252 *N.Y.S.* 2d 705 (Sup. Ct. 1962); *see generally* Annot., "Power Of Courts Or Other Public Agencies, In The Absence Of Statutory Authority, To Order Compulsory Medical Care for Adult," 9 *A.L.R.* 3d 1391 (1966); forbid exposure to death from handling virulent snakes or ingesting poison (interfering with deeply held religious sentiments in such regard), *e.g., Hill* v. *State*, 38 *Ala. App.* 404, 88 *So.* 2d 880 (Ct. App.), *cert. den.*, 264 *Ala.* 697, 88 *So.* 2d 887 (Sup. Ct. 1956); *State* v. *Massey*, 229 *N.C.* 734, 51 *S.E.* 2d 179 (Sup. Ct.), appeal dismissed *sub nom., Bunn* v. *North Carolina*, 336 *U.S.* 942, 69 *S.Ct.* 813, 93 *L.Ed.* 1099 (1949); *State ex rel. Swann* v. *Pack*, ____ *Tenn.* ____, 527 *S.W.* 2d 99 (Sup. Ct. 1975), *cert. den.*, ____ *U.S.* ____, ____ *S.Ct.* ____, ____ *L.Ed.* 2d ____ (44 *U.S.L.W.* 3498, No. 95-956, (March 8, 1976)); and protect the public health as in the case of compulsory vaccination (over the strongest of religious objections), *e.g., Wright* v. *DeWitt School Dist. 1*, 238 *Ark.* 906, 385 *S.W.* 2d 644 (Sup. Ct. 1965); *Mountain Lakes Bd. of Educ.* v. *Maas*, 56 *N.J. Super.* 245 (App. Div. 1959), *aff'd o.b.*, 31 *N.J.* 537 (1960), *cert. den.*, 363 *U.S.* 843, 80 *S.Ct.* 1613, 4 *L.Ed.* 2d 1727 (1960); *McCartney* v. *Austin*, 57 *Misc.* 2d 525, 293 *N.Y.S.* 2d 188 (Sup.

Ct. 1968). The public interest is thus considered paramount, without essential dissolution of respect for religious beliefs.

We think, without further examples, that, ranged against the State's interest in the preservation of life, the impingement of religious belief, much less religious "neutrality" as here, does not reflect a constitutional question, in the circumstances at least of the case presently before the Court. Moreover, like the trial court, we do not recognize an independent parental right of religious freedom to support the relief requested. 137 *N.J. Super.* at 267-68.

II.

Cruel and Unusual Punishment

Similarly inapplicable to the case before us is the Constitution's Eighth Amendment protection against cruel and unusual punishment which, as held by the trial court, is not relevant to situations other than the imposition of penal sanctions. Historic in nature, it stemmed from punitive excesses in the infliction of criminal penalties.[6] We find no precedent in law which would justify its extension to the correction of social injustice or hardship, such as, for instance, in the case of poverty. The latter often condemns the poor and deprived to horrendous living conditions which could certainly be described in the abstract as "cruel and unusual punishment." Yet the constitutional base of protection from "cruel and unusual punishment" is plainly irrelevant to such societal ills which must be remedied, if at all, under other concepts of constitutional and civil right.

So it is in the case of the unfortunate Karen Quinlan. Neither the State, nor the law, but the accident of fate and nature, has inflicted upon her conditions which though in essence cruel and most unusual, yet do not amount to "punishment" in any constitutional sense.

Neither the judgment of the court below, nor the medical decision which confronted it, nor the law and equity perceptions which impelled its action, nor the whole factual base upon which it was predicated, inflicted "cruel and unusual punishment" in the constitutional sense.

III.

The Right of Privacy[7]

It is the issue of the constitutional right of privacy that has given us most concern, in the exceptional circumstances of this case. Here a loving parent, *qua* parent and raising the rights of his incompetent and

303

profoundly damaged daughter, probably irreversibly doomed to no more than a biologically vegetative remnant of life, is before the court. He seeks authorization to abandon specialized technological procedures which can only maintain for a time a body having no potential for resumption or continuance of other than a "vegetative" existence.

We have no doubt, in these unhappy circumstances, that if Karen were herself miraculously lucid for an interval (not altering the existing prognosis of the condition to which she would soon return) and perceptive of her irreversible condition, she could effectively decide upon discontinuance of the life-support apparatus, even if it meant the prospect of natural death. To this extent we may distinguish *Heston, supra,* which concerned a severely injured young woman (Delores Heston), whose life depended on surgery and blood transfusion; and who was in such extreme shock that she was unable to express an informed choice (although the Court apparently considered the case as if the patient's own religious decision to resist transfusion were at stake), but most importantly a patient apparently salvable to long life and vibrant health;—a situation not at all like the present case.

We have no hesitancy in deciding, in the instant diametrically opposite case, that no external compelling interest of the State could compel Karen to endure the unendurable, only to vegetate a few measurable months with no realistic possibility of returning to any semblance of cognitive or sapient life. We perceive no thread of logic distinguishing between such a choice on Karen's part and a similar choice which, under the evidence in this case, could be made by a competent patient terminally ill, riddled by cancer and suffering great pain; such a patient would not be resuscitated or put on a respirator in the example described by Dr. Korein, and *a fortiori* would not be kept *against his will* on a respirator.

Although the Constitution does not explicitly mention a right of privacy, Supreme Court decisions have recognized that a right of personal privacy exists and that certain areas of privacy are guaranteed under the Constitution. *Eisenstadt* v. *Baird*, 405 *U.S.* 438, 92 *S.Ct.* 1029, 31 *L.Ed.* 2d 349 (1972); *Stanley* v. *Georgia*, 394 *U.S.* 557, 89 *S.Ct.* 1243, 22 *L.Ed.* 2d 542 (1969). The Court has interdicted judicial intrusion into many aspects of personal decision, sometimes basing this restraint upon the conception of a limitation of judicial interest and responsibility, such as with regard to contraception and its relationship to family life and decision. *Griswold* v. *Connecticut*, 381 *U.S.* 479, 85 *S.Ct.* 1678, 14 *L.Ed.* 2d 510 (1965).

The Court in *Griswold* found the unwritten constitutional right of privacy to exist in the penumbra of specific guarantees of the Bill of

Rights "formed by emanations from those guarantees that help give them life and substance." 381 *U.S.* at 484, 85 *S.Ct.* at 1681, 14 *L.Ed.* 2d at 514. Presumably this right is broad enough to encompass a patient's decision to decline medical treatment under certain circumstances, in much the same way as it is broad enough to encompass a woman's decision to terminate pregnancy under certain conditions. *Roe* v. *Wade*, 410 *U.S.* 113, 153, 93 *S.Ct.* 705, 727, 35 *L.Ed.* 2d 147, 177 (1973).

Nor is such right of privacy forgotten in the New Jersey Constitution. *N.J. Const.* (1947), Art. I, par. 1.

The claimed interests of the State in this case are essentially the preservation and sanctity of human life and defense to the right of the physician to administer medical treatment according to his best judgment. In this case the doctors say that removing Karen from the respirator will conflict with their professional judgment. The plaintiff answers that Karen's present treatment serves only a maintenance function; that the respirator cannot cure or improve her condition but at best can only prolong her inevitable slow deterioration and death; and that the interests of the patient, as seen by her surrogate, the guardian, must be evaluated by the court as predominant, even in the face of an option *contra* by the present attending physicians. Plaintiff's distinction is significant. The nature of Karen's care and the realistic chances of her recovery are quite unlike those of the patients discussed in many of the cases where treatments were ordered. In many of those cases the medical procedure required (usually a transfusion) constituted a minimal bodily invasion and the chances of recovery and return to functioning life were very good. We think that the State's interest *contra* weakens and the individual's right to privacy grows as the degree of bodily invasion increases and the prognosis dims. Ultimately there comes a point at which the individual's rights overcome the State interest. It is for that reason that we believe Karen's choice, if she were competent to make it, would be vindicated by the law. Her prognosis is extremely poor,—she will never resume cognitive life. And the bodily invasion is very great,—she requires 24-hour intensive nursing care, antibiotics, and the assistance of a respirator, a catheter and feeding tube.

Our affirmance of Karen's independent right of choice, however, would ordinarily be based upon her competency to assert it. The sad truth, however, is that she is grossly incompetent and we cannot discern her supposed choice based on the testimony of her previous conversations with friends, where such testimony is without sufficient probative weight. 137 *N.J. Super.* at 260. Nevertheless we have concluded that Karen's right of privacy may be asserted on her behalf by her guardian under the peculiar circumstances here present.

If a putative decision by Karen to permit this non-cognitive, vegetative existence to terminate by natural forces is regarded as a valuable incident of her right of privacy, as we believe it to be, then it should not be discarded solely on the basis that her condition prevents her conscious exercise of the choice. The only practical way to prevent destruction of the right is to permit the guardian and family of Karen to render their best judgment, subject to the qualifications hereinafter stated, as to whether she would exercise it in these circumstances. If their conclusion is in the affirmative this decision should be accepted by a society the overwhelming majority of whose members would, we think, in similar circumstances, exercise such a choice in the same way for themselves or for those closest to them. It is for this reason that we determine that Karen's right of privacy may be asserted in her behalf, in this respect, by her guardian and family under the particular circumstances presented by this record.

Regarding Mr. Quinlan's right of privacy, we agree with Judge Muir's conclusion that there is no parental constitutional right that would entitle him to a grant of relief *in propria persona. Id.* at 266. Insofar as a parental right of privacy has been recognized, it has been in the context of determining the rearing of infants and, as Judge Muir put it, involved "continuing life styles." *See Wisconsin* v. *Yoder,* 406 *U.S.* 205, 92 *S.Ct.* 1526, 32 *L.Ed.* 2d 15 (1972); *Pierce* v. *Society of Sisters,* 268 *U.S.* 510, 45 *S.Ct.* 571, 69 *L.Ed.* 1070 (1925); *Meyer* v. *Nebraska,* 262 *U.S.* 390, 43 *S.Ct.* 625, 67 *L.Ed.* 1042 (1923). Karen Quinlan is a 22 year old adult. Her right of privacy in respect of the matter before the Court is to be vindicated by Mr. Quinlan as guardian, as hereinabove determined.

IV.

The Medical Factor

Having declared the substantive legal basis upon which plaintiff's rights as representative of Karen must be deemed predicated, we face and respond to the assertion on behalf of defendants that our premise unwarrantably offends prevailing medical standards. We thus turn to consideration of the medical decision supporting the determination made below, conscious of the paucity of pre-existing legislative and judicial guidance as to the rights and liabilities therein involved.

> A significant problem in any discussion of sensitive medical-legal issues is the marked, perhaps unconscious, tendency of many to distort what the law is, in

306

pursuit of an exposition of what they would like the law to be. Nowhere is this barrier to the intelligent resolution of legal controversies more obstructive than in the debate over patient rights at the end of life. Judicial refusals to order lifesaving treatment in the face of contrary claims of bodily self-determination or free religious exercise are too often cited in support of a preconceived 'right to die,' even though the patients, wanting to live, have claimed no such right. Conversely, the assertion of a religious or other objection to lifesaving treatment is at times condemned as attempted suicide, even though suicide means something quite different in the law. [Byrn, "Compulsory Lifesaving Treatment For The Competent Adult," 44 *Fordham L. Rev.* 1 (1975)].

Perhaps the confusion there adverted to stems from mention by some courts of statutory or common law condemnation of suicide as demonstrating the state's interest in the preservation of life. We would see, however, a real distinction between the self-infliction of deadly harm and a self-determination against artificial life support or radical surgery, for instance, in the face of irreversible, painful and certain imminent death. The contrasting situations mentioned are analogous to those continually faced by the medical profession. When does the institution of life-sustaining procedures, ordinarily mandatory, become the subject of medical discretion in the context of administration to persons *in extremis*? And when does the withdrawal of such procedures, from such persons already supported by them, come within the orbit of medical discretion? When does a determination as to either of the foregoing contingencies court the hazard of civil or criminal liability on the part of the physician or institution involved?

The existence and nature of the medical dilemma need hardly be discussed at length, portrayed as it is in the present case and complicated as it has recently come to be in view of the dramatic advance of medical technology. The dilemma is there, it is real, it is constantly resolved in accepted medical practice without attention in the courts, it pervades the issues in the very case we here examine. The branch of the dilemma involving the doctor's responsibility and the relationship of the court's duty was thus conceived by Judge Muir:

Doctors *** to treat a patient, must deal with medical tradition and past case histories. They must be guided by what they do know. The extent of their training, their experience, consultation with other physicians,

307

must guide their decision-making processes in providing care to their patient. The nature, extent and duration of care by societal standards is the responsibility of a physician. The morality and conscience of our society places this responsibility in the hands of the physician. What justification is there to remove it from control of the medical profession and place it in the hands of the courts? [137 *N.J. Super.* at 259].

Such notions as to the distribution of responsibility, heretofore generally entertained, should however neither impede this Court in deciding matters clearly justiciable nor preclude a re-examination by the Court as to underlying human values and rights. Determinations as to these must, in the ultimate, be responsive not only to the concepts of medicine but also to the common moral judgment of the community at large. In the latter respect the Court has a non-delegable judicial responsibility.

Put in another way, the law, equity and justice must not themselves quail and be helpless in the face of modern technological marvels presenting questions hitherto unthought of. Where a Karen Quinlan, or a parent, or a doctor, or a hospital, or a State seeks the process and response of a court, it must answer with its most informed conception of justice in the previously unexplored circumstances presented to it. That is its obligation and we are here fulfilling it, for the actors and those having an interest in the matter should not go without remedy.

Courts in the exercise of their *parens patriae* responsibility to protect those under disability have sometimes implemented medical decisions and authorized their carrying out under the doctrine of "substituted judgment." *Hart* v. *Brown*, 29 *Conn. Super.* 368, 289 *A.* 2d 386, 387-88 (Super. Ct. 1972); *Strunk* v. *Strunk*, 445 *S.W.* 2d 145, 147-48 (Ky. Ct. App. 1969). For as Judge Muir pointed out:

> "As part of the inherent power of equity, a Court of Equity has full and complete jurisdiction over the persons of those who labor under any legal disability ***. The Court's action in such a case is not limited by any narrow bounds, but it is empowered to stretch forth its arm in whatever direction its aid and protection may be needed. While this is indeed a special exercise of equity jurisdiction, it is beyond question that by virtue thereof the Court may pass upon purely personal rights." [137 *N.J. Super.* at 254 (quoting from *Am.Jur.* 2d, Equity § 69 (1966))].

But insofar as a court, having no inherent medical expertise, is called upon to overrule a professional decision made according to prevailing medical practice and standards, a different question is presented. As mentioned below, a doctor is required

> "to exercise in the treatment of his patient the degree of care, knowledge and skill ordinarily possessed and exercised in similar situations by the average member of the profession practicing in his field." *Schueler* v. *Strelinger*, 43 *N.J.* 330, 344 (1964). If he is a specialist he "must employ not merely the skill of a general practitioner, but also that special degree of skill normally possessed by the average physician who devotes special study and attention to the particular organ or disease or injury involved, having regard to the present state of scientific knowledge." *Clark* v. *Wichman*, 72 *N.J. Super.* 486, 493 (App. Div. 1962). This is the duty that establishes his legal obligations to his parents. [137 *N.J. Super.* at 257-58].

The medical obligation is related to standards and practice prevailing in the profession. The physicians in charge of the case, as noted above, declined to withdraw the respirator. That decision was consistent with the proofs below as to the then existing medical standards and practices.

Under the law as it then stood, Judge Muir was correct in declining to authorize withdrawal of the respirator.

However, in relation to the matter of the declaratory relief sought by plaintiff as representative of Karen's interests, we are required to reevaluate the applicability of the medical standards projected in the court below. The question is whether there is such internal consistency and rationality in the application of such standards as should warrant their constituting an ineluctable bar to the effectuation of substantive relief for plaintiff at the hands of the court. We have concluded not.

In regard to the foregoing it is pertinent that we consider the impact on the standards both of the civil and criminal law as to medical liability and the new technological means of sustaining life irreversibly damaged.

The modern proliferation of substantial malpractice litigation and the less frequent but even more unnerving possibility of criminal sanctions would seem, for it is beyond human nature to suppose otherwise, to have bearing on the practice and standards as they exist. The brooding presence of such possible liability, it was testified here, had no part in the decision of the treating physicians. As did Judge Muir, we afford this testimony full credence. But we cannot believe that the stated factor has not had a strong influence on the standards, as the literature on the subject plainly reveals. (See footnote 8, *infra*). Moreover our attention is drawn not so much to the recognition by Drs. Morse and Javed of the extant practice and standards but to the widening ambiguity of those standards themselves in their application to the medical problems we are discussing.

The agitation of the medical community in the face of modern life prolongation technology and its search for definitive policy are demonstrated in the large volume of relevant professional commentary.[8]

The wide debate thus reflected contrasts with the relative paucity of legislative and judicial guides and standards in the same field. The medical profession has sought to devise guidelines such as the "brain death" concept of the Harvard Ad Hoc Committee mentioned above. But it is perfectly apparent from the testimony we have quoted of Dr. Korein, and indeed so clear as almost to be judicially noticeable, that humane decisions against resuscitative or maintenance therapy are frequently a recognized *de facto* response in the medical world to the irreversible, terminal, pain-ridden patient, especially with familial consent. And these cases, of course, are far short of "brain death."

We glean from the record here that physicians distinguish between curing the ill and comforting and easing the dying; that they refuse to treat the curable as if they were dying or ought to die; and that they have sometimes refused to treat the hopeless and dying as if they were curable. In this sense, as we were reminded by the testimony of Drs. Korein and Diamond, many of them have refused to inflict an undesired prolongation of the process of dying on a patient in irreversible condition when it is clear that such "therapy" offers neither human nor humane benefit. We think these attitudes represent a balanced implementation of a profoundly realistic perspective on the meaning of life and death and that they respect the whole Judeo-Christian tradition of regard for human life. No less would they seem consistent with the moral matrix of medicine, "to heal," very much in the sense of the endless mission of the law, "to do justice."

Yet this balance, we feel, is particularly difficult to perceive and apply in the context of the development by advanced technology of sophisticated and artificial life-sustaining devices. For those possibly curable, such devices are of great value, and, as ordinary medical procedures, are essential. Consequently, as pointed out by Dr. Diamond, they are necessary because of the ethic of medical practice. But in light of the situation in the present case (while the record here is somewhat hazy in distinguishing between "ordinary" and "extraordinary" measures), one would have to think that the use of the same respirator or like support could be considered "ordinary" in the context of the possibly curable patient but "extraordinary" in the context of the forced sustaining by cardio-respiratory processes of an irreversibly doomed patient. And this dilemma is sharpened in the face of the malpractice and criminal action threat which we have mentioned.

We would hesitate, in this imperfect world, to propose as to physicians that type of immunity which from the early common law has surrounded judges and grand jurors, *see, e.g., Grove* v. *Van Duyn*, 44 *N.J.L.* 654, 656-57 (E. & A. 1882); *O'Regan* v. *Schermerhorn*, 25 *N.J. Misc.* 1, 19-20 (Sup. Ct. 1940), so that they might without fear of personal retaliation perform their judicial duties with independent objectivity. In *Bradley* v. *Fisher*, 80 *U.S.* (13 *Wall.*) 335, 347, 20 *L.Ed.* 646, 649 (1872), the Supreme Court held:

> [I]t is a general principle of the highest importance to the proper administration of justice that a judicial officer, in exercising the authority vested in him, shall be free to act upon his own convictions, without apprehension of personal consequences to himself.

Lord Coke said of judges that "they are only to make an account to God and the King [the State]." 12 *Coke Rep.* 23, 25, 77 *Eng. Rep.* 1305, 1307 (S.C. 1608).

Nevertheless, there must be a way to free physicians, in the pursuit of their healing vocation, from possible contamination by self-interest or self-protection concerns which would inhibit their independent medical judgments for the well-being of their dying patients. We would hope that this opinion might be serviceable to some degree in ameliorating the professional problems under discussion.

A technique aimed at the underlying difficulty (though in a somewhat broader context) is described by Dr. Karen Teel, a pediatrician and a director of Pediatric Education, who writes in the *Baylor Law Review* under the title "The Physician's Dilemma: A Doctor's View: What The Law Should Be." Dr. Teel recalls:

> Physicians, by virtue of their responsibility for medical judgments are, partly by choice and partly by default, charged with the responsibility of making ethical judgments which we are sometimes ill-equipped to make. We are not always morally and legally authorized to make them. The physician is thereby assuming a civil and criminal liability that, as often as not, he does not even realize as a factor in his decision. There is little or no dialogue in this whole process. The physician assumes that his judgment is called for and, in good faith, he acts. Someone must and it has been the physician who has assumed the responsibility and the risk.

311

I suggest that it would be more appropriate to provide a regular forum for more input and dialogue in individual situations and to allow the responsibility of these judgments to be shared. Many hospitals have established an Ethics Committee composed of physicians, social workers, attorneys, and theologians, *** which serves to review the individual circumstances of ethical dilemma and which has provided much in the way of assistance and safeguards for patients and their medical caretakers. Generally, the authority of these committees is primarily restricted to the hospital setting and their official status is more that of an advisory body than of an enforcing body.

The concept of an Ethics Committee which has this kind of organization and is readily accessible to those persons rendering medical care to patients, would be, I think, the most promising direction for further study at this point. ***

*** [This would allow] some much needed dialogue regarding these issues and [force] the point of exploring all of the options for a particular patient. It diffuses the responsibility for making these judgments. Many physicians, in many circumstances, would welcome this sharing of responsibility. I believe that such an entity could lend itself well to an assumption of a legal status which would allow courses of action not now undertaken because of the concern for liability. [27 *Baylor L. Rev.* 6, 8-9 (1975)].

The most appealing factor in the technique suggested by Dr. Teel seems to us to be the diffusion of professional responsibility for decision, comparable in a way to the value of multi-judge courts in finally resolving on appeal difficult questions of law. Moreover, such a system would be protective to the hospital as well as the doctor in screening out, so to speak, a case which might be contaminated by less than worthy motivations of family or physician. In the real world and in relationship to the momentous decision contemplated, the value of additional views and diverse knowledge is apparent.

We consider that a practice of applying to a court to confirm such decisions would generally be inappropriate, not only because that would be a gratuitous encroachment upon the medical profession's field of competence, but because it would be impossibly cumbersome. Such a requirement is distinguishable from the judicial overview traditionally required in other matters such as the adjudication and commitment of mental incompetents. This is not to say that in the case of an otherwise justiciable controversy access to the courts would be foreclosed; we speak rather of a general practice and procedure.

And although the deliberations and decisions which we describe would be professional in nature they should obviously include at some stage the feelings of the family of an incompetent relative. Decision-making within health care if it is considered as an expression of a primary obligation of the physician, *primum non nocere*, should be controlled primarily within the patient-doctor-family relationship, as indeed was recognized by Judge Muir in his supplemental opinion of November 12, 1975.

If there could be created not necessarily this particular system but some reasonable counterpart, we would have no doubt that such decisions, thus determined to be in accordance with medical practice and prevailing standards, would be accepted by society and by the courts, at least in cases comparable to that of Karen Quinlan.

The evidence in this case convinces us that the focal point of decision should be the prognosis as to the reasonable possibility of return to cognitive and sapient life, as distinguished from the forced continuance of that biological vegetative existence to which Karen seems to be doomed.

In summary of the present Point of this opinion, we conclude that the state of the pertinent medical standards and practices which guided the attending physicians in this matter is not such as would justify this Court in deeming itself bound or controlled thereby in responding to the case for declaratory relief established by the parties on the record before us.

V.

Alleged Criminal Liability

Having concluded that there is a right of privacy that might permit termination of treatment in the circumstances of this case, we turn to consider the relationship of the exercise of that right to the criminal law. We are aware that such termination of treatment would accelerate Karen's death. The County Prosecutor and the Attorney General stoutly maintain that there would be criminal liability for such acceleration. Under the statutes of this State, the unlawful killing of another human being is criminal homicide. *N.J.S.A.* 2A:113-1, 2, 5. We conclude that there would be no criminal homicide in the circumstances of this case. We believe, first, that the ensuing death would not be homicide but rather expiration from existing natural causes. Secondly, even if it were to be regarded as homicide, it would not be unlawful.

313

These conclusions rest upon definitional and constitutional bases. The termination of treatment pursuant to the right of privacy is, within the limitations of this case, *ipso facto* lawful. Thus, a death resulting from such an act would not come within the scope of the homicide statutes proscribing only the unlawful killing of another. There is a real and in this case determinative distinction between the unlawful taking of the life of another and the ending of artificial life-support systems as a matter of self-determination.

Furthermore, the exercise of a constitutional right such as we have here found is protected from criminal prosecution. *See Stanley* v. *Georgia, supra*, 394 *U.S.* at 559, 89 *S.Ct.* at 1245, 22 *L.Ed.* 2d at 546. We do not question the State's undoubted power to punish the taking of human life, but that power does not encompass individuals terminating medical treatment pursuant to their right of privacy. *See id.* at 568, 89 *S.Ct.* at 1250, 22 *L.Ed.* 2d at 551. The constitutional protection extends to third parties whose action is necessary to effectuate the exercise of that right where the individuals themselves would not be subject to prosecution or the third parties are charged as accessories to an act which could not be a crime. *Eisenstadt* v. *Baird, supra*, 405 *U.S.* at 445-46, 92 *S.Ct.* at 1034-35, 31 *L.Ed.* 2d at 357-58; *Griswold* v. *Connecticut, supra*, 381 *U.S.* at 481, 85 *S.Ct.* at 1679-80, 14 *L.Ed.* 2d at 512-13. And, under the circumstances of this case, these same principles would apply to and negate a valid prosecution for attempted suicide were there still such a crime in this State.[9]

VI.

The Guardianship of the Person

The trial judge bifurcated the guardianship, as we have noted, refusing to appoint Joseph Quinlan to be guardian of the person and limiting his guardianship to that of the property of his daughter. Such occasional division of guardianship, as between responsibility for the person and the property of an incompetent person, has roots deep in the common law and was well within the jurisdictional capacity of the trial judge. *In re Rollins*, 65 *A.*2d 667, 679-82 (N.J. Cty. Ct. 1949).

The statute creates an initial presumption of entitlement to guardianship in the next of kin, for it provides:

> In any case where a guardian is to be appointed, letters of guardianship shall be granted *** to the next of kin, or if *** it is proven to the court that no appointment from among them will be to the best interest of

314

the incompetent or his estate, then to such other proper person as will accept the same. [*N.J.S.A.* 3A:6-36. *See In re Roll*, 117 *N.J. Super.* 122, 124 (App. Div. 1971)].

The trial court was apparently convinced of the high character of Joseph Quinlan and his general suitability as guardian under other circumstances, describing him as "very sincere, moral, ethical and religious." The court felt, however, that the obligation to concur in the medical care and treatment of his daughter would be a source of anguish to him and would distort his "decision-making processes." We disagree, for we sense from the whole record before us that while Mr. Quinlan feels a natural grief, and understandably sorrows because of the tragedy which has befallen his daughter, his strength of purpose and character far outweighs these sentiments and qualifies him eminently for guardianship of the person as well as the property of his daughter. Hence we discern no valid reason to overrule the statutory intendment of preference to the next of kin.

DECLARATORY RELIEF

We thus arrive at the formulation of the declaratory relief which we have concluded is appropriate to this case. Some time has passed since Karen's physical and mental condition was described to the Court. At that time her continuing deterioration was plainly projected. Since the record has not been expanded we assume that she is now even more fragile and nearer to death than she was then. Since her present treating physicians may give reconsideration to her present posture in the light of this opinion, and since we are transferring to the plaintiff as guardian the choice of the attending physician and therefore other physicians may be in charge of the case who may take a different view from that of the present attending physicians, we herewith declare the following affirmative relief on behalf of the plaintiff. Upon the concurrence of the guardian and family of Karen, should the responsible attending physicians conclude that there is no reasonable possibility of Karen's ever emerging from her present comatose condition to a cognitive, sapient state and that the life-support apparatus now being administered to Karen should be discontinued, they shall consult with the hospital "Ethics Committee" or like body of the institution in which Karen is then hospitalized. If that consultative body agrees that there is no reasonable possibility of Karen's ever emerging from her present comatose condition to a cognitive, sapient state, the present life-support system may be withdrawn and said action shall be without any civil or criminal liability therefor on the part of any participant, whether guardian, physician, hospital or others.[10] We herewith specifically so hold.

315

CONCLUSION

We therefore remand this record to the trial court to implement (without further testimonial hearing) the following decisions:

1. To discharge, with the thanks of the Court for his service, the present guardian of the person of Karen Quinlan, Thomas R. Curtin, Esquire, a member of the Bar and an officer of the court.

2. To appoint Joseph Quinlan as guardian of the person of Karen Quinlan with full power to make decisions with regard to the identity of her treating physicians.

We repeat for the sake of emphasis and clarity that upon the concurrence of the guardian and family of Karen, should the responsible attending physicians conclude that there is no reasonable possibility of Karen's ever emerging from her present comatose condition to a cognitive, sapient state and that the life-support apparatus now being administered to Karen should be discontinued, they shall consult with the hospital "Ethics Committee" or like body of the institution in which Karen is then hospitalized. If that consultative body agrees that there is no reasonable possibility of Karen's ever emerging from her present comatose condition to a cognitive, sapient state, the present life-support system may be withdrawn and said action shall be without any civil or criminal liability therefor, on the part of any participant, whether guardian, physician, hospital or others.

By the above ruling we do not intend to be understood as implying that a proceeding for judicial declaratory relief is necessarily required for the implementation of comparable decisions in the field of medical practice.

Modified and remanded.

[1] The importance of the preservation of life is memorialized in various organic documents. The Declaration of Independence states as self-evident truths "that all men *** are endowed by their Creator with certain unalienable Rights, that among these are Life, liberty and the pursuit of happiness." This ideal is inherent in the Constitution of the United States. It is explicitly recognized in our Constitution of 1947 which provides for "certain natural and unalienable rights, among which are those of enjoying and defending life *** ." *N.J. Const.* (1947), Art. I, par. 1. Our State government is established to protect such rights, *N.J. Const.* (1947), Art. I, par. 2, and, acting through the Attorney General (*N.J.S.A.* 52:17A-4(h)), it enforces them.

[2] Dr. Julius Korein, a neurologist, testified:

A. *** [Y]ou've got a set of possible lesions that prior to the era of advanced technology and advances in medicine were no problem inasmuch as the patient would expire. They could do nothing for themselves and even external care was limited. It was—I don't know how many years ago they couldn't keep a person alive with intravenous feedings because they couldn't give enough calories. Now they have these high caloric tube feedings that can keep people in excellent nutrition for years so what's happened is these things have occurred all along but the technology has now reached a point where you can in fact start to replace anything outside of the brain to maintain something that is irreversibly damaged.

Q. Doctor, can the art of medicine repair the cerebral damage that was sustained by Karen?

A. In my opinion, no. ***

Q. Doctor, in your opinion is there any course of treatment that will lead to the improvement of Karen's condition?

A. No.

317

³The Harvard Ad Hoc standards, with reference to "brain death," will be discussed *infra*.

⁴Dr. Robert J. Morse, a neurologist, and Karen's treating physician from the time of her admission to Saint Clare's Hospital on April 24, 1975 (reference was made *supra* to "treating physicians" named as defendants; this term included Dr. Arshad Javed, a highly qualified pulmonary internist, who considers that he manages that phase of Karen's care with primary responsibility to the "attending physician," Dr. Morse).

⁵DEATH. The cessation of life; the ceasing to exist; defined by physicians as a total stoppage of the circulation of the blood, and a cessation of the animal and vital functions consequent thereon, such as respiration, pulsation, etc. *Black's Law Dictionary* 488 (rev. 4th ed. 1968).

⁶It is generally agreed that the Eighth Amendment's provision of "[n]or cruel and unusual punishments inflicted" is drawn verbatim from the English Declaration of Rights. *See* 1 Wm. & M., sess. 2, c. 2 (1689). The prohibition arose in the context of excessive punishments for crimes, punishments that were barbarous and savage as well as disproportionate to the offense committed. *See generally* Granucci " 'Nor Cruel and Unusual Punishments Inflicted:' The Original Meaning," 57 *Calif. L. Rev.* 839, 844-60 (1969); Note, "The Cruel and Unusual Punishment Clause and the Substantive Criminal Law," 79 *Harv. L. Rev.* 635, 636-39 (1966). The principle against excessiveness in criminal punishments can be traced back to Chapters 20-22 of the *Magna Carta* (1215). The historical background of the Eighth Amendment was examined at some length in various opinions in *Furman* v. *Georgia*, 408 *U.S.* 238, 92 *S.Ct.* 2726, 33 *L.Ed.* 2d 345 (1972).

The Constitution itself is silent as to the meaning of the word "punishment." Whether it refers to the variety of legal and nonlegal penalties that human beings endure or whether it must be in connection with a criminal rather than a civil proceeding is not stated in the document. But the origins of the clause are clear. And the cases construing it have consistently held that the "punishment" contemplated by the Eighth Amendment is the penalty inflicted by a court for the commission of a crime or in the enforcement of what is a criminal law. *See, e.g., Trop* v. *Dulles*, 356 *U.S.* 86, 94-99, 78 *S.Ct.* 590, 594-97, 2 *L.Ed.* 2d 630, 638-41 (1957). *See generally* Note, "The Effectiveness of the Eighth Amendment: An Appraisal of Cruel and Unusual Punishment," 36 *N.Y.U.L. Rev.* 846, 854-57 (1961). A deprivation, forfeiture or penalty arising out of a civil proceeding or otherwise cannot be "cruel and unusual punishment" within the meaning of the constitutional clause.

[7]The right we here discuss is included within the class of what have been called rights of "personality." *See* Pound, "Equitable Relief against Defamation and Injuries to Personality," 29 *Harv. L. Rev.* 640, 668-76 (1916). Equitable jurisdiction with respect to the recognition and enforcement of such rights has long been recognized in New Jersey. *See, e.g., Vanderbilt* v. *Mitchell,* 72 *N.J. Eq.* 910, 919-20 (E. & A. 1907).

[8]*See, e.g., Downing, Euthanasia and the Right to Death* (1969); *St. John-Stevas, Life, Death and the Law* (1961); *Williams, The Sanctity of Human Life and the Criminal Law* (1957); Appel, "Ethical and Legal Questions Posed by Recent Advances in Medicine," 205 *J.A.M.A.* 513 (1968); Cantor, "A Patient's Decision To Decline Life-Saving Medical Treatment: Bodily Integrity Versus The Preservation of Life," 26 *Rutgers L. Rev.* 228 (1973); Claypool, "The Family Deals with Death," 27 *Baylor L. Rev.* 34 (1975); Elkington, "The Dying Patient, The Doctor and The Law," 13 *Vill. L. Rev.* 740 (1968); Fletcher, "Legal Aspects of the Decision Not to Prolong Life," 203 *J.A.M.A.* 65 (1968); Foreman, "The Physician's Criminal Liability for the Practice of Euthanasia," 27 *Baylor L. Rev.* 54 (1975); Gurney, "Is There A Right To Die?—A Study of the Law of Euthanasia," 3 *Cumb.—Sam. L. Rev.* 235 (1972); Mannes, "Euthanasia vs. The Right To Life," 27 *Baylor L. Rev.* 68 (1975); Sharp & Crofts, "Death with Dignity and The Physician's Civil Liability," 27 *Baylor L. Rev.* 86 (1975); Sharpe & Hargest, "Lifesaving Treatment for Unwilling Patients," 36 *Fordham L. Rev.* 695 (1968); Skegg, "Irreversibly Comatose Individuals: 'Alive' or 'Dead'?," 33 *Camb. L.J.* 130 (1974); Comment, "The Right to Die," 7 *Houston L. Rev.* 654 (1970); Note, "The Time of Death—A Legal, Ethical and Medical Dilemma," 18 *Catholic Law.* 243 (1972); Note, "Compulsory Medical Treatment: The State's Interest Re-evaluated," 51 *Minn. L. Rev.* 293 (1966).

[9]An attempt to commit suicide was an indictable offense at common law and as such was indictable in this State as a common law misdemeanor. 1 *Schlosser, Criminal Laws of New Jersey* § 12.5 (3d ed. 1970); *see N.J.S.A.* 2A:85-1. The legislature downgraded the offense in 1957 to the status of a disorderly persons offense, which is not a "crime" under our law. *N.J.S.A.* 2A:170-25.6. And in 1971, the legislature repealed all criminal sanctions for attempted suicide. *N.J.S.A.* 2A:85-5.1. Provision is now made for temporary hospitalization of persons making such an attempt. *N.J.S.A.* 30:4-26.3a. We note that under the proposed New Jersey Penal Code (Oct. 1971) there is no provision for criminal punishment of attempted suicide. *See* Commentary, § 2C:11-6. There is, however, an independent offense of "aiding suicide." § 2C:11-6b. This provision, if enacted, would not be incriminatory in circumstances similar to those presented in this case.

[10]The declaratory relief we here award is not intended to imply that the principles enunciated in this case might not be applicable in divers other types of terminal medical situations such as those described by Drs. Korein and Diamond, *supra,* not necessarily involving the hopeless loss of cognitive or sapient life.

319

In The

SUPERIOR COURT OF NEW JERSEY

Chancery Division, Morris County

Docket No. C-201-75

IN THE MATTER OF KAREN QUINLAN,
AN ALLEGED INCOMPETENT

REPLY BRIEF OF THE PLAINTIFF

Paul W. Armstrong, Esquire
801 Lindsley Drive
Morristown, New Jersey
Attorney for the Plaintiff

James M. Crowley, Esquire
Of the New York Bar
Of Counsel

REPLY BRIEF OF THE PLAINTIFF

In its trial brief submitted to this Honorable Court plaintiff states at page 17:

> "There is no New Jersey statute, nor any court decision that requires a competent adult to submit to medical treatment which offers no reasonable hope of relief or cure."

Plaintiff also contends at page 25:

> "The State has no compelling secular interest in prohibiting [the withdrawal of the treatment currently being administered to Karen Ann Quinlan]".

Briefs submitted by learned counsel for other parties to the instant proceeding have disputed such contentions. Their argument has been based in large part on the case of *John F. Kennedy Memorial Hospital* v. *Heston*, 58 N.J. 576, 279 A.2d 670 (1971). In that case an unmarried young woman who had been severely injured in an automobile accident was admitted to the plaintiff hospital, where it was determined that surgery and a blood transfusion would be necessary to save her life. The patient's family informed the hospital that the transfusion was forbidden by the religion to which they all belonged and objected to the administration thereof. The hospital petitioned for the appointment of a guardian to consent to the transfusion. The Petition was granted, the transfusion was administered, surgery was performed and the patient recovered.

In affirming the denial of a motion to vacate the guardianship order, the court observed:

> "it seems correct to say there is no constitutional right to choose to die ... nor is a constitutional right established by adding that one's religious faith ordains his death"
> 58 N.J. at 580, 279 A.2d at 672.

The *Heston* case, however, is clearly distinguishable from the one at hand. The above-quoted dicta of *Heston* should not be considered as dispositive of the instant proceeding.

Discussion

It appears that three questions have been relevant in deciding whether a patient may refuse treatment:

1. What is the nature and the prognosis of the ailment?
2. What is the nature of the proposed treatment?
3. What are the social responsibilities of the patient?

Depending on the answers to the foregoing questions, State interest may or may not be sufficiently compelling to over-balance individual choice.

Where a patient is considered to have a poor prognosis without treatment, a good chance of recovery with such treatment, and the treatment is not deemed essential, the right of a patient to refuse treatment has been upheld. *Erickson* v. *Dilgard*, 44 Misc. 2d. 27, 252 N.Y.S.2d. 705 (Sup. Ct. 1962); *In re Nemser*, 51 Misc. 2d. 616, 273 N.Y.S.2d. 1964, (Sup. Ct. 1966).

Even in an emergency situation, where the prognosis was that death would ensue if treatment were not administered, the court, in *In re Estate of Brooks*, 32 Ill. 2d. 361, 205 N.E.2d 435 (1965), upheld a patient's refusal of treatment where such refusal created no clear and present danger to public health, welfare or morals. 32 Ill. 2d. at 373, 205 N.E.2d at 441.

Even more clear is the situation where death is inevitable despite any proposed treatment. In *Palm Springs General Hospital, Inc.* v. *Martinez*, Civil No. 71-12687 (Dade Co. Cir. Ct., filed July 2, 1971) the court refused to order surgery for a 72-year-old woman where such medical procedures might have prolonged her life, but there was no hope of a cure. The patient had "begged her family not to 'torture me any more' with further surgery". *Wash. Post*, July 5, 1971 at 1, Column 1. The Court stated:

> "Based upon [her] physical condition ... and the fact that performance of surgery ... and the administration of further blood transfusions would only result in the painful extension of her life for a short period of time, it is not in the interest of justice for this Court of

323

Equity to order that she be kept alive against her will''. *Palm Springs Gen. Hosp., Inc.* v. *Martinez, supra,* citing *Erickson* v. *Dilgard, supra* at 27 and 705.

The *Heston* situation on the other hand was quite different. In *Heston,* treatment was relatively uncomplicated, and the prognosis for recovery with such treatment was very good. In such a case it is not difficult to see that the state's admitted interest in preserving life could overcome a patient's objection to treatment. Moreover, if a patient, in addition to being quite curable, had significant social or familial responsibilities, the state's case would be even stronger, *Raleigh Fitkin—Paul Morgan Memorial Hospital* v. *Anderson,* 42 N.J. 421 (1964), *cert. den.* 377 U.S. 985 (1964).

In the instant proceeding, however, the situation is more similar to *Erickson, Nemser, Brooks* and *Martinez* than it is to *Heston.* Karen Quinlan is in an irreversible coma. The chances for her recovery are nil, she has no family to provide for, no children, and the advent of her death is merely a matter of time. For the court to accept the above-quoted statements from *Heston* as controlling in the present case would be to misapply an uncontested general principle. A more profitable use of the court's opinion in *Heston* could be made by realizing that while the court considered refusal of treatment in Miss Heston's case to be tantamount to suicide, it realized that the situation would be "arguably different when an individual, overtaken by illness, decides to let it run a fatal course." 58 N.J. at 582.

In summary, while plaintiff agrees with and venerates the principal that life is sacred and that it is to be preserved through all reasonable means, he feels that there is no reason to continue treatment in the present circumstances, that Karen could lawfully discontinue such treatment if competent, that the Court can thus consent thereto on her behalf, and that the cases which are relied upon for the opposite proposition cannot support a denial of plaintiff's request if proper weight is given to the facts before this Court.

PAUL W. ARMSTRONG
JAMES M. CROWLEY